CORPORATIONS AND
CRIMINAL RESPONSIBILITY

Corporations and Criminal Responsibility

Second Edition

CELIA WELLS

OXFORD
UNIVERSITY PRESS

This book has been printed digitally and produced in a standard specification
in order to ensure its continuing availability

OXFORD
UNIVERSITY PRESS

Great Clarendon Street, Oxford OX2 6DP

Oxford University Press is a department of the University of Oxford.
It furthers the University's objective of excellence in research, scholarship,
and education by publishing worldwide in

Oxford New York

Auckland Cape Town Dar es Salaam Hong Kong Karachi
Kuala Lumpur Madrid Melbourne Mexico City Nairobi
New Delhi Shanghai Taipei Toronto
With offices in
Argentina Austria Brazil Chile Czech Republic France Greece
Guatemala Hungary Italy Japan South Korea Poland Portugal
Singapore Switzerland Thailand Turkey Ukraine Vietnam

ISBN 0-19-924619-X

General Editor's Introduction

It is a great pleasure to be able to contribute, for the first time, a short introduction to a second edition of a book in the series of Oxford Monographs on Criminal Law and Justice. The first edition of Celia Wells's book was a resounding success, not just in making sense of the diverse issues surrounding corporate criminal responsibility, but also in influencing the debate that has taken place in this country and in many other jurisdictions in the past decade. The second edition is much more than an up-dating. It draws upon wider comparative research and on developments in theory and research to present some re-worked and some sharpened arguments on corporate liability, and deals specifically with the role of the criminal law in responses to corporate killings. It is with great enthusiasm that I commend a book that is sure to retain its position as the leading study of this area of criminal liability.

Andrew Ashworth

Preface to the Second Edition

Corporate liability for crime is never going to occupy a very large space in either company law or criminal law. But over the past ten years it has emerged from the cracks between those large unwieldy edifices to claim at least a small outbuilding of its own.

In the transition from the esoteric to the familiar, some of the underlying arguments for holding corporations responsible in criminal law may become confused. It is easy to think solely in instrumental terms. This I believe is a mistake. The reduction of risks and the delivery of safety will not happen through criminal blame. That does not mean that criminal blame should not have a role. Indeed, the role that criminal law has in any area reflects our fears and uncertainties, and that is why the current mood in favour of corporate liability is fascinating. Ask not what criminal justice does for you, ask what you can do for criminal justice, to adapt John Kennedy's aphorism. The main argument for developing corporate liability principles is on firmer ground when the expressive or symbolic function is brought to the fore.

Corporate liability has been under active consideration by courts, legislatures, law reform bodies, and international organizations in the last two decades. I have attempted to reflect those debates in this new edition of the book, which retains the same core structure as the first. As well as updating, I have added new chapters on corporate manslaughter and on comparative and international responses. In the process it has been necessary to move some sections to different chapters. The opportunity to participate in international conferences and colloquia has enabled me to move from my Dark Ages comprehension of non-English speaking jurisdictions. How far I have moved is a matter for them to judge, but I am especially grateful to Albin Eser and Barbara Huber of the Max Planck Institute in Freiburg, Alberto Cadoppi of the University of Parma, and Mark Pieth of the University of Zurich, for leading the way.

I have been much assisted by the kind reviewers of the first edition who helped me to believe that it was worthwhile producing this new version. I have benefited from excellent research assistance, funded by Cardiff Law School, over the last few years, in particular from Helen Wright, Justine Davidge, and Oliver Quick. I would like to thank them for translating my vague instructions into coherent advice. I am additionally grateful to Oliver Quick for allowing me to draw on some of his published work, and to Fiona Donson and Bob Lee for reading drafts of my work and for their friendship. Tony Caffel is to be congratulated on his talent for mediation whenever relations between me and my word processor take a nasty turn, and the information services staff at Cardiff University, especially Duncan Montgomery in the law library, continue to win my admiration and gratitude for their willingness to answer daft queries at inconvenient times.

Derek Morgan continues very skilfully to negotiate the path of colleague and partner. His editorial suggestions are always helpful, though I may not always see them that way at the time. And lastly, I want to thank Lydia, our last remaining child at home, for enduring without dilution incessant 'law-talk' from her parents.

8 December 2000

Contents

Table of Cases

Table of Statutes

1

Safety and Public Welfare

> Corporate bodies are more corrupt and profligate than individuals, because
> they have more power to do mischief, and are less amenable to disgrace or
> punishment. They neither feel shame, remorse, gratitude nor goodwill.[1]

This is a book about the criminal liability of corporations, rather than about the
phenomenon of corporate crime. The term 'corporate crime' describes corporate
activities which are perceived to involve a transgression of some aspect of criminal law. A broad division is often made in criminal law between what are known
as regulatory offences and those which are thought of as conventional crime.
'Corporate crime' is commonly used to denote breaches of regulatory offences.
'Corporate crime' also conjures images of fraud and other illegal endeavour,
which offend against laws which are of general application.

Not all business enterprises are incorporated: there exist also partnerships and
other types of unincorporated organization. Regulatory offences apply equally
to these firms, so that for example all employers have to comply with the Health
and Safety at Work Act 1974. But in relation to these unincorporated businesses
any liability will be incurred by an individual, not by the firm itself. The corporation is thus an important concept because it enables legal liability, whether criminal or civil, to attach to the enterprise itself rather than, or as well as, to any one
person within it. It is with this type of liability that I am concerned.[2]

My focus will be on how and why a corporation could be regarded as criminally
liable together with an attempt to explain the reluctance to bring corporate behaviour under the criminal law except in the regulatory sphere. This involves an examination of criminal law and its reliance on an individualistic model of responsibility.
The significance of this individualistic bias can be seen on a number of planes: it
affects ideas about the role of criminal laws; it affects definitions of criminal behaviour; it affects the application of those laws to the collective concept represented by
the corporation; and it affects perceptions about the activities to which those
definitions should be applied. These four implications of the underlying individualism of criminal law are broadly reflected in the structure of what follows. The book
takes what might be called a panoptic approach to the subject. Corporations and
their susceptibility to criminal law are examined from sociological, psychological,
philosophical, and organizational prespectives as the book progresses.

---

[1] Hazlitt (1821) 1901: 359.

[2] There are numerous ways in which a group can be incorporated, including by charter and by
statute, as well as through registration under the Companies Acts.

I discuss in Chapter 2 some of the principal justifications and arguments for a system of criminal law and punishment. These are placed in the context of corporate pursuits including an examination of sanctions which might appropriately be applied. The cultural and psychological processes by which social perceptions of corporate harm have developed are then discussed in Chapter 3. Because they are intimately related to attribution I look in this chapter at issues of causation and at the legal institutional framework for determining blame. Chapter 4 introduces an account of criminal responsibility and the nature of the corporate entity. These chapters lay the groundwork for developing an analysis of core questions concerning the nature and development of corporate fault in criminal law. An account of the historically contingent and arguably haphazard development of corporate liability for crime follows in Chapter 5, while Chapter 6 is devoted to aspects of corporate manslaughter as it has emerged in England and Wales. This chapter includes a discussion of risk, a concept central both to safety and to responsibility. Chapter 7 deals with developments in corporate liability in other common law jurisdictions, in the civil law states of Europe, and introduces international and supra national efforts to combat corporate crime through harmonized responses. Models of corporate criminal liability are the subject of Chapter 8. Here the nature of corporate liability, the extent to which it should be regarded as vicarious and the appropriate relationship between the corporation and the individuals within it are considered. Two different questions are raised here: as well as the need to consider how responsibility should be properly distributed between a corporation and the individuals who work for it, there is a further issue of whether in some circumstances an individual's responsibility should be mitigated because of the corporation's demands. In the concluding sections I draw together the arguments which have been gestating or left unconcluded in the earlier parts of the book. In this introductory chapter I attempt to highlight some general themes which inform the later discussions and arguments.

The concerns of this book are an example of a wider problem identified by Friedmann: 'The sociological and juristic aspects of the problem of group power within the state have largely remained hidden behind accidents of legal form, especially in the Anglo-American system.'[3] The 'cloaking factors' exploited by powerful organizations included their ability to remain unincorporated, in which they were aided and abetted by the versatility of the trust device, and the limitations of equitable remedies which left them relatively protected against actions for abuse of power.[4] Their immunity from criminal prosecution has relied on a rather different set of forces: incorporation as juristic 'persons' has proved an asset to these powerful organizations in this context. As a 'capital-pooling device', the corporation's rise in legal fiction 'is an essential part of economic development'.[5] Recognition as a legal person has largely carried with it protections without the imposition of corresponding responsibilities or obligations.[6]

---

[3] Friedmann 1972: 312.   [4] Ibid.
[5] Tigar 1990: 212; see also Hadden 1977: chs. 1, 2.   [6] Kramer 1989: 157.

It is important initially to explain and unravel the distinction already referred to between regulatory and conventional crime, since it both informs and distorts much discussion of corporate criminal liability.[7] The descriptive categories of regulatory and non-regulatory prohibitions are used to distinguish those offences which are subject to separate regulatory control from those which more traditionally are enforced by the state police. While regulation might be the most common forum in which corporations are confronted by criminal sanction, it should not be assumed that it is the only type of criminal law which might apply.

1. REGULATORY OFFENCES

Regulatory agencies are many and diverse. Some have their origins in the nineteenth century but most have been established since the Second World War, and they are particularly a phenomenon of the 1960s onwards.[8] They are staffed by health and safety inspectors, environmental health officers, trading standards officers, and many others.[9] They are either, as with health and safety at work legislation, concerned with one aspect of any corporate enterprise activity, or, as with food safety, with a particular industry. Where regulation seeks directly to prevent or deter a corporation from engaging in activities regarded as socially harmful it can be said to fulfil a social control role.[10] Where the object is to provide coordination and mediation to improve the performance of corporations or markets, then regulation takes the form of a service.[11]

In the light of such different functions it is not surprising that there is considerable variation between agencies both in terms of structure and statutory responsibility. Some generalization is possible about the organizational features which distinguish the regulatory bodies from the formal criminal law enforcement agency the police.[12] These administrative, substantive, and evidential differences, discussed further below, more often than not reflect a wider state ambivalence towards the regulation of capitalism.[13] What Snider calls the 'complex dialectical process'[14] by which regulatory mechanisms develop results in an uneasy compromise between the demands of capitalism for unfettered control of resources and labour and those of pressure groups which can ultimately 'force the state's agenda, threaten legitimacy, and arouse and channel dissent'.[15]

It is important not to lose sight of the observation that, while we do not call regulatory inspectors 'police' they 'are in fact special police forces for industry'.[16] Often of comparatively recent origin, regulatory bodies lack the shared 'professionalization' of the police and there are few accepted notions in terms of the

---

[7] Carson 1979 provides an excellent introduction to many of the issues discussed here.
[8] Rowan-Robinson *et al.* 1990: 5.
[9] See the useful collection of essays in Baldwin and McCrudden 1987; see also Ogus 1994; Haines 1997; and Gunningham and Johnstone 1999.
[10] Frank and Lombness 1988: 9.   [11] Ibid.   [12] See generally Kagan 1984.
[13] Snider 1991; Haines 1997.   [14] Snider 1991: 212.   [15] Ibid. 211.
[16] Kagan 1984: 37.

norms which should govern inspectors' conduct.[17] Regulatory bodies are specifically charged with the enforcement of the legislation which begets them. This is one distinct difference. The police enforce both common law and statutory offences as part of their general duty to enforce the law of the land.[18] By contrast, regulatory agencies deal only with statutory offences within their scheme. The legislative aim may, as with the Health and Safety at Work Act 1974, be explicitly premised on an ideology of co-operation based on the unsubstantiated view that 'accidents' at work are largely the result of apathy not recklessness.[19]

The investigation practices employed by regulators can differ from those of the police, although it is in the actual enforcement strategies that the more marked dissimilarity emerges. Like the police they use a mix of reactive and proactive strategies. This is partly related to the visibility of the violations, but also to resources. The disadvantage of relying on the public is that the most obvious violations may not be the most serious.[20] In his study of pollution control Hawkins described proactive investigation; it included monitoring, regular sampling of rivers, and physical inspection of waterways. Reactive inquiries had to be taken seriously because of the potential for scandal. This meant that complaint cases took priority over proactive work and at the same time the inspectors were concerned to try to prevent any pollution coming to the notice of the public. This resulted in a 'collusive' relationship between polluters and controllers whereby the polluters were encouraged to report any potential problems. This kind of collusion is not directly apparent in police work, but the agency's dependence on the regulated industry for information has echoes in the police use of informers.

It is in the enforcement strategies that the real differences between the regulatory and the police mode begins to emerge, and are regarded by some commentators as central: 'The distinction between compliance and deterrence systems of social control is fundamental to the problem of implementing regulatory policy.'[21] Although in a few cases such as rape and domestic violence, police reluctance to pursue all the cases reported to them—employing techniques ranging from discouragement to obstruction—has at least in the past been notorious, the expected police response where the identity of the criminal is known to them is to prepare a case for prosecution. Many regulatory agencies on the other hand employ mainly a strategy of compliance. The contrast between compliance and deterrence strategies is not unproblematic, and is discussed in more detail in Chapter 2, Section 3. iii.

It is often alleged that regulatory agencies run the risk of capture; the collusive relationship can become cemented. Discretionary enforcement clearly assists this.

A captured agency no longer mediates between the interests of the public, which is to be protected through regulation, and the interests of the regulated industry. Instead it uses its discretion to advance the goals of regulation only so far as industry interests permit.[22]

---

[17] Kagan 1984: 38.
[18] *R.* v *Metropolitan Police Commr,* ex parte *Blackburn (no. 3)* (1973) per Lord Denning at 254.
[19] Robens 1972.   [20] Hawkins 1984.   [21] Hawkins and Thomas 1984: 13.
[22] Frank and Lombness 1988: 97.

Although enforcement patterns adopted by regulatory agencies can be contrasted with those of the police, it is important to bear in mind that the police use discretion too, if in less clearly articulated ways.[23] It could also be argued that they too are 'captured': by allowing the Health and Safety Executive to subordinate their role in relation to deaths at work, they avoid prosecuting what might be called 'professional' manslaughter in favour of what they see as 'real' crime. 'The police and the Crown Prosecution Service display an almost inexplicable insouciance towards death at work.'[24] The agreement of a protocol for the investigation of workplace deaths by the HSE, the police, and the CPS in 1998 will facilitate but not guarantee a change in attitude.[25] Corporate collusion with those who are charged with controlling them is arguably an inevitable and therefore unavoidable fact of a capitalist economy. An interesting variation on this argument is that corporations, while adept at avoiding prosecution, are active participants in the criminal process as victims. In other words, they pursue voraciously through the courts those who commit crimes against them.[26]

2. REAL CRIME AND REAL PERSONS

Also informing debate about the role of regulatory agencies and their relationship with other parts of the criminal justice system is the concept of 'real' crime. One of the distinctive features of regulatory offences is the form in which they are drafted.[27] There will be variations between different schemes. Sometimes detailed standards will be preferred, but the legislation may resort to general exhortations such as 'best practicable means', or use terms such as 'unwholesome'.[28] While allowing flexibility and responsiveness on the part of the agency, vague provisions can make it difficult for businesses to know whether they have complied.[29] But at a more general level it is often observed that whereas so-called conventional offences are defined in relation to a specific harm (causing death, causing grievous bodily harm, damaging property, and so on), regulatory offences use an inchoate mode. Health and safety offences, for example, do not refer to the result which the unguarded machine might engender, they prohibit the failure to guard.[30] The anxious regulator may be deterred from pursuing charges because of the very vagueness of the regulatory scheme.[31] The justifications for the inchoate mode here are not any different from the arguments given for the general inchoate offences such as attempt. And there are many

---

[23] Cf. Home Office Circular (1994) *Caution Policy* 18/994.

[24] See Bergman (1990*a* and *b*).

[25] Between 1992 and 1998, 59 cases investigated by the Health and Safety Executive were referred to the CPS for possible manslaughter charges. Eighteen prosecutions were brought. Four were successful, mostly against individuals.

[26] Hagan 1988: 42. [27] Ashworth 1989: 41.

[28] Rowan Robinson 1988: 212–13. Rowan-Robinson 1990: ch. 8. Veljanowski refers to the over-inclusiveness of many offences, 1984: 173.

[29] Alldridge 1990. [30] Factories Act 1961, ss. 12–14. [31] Hawkins 1989.

examples of offences which themselves take the inchoate mode,[32] but it is unusual for them not be one of a pair, one of which is result-based. Ashworth suggests a historical explanation for some of these inchoate offences: they owe their origin to nineteenth-century enactments, a time when the general law of attempt was not clearly delineated.[33]

One justifying reason advanced for inchoate liability is that harm can be prevented if law enforcement personnel can intervene and charge with an offence of attempt murder before the knife is plunged into the victim and it becomes a murder. Another reflects the principle that a person's intentions, as evidenced by their actions, are culpable even where harm does not occur. The inchoate mode used for regulatory offences probably owes more to the first, utilitarian, argument. But regulatory schemes differ in that they often stop at the inchoate stage, so that there is no offence which reflects the seriousness of harm which actually ensues as opposed to the risk of that harm. So, for example, three workers were killed during the first three years of construction of the channel tunnel. Prosecutions were brought under the Health and Safety at Work Act 1974, but they did not reflect the fact that deaths were caused.[34] This, in its own way, is one contributory reason for the social construction of health and safety violations as something separate and distinct from manslaughter. The prevalence of the inchoate form in regulatory offences helps to perpetuate a bifurcation between safety and harm.

The emphasis on safety was also assisted as regulatory offences came to be known as 'public welfare' offences.[35] The use of this term reinforces the sense that these are not merely subject to a different operational or enforcement framework but that they are of a different order from ordinary crime. The offences are concerned in some way with 'public safety'. This characterization obscures rather than illuminates. Homicide, assault, wounding, rape, and burglary are not unconnected with public safety. The police enforcement of criminal law and the existence of a public prosecution system bear witness to the public nature of criminal law generally.

The assertion of a category of 'public welfare offences' is then deeply symbolic for it suggests that conventional crimes such as homicide, assault and rape are not to do with public welfare but with individuals. Yet the state asserts its interest in the prosecution of such offences through a state system of enforcement on the very ground that there is a public interest. There is a public welfare in prevention of harm done to individuals by individuals as well as in that done to individuals by collectivities and that done to the 'community' by collectivities. The state has a legitimate interest in all these.

The distinction between preventive offences and result offences does not derive from the regulatory system. It may be that there is an increased use of criminal law sanctions in areas of public safety which previously were left to individ-

---

[32] Ashworth 1987: 12.   [33] Ibid.
[34] See Bergman 1990*a*, who describes the death of a worker as the result of a failure to earth a boring machine as required under British Standard regulations.
[35] e.g. Sayre (1933); Hall 1947; Williams 1961; Scwenk 1943.

ual choice, as for example with safety belt legislation, or the Horses (Protective Headgear for Young Riders) Act 1990.[36] But whether these come under a regulatory agency depends as much on historical and administrative factors as on any inherent distinction between regulation being for 'public safety' and 'other' criminal law being for something different.

The association of regulation with 'public welfare' and safety does, however, help to sustain the distinction between 'real' and 'quasi' crime. Another way of making a similar distinction is the use of the terms *mala in se* and *mala prohibita*.[37] It is sometimes claimed that 'quasi' crime or *mala prohibita* plays a less significant role in the criminal justice empire.

This type of offence, while going under the general label of criminal law, is of an essentially different character from the criminal offences based on individual wrongdoing. Like all law, the conditions under which criminal liability is imposed depend on a balance of values in a given society.'[38]

In asserting these different categories examples are used, offences such as murder, rape, and theft are placed clearly in the category of 'real' crime or *mala in se* while 'quasi' crime/*mala prohibita* includes road traffic offences, health and safety legislation, food and drug regulation, and so on.[39] Attempts to categorize the different harms or activities which criminal laws seek to deter, prevent, or control are not themselves a problem. What is problematic is the labelling of some criminal laws as better grounded in moral seriousness or heinousness than others, purely as a result of their different administration. Morals are historically and culturally contingent; what appears to lie behind the 'true' crime/'quasi' crime distinction is an unarticulated argument that, if an activity was not traditionally a matter for the criminal law, then it cannot achieve the status of the 'true' crime. It is not necessary to argue that all criminal laws are of equal gravity or that all breaches of them are equally harmful in order to see the objection to a categorization which denies the very feature that unites these laws; that they are prohibitions which carry criminal penalties. In the words of Lord Atkin:

The domain of criminal jurisprudence can only be ascertained by examining what acts at any particular period are declared to be crimes by the State, and the only common nature they will be found to possess is that they are prohibited by the State and that those who commit them are punished.[40]

The labelling of statutory offences as *mala prohibita* can be seen more as a reflection of the common lawyer's aversion to legislative creation than of any inherent distinction in relative harm. The use of regulatory enforcement should not be used as the basis for determining offence seriousness.[41]

---

[36] Also Entertainments (Increased Penalties) Act 1990, which increases to 6 months penalties for various offences, and the Food Safety Act 1990, see editorial, *Criminal Law Review*, 1990: 153.

[37] Wootton 1982; Skolnick 1968.   [38] Friedmann 1972: 202.

[39] For an example of such categorization, see Tigar 1990: 213.

[40] *Proprietary Articles Trade Association v Att-Gen for Canada* (1931) 324.

[41] Ashworth 1999: 40.

Hand in hand with the 'real' crime/ 'quasi' crime distinction, with its dependence on the unsubstantiated concept of 'public welfare', is the emphasis on the use of strict liability in regulatory 'public welfare' offences. One of the common features of a regulatory scheme is the use of strict liability. By this is meant that a mental element (intention, knowledge, recklessness, or negligence) need not be proved. The connection between 'public welfare'/ 'quasi' crime and strict liability is self-fulfilling at both a legislative and an interpretive level. The imposition of strict liability in the first place is seen as justified because the prohibited activity is not thought to be 'real' crime. At the same time, the fact that an offence is not thought to be 'real' crime is used as evidence that Parliament must have intended strict liability. (Or of course it can be used the other way: this is a 'real' crime, therefore Parliament must have intended it to have a mental element). Many regulatory schemes are based on a clear legislative (governmental) commitment to strict liability. This paves the way for an undervaluing of the seriousness of corporate misbehaviour.[42] It is a clear dilemma, for the regulatory scheme may well have been designed with strict liability precisely because of the seriousness of the potential (and actual) harm caused by poor corporate standards.[43] Regulatory schemes have often been adapted to include strict liability offences as a result of lobbying by the regulatory inspectors who were confronted by the reluctance of local magistrates to convict.[44] The empirical data suggests that strict liability is of evidential rather than substantive importance. Regulatory prosecutions for faultless behaviour are rare.[45] The use made of the concept of *mens rea* (of which strict liability is the antithesis) in criminal law is discussed in more detail in Chapter 4, Section 2. But it can be noted here that the consonance between regulatory offences and strict liability falls down in two ways. First, strict liability permeates, under disguise, offences which on their face require proof of a mental element.[46] Secondly, many strict liability offences, road traffic for example, are not enforced through separate regulatory mechanisms and apply to individuals as much as to businesses.

3. CORPORATIONS AND CRIME

The descriptive model which results from the dichotomies between regulation and crime, between 'quasi' and 'real' crime and between strict liability and *mens rea* is false and misleading. The words 'crime' and 'criminal law' commonly evoke images of what might be called the serious 'moral' offences, that is murder, rape, or burglary. These offences are characterized by having identifiable victims and by their investigation and prosecution by the dedicated detectives seen in fictional portrayals of the police. Such representation rarely reveals or acknow-

---

[42] Although Ashworth commends separate treatment of corporations and individuals, 1989: 52, see the comment in Ch 4 below, n. 39.

[43] i.e. the pursuit of profit at the cost of harm to others, Carson 1982.

[44] Carson 1979 and Paulus 1974.   [45] Richardson 1987: 302.   [46] Wells 1982.

ledges the mundane reality of police work with its daily diet of public order, traffic control, 'street cleaning' operations against drunks, those working as prostitutes, and male solicitation, and last but not least responding to victim reports. It is important to bear in mind the fictional image when thinking about corporate liability for crime: a subject which rarely enters either the fiction or reality of police activity. There are of course important differences in the ways in which corporations are able to experience the processes of criminal justice. The corporation's non-human form rules out certain types of sanction and there are some crimes which by their nature could not be committed by a corporation; rape is (possibly) an example.[47] But there are fewer of these than perhaps are often imagined. Corporate enterprise takes its own toll in terms of workplace death and injury, as well as injury to the person and damage to the property of consumers and other members of the public.[48] For example, every year over 300 people die at work in the United Kingdom, and not just in traditionally dangerous industries. As the Health and Safety Commission has been keen to point out, many of these deaths occur during 'seemingly innocuous' activities.[49] The persistent failure to perceive these harms as giving rise to potential liability for homicide or other offences against the person or property will be a recurrent theme.[50] While the idea of corporate manslaughter has undoubtedly gained some purchase in popular vocabulary over the last fifteen years, it is still unusual for such a prosecution to be considered or pursued. And, what is more astonishing, despite the HSE's own research into safety in specific industries which concludes that between 70 and 85 per cent of workplace deaths were preventable, fewer than 20 per cent result in a prosecution even for a health and safety offence.[51]

Turning for a moment specifically to corporate interference with the property of others, we have no difficulty in accepting the fraudster as the classic white-collar criminal,[52] of whom the corporation will often be the victim. And, although when attention is turned to the corporation as perpetrator, economic crime is the most obvious example, what comes to mind is rarely an offence of straightforward dishonesty but some complex tax or price-fixing violation.[53] There is evidence that frauds of this sort are prosecuted with less alacrity than are, for example, social security offences.[54] It is only relatively recently that the problem of white-collar fraud has been tackled through the establishment of specialist police departments. Beginning in 1946 with the Company Fraud Departments in the Metropolitan and City of London police forces, gradually all police forces developed their own Fraud Squads, although some had as few as

[47] As a principal offender; it is a moot point whether a corporation could aid and abet a rape.
[48] Box 1983: ch. 2; Hills 1987; Cullen *et al.* 1987: ch. 2.
[49] Health and Safety Commission 1991: 1.   [50] See particularly Ch 3.
[51] Slapper and Tombs 1999: 74–7. See Chs 2 and 6.   [52] Sutherland 1983.
[53] A possible exception was the Blue Arrow share fraud trial which began in 1991 with three corporate defendants and seven individuals charged with conspiracy to defraud. (The appropriate offence would now be s. 47 Financial Services Act 1986.) But all three corporate defendants and two individuals were acquitted on the judge's direction. *Independent on Sunday*, 2 Feb. 1992.
[54] Cook 1989 and Taylor 1997: 297a.   [55] Levi 1987

two officers.[55] The Serious Fraud Office was established in 1986.[56] So the extent of white-collar fraud investigation has been relatively limited, certainly compared with more traditional police work. Of course, the nature of the offence means that its victims may not be aware that an offence has been committed against them and police enforcement is heavily dependent on victim reporting.[57]

While operational factors help to explain the slow development of fraud prosecutions, they do not account for the different language applied to the white-collar offender. The word 'fraud' is an anaesthetizing generic term for a number of offences, including theft.[58] If we do not call a white-collar thief a thief then we should not be surprised that it sounds a little odd to talk of a corporation stealing (or as discussed above wounding or killing). The idea is difficult to contemplate because our 'image' of the thief is of an individual physically taking the property of another. There is a conflict between the images, reinforced by the choice of language, of different types of offence and offender and the possible categories into which they could legally be placed. The contrast between the social and legal constructions of crime prevents us from seeing corporations as real criminals and highlights a paradox. Theft is the dishonest appropriation of property belonging to another. Yet we could with justification describe corporate aims as the appropriation of property belonging to another. Much of what corporations do legitimately is the lawful pursuit of that which done dishonestly would be regarded as anti-social. Corporate goals are directed towards making profits at another's expense. For this reason some economists find the prohibition against insider trading difficult to understand.[59] The line between acceptable and unacceptable appropriation then may be a fine one.[60] The process whereby class and wealth determine the enthusiasm with which undesirable activities are repressed is what Foucault dubbed 'the restructuring of the economy of illegalities'.[61]

And this great redistribution of illegalities was even to be expressed through a specialization of the legal circuits: for illegalities of property—for theft—there were the ordinary courts and punishments; for the illegalities of rights . . . special legal institutions applied with transactions, accommodations, reduced fines etc.[62]

Likewise modern states are dependent on the capital which business enterprise yields; capitalism relies on them for jobs, investment, and wealth.[63]

When criminologists turned their focus to corporations in the late 1970s they soon discovered what Sutherland had noted thirty years earlier, that the study of 'white collar' or corporate crime requires an examination of illegal acts outside

---

[56] Levi 1987: 284–91.

[57] Ibid. 121. It is suggested that four-fifths of offences which come to the attention of the police are reported by the public, Ashworth 1999: 8.

[58] Ernest Saunders *et al.*, the defendants in the Guinness trial (the City *cause célèbre* of 1990) were convicted of theft, conspiracy to defraud, and false accounting.

[59] The Companies Securities (Insider Dealing) Act 1985, ss. 1 and 2. See Rider 1989 and Campbell 1996.

[60] Durkheim 1898: 1951.

[61] Foucault 1977: 87.

[62] Ibid., quoted in Carson 1979: 37.

[63] Snider 1991: 211.

the normally accepted boundaries of the criminal law.[64] Friedmann, amongst others, pointed out the 'giant and powerful forces' which organized industry and organized labour had become,[65] he did not refer to the harms and injuries which this vast corporate power was capable of inflicting, nor consider whether that should be reflected through criminal liability. By the early 1980s, however, there was a growing body of literature connecting corporations and crime.[66]

Exploring some of the conflicting images and ideas about conventional crime and acceptable corporate goals provides a helpful prelude to an analysis of the criminal liability of corporations. Definitions of crime reflect a moral agenda; choices are made not only as to which acts to proscribe but also as to the legal mechanism (criminal, civil, or administrative) through which those proscriptions should be communicated.[67] Snider, who is otherwise sceptical about the likelihood of criminal laws being strictly enforced against corporations, acknowledges that a strategy of criminalization provides 'leverage and moral legitimacy' for regulatory watchdogs and other pressure groups.[68] An additional point is that discussions of corporate crime often ignore altogether the possibility that corporate activity might breach not just regulatory codes but the criminal law 'code' itself.[69] The irony is that early factory legislation failed precisely because it was perceived by those charged with its enforcement, local Justices of the Peace, as an inappropriate use of the criminal penalty.[70] The present infrastructure of regulation in this area thus owes its origin directly to the same kinds of resistance to the imposition of criminal sanctions on business enterprises as is evidenced now in the reluctance to perceive corporate harm as a type of criminal violence.

The assumptions we make about the role of criminal law are connected with our understanding of the world; an understanding increasingly mediated by technological knowledge and risk evaluations. The social construction of behaviour and events results from a complex interaction between a number of factors, including cultural predispositions, media representations, and legal rules, decisions, and pronouncements. Through the use of language different messages and meanings are communicated. 'Mugging', 'joyriding', 'shoplifting', 'glassing', 'vandalism' are examples of the many colloquial terms in use for conveying the social meanings of behaviour; each has an equivalent legal term and definition. The social vocabulary for corporate harms is less well-developed. The word 'accident' frequently appears: 'accidents' at work; road 'accidents'. The legal impediments to prosecutions for manslaughter following negligent workplace deaths or other negligent deaths caused by corporate activity are reinforced by such constructions. If the deaths are called accidents then they are less likely to be

---

[64] See the discussion of Sutherland's contribution in Hagan 1988: 3–4, 19–20.

[65] Friedmann 1972: 320.

[66] Carson 1979; Coffee 1977; Ermann and Lundman 1978; Fisse 1978.

[67] Kramer 1989: 148.   [68] Snider 1991: 221.

[69] e.g. the subtitle to Frank and Lombness's book *Corporate Illegality* is 'The Regulatory Justice System' (1988). Exceptions to this are Schrager and Short 1980, and Pearce and Snider 1995.

[70] Carson 1979: 40.

seen as potentially unlawful homicides; if they were seen as potentially unlawful homicides they would be less likely to be called accidents. Enforcement processes are influenced and partly determined by stereotypes of crime and criminals: corporations are not stereotypical deviant offenders. Whichever came first, the chicken or the egg, is not a question which we are likely to be able to answer, but the deployment of words such as 'accident' rather than 'violence' to describe the outcome of corporate risk-taking will undoubtedly influence the construction which is placed upon it.[71] For these reasons, it is proposed to use the term 'violence' as one way of describing negligently caused corporate deaths and physical injuries.[72] Media reporting of transport and other disasters in the last twenty years demonstrates the significance of cultural and social perceptions. There is now far more likely to be talk of the possibility of a corporate manslaughter prosecution. This has been accompanied by changes in the nature of news reporting as well as its content. In place of dry, factual reporting, is the rise of comment, analysis, and opinion-forming. Whereas earlier broadsheet reporting was intensely 'factual', all newspapers now, to a greater or lesser degree, provide a custom-made vocabulary of emotional response which finds a welcome reception in a blamist culture.[73]

4. CONCLUSION

The distinctions and differences which interweave, interact, and penetrate discussions of corporate illegality are often relayed and relied upon uncritically and provide an unseen and unacknowledged backdrop. In bringing them to the fore and introducing them here I hope to avoid the blurring which has afflicted some approaches to corporate criminal liability. Drawing a line between crime and regulation has a powerful ideological impact. A large and diverse range of terms helps perpetuate the separation between the criminal and the mere law-breaker: 'real' crime is contrasted with 'quasi' crime; *mala in se* with *mala prohibita*; morals with public welfare; *mens rea* with strict liability; common law with statutory offences, and so on. Clearly regulatory schemes with their different enforcement and offence structures play an important role in the construction of criminal justice. Acknowledging the ideological dimension of their separation from conventional crime is crucial to a productive consideration of corporations and criminal responsibility.

---

[71] For a philosophical exploration of the term, see Cotta 1985.
[72] As does Hills 1987.   [73] Cathcart 1997.

2

The Role of Criminal Law

A philosopher produces ideas, a poet poems, a clergyman sermons, a professor compendia and so on. A criminal produces crimes. If we take a closer look at the connection between this latter branch of production and society as a whole, we shall rid ourselves of many prejudices. The criminal produces not only crime but also criminal law, and with this also the professor who gives lectures on criminal law and in addition to this the inevitable compendium in which this same professor throws his lectures on to the general market as 'commodities' . . . The criminal moreover produces the whole of the police and of criminal justice, constables, judges, hangmen, juries, etc; and all these different lines of business, which form just as many categories of the social division of labour, develop different capacities of the human mind, create new needs and new ways of satisfying them. . . . The effects of the criminal on the development of productive power can be shown in detail. Would locks ever have reached their present degree of excellence had there been no thieves? Would the making of banknotes have reached its present perfection had there been no forgers? . . . And if one leaves the sphere of private crime, would the world market ever have come into being but for national crime? [H]as not the Tree of Sin been at the same time the Tree of Knowledge ever since the time of Adam? [1]

People rarely stop to ask why we have a system of criminal law. When someone is murdered all sorts of questions might be raised: what powers should be given to the police to find the murderer and to garner sufficient evidence to prosecute? Should there be a difference between murder and manslaughter, and if so, what? What is an appropriate sentence for murder? But it is unusual to hear anyone ask 'what is the point of punishing a murderer?'[2] In contrast the question 'why punish a corporation?' is commonly put. There are those whose answer would be that there is no justification for punishment, that it cannot be justified as a 'necessary evil'.[3] Nonetheless we do find the idea of a corporation being punished more odd than that of a murderer or a rapist being sent to prison. Lederman claims that the whole idea of corporate criminal liability challenges 'the ideological and normative basis of criminal law and its mode of expression and operation'.[4] His 'premature assumption'[5] should, however, be seen as a challenge rather than an

---

[1] Karl Marx, *Theories of Surplus Value*, quoted in Wheen 1999: 308.
[2] Cf. de Haan 1990. For some insights into the impact of sentence on the murderers themselves, see Parker 1990.
[3] de Haan 1990: 104. [4] 1985: 296. [5] Fisse 1990.

obstacle to the development of a coherent theory of corporate liability. We should not be surprised that the language and ideas of criminal law are in the grip of individualism. There are, of course, a number of different levels at which the question 'why punish a corporation?' can be asked. It could be taken as asking why there should be any punishment at all for corporate illegal activities. Or it could mean why should the corporation itself rather than the individual miscreants within it be punished? These questions are addressed in Chapter 8. Here I am more concerned with the question of how corporations fit into a system of criminal justice at a general level. This is done first through an exploration of the institutions of criminal law and punishment, followed by a detailed discussion of the relationship between crime and regulation. The chapter concludes with an introduction to some ideas about appropriate sanctions for a corporate offender.

1. Why criminal law?

It is not possible to address these 'why, how, and whom' questions about punishing corporations without initially confronting more general issues about criminal law and punishment. One of the persistent problems in the search for an adequate and coherent account of the justifications of the institution of punishment has been the tendency to deny its connection with the system of criminal law.[6] It has been assumed that punishment can be separated from the laws for which it is imposed and vice versa. More realistically, the relationship between criminal law and punishment should be seen as symbiotic rather than serial.[7] The term 'criminal law' itself misleadingly presupposes a unitary concept. Criminal laws arise in specific social and political contexts and the most we can hope for in a normative theory is that it provides the minimum conditions for the imposition of such liability.[8]

At a very broad level criminal laws can be seen as either instrumental or symbolic (or ideological); that is, criminal laws can be seen as there to achieve a purpose or to make a (moral) statement. The utilitarian harm principle espoused by Mill long informed and dominated liberal debate about criminal law. Mill's 'principle of liberty'[9] dictated that the justifying purpose of any social institution was the maximization of happiness. Applied to criminal law this leads to a view that it should be devoted to 'minimising human suffering via the prevention of crime by the most efficient means possible'.[10] This enterprise had to be limited by the harm principle that the coercive powers of the state should only be invoked to prevent 'harm to others'. The influence of the harm principle on perceptions about the legitimate role of criminal law cannot be underestimated. But it presents difficulties which are confirmed by the context and nature of corporate activity.

---

[6] Lacey 1984: 29 and 1988: 98 ff.   [7] Davis 1985: 122.   [8] Lacey and Wells 1998: 6.
[9] Mill 1859.   [10] Lacey and Wells 1998: 6.

The language of the harm debate assumes that the state's coercion is to be exercised against an individual and that the harm which that individual might bring about will injure other specific individuals. Corporate activities do not fit that paradigm. The harm which is caused does not, in the corporate context, have to be balanced against state coercion of an individual but against control of a profit-generating enterprise. Harm itself is a question-begging term. Traditionally criticism has been based on the use of examples such as offence to others or the creation of risk. It is not always appropriate to see pollution, for example, which has only been recognized relatively recently as a threat both to individual and to collective interests, as harm *to others*. It may not discriminate in the harm it does except in the broadest geographical sense. Wealth and power allow a certain measure of choice in determining the degree of exposure to harmful pollutants, although in the long term environmental harms will, like time and tide, wait for no man. This highlights an additional problem with Mill's conception, that it makes an artificial distinction between individual and social interests.[11] Not only is it inappropriate always to conceive criminal justice powers of the state as a threat to an individual's liberty (rather than to a corporation's operational autonomy), but the interests harmed may need to be more broadly conceived.

A symbolic conception in contrast regards criminal law as representing a statement of moral or other values. This type of conception has been associated with what are often thought of as aspects of private morality, in particular whether certain sexual practices should be regulated.[12] But again it is a mistake to associate a broad theory too closely with the examples to which it has been commonly applied. In any case, the notion of 'private' and 'public' spheres is a contested one in itself, as is the concept of consensual behaviour in a society where individuals are of unequal socio-economic status.[13] The ideological significance of criminal law in a wider sense is often underestimated. Debates about the boundaries of sexual behaviour divert attention from the centrality of the symbolic nature of criminal prohibitions and judicial pronouncements.

But sight should not be lost of the common ground shared by both symbolic and harm theories. Arguments about the control of corporate crime commonly, but not exclusively, revolve around notions of harm reduction: 'If nothing more', wrote Elkins, 'the utilization of the criminal justice system serves to call public attention to the crying need to reduce harm-producing corporate activities.'[14] No utilitarian would dismiss the ideological power of law if it achieved her purpose (the reduction of harm). Similarly, a symbolist is not uninterested in the reduction of harm. What is often at stake in the argument, apart from the obvious difference in starting point, is where the outer boundaries of each theory extends. Since a theory of the criminal liability of corporations can survive either account it is unnecessary to do more than rehearse these different conceptions of the nature of the criminal justice enterprise.

[11] Lacey 1988: 159.
[13] O'Donovan 1985: 207–8.

[12] Hart 1968a; Devlin 1968; Feinberg 1984–5.
[14] Elkins 1976: 77.

It might, however, be worthwhile to dwell on the potential benefits and dis-benefits of deploying blame and punishment especially in the safety context. Here arguments about the justness of holding corporations to account are sometimes confused with arguments that corporate accountability would lead to the world being a safer place. A system of blame may be less effective in terms of safety delivery than one which encourages prevention through reporting of near-misses for example.[15] And some argue that liability regimes may have the opposite effect to that intended.[16] The deterrent potential of strict enforcement depends on many factors: the industry concerned, the size and type of organization, particular sectors or individuals within the organization, as well as the size of the penalty imposed.[17]

It is puzzling that there is so little conversation between the sociologists of mistake and disaster and critical lawyers. The literature on disasters and errors reveals a continuing tension between individual and organizational approaches in explanations of disastrous mistakes. Mistakes are a predictable and inevitable property of work.[18] Human errors, Reason argues, divide into two categories: active and latent failures.[19] Active failures are unsafe acts committed by individuals, such as pilots, train drivers, and surgeons, at the 'sharp end' of the action. Latent failures, on the other hand, involve decisions taken by management, with the consequences lying dormant for some time and triggered by active failures. Broadly speaking, this classification of error as active or latent fits with individual and organizational approaches to understanding such incidents. Typically, the individual 'rational choice' model isolates individual culprits and pursues a strategy of blame, punishment, and deterrence. Operators at the sharp end of the action are generally deemed responsible. For adherents of this approach, quality is improved by rooting out so-called 'bad apples'.[20] Advocates of this approach are typically supportive of disciplinary mechanisms for dealing with individual failings. The legal processes of the civil and criminal justice systems are regarded as necessary in delivering appropriate punishment.

However, sociologists and psychologists have challenged the individual blamist approach, preferring to concentrate on organizational or systems analyses. The claim here is predicated on the notion that individual human errors are inevitable. Rarely, according to this argument, are errors and disasters the product of the active error, the last link in the chain. Rather, in order to understand why the individual failed, we must search for extrinsic factors and, in the words of Berwick, pursue a policy of continuous improvement.[21] The argument here is premised on the fact that all systems have a number of latent failures, generally management and communication problems, and the more complex, interactive,

---

[15] I am grateful to my co-authors for allowing me to draw in this section from Wells, Morgan, and Quick 2000: 499–503.

[16] Khanna 1996; Parker 1996.   [17] Gunningham and Johnstone 1999: 188–9.

[18] Hughes 1958.

[19] Reason 1990: 173. Reason now prefers the label 'latent conditions', since this does not necessarily involve error or failure, Reason 1997: 9.

[20] Berwick 1989.   [21] Ibid.

and opaque the system, the greater number of latent errors it is likely to contain.[22] Instead of regarding errors as negative events requiring some sort of sanction, this approach encourages the open disclosure of all such incidents—the so-called 'error as treasure approach'. The key question then becomes under what conditions do such errors occur, and whether the benefits of a particular technology or procedure outweigh its risks? This requires attention to the design, procedures, and cultures of organizations. Law and legal institutions have a clear role to play; this is not an all-or-nothing choice. It is partly a question of determining the appropriate roles of individual and organizational accountability and partly one of determining the balance between administrative, regulatory, punitive, remedial, and compensatory legal mechanisms.[23]

This relates to another frequently made argument. Law, it is claimed, is only one of a number of strategies of social control, and while it may be preferable to some, such as torture or terrorism, it clearly is not an alternative but is complementary to other institutions such as school, religion, family, and peer group, all of which use the currency of guilt, shame, and anxiety. No-one would claim that the criminal law should be regarded as the sole means of developing social responsibility, whether of corporations or any other groups or individuals.[24] But some of the mechanisms by which such a sense of responsibility are encouraged may have less relevance for corporations: the corporate 'conscience' is not so readily identifiable nor so accessible.[25] Two counter arguments can be made. First, that corporations do operate in a cultural climate albeit a different one from individuals. The market, customers, trade associations, insurance companies, sellers of safety devices, trade unions and professionals employed by corporations all exert pressures of one kind or another to behave responsibly.[26] Secondly, that criminal sanctions may have indirect effects such as providing victims with an easier route to compensation, either by strengthening a civil claim or through the use of criminal compensation orders.[27] This could be regarded as a legitimate use of the publicly funded criminal justice system.[28] In fact this point could be more strongly made the other way; that since many of the victims of corporate wrongdoing are unaware of the source of the harm done to them and therefore cannot invoke the criminal enforcement system as do victims of burglary, there is a state obligation to provide that mechanism for them in the form of proactive investigation backed up by effective sanction.[29] It is because safety should be rated highly in assessing the seriousness of crimes,[30] that an appropriate system of criminal justice should be devised which reflects its importance both symbolically and instrumentally. The problem has been that the opposite has occurred. With health and safety for example, the statutory offences often fail to

---

[22] Reason 1990: 198.   [23] Galanter 1994.   [24] Elkins 1976: 77.
[25] Stone 1975: 35. See also the discussion below in Ch. 4.4.
[26] Kagan and Scholz 1984: 71.   [27] Haines 1997.   [28] Tigar 1990: 217.
[29] Similarly, those injured through employer recklessness should not be deprived of a police investigation through the monopolization of this area by the HSE, see Bergman 1990a and b, Slapper 1999.
[30] Ashworth 1999: 39.

reflect the actual seriousness of the injuries caused by employer recklessness and the structure and practice of enforcement fails to reinforce the message that these are serious criminal offences. While safety prevention requires a full and searching acknowledgement of all the factors leading to a death, the need to limit liability discourages the production of comprehensive written records of all possible contributing causes.

2. THEORIES OF PUNISHMENT

The criminal justice enterprise is predicated on a system of state enforced penalties.

What is punishment? It is an evil satisfying these six conditions:

1. There is a body of rules capable of guiding action ('primary rules');

2. There are beings ('persons') capable of following these rules or not as they choose, capable of choosing on the basis of reasons, and capable of treating the prospect of suffering specified evils as a reason against doing an act (to be weighed with other reasons for and against);

3. There is a procedure ('authority') for inflicting types of evil ('penalties') upon a person if he does not follow the rules;

4. There are ('secondary') rules connecting failure to follow primary rules ('crimes' or 'offences') with certain penalties;

5. Both the primary and secondary rules are supposed to be known to the persons subject to them (in general, at least); and

6. Imposition of the penalty is (in general, at least) justified by the person's not having followed the appropriate rule when he could have.[31]

Seen thus, the justification of the institution of punishment follows from the existence of a system of criminal law. The interconnection between the aims of criminal law and the purposes of punishment does not mean that they are one and the same;[32] the agenda for a satisfactory theory of punishment, Lacey argues, 'has to be made out in consequentialist terms within the framework of an endstate political philosophy'.[33] The contingent relationship between obligations and sanctions, she argues, 'makes the justification of punishment dependent upon at least part of a general political philosophy which would provide a justification for the maintenance of a legal system'.[34] Echoing the debate between the instrumental and symbolic role of criminal law are arguments about the justifications for and purposes of punishment. The debate about punishment is (mainly) conducted between deterrent and retributive theories.

Most people agree that a system of criminal law is to be preferred to a system of terror or incapacitation as a means of social control. In reaching the conclusion that the 'criminal law thus strikes the best balance between protecting persons and respecting them' it is not necessary to be committed to a deterrent or a

---

[31] Davis 1985: 121.   [32] Hart 1968: ch. 1.   [33] 1984: 29.   [34] Lacey 1988: 96.

retributive theory of punishment.[35] In other words, the justification can be found by either route. The retributive theory of punishment 'seeks to justify punishment, not in terms of social utility, but in terms of a cluster of moral concepts: rights, desert, merit, moral responsibility, and justice'.[36] What is often seen as at stake is the justness versus the social usefulness of punishment. As a justifying reason for the punishment of individuals utilitarianism has fallen from favour.[37] Doubts have arisen both about the empirical soundness of deterrence and, of more concern perhaps, about the ethics of imposing severe penalties on individual offenders in order to deter. It is from these doubts that just deserts theories have grown and rapidly flourished in the last two decades. Desert sentencing has been officially endorsed on both sides of the Atlantic.[38] The impact has, however, not been as great in England for two reasons: sentencing practice has traditionally been tariff-based and there has been greater reluctance to interfere with judicial sentencing discretion.[39] Although just deserts has its origins in retributive or at least deontological theories and emerged as a clear departure from deterrence-based ideas, in its maturation it has feet in both camps. There is nothing particularly strange about this; there has been a long-standing debate as to whether retributivism is to be used as a limiting principle of a deterrence-based system (what has been called weak or negative retributivism)[40] or whether it should be a full-blown justification in its own right. The most coherent and secure arguments in favour of just deserts depend on a combination of justice or fairness and utility.[41] Punishment is justified as an expression of censure, blame, or disapproval; in the words of von Hirsch, 'Even if punishment exists wholly for preventive reasons, one of its principal features is to censure or condemn. Such a condemnatory sanction should be allocated according to how blameworthy the conduct is.'[42]

Much of the foregoing argument should have prepared the way for acknowledging that the quest is multi-faceted and multi-layered. The objective should not be the discovery of an independent theory of punishment—after all that was not one of the more successful philosophical enterprises of the last millennium. Depending on our view of the state, and of the function particularly of criminal law within the state, we will have different ideas about the purposes and justifications of punishment.[43] What is necessary if we are to think about corporations and crime is to appreciate the complexities of these questions and to acknowledge the historical and philosophical contingency of many of the answers which Western legal systems seem to take for granted. While retributivism has undergone a revival in its hold on late twentieth-century thinking about crime, the language of penal policy draws on notions of deterrence as well.[44] The characterization of deterrence as forward looking and retributivism as backward looking is helpful so long as it is remembered that it is always

[35] Davis 1985: 122.   [36] Murphy 1985: 158.   [37] But see Walker 1991.
[38] By the Sentencing Reform Act 1984 18 USC and in the UK by the Criminal Justice Act 1991.
[39] See generally Ashworth 2000.   [40] Hart 1968: 77 ff.   [41] Lacey 1988: 22–4.
[42] von Hirsch 1990.   [43] See generally Garland 1990.
[44] Walker 1991: 49 suggests that scepticism about deterrence resulted from exaggerated interpretations of empirical evidence.

possible to turn round and scan the other horizon. Because punishment is a complex social institution it may not be feasible or desirable to develop unitary theories in relation to its justification, purpose, or social role.[45]

What does need to be considered is whether there are reasons for treating corporations differently from individual subjects. Corporations present their own challenge to the justifications for criminal law and punishment. Deterrent arguments may not be open to the same objections when applied to corporations as to individuals. The efficacy of deterrent penalties may well be different for corporations,[46] or for different corporations.[47] Although there is disagreement about whether profit maximization is all that motivates senior management, there is no doubt that it plays a significant role in business corporations. The ethics of deterrence could be different too. Concern about the imposition of a long prison sentence is not relevant. Corporations already enter the criminal justice process with the advantage that they cannot have imposed upon them the hardship and degradation which incarceration entails. Arguments based on unfairness also have less sway where the entity on whom the penalty has been inflicted has consciously chosen to submit itself to the criminal laws of the jurisdiction in which it operates. Individuals do not generally have the opportunity to make that particular choice.[48] Neither of these points should be regarded as determinative of a deterrent justification for corporate offenders. The expressive form of just deserts theory can have application in the corporate debate. Given that corporations are immune from the degrading aspects of incarceration, there could be benefits in demonstrating that censure does not have to be accompanied by the debasement which is associated with punishment of individuals. Attention would then be drawn to the failure of imagination which has characterized modern penal policy (in its execution and design if not in its rhetoric).

Just deserts theory has been criticized on the ground that it ignores the essential reality of the criminal justice process, which is that only a minority of offenders is ever caught.[49] This is particularly true of white-collar crime which leads Braithwaite and Pettit to conclude that to apply just deserts to it is neither desirable nor feasible.[50] They suggest that not only is the hidden figure for white-collar crime greater, but that overall there is more white-collar crime: 'If we exclude victimless crimes and traffic violations, we think that the inference, even in the absence of systematic data, is not only plausible, but overwhelming.'[51] Some of the implications of their consequentialist version, presented as an integrated theory of criminal justice, are discussed below.[52]

The conclusion to this part of the discussion is that theories of punishment have to take account not only of the legal and political context with which they intimately relate but also of the argument that corporate crime has to be brought

---

[45] Garland 1990.   [46] Khanna 1996.
[47] Gunningham and Johnstone 1999: ch 4.
[48] This is not of course to suggest that they have no say at all in the political process, although it has to be acknowledged that it is usually an extremely limited one.
[49] Braithwaite and Pettit 1990.   [50] Ibid.   [51] Ibid. 186.   [52] In s. 3. ii.

into the criminal justice story and not left as an awkward afterthought. Apart from the obvious point that most discussions of punishment address the individual and not the corporate offender, the regulatory background has been one of the factors obscuring the debate. The existence of regulatory schemes prevents an argument that no notice at all is taken of the harms caused by industry. On the other hand, regulation is seen as distinctive from ordinary crime control. The other difficulty confronting debate about corporate crime is that the penalties applied to individuals may be neither available nor suitable for corporate offenders. It is to these points that I turn in the next two sections.

3. Crime and Regulation

Over-reliance on philosophical critique can obscure the empirical reality of the criminal justice process with its dependence on discretion and administrative procedures.[53] The tendency to separate 'crime' from 'regulation', the ideological significance of which was highlighted in Chapter 1, has exerted a powerful hold over the imagination of scholars in the field. Although regulatory systems involve the laying down of offences and a system of enforcement pursued through criminal courts, in other words they have characteristics commonly associated with (conventional) criminal law, they are not always analysed within a criminal justice perspective.[54] There is often more emphasis on the distinctiveness of regulation than on the similarities it shares with the policies and practices of traditional police methods.[55] There is a tendency to assume that criminal law is bounded by two characteristics: that it is enforced by the police and that it addresses individuals. Regulation, conversely, is assumed to be concerned only with business corporations.[56] Regulation could instead be conceived as part of criminal law; more acknowledgement could be given to the fact that corporations are, or should be, subject both to conventional policing and to regulatory control. Additionally, it should be recognized that regulation also addresses individuals, both as sole traders and as employees.

It would be foolish to deny that in a descriptive sense, of course, regulation has developed many distinct features.[57] The difficulties arise when those distinctions become ensnared in normative assertions about the appropriate methods of control of certain types of activity. Four models of regulation can be identified, the criminal justice, the rational-legal, the economic, and the conflict models.[58]

(*a*) Under the criminal justice model, regulation is viewed as a system of social control. This approach would lend itself to descriptions of the processes of investigation, of adjudication, and punishment with a focus on discretion, due process, and effectiveness.

---

[53] Nelken 1987: 140.   [54] See generally Hutter 1988 and Hawkins 1984*a*, 1989, 1990.
[55] See Kagan 1984 for a useful comparison of police and regulatory systems.   [56] Ibid. 44.
[57] Although regulatory practice is far from uniform, Gunningham 1987: 69; Baldwin and McCrudden 1987; Ogus 1994.
[58] Frank and Lombness 1988: 5.

(*b*) The rational-legal model asserts that law provides a rational and definitive solution to legal problems. Whenever a problem is identified, lawmakers create rules to eliminate the problem. Problems are identified either through societal consensus or through the wisdom of lawmakers. Enforcement is taken for granted as a natural consequence of law and the discovery of a violation and is viewed as impartial and objective.

(*c*) The economic model invokes the goal of efficiency. Regulation should maximize social benefits and minimize social costs. The economic model prefers maximization of choice over legal controls.

(*d*) the conflict model sees the regulatory system as a method by which certain groups gain privileges and advantages. Whether a problem is recognized depends on the balance of interests affected. Powerful groups can on this model use their influence to ensure that activities which harm them are controlled or that regulation which will harm them is prevented or frustrated.

These models help to demonstrate the connections between systems of regulation and the practice of the criminal justice system in general. They could be used profitably as models of criminal law (including regulation). This would then allow us to perceive not only differences within conceptions of regulation but also the similarities between some aspects of (traditional) criminal law and of regulatory concerns. For example, traditional property offences are enforced by police largely against individual offenders for reasons that can be related to three of the four models: (*a*), (*b*), and (*d*). An important point then is that what appears to be an instructive analysis of regulation turns out to be equally successful if applied to the content of traditional criminal law. Regulation and traditional criminal law share more than is often supposed. Instead of asking what it is about regulation that is different, we should perhaps pursue the parallel question of why it attracts a distinctive analysis; conversely we should perhaps ask what is it about traditional criminal law that causes so many aspects to be taken for granted. It is rather as though the 'grand' questions in the traditional discourse assume the existence of the institution of criminal law but agonize over how to justify the concomitant infliction of punishment. For regulation, the 'grand' issue is over the necessity for its existence as part of criminal law. If it does not start out as a recognized part of traditional discourse, then it 'needs' to be justified at a much earlier stage. While criminologists worry about the effectiveness of imprisonment, fines, and community service, students of regulation describe in intimate detail the enforcement strategies of the regulators. When the police are studied, it forms a separate sub-topic. When regulation is studied, enforcers are the topic. Of course, we do need to look at the development of the different strategies, at why regulators are as concerned to 'tell' violators to obey the law in the future as the conventional criminal justice is to place offenders in positions where they have no option one way or the other. But it is instructive in doing so to note that it is rare for the comparisons to be on equal terms. Three arguments are pursued below:

(i) that the types of activity controlled through regulation are often historically contingent,

(ii) that regulation reinforces social constructions, and

(iii) (a connected argument) that the categories of compliance and deterrence
enforcement styles are accepted too uncritically.

i. THE HISTORICAL AND POLITICAL CONTINGENCY OF REGULATION

The distribution of criminal law enforcement between the police and regulatory
agencies is historically contingent. Not all corporate offending comes under the
aegis of a regulatory body. Corporate fraud for example may not be probed as
assiduously as house burglary, but when it is investigated the inquiry is conducted under police auspices. On the whole, though, the police deal with individuals while business enterprise is regulated by specialist agencies. Why should
this be so?

Obviously, the type of conduct that a particular society considers as sufficiently worthy of
condemnation to prohibit it by criminal sanctions, is deeply influenced by the values governing that society.[59]

Friedmann cited economic crime as an example. Protection of private property,
whether owned by individuals or by corporate businesses, has been a prime concern of criminal laws. Fraudulent conversion of such property threatens the security on which the market system depends. Ashworth gives the classic account of
the aims of criminal law:

The first is to protect those interests which are most central to life in society (leaving less
important interests to be protected by government regulation or civil actions, and others
still by informal pressures) . . . The second aim of the criminal law is to establish an authoritative framework for the official response to lawbreaking.[60]

Unlike threats to private property, the waste of resources is, like its accumula-
tion, in times of laissez-faire, a matter of private concern; 'the growing recognition of the social function and use of property has led to more permanent changes
in legal values'.[61] The protection of resources and commodities has in non-social-
ist societies mainly developed through regulatory measures,[62] reflecting presumably, if we accept Ashworth's view, that they are 'less important'. Individual
property ownership rapidly produces individual property laws such as those
prohibiting criminal damage and theft, while industrial production and complex
financial markets slowly attracted broad-ranging regulation. The institutions of
private property and the 'free market' of exchange are core concepts of liberal
capitalist society.[63] Corporate harms such as pollution and safety violations are
not perceived as crimes partly because they are not described or labelled as such.
The prophecy becomes self-fulfilling, if the starting point is that criminal law is

---

[59] Friedmann 1972: 194. [60] Ashworth 1987: 8. [61] Friedmann 1972: 195.
[62] Ibid., ch. 2. [63] Lacey and Wells 1998: 221.

essentially a system for upholding a certain social order[64] and underwriting individual property rights.[65] The inherent nature of corporate activity, in terms both of its size and content, is such that the assertion of such rights is far more likely to involve damage either to collective or individual interests of others, whether workers, consumers, or members of the public. While police work contains the 'dangerous classes',[66] corporate control has inevitably trodden a delicate line between maintaining and disciplining.

Police departments were established in Anglo-American jurisdictions in the nineteenth century, Kagan argues, largely to protect institutions of private property from the threat posed by the 'dispossessed masses of burgeoning urban centres', and as a result 'hold the fort and quell outbursts of anarchy'.[67] In contrast, regulatory legislation aims to change systematic practices.[68] Others assert the public order role of regulation.[69] Of course, the different ways in which regulatory bodies go about their tasks vary both amongst themselves and in important respects contrast with police methods. Many of the factors contributing to these differences affect conventional policing as well. Regulatory ideology is characterized by an identification between the regulators and the regulated: 'regulatory control may lack the moral mandate necessary for the legitimacy of an agency's enforcement work.'[70] Such identification is not wholly absent from policing ideology, but is found only in specific aspects of their work, such as traffic control.[71]

The differential resourcing of regulatory bodies and the police is also of significance.[72] Whatever strategy such agencies adopt, this is one measure of how seriously corporate crime is taken. The Health and Safety Executive in 1996 had 1,500 inspectors;[73] while police numbers increased throughout the 1980s, the HSE had its staff cut by 20 per cent between 1980 and 1985,[74] a period which coincided with a rise in the number of workplace fatalities and major injuries.[75] Although this trend has been reversed, with one inspector to every 1,000 worksites in 1996 compared with one to 420 in 1984, the HSE is undoubtedly under-resourced.[76] The rise in the number of small businesses partly accounts for this dramatic change in the ratio of inspectors to workplace.[77] Between 1979 and 1993 the total number of small businesses in the UK rose from 1.8 to 3.6 million. By the late 1990s 99 per cent of all firms employed fewer than fifty people. Small businesses often find it most difficult to ensure safe working systems.[78] The business may have come and gone before the HSE is aware of its existence. At the other end of the scale many of those whom the HSE are attempting to 'police' have vast resources of their own with which to cover up their crimes and with which to fight

---

[64] Ibid.: ch. 2 and Malcolm Young 1991.   [65] Kagan 1984: 43.

[66] Young 1991: 1–3.   [67] Kagan 1984: 43.   [68] Ibid. 44.

[69] Weinfeld 1982: 667.   [70] Hawkins and Thomas 1984: 8.

[71] Although, this is subject to change, witness the changing attitude to drink-driving offences, domestic violence, and marital rape.

[72] See Rowan-Robinson *et al*. 1990: 215 for a discussion of resourcing amongst different agencies.

[73] Gunningham and Johnstone 1999: 374.   [74] Rimington 1991.

[75] Gunningham and Johnstone 1999: 113.   [76] Ibid. 105.   [77] Ibid. 3.

[78] HSE 1995: 15.

any prosecution which is mounted. Sanctions are often limited too. The maximum fine for health and safety offences tried in the magistrates' courts is £20,000, hardly a large sum to a business enterprise, even if it were routinely imposed.[79]

ii. REGULATION AND SOCIAL CONSTRUCTIONS

The essentially protective and preservationist approach to regulation has been explained by the false view that corporate wrongdoing is closer to legitimate conduct than ordinary crime. Richardson, for example, suggests that 'Much protective regulation creates offences which may be regarded as morally neutral in the sense that the conduct can closely resemble acceptable business practice.'[80] There are a number of problems with this. One is that it assumes that 'acceptable business practice' is an unproblematic concept: but who are the determinants of this acceptability, how much do we know of business practice in any case. Business cannot determine the morality of its own behaviour, for this would be like saying that rape is morally neutral since most rapists feel no remorse.[81] The rape analogy points to another problem, which is the idea that ordinary crime is far removed from 'acceptable' behaviour. But this way of looking at crime is itself part of the ideology of 'otherness' which traditional criminal law and its enforcement encourages. The fact that white-collar crime had to be 'discovered'[82] is sufficient to remind us that our notions of crime and criminals derive not from definitions but from constructions of everyday behaviour.

It is often extremely difficult to escape the confines of those social constructions. For example, Hawkins and Thomas write as though something inherent about regulation leads to its being regarded as an administrative matter with very different concerns from those of criminal law: '[T]he concept of regulation implies a toleration of conduct that causes, or possesses the potential for harm, not the eradication of existing harmful acts.'[83] The contrast here between the de-emphasis on harmful results and the toleration of potential hazard seems inappropriate. What they actually appear to be concerned with, and seems of more importance, is whether the focus of regulation is on the pre-emptive control of potential harm or on a retrospective enforcement of a penalty for causing a harmful result, a contrast between what Reiss calls the premonitory and postmonitory systems of enforcement.[84] As we have already seen, part of the explanation for the premonitory pre-emptive style may be found in the legislative scheme itself. The regulatory agency may only have in its armoury offences which anticipate harm, such as 'failure to fence dangerous machinery' or 'failure to keep a proper

---

[79] Health and Safety at Work Act 1974, s. 33 (1A) inserted by Offshore Safety Act 1992, s. 4(2), which also introduced the power to imprison to a maximum of 2 years. Most health and safety prosecutions for triable-either-way offences, even where a worker has been killed, are proceeded with summarily, Bergman 1991, 35; but see *R v Howe and Sons* (1999), below s. 4.i.

[80] Richardson 1987: 299.   [81] *Guardian*, Mar. 1991.

[82] Sutherland 1937 and 1983. And see Levi 1987: 354–7.   [83] Hawkins and Thomas 1984: 8.

[84] Reiss 1984: 24.

lookout'. So it is important to distinguish between the enforcement styles adopted within the context of the scheme of offences available. Both criminal law generally and regulation in particular can be regarded as exercises in harm prevention; what is lacking in the regulatory sphere is the element of social control and of denunciation or censure. What then is the true relationship between the social construction of corporate crime and the regulatory edifice? Are regulatory offences perceived as relatively unimportant because they are regulatory and because they are enforced by agencies which work a compliance strategy, or are they enforced and labelled in these ways because they are perceived as relatively unimportant? This conundrum can only be penetrated by unravelling some underlying confusions and distortions in the compliance debate.

iii. ENFORCEMENT STRATEGIES

In a scheme based largely on an inchoate style of offence definition, there will arguably be more room for a choice between what have been identified as the compliance and deterrence strategies of enforcement. It is sometimes assumed that, because of their inchoate form, regulatory offences produce no victims. In seeking to explain the preference for compliance strategies Hawkins and Thomas emphasize that they are more likely where there are no obvious victims. The emphasis needs to be on the 'obvious'; there are indeed victims of corporate crime. Those who are exposed to harmful pollutants do not realize that their illnesses may be attributable to illegal corporate behaviour; those whose lives, health, or livelihood are endangered by poor safety policies and practices may realize too late; consumers may not appreciate that part of the price they pay for goods is helping to finance a corporate fraud and so on. Regulatory breaches are victimless only in a formal, substantive sense, only because there are no result offences to enforce alongside the 'preventive' inchoate offences.[85]

It is also argued that compliance is a more appropriate strategy where there is a possibility of a continuing relationship with the rule-breakers.[86] Perhaps there is an analogy where police adopt a similar approach in their dealings with drunks, vagrants, and prostitutes.[87] While it is certainly true that these groups are more likely to be subjected to policing at the compliance end of the spectrum, they are different in two respects from those who are 'regulated'. The first point is that this perspective ignores the extent to which the police define these groups in the first place. There is an assumption that, in the same way as there is an identifiable group of manufacturers, there is an identifiable group of vagrants, when in truth, vagrants are people whom the police regard as vagrants. Or to give a more contemporary example, the definition of the offence of harassment in the Public Order Act 1986, 'behaviour likely to cause harassment, alarm or distress',

---

[85] In contrast, the US Occupational Safety and Health Act provides for penalties for wilful violations of the act causing death, 29 USC 666(e).

[86] Hawkins and Thomas 1984: 8.   [87] Ibid. and see Uglow 1988: ch. 6.

seems as likely to create a 'criminal' as to catch one.[88] Secondly, they do not engage in potentially harmful behaviour. There does not seem to be a close match between police use of compliance and its adoption as a *modus operandi* by regulators.

It is helpful to outline the range of powers a regulator might have at her disposal. The HSE for example can begin a formal prosecution against an employer in breach of the duties imposed in the 1974 Health and Safety at Work Act. Approximately 3,000 such prosecutions are brought each year and these are mainly reserved for serious breaches, that is flagrant, wilful, or reckless failures to comply. Much more common are the administrative improvement and prohibition notices which they are empowered to issue. Over 6,000 improvement notices and 4,000 prohibition notices are issued each year. An improvement notice can be issued if there is a contravention of any of the relevant statutory provisions and directs the employer to remedy the fault within a given time. A prohibition notice may be issued when the activity or practice involves a risk of serious personal injury and directs that it be stopped either immediately or within a specified time.[89]

The extensive literature on regulatory forms in different jurisdictions discloses a growing debate about the efficacy of regulators' reluctance to adopt a strict policy of enforcement.[90] A conventional account holds that three theories of corporate violators inform inspectors' enforcement practices: (*a*) that the violator is an 'amoral calculator' who will violate regulations whenever the benefits exceed the punishment; (*b*) that the violation was unintentional but they had failed to develop an organizational structure which was capable of implementing an effective compliance system; and (*c*) the regulatory equivalent of civil disobedience, a principled disrespect.[91] Kagan and Sholz reject strict, 'going by the book', police-like enforcement which the amoral calculator theory would indicate on the ground that most businesses (including the violators) are committed to social responsibility. Such a view is instructive in understanding the disregard in which many regulatory officials hold formal action: they argue that it causes delays, creates excessive work for the agency, and increases the resistance of regulated firms. Formal action then is seen as counter-productive and an unnecessary and/or ineffective deterrent. A similarly developed argument about the motivations of most burglars might lead the police to the conclusion that strict enforcement is inappropriate . . .

'The real effectiveness of legal sanctions depends . . . above all on the degree and methods of their practical implementation,' wrote Friedmann.[92] Considerable evidence is available of a low level of compliance with regulatory

---

[88] Section 5. A common use of the section is to criminalize people who swear at police officers, Ashworth 1999: 25.

[89] See generally Wright 1997. The maximum fine for failure to comply with such notices is £20,000 or 6 months' imprisonment or both, s. 33 (2A) Health and Safety at Work Act 1974.

[90] See Haines 1997; Gunningham and Johnstone 1999.

[91] Kagan and Sholz 1984: 67; these are extensively criticized by Pearce and Tombs 1990.

[92] 1972: 198.

laws accompanied by a low number of prosecutions.[93] It can be observed both that most major corporations regularly breach criminal/regulatory laws,[94] and that many regulatory agencies exercise only rarely the power to prosecute. A three-year study of ninety-six Australian regulatory agencies found that a third had not launched a single prosecution during that time.[95]

When GEC and Westinghouse were prosecuted in the United States for price fixing, the top executives were exonerated on their assertion of ignorance while middle executives were given short sentences of imprisonment.[96] A compliance strategy of enforcement relies more on the threat than the reality of sanction. In their study of the British Columbia Workers' Compensation Board (WCB) and the Waste Management Branch of the Ministry of Environment, Brown and Rankin looked both at long-term compliance records and at whether those who proved resistant to persuasion were ultimately punished.[97] The compliance history of both disclosed that a substantial number repeatedly contravened regulatory requirements.[98] In dealing with this 'compliance deficit' the WCB has the unusual power to impose administrative monetary penalties without recourse to the courts. It emerged that the WCB invoked this power more frequently and with higher tariffs than were achieved by the Waste Management Branch's recourse to the criminal courts. Two of the reasons suggested for the different rate of penalty enforcement were that the administrative process is better geared towards recognizing the dangers of a risky work practice while the criminal courts are conditioned to dealing only with harm *ex post facto*, and that regulatory officials would be more reluctant to invoke a criminal process because of the stigma involved. But in what direction would such conclusions lead? If courts are reluctant to recognize the potential and actual harm of risky practices, then perhaps an administrative process might be preferred. But if stigma is an important aspect of the deterrent function of penalties then access to the criminal courts is necessary. The United States Department of Justice certainly believes that the very fact of indicting a corporation will lead to the introduction of immediate remedial steps in other corporations in that industry.[99]

This highlights a further confusion arising from the compliance and deterrence distinction. This concerns the implication that the underlying aims of each strategy differs.[100] A compliance system, say Hawkins and Thomas, 'is primarily concerned with preventing violations and remedying underlying problems' whereas deterrence involves 'detecting offences and punishing violators'.[101] This might be put differently: that deterrence achieves the aim of preventing violations and remedying problems *by punishing* those who violate whereas compliance *condones* violations in the hope of preventing future violations and in order to rem-

---

[93] Rowan-Robinson *et al.* 1990: ch. 8.   [94] Braithwaite and Pettit 1990: 184.
[95] Grabosky and Braithwaite 1986.   [96] Walton and Cleveland 1964.
[97] Brown and Rankin 1990.[98] Ibid. 336.   [99] US Department of Justice 1999: para 1.
[100] Reiss 1984 acknowledges the congruity in their aims.
[101] Hawkins and Thomas 1984: 13.

edy problems. In other words, the underlying goal is similar (both are aimed at compliance): what differs is the means adopted to achieve it. The enforcement pyramid advocated by Braithwaite and others provides a more integrated picture of compliance and deterrence.[102] Regulators under this model would begin with compliance measures such as advice, formal directions, and warnings on the assumption that the corporation has virtue. Only when this fails would the regulator move up the pyramid and deploy deterrent measures such as prohibition notices and fines. Prosecution would only be used as a last resort. In their thorough critique of this mixed 'carrots and sticks' model, Gunningham and Johnstone point to 'the large gap between theory and practice'. They point out that 'escalation' up the enforcement pyramid will be most needed against 'the intransigent, with the irrational, and most important, with the rational calculators, who believe it is not in their self-interest (usually financially defined) to comply voluntarily, and who are only likely to respond when the costs outweigh the benefits'.[103] These strategic 'game-players' are not susceptible to compliance strategies and the practical limitations on most regulators' activities make tough deterrence unlikely. Even where there appears to be an enforcement pyramid, a range of measures from advice to prosecution, the reality is that few businesses are ever subjected to the whole scale. Instead, the compliance base is used as a discrete set of measures for routine enforcement, while the deterrence top half comes into play only when there is a specific workplace injury. This leaves the 'rational calculators' with every incentive not to comply with their legal obligations.[104] A further limitation in the pyramid theory is that it is difficult to take account of the huge differences in attitudes to safety between, and even within, organizations.

The assumption implicit in much of the regulatory literature that the compliance/deterrence contrast reflects rather than helps to generate the difference in social construction between regulatory and conventional (police) enforcement should therefore be questioned. It is more likely that the so-called 'compliance' strategy is justified by *and* at the same time reproduces the view that the kinds of harms caused by industry are less worthy of condemnation than traditional crimes. Taken together with the characteristic form of regulatory schemes, the compliance/regulatory distinction can at most be seen as evidence of a much broader process of social construction. And, as I argue in more depth in Chapter 3, this inevitably interacts with legal and official responses to corporate harm.

The on-going argument within the regulatory literature as to whether compliance is either necessary or effective bears witness to the political stage on which the debate about corporate illegality takes place.[105] The details of that debate are not of concern here; what is important is to attempt to see the multi-faceted nature of the regulation/crime distinction. The failure rigorously to enforce

---

[102] Braithwaite, 1991; Sigler and Murphy 1989. See also Haines 1997 and Gunninghan and Johnstone 1999.
[103] Gunningham and Johnstone 1999: 121.   [104] Ibid. 123.
[105] Pearce and Tombs 1990; Hawkins 1990; Haines 1997; Gunningham and Johnstone 1999.

regulatory schemes taken together with the paucity of available penalties can be used to support the argument that crimes of the powerful are condoned and effectively, or even deliberately, de-criminalized. An accusation made against adherents of compliance strategies is that they have assumed both the legitimacy of the capitalist economic system and the illegitimacy of its being policed.[106] Furthermore, in choosing to take uncritically the enforcers' arguments that strict policing will not work it could be said that they stifle further debate and allow the agencies they study to continue believing their own rhetoric. It may also be necessary to readjust thinking about criminal responsibility to cater for the different challenge corporations bring; part of the difficulty may arise because corporations are often given the same due process safeguards as individuals.[107] Since they are not subject to pre- or post-trial incarceration and are not usually given to making false confessions it may be that these are unnecessary. The debate about the relationship between criminal justice and corporations will not advance unless some of these differences are taken on board.[108]

This contrasts with the realist approach taken by Braithwaite and Pettit: 'While there are important differences of degree, there is almost a sociological inevitability that ruling-class constituencies will mobilize their political and economic power so that enforcement directed against them will be more muted than that which the police deliver against the working class.'[109] Their diagnosis is similar to that of the compliance critics (that business is powerful enough to subvert regulation), but their solution is radically different. Instead of solving the perceived problem with more enforcement or with a socio-economic realignment they endorse a system of persuasion as more likely to achieve better results.[110] I have already discussed some of the theoretical and practical problems with this approach. Another difficulty is that it ignores the declaratory effect of criminal law enforcement. One of the reasons, but by no means the only one, that corporate crime has attracted little attention is that it is relatively recent. The public nature of criminal prosecution plays an important role in conveying cultural messages about types of behaviour and offences. A policy of persuasion can only be part of such a system of communication.

Thus, too much (or the wrong things) can be made of the distinctiveness of regulation.[111] Regulation should be seen as a type of enforcement of criminal law, not a separate notion altogether. While attempting to control the criminal activities of corporations does raise quite distinct issues, the ideological separation of crime and regulation does little to assist. The police do have the additional public order function, but this does not yield sufficient explanatory force to account for the discrete discourse of regulation. There is much ambiguity in the

---

[106] Pearce and Tombs 1990: 429–30.

[107] Nijboer 1999, and see *EPA* v. *Caltex* 1993 in which the High Court of Australia held that the privilege against self-incrimination was a *human* right.

[108] Box 1983: 70; Dan-Cohen 1986: ch. III; Ashworth 1999: 93–5; see the discussion below, Chs. 4 and 7.

[109] 1990: 191.   [110] Ibid. 192.   [111] See Pearce and Tombs 1990.

roles assigned to the regulatory agencies. The complex web of argument which has been woven above can perhaps best be encapsulated in the words of Pearce and Tombs, that there has been 'a failure to question, and to open up the possibility of transcending, the hegemony of corporate ideology'.[112]

4. CORPORATE SANCTIONS

It is interesting that the word 'punishment' is replaced when corporations are the object of criminal enforcement by the altogether less emotive 'sanction'. The words are sometimes used interchangeably, but while lawyers talk of civil sanctions they never speak of civil punishment. If we accept Garland's persuasive thesis that the social institution of punishment (what he terms 'penality') 'communicates meaning not just about crime and punishment but also about power, authority, legitimacy, normality, morality, personhood, social relations and a host of other tangential matters',[113] then the distinction becomes of significance. The process is interactive, and cultural changes are reflected in the structure of punishment.[114] This is partly what makes the argument about corporate liability so difficult, because it has to rely ultimately on changes in wider cultural perceptions and concerns. Blaming and punishing individuals inevitably has a longer history than talk of corporate liability. Business corporations and the technology they employ are relatively recent phenomena; they bring both benefit and potential disaster. As I argue in Chapter 4, notions of responsibility are part of the cultural reproductive process and cannot be isolated for the purposes of legal analysis. Punishment is similarly culturally constituted and reconstituted; the contemporary call for corporate punishment fits into that procreative cycle. When the wheel is stopped and a spoke, such as punishment, examined, it is salutary to remind oneself that its meaning depends on its relationship with the other radials, as well as the wheel itself being one part of a larger and more complex mechanism. It may seem premature to discuss types of corporate sanction before making an argument about corporate fault or about the nature of the corporate entity. The justification for this reverse logic is that, until some of the sentencing options are known, it is difficult to respond sensibly to arguments about accountability and fault. The common misconception is that corporate sanctions can only be exacted in the form of financial penalty is yet another consequence or manifestation of the individualist bias in criminal justice discourse. The notion of criminal law is predicated on the existence of a system of penalties.

Leaving aside for the moment what are undoubtedly polarities in our perceptions of individual and corporate crime, it is clear that the application of a penalty to a corporation raises a different set of problems. Determining the role of moral blame in the context of corporate punishment has proved a difficult although not insuperable task.[115] Most corporate crime theory has been

---

[112] Ibid. 430.   [113] Garland 1990: 252.   [114] Ibid. 250.
[115] Schlegel 1990: 15. And see Ch. 4.

deterrence based, in the sense that the purpose of instituting sanctions has been to discourage violations and encourage good practice. As we have seen, latterly arguments for invoking a just desert theory into corporate control have emerged.[116] There is sometimes a confusion between the use of the concept of deterrence as a broad justifying principle of punishment and its use at ground level to assist in describing enforcement practice. It is in the latter context that deterrence is contrasted with compliance. But as suggested earlier these alternative styles would perhaps be better seen as different or possibly complementary instruments, one the stick and the other the carrot, employed to achieve the same end.

Theories of sentencing have generally been slower to develop than theories of liability. For both individual and corporate defendants the rhetoric of due process ends on conviction: the sentencing stage has been far less circumscribed by procedural nicety. More effort does, however, seem to be made to relate sentence to the circumstances of the individual offender than to those of the corporate offender. Social inquiry reports are frequently prepared before sentencing individual defendants in both magistrates' and crown courts. With corporate defendants, however, no attempt is generally made to investigate their background or their assets; fines do not seem to be related to the corporation's means nor necessarily related to the severity of harm caused.[117]

i. FINANCIAL SANCTIONS

It is appropriate to begin with the fine since it is the main sanction employed against corporate offenders in England and Wales.[118] Other corporate sentencing options are explored in the following section.

The average fine imposed on companies following an HSE prosecution for a workplace death in the years 1996 to 1998 was £13,032.[119] Both the level of fines and the percentage of prosecutions brought in the magistrates' courts (where the maximum fine is £20,000) has increased since 1990.[120] At the same time there have been some notably large fines and each year the previous maximum appears to be exceeded. Fines in excess of a million have been known but these are rare birds indeed.[121] For health and safety breaches generally the average fine has been slowly increasing but had still only reached the level of £5,421 (or £3,266 when adjusted for exceptional fines).[122] The appellate courts have begun to show con-

---

[116] Ibid. See also Fisse 1983 and 1990.

[117] Bergman 1991: 35.

[118] Regulatory agencies have powers to issue prohibition and other notices but these are not court-ordered sanctions.

[119] Centre for Corporate Accountability 1999. There were 96 prosecutions (of which 75% were tried summarily) during this period.

[120] Bergman's figures for 1988–90 were an average fine of £1,940 with 61% tried summarily.

[121] For example, Balfour Beatty were fined £1.7 million following the collapse of a tunnel they were building for the Heathrow express link, 15 Feb. 1999, and GWT £1.5 million after the Southall rail crash in 1997.

[122] Health and Safety Bulletin Feb. 1998: 266.

cern at the low level of fines imposed and described as 'derisory' the fine of £100 handed out to British Steel for a breach of safety regulations which led to a worker's death.[123] Of course, part of the reason for the failure to link the fine to the harm relates back to the point mentioned already, that the offences with which corporations are charged are drawn almost exclusively from the regulatory calendar and the harm is often not part of the offence description. This would certainly be the case with the HSE prosecutions referred to. Additionally, the vast majority of health and safety prosecutions take place in the magistrates courts rendering the fines subject to statutory maxima. Almost half the fines in magistrates courts in 1997–8 were below one-quarter of the maximum.[124] However, there is no reason why these should be set at the same level for corporate defendants. Even the very large exemplary fines in the crown court often represent a tiny fraction of the company's turnover. Gobert points out that the £750,000 fine on BP in 1987 amounted to 0.05 per cent of the company's after tax profits.[125]

The sentencing guidance in health and safety offences recently provided by the Court of Appeal may herald a new era of more punitive sentencing.[126] The court outlined as aggravating features: causing death, failure to heed warnings, and taking risks to maximize profits. Mitigating factors include prompt admission of responsibility, timely guilty plea, evidence of having taken steps to remedy the deficiency, and a good safety record. Because the objective is to achieve a safe working environment, fines need to be large enough, the court said, to bring home the message not only to managers but also to shareholders. The fine should not be so large as to imperil earnings of employees, but there may be cases where the offence was so serious that the defendant ought not to be in business. Mr Justice Scott Baker added some interesting observations: 'As to the level of fines imposed generally for offences of this nature, it is the view of each member of this court that they are too low and therefore not an appropriate yardstick for determining the level of fine in the present case.'[127] Any fine should reflect not only the gravity of the offence but also the means of the offender,[128] and this applies just as much to corporate defendants as to any other. He added further that magistrates should always think carefully before accepting jurisdiction in health and safety at work cases, 'where it is arguable that the fine may exceed the limit of their jurisdiction or where death or serious injury has resulted from the offence'.[129] This strong message from the Court of Appeal will take time to filter through to the agencies involved in determining the mode of trial and the level of fines sought (the HSE, the magistrates, and crown courts).

But it will be necessary to go further and to relate the fine concept to the reality of corporate finances rather than to assume that the same limits should apply to

---

[123] *R v. British Steel* (1995).
[124] *R v. Howe and Sons (Engineers)* (1999), per Scott Baker J.
[126] *R v. Howe and Son (Engineers) Ltd* (1999).
[128] Criminal Justice Act 1991, s. 18(3).
[129] *R v. Howe and Sons*, (1999) per Scott Baker J at p. 255.

[125] Gobert 1994a: 394.
[127] At 253.

business enterprises as to individuals. Precedent for differential fines for corporations can be found in the Australian Commonwealth Crimes Act 1914, section 4B which provides:

> 2A Where a natural person is convicted of an offence against a law of the Commonwealth in respect of which a court may impose a penalty of imprisonment for life, the court may, if the contrary intention does not appear and the court thinks it appropriate in all the circumstances of the case, impose, instead of, or in addition to, a penalty of imprisonment, a pecuniary penalty not exceeding $200,000.
>
> 3 Where a body corporate is convicted of an offence against a law of the Commonwealth, the court may, if the contrary intention does not appear and the court thinks fit, impose a pecuniary penalty not exceeding an amount equal to 5 times the amount of the maximum pecuniary penalty that could be imposed by the court on a natural person convicted of the same offence.

A provision such as this ensures that corporations can be more effectively punished for serious offences, such as those carrying life imprisonment, and that for other offences it is permissible to introduce a multiplier to reflect their different resources.[130] Another solution to this problem is that adopted by EU antitrust laws which allow fines to amount to up to 10 per cent of the offending company's previous year's global turnover.[131] This also overcomes the criticism that the effect of fine can be minimized through the use of subsidiary companies. However, enforcement ultimately depends on seizure of assets, which will be locally limited.[132]

The use of financial penalties often implies the assumption of a model of the corporation as 'profit maximizer'. Stone alerts us to two problems with this.[133] One is that a sum which will be big enough to deter will often also make the enterprise unworthwhile. Because, unlike a human person, a corporation cannot be threatened with imprisonment in default of payment, a wealth boundary or 'deterrence trap' limits the impact of fines.[134] The other is that the assumption itself may be faulty. Corporations, even if goal orientated, do not necessarily have only one goal in mind. Once survival is secure, the corporation will seek 'a *satisfactory* level of profits—that is, enough profits to stave off shareholder insurrections. . .'.[135] Even if it makes sense to threaten profits, legal sanctions have to be sensitive to the fact that, comparatively, they are of very little significance to a large corporation. Profits can be increased or undermined from many more sources: through personnel policies, competitors' moves, investment or not in production and so on.

The most developed system of corporate fines is found in the Federal Sentencing Guidelines in the United States, which also has some of the most draconian liability principles as well.[136] The Guidelines reward companies which have an effective compliance plan in place and for reporting the breach with up to

---

[130] Corns 1991: 354.
[132] Fisse 1990: 229.
[134] Coffee 1981; 390; Fisse 1990: 217.
[136] Summarized in Coffee 1999.

[131] Fisse 1990: 228. EEC Council Reg., art. 15(2).
[133] 1975: 36–9.
[135] Stone 1975, 39.

90 per cent reduction in the fine for which the company would otherwise be liable.[137] The effect of these provisions is to introduce an affirmative partial defence to an otherwise strict liability regime.

The sanction of fine has to be viewed in the context of the conviction it accompanies.[138] To the extent that criminal penalties have an impact or influence on a corporation's standing or reputation then a stigmatic effect can be claimed. As with individual offenders there will be a complex interaction between social and legal constructions of behaviour. Raising the consciousness of victims and the public to the nature of corporate crime is both necessary in order for sanctions to be effective but also could result from the imposition of some of those sanctions particularly if publicity were a major factor.[139] Not all corporations operate in the same social and business milieu but it would be wrong to claim that criminal prosecution (even where only followed by a fine) might never adversely affect business reputation.

However, the effectiveness of the fine as a deterrent or its appropriateness as a retributive penalty is clearly open to question. A less cogent argument raised against many suggested corporate penalties, including fines, is that they incur undesirable and/or unfair secondary harmful effects. For example, when British Rail was fined £250,000 and ordered to pay £55,000 prosecution costs for an admitted failure to ensure the safety of employees and passengers following the Clapham rail collision in 1987, the trial judge confessed that he faced an 'acute problem'. Since BR was funded by the taxpayer and its customers, the fine could only be met either by increasing the burden on fare-paying passengers which was hardly logical or by reducing the finance available for improvements to the railway system. He concluded that he had to take into account the necessity of marking society's disapproval of BR's failures.[140] This is reminiscent of how the unfair secondary costs of individual criminal punishment are justified or at least explained, and suggests that there is no reason to give it more weight in relation to corporate defendants. The argument that it is unfair to pass on the costs of corporate penalties to the consumer can be conversely argued: that it is unfair that consumers should benefit from the crimes of corporations. 'Unless the corporate enterprise is punished for crimes perpetrated on its behalf', writes Fisse, 'the price of its goods and services will not accurately reflect the cost of production; instead the social cost of corporate crime will be passed on to society as a whole or to particular segments of the public.'[141]

Other groups affected by corporate sanctions are shareholders and employees. From a deterrence perspective could it be argued that this is irrelevant, since the goals of those punished indirectly (the corporation's officers, employees, and shareholders) are the same as those of the corporation itself?[142] Stone, focusing particularly on shareholders, disagrees. Their absence of identity with the

---

[137] US Sentencing Guidelines manual, ch. 8. para. 8A1.2 and Federal Principles of Prosecution of Corporations, Department of Justice 1999.

[138] Ibid. 229.   [139] Box 1983: 66.   [140] *Guardian*, 15 June 1991.

[141] Fisse 1990: 212.   [142] Schlegel 1990: 25.

corporation is reflected in two of the basic notions of corporate status, limited liability and bankruptcy.[143] Their insulation means that they are unlikely to take the action to protect their (unthreatened) interests. It seems strange, however, to protect shareholders on the ground that they are already protected (by limited liability and so on). The argument slips uneasily from one based on effectiveness (on which he has a point) to one based on fairness (on which he does not). 'Controlling through law becomes not only, as behaviourists would say, a misplaced faith on "negative reinforcement" (trying to teach people through punishing undesired acts rather than by rewarding good ones) but it is also the least effective sort of negative reinforcement, one administered almost randomly (or so it seems) by a nonrespected source.'[144] But this could equally be deployed as a telling argument against the use of fines or any other criminal penalty for individual offenders. There is no reason, Pearce writes, 'why shareholders should not bear these costs since they benefit from corporate crime, have all the privileges associated with limited liability and rarely suffer the environmental hazards produced by their corporations'.[145]

The unfairness argument gains more ground in so far as penalties impose costs on employees.[146] One deterrent financial penalty which it is claimed avoids inappropriate, ill-directed secondary damage is the equity fine.[147] This would be levied in equity securities rather than in cash and would consist of a block of new common stock in the corporation. This would be issued to a state crime-victim compensation scheme. The resulting stock-dilution would have impact on shareholders rather than on employees or consumers.[148] This also overcomes the problem that the maximum meaningful fine (in deterrence terms) is necessarily bounded by a corporation's wealth.

Although equity fines are specifically designed as a form of corporate sanction they would not represent a radical rethinking of the problems criminal justice systems face when confronted by corporate wrongdoing. They suffer the same deterrent weakness as conventional fines, which is that risk of apprehension and punishment is likely to be the major deterrent factor. Additionally, they make no contribution to reform of the corporation's internal procedures nor necessarily ensure that individuals within the company are disciplined.

It is essential that any discussion of corporate sanctions addresses whether there should be more variety in the calendar of penalties.[149] The selection of penalty will to some extent be a function of the aim. The use of prison for individuals has been partly explained by a traditional emphasis on the socially undesirable nature of offences.[150] Therefore it is inconsistent to use fines as the only punishment for corporate offences. 'Fines do not emphatically convey the message that serious corporate offences are socially intolerable. Rather they create

[143] Stone 1977: 58.   [144] Ibid. 42.
[145] Pearce 1987: 127; and see Dunford and Ridley 1996: 11.
[146] And increasingly these groups may overlap.
[147] Coffee 1981: 413; Heine 1999: 248.   [148] Fisse 1985: 142.
[149] Gobert 1998.   [150] Fisse 1990: 219.

the impression that corporate crime is permissible provided the offender merely pays the going price.'[151]

ii. NON-FINANCIAL SANCTIONS

The spectrum of possible penalties here runs from incapacitation in the form of corporate dissolution, corporate 'imprisonment', through to probation, adverse publicity, community service, direct compensation orders, and punitive injunctions.[152] 'These approaches are promising because they increase the variety of deterrent, retributive, and rehabilitative measures available against corporations and in so doing circumvent some of the major limitations of monetary sanctions . . . [T]he anatomy of corporate crime is so diverse that effective sentencing requires a range of sanctions.'[153] It can be noted that the penalties for the proposed corporate killing offence include the power to make remedial orders to ensure a safer system in the future.[154]

Incapacitation through compulsory winding up or closure is the most drastic penalty available and is used in some jurisdictions against corporations formed for an illegal purpose.[155] US federal courts have used the option of 'imprisonment', restraining the corporation from acting in specified ways, since 1988.[156] Described as 'judicially mandated restructuring of internal corporate processes', corporate probation can also be regarded no less efficient than a fine.[157] Probation orders have been used in Canada either separately with the imposition of conditions or in combination with other types of order. They are 'potentially powerful instruments' which can include punitive as well as rehabilitative elements.[158] The costs of probation can be charged to the company and at the same time the probation conditions can require corporate decision-making to be restructured. Corporate probation orders are authorized in the United States under the Sentencing Reform Act 1984.[159] Braithwaite, developing his theory of 'republican' criminology,[160] contends that business regulation would be more effective if instead of a bipartite game between the state and a regulated industry a third element were introduced, a community group with active interest in the regulatory domain. The proposal involves the use of the enforcement pyramid discussed above through which the state signals that it has a range of sanctioning possibilities. The first level is persuasion and the ultimate (capital punishment) is 'license revocation', with warning letter, civil penalty, criminal penalty, and licence suspension in between.

Adverse publicity could also be used as part of the strategy to combat corporate disregard of criminal law and as a backup to probation. This is an old idea writ new; as Fisse reports the nineteenth-century Bread Acts incorporated the

---

[151] Ibid. 220.
[152] Ibid. 249; Heine 1999; Gunningham and Johnstone 1999: 262–77.
[153] Fisse 1990.
[154] *Draft Involuntary Homicide Bill*, Clause 5, Home Office 2000.
[155] Heine 1999: 246.
[156] *US v. Allegheny Bottling Co.* (1988).
[157] Note, Yale 1979: 365.
[158] Prefontaine 1999: 280.
[159] 18 USC para 3551.
[160] Braithwaite and Pettit 1990.

same notion.[161] The importance of prestige and status to many corporations is evidenced both by their extensive use of brand-image in advertising and by their efforts to regain a 'clean' image after a major disaster is associated with their name. Examples of extensive post-disaster advertising include PanAm following Lockerbie and P&O following the *Herald of Free Enterprise* at Zeebrugge.

Preventive sanctions are increasingly favoured.[162] The US Sentencing Guidelines as I have noted encourage compliance through rewarding monitoring and self-reporting. The recognition inherent in these ideas, that regulation often lacks punitive bite whereas conventional enforcement often ignores the possibilities of negotiation, is useful. But, as with earlier proposals for the appointment of independent directors to monitor corporate behaviour,[163] any suggestion of this sort has to counter the forceful argument that the underlying problem of economic dominance by some large corporations is still there. Where they are premised on an attempt to reform companies from within, such measures have been dubbed under the broad head of 'the social responsibility movement'.[164] These in turn have attracted the criticism that they are based on a misunderstanding of the nature of capitalism.[165] Based on the assumption that corporate deviance arises from the nature and structure of business organizations, these proposals aim at encouraging companies to take into account and absorb in their decision-making matters such as safety and consumer protection, factors which might otherwise be neglected. Public corporations, it is argued, are owned by a dispersed range of shareholders who have little or no control over the day-to-day or even year-to-year management. Managers have control over resources which they do not own and on a scale which no one individual would ever likely own. In addition, the organizational structure is such that knowledge and control is disaggregated: corporate goals are the responsibility of a large number of individuals who may not know what other individuals are doing.[166] Recognition of these factors leads to suggestions for new types of corporate fault, for broader-based forms of corporate liability,[167] as well as for internal reformative programmes. Glasbeek writes of Canada, but his points are relevant in any Western economy with large national or multi-national businesses:

In a democracy, elected government is to set the standards and norms for economic and social behaviour. In [the Canadian] democracy, the profit-maximisation by individual economic actors is accepted by government to be the motor of our economy. In an economy with many independent, unrelated economic actors, this should leave government free to set standards and norms. The problem is that the Canadian economy is not of that kind. Democratic control has to be subjugated to large private interests which can determine the level of economic activity and general welfare. . . . [I]n the ideal, to recapture democratic control over the state, a curtailment of existing economic power is imperative.[168]

---

[161] Fisse 1990, 240; 6 & 7 Will. ch. 37 ss. 8, 12 (1836); 1 & 2 Vict. ch. 28 ss. 7, 11 (1838); Dunford and Ridley 1996: 13.

[162] Heine 1999: 252.   [163] Stone 1975.   [164] Glasbeek 1988; Ryan 1990; Haines 1997.

[165] Glasbeek 1988.   [166] Ryan 1990: 358–9.   [167] See the discussion, Ch. 8.

[168] Glasbeek 1988: 400–1.

In the end, just as the analysis of punishment itself has to draw on a number of perspectives, so also there will be different types of sanction within the broader social institutions they serve. While Glasbeek may be right that any attempt to curtail corporate wrongdoing within current politico-economic structures will be of token effect overall, there is still something to be said for small gains. Not all corporations are huge multi-national organizations although there would be something distasteful about a system which self-consciously targeted the small fry through a sense of powerlessness over the big. An analysis which acknowledges the complexities and contradictions of modern politico-economic formations might well recognize that a single solution is a blind alley. Much theorizing about criminal punishment is open to the criticism that it holds constant factors which are obstinately mobile in the real world. This is particularly so when it comes to deterrent arguments for which is there is not a great deal of empirical support.[169]

[169] Dandurand 1999: 273.

3

Attribution of Responsibility

The construction of events, their translation into 'accidents' or 'crimes', responses of blaming others, self-blame, or stoic acceptance of 'fate', can be seen as the life blood of a legal system. While the following chapter focuses on the legal minimum before criminal accountability can attach, here the stress is on social or cultural perceptions of behaviour. It is a commonplace that the legal prohibition of behaviour does not necessarily mean the enforcement or even public acceptance of the undesirability of such behaviour. This sometimes reflects moral, religious, or class differences. The processes of social construction by which deaths come to be seen as examples of culpable homicide rather than 'accidents' are complex and involve all sorts of institutions: media; official inquiries; regulatory bodies; legal processes such as inquests as well as more diverse cultural influences. In the first section I examine at a broad level the social construction of corporate harms; I then move to psychological explanations of blame attribution before discussing in the third section the interaction between social construction, blame attribution, and legal causation. I conclude the chapter with an assessment of the roles played by formal state institutions such as inquests and public inquiries in forging and responding to public awareness and fears of technological risk.

1. SOCIAL CONSTRUCTIONS OF CRIME

Media news selection is gauged to be one of the most powerful methods by which people form their ideas and conceptions of crime and criminals.[1] Certain types of death are presented through personified versions of events with victim and perpetrator often given stereotyped descriptions such as 'gangland feud' or 'domestic tiff', while others are rendered less alarming by the use of statistical presentation.[2] Stereotypes enable conceptions of crime to be diffused.[3] As a result the victims of corporate crime may not see themselves as such at all.[4] Corporate criminal activity suffers (or benefits) from this.[5] Disasters are the most publicized form of corporate damage; employee injury, consumer harm, and environmental pollution are not always associated with corporate activity.

It is helpful initially to reflect on some of the reasons why these days we are more likely to turn to blaming corporations when things go wrong. Drawing on

---

[1] Quinney 1970: 282. [2] Schur 1980: 174. [3] Quinney 1970: 286.
[4] Clinard and Yeager 1980: 9. [5] Hills 1987.

the analysis developed by Felstiner, Abel, and Sarat[6] on the transformation of a personal injury into a legal dispute, three stages—naming, blaming, and claiming—can be observed in the move from acceptance of death and disaster to the wide-felt need to blame. The 'naming' is the recognition that disastrous events are more than 'accidents' or 'acts of God'—this is where cause becomes a vital issue. The 'blaming' occurs through changing ideas about human behaviour and social groupings; a systems-based conception of organizational behaviour has gradually come to replace the assumption that individuals act either alone or as atoms in a wider group. The third stage in this adaptation of their thesis, the stage at which criminal law is deployed, is perhaps better termed 'de-claiming' to emphasize its symbolic dimension.

A shift in the political and social frameworks of blame has placed responsibility for untoward events at the door of organizations rather than at those of individuals, and has resulted in the use of criminal rather than or in addition to civil remedies. Technological advances, leading to completely different hazards, can be identified as the first stage in this process. Greater mobility through mass transport introduces an increased likelihood of collisions and explosions of near universal threat. Combined with the associated transmission and publicity this means that we are more aware of the threat. Changes in cultural beliefs have affected the process of attributing cause and therefore blame. The boundaries between what is natural and what is man-made are increasingly questioned. There are more man-made events as technology grows, but technology also affects the previously 'natural'; flooding or forest fires present good examples. What looks like a natural disaster is often attributable to some human industrial or agricultural activity further upstream. Then there is the illusion of control. At first technological development was relatively localized and mechanically within the grasp of individuals. Compared with so-called natural disasters which, though powerful and sudden are familiar and inflict damage which is visible, technological disaster can be invisible, and universally threatening.[7] We know that people will take and therefore accept greater risks if they believe they are in control and if they believe the activity is voluntary. Technological catastrophes arise when systems which were thought to be under control fail.[8] 'Not having control when one expects to have it appears to have different psycho-physiological consequences than does not having control when one had no expectations for it.'[9] Connected to this is the finding that the risks which people are prepared to take vary in relation to their voluntariness; there is far greater tolerance of chemicals when consumed voluntarily in food than of lower-risk environmental chemicals.[10] Familiarity also alters our perceptions of risk which perhaps explains how we ever bring ourselves to make a journey by car or why people are resistant to move from earthquake-prone areas. High personal cost is traded off (although not in algebraic terms) against benefits such as maintaining

---

[6] Felstiner, Abel, and Sarat 1980. [7] Baum *et al.* 1983: 334. [8] Ibid. 346.
[9] Ibid. 348. [10] Katzman 1986.

a lucrative lifestyle and not having to move. People select and distort what they attend to, and many do so differentially according to their preference for risk, in order to reduce conflict. They may completely suppress any thoughts about the undesirable aspects of a hazard.[11] Advanced transport systems, industrial development generally, and widespread interdependence means that more and more areas of life are not perceived as within individual control. This leads to an increase in blaming others.

Attitudes to safety and risk affect both the propensity to blame and the target of it. The importance both of risk perception and of the part played by perception in what have hitherto been accepted as objective risk assessments is being increasingly recognized.[12] Ulrich Beck's 'risk society' thesis provides powerful insights into the role and focus of blame in contemporary society.[13] One of Beck's interlocutors has recently distilled the concept of 'risk society' in a way that may be more accessible for a legal audience. Anthony Giddens has cautioned that the idea of 'risk society' might suggest a world which has become more hazardous, but this is not necessarily so. Rather, it is a society increasingly preoccupied with the future (and also with safety), which generates the notion of risk; the use of 'risk' is taken to represent a world 'which we are both exploring and seeking to normalise and control'.[14] In this understanding, 'risk society' suggests a society which increasingly 'lives on a high technological frontier which absolutely no one completely understands and which generates a diversity of possible futures'.[15] The risk society derives from two fundamental transformations connected to the increasing influence of science and technology: 'the end of nature' and the 'end of tradition'.[16] The 'risk society' is one that creates manufactured risk. Science and technology create as many uncertainties as they dispel.

Risk society raises issues of trust, accountability, and personal responsibility. The social institutions associated with law themselves play a significant role in risk management and the production of risk knowledge. Concern with risk is not merely to do with knowledge of probability, it is to do with cultural attitudes to the acceptability of different hazards. The relationship between risk and blame can be understood in this way. Perceptions of risk affect the ways in which societies respond to different threats, how they distribute institutional authority; and they additionally provide the focus for debates about morality and identity.[17]

It is the tension between vulnerability and powerlessness and the illusion of voluntariness and control that characterizes the risk society. Technological innovation leads to an acceptance of and reliance upon others. Risk increases but it is also under control. In societies where risk is privatized, it is a matter for individual judgement, as well as an issue of institutional trust. Individual situations are also institutional because, as Beck argues, 'the liberated individual is dependent on a series of secondary agencies and institutions'.[18] The relationship between the individual and institutions affects all aspects of the question we are consider-

---

[11] Lee 1981.   [12] Hood and Jones 1996.   [13] Beck 1992 and Giddens 1991.
[14] Giddens 1999.   [15] Ibid. at 3.   [16] Ibid.
[17] Douglas 1992.   [18] Beck 1992: 130–2.

ing here. It affects the social, economic, and cultural context in which people live their lives; it affects their perception of risk; and it affects their understanding of the causes of untoward events. The changing relationship between individual citizens and community, and between social and state institutions, inevitably brings shifts in our understanding of those institutions themselves.

The example of the BSE/CJD crisis as it developed in the United Kingdom in the 1990s illustrates well our preoccupation with risk and its deployment as a cultural resource, including its potential to provide a vocabulary with which to make sense of seemingly uncontrollable hazards.[19] On the one hand, technological innovation has transformed the food economy into a major international business reliant on mass-production methods and transportation—hence the emergence of the risk of widespread (invisible) contamination. On the other hand, our familiarity with and reliance on risk analysis leads to the belief that danger is quantifiable and predictable. BSE has shaken those beliefs and at the same time confirmed that bringing hazard under control is both individualized and reliant on expert knowledge. Even in the wake of the total scandal of government ignoring the possibility that BSE was transmissible to humans,[20] there was still considerable objection to the ban on the sale of beef on the bone in 1998.

2. BLAME ATTRIBUTION

Psychological attribution theories assume that an individual's perception of the causal relations in the environment is an important determinant of that person's reaction to environmental events. These attributions are often distorted by the perceiver's personal motivations.[21] Motivational explanations may, states Burger, bias the perception of responsibility for tragic consequences, such as those caused by natural disasters, disease, crime, and accidents.[22] This, of course, begs all the questions which cultural analysis raises such as what is the line between nature and man-made, when is an accident avoidable or not, and so on. Victim blaming, for example, serves the useful purpose, especially if the victim dies, of 'silencing indictment of the whole social system.'[23] Psychological reactions will tell us something about individual responses to misfortune but will also be derived from and possibly informative of the cultural infrastructure. Reactions to victims of serious 'accidents' have then to be regarded as socially or culturally contingent but nonetheless contribute to a better understanding of public responses to examples of major disasters and other harms.

Common theories of adjustment to major traumas include those of, *just world*, *control*, and *defensive* attribution.[24]

(*a*) The *just world* hypothesis asserts that because we have a need to believe that people get what they deserve and deserve what they get; if subjects are

---

[19] Cooke 1999. [20] See Phillips Report 2000. [21] Burger 1981.
[22] Ibid. [23] Ibid. 56 [24] Janoff-Bulman and Wortman 1977.

exposed to a victim of misfortune, they will either blame or derogate the victim.[25]

(*b*) Walster's *control* theory argues that as the consequences of an accident become increasingly severe, people become motivated to assign blame to someone possibly responsible for the accident.[26] This reassures people that they will be able to avoid similar disasters. If causality is assigned to an unpredictable, uncontrollable set of circumstances, individuals are forced to concede that such an event might happen to them.[27] Viewing the event as a predictable, controllable one, deciding that '*someone* was responsible for the unpleasant event, will allow the observer to feel somewhat more able to avert such a disaster'.[28] Subsequent research has not been successful in replicating Walster's results. Shaver introduced two new variables: personal and social similarity.[29] He argued that before motivational distortion can occur, observers must feel a degree of situational similarity.

(*c*) Shaver coined the term *defensive attribution* to describe the hypothesis that people assign causality in order to maintain or enhance their self-esteem; their reactions are affected by their desire to avoid blame for their own future accidents.[30]

The more people believe that they may one day find themselves in the perpetrator's (or victim's) shoes, the more they will prefer to attribute the perpetrator's (or victim's) behaviour to chance. Such an attribution implies that they too will be protected from blame.[31]

Just-world and defensive attribution are similar in that they are 'based on the same self-protective motive'.[32] Both theories emphasize the need to attribute the accident to chance as a way of avoiding harm in the future. This need increases as the similarity between the perceiver's and the victim's 'worlds' increases.[33]

These are reactions of others. What about reactions of victims? The motives and attitudes of, for example, survivors and relatives following major disasters could be examined with such a perspective. If just-world theory were applied we might expect victims to be motivated to believe that they deserved the outcome and would blame themselves. Control theory would lead them to blame those factors that are most within their control. To attribute it to chance would be unlikely as that is not in their control. Defensive attribution would also be likely to lead to a need to blame others. In their study of spinal cord accident victims which attempted to relate blame attribution with coping, Janoff-Bulman and Wortman found that 'the results provide clear evidence for a correlation between the attributions of blame made by the victims and their ability to cope with victimization. Individuals who blamed another for their accident also showed great difficulty in coping.'[34] This unexpected pattern of relations emerged between feelings of

---

[25] Lerner and Simmons 1966.
[26] Walster 1966.
[27] See also systematic treatment by Kelley 1971.
[28] Walster 1966: 74.
[29] Shaver 1970.
[30] Ibid.
[31] Janoff-Bulman and Wortman 1877: 351.
[32] Burger 1981: 507.
[33] But note that Shaver (1970) found that 'instead of altering their perceptions of accident responsibility, individuals who witness a severe accident perpetrated by a person similar to themselves may simply deny the similarity'.
[34] Janoff-Bulman and Wortman 1977.

perceived avoidability, self-blame for the accident, and coping is at odds with the conventional view that litigation may be therapeutic. On the other hand, there was a complex relationship between self-blame, avoidability, and coping. Individuals who blamed themselves for the accident also tended to feel that they could have avoided it; but perceived avoidability was negatively correlated with effective coping whereas self-blame was positively correlated.[35] In trying to decide whether they could have avoided the accident, many respondents appeared to consider whether the activity they had been engaging in was a common one for them or one they just happened to be doing when the accident occurred. If it was common, for example swimming or sport, then they saw it as unavoidable. If it was unusual for them, then they saw it as avoidable. There was also correlation with enjoyable, regular leisure activities and lack of self-blame and good coping. The study found little evidence for defensive attribution, they seemed to attribute more blame to themselves than objective circumstances would warrant.[36]

The unexpected amount of self-blame was consistent with just-world and control hypotheses, with the conclusion that the data was more indicative of a need for an orderly and meaningful world than a need for a controllable one. These victims were going to live with the results of the accident for the rest of their lives; what about other victims. The same authors found that rape victims explained their attack with behavioural self-blame which enabled them to see future attacks as avoidable.[37] The accidents were from a variety of causes but the sample was selected because of their 'chance' or 'freak' natures. At first sight this might render the study unilluminating in the present context. The categorization is, however, somewhat problematic since determination of cause is a function of the depth of inquiry; the National Coal Board initially attributed Aberfan to freak geology. One hundred and forty-four people, most of whom were children, were suffocated when slagheap slurry cascaded onto a village in South Wales. The NCB blamed 'a coincidence of a set of geological factors, each of which in itself is not exceptional but which collectively created a particularly critical geological environment'.[38] The Tribunal of Inquiry commented that:

This was the starting point of an attempt persisted in for many weeks by the National Coal Board, to persuade acceptance of the view that the concatenation of geological factors on Merthyr mountain was such as could not reasonably have been expected to exist. The observation . . . might conceivably have had some bearing on our task had there ever been an attempt to ascertain what the geological features were; but, since there was no investigation and no thought devoted to the subject, the claim carried one nowhere.[39]

Perhaps this earlier experience with apathy explains why the Robens Report on health and safety at work went on to conclude that

the traditional concepts of the criminal law are not readily applicable to the majority of infringements which arise under this type of legislation. . . . [Few offences] arise from

---

[35] Ibid. 362. [36] Ibid. 367. [37] Janoff-Bulman 1979.
[38] Report of Tribunal of Inquiry, 1967: para 190; see generally McLean and Johnes 2000.
[39] Ibid.

reckless indifference to the possibility of causing injury . . . The typical infringement . . . arises rather through carelessness, oversight or lack of knowledge or means, inadequate supervision or sheer inefficiency.[40]

Since control and avoidability come out strongly as motivating forces behind patterns of blaming it would be possible to explain the increased tendency to blame corporations for disasters which previously were dismissed as fate, nature, or 'one of those things', in these functional terms. The variable of identification with the victims' fate is also of interest.[41] It might be thought to be one factor which helps to explain the way Aberfan was constructed compared with later disasters such as the *Herald of Free Enterprise*, Hillsborough Stadium, and the Southall rail crash.[42] Living in the shadow of an NCB tip is experienced by relatively few people compared with the numbers using public transport or watching football matches (even if only on television). Aberfan was also extremely localized whereas transport and football disasters have a much wider geographical range. Of course, the constellation of factors operating at any one time is complex. Not so many people use ferries but those who do are relatively affluent, therefore able to organize their protest, voice their complaints; and their experience would be amplified by their lack of control over the situation. Road accidents are often thought to be perceived differently (and feared less) not only because they happen frequently but rarely kill large numbers at the same time, but also because drivers believe themselves to be in control. In the case of the *Herald*'s capsize at Zeebrugge a blindingly simple causative factor combined with the sense of trust which passengers have to place in those in charge would also have contributed to the horror. Secularization of society may be regarded as an underlying ingredient too. Taylor has suggested that fear of crime is a metaphor for the generalized anxiety caused by lack of a secular ethic with which 'to make sense both of our fragility and our unique importance as diverse human beings'.[43] Blaming corporations could be seen in these terms, that it is a process reflecting the unease and vulnerability which life inevitably entails.

The combination of psychological data and socio-cultural theories gives insights, which in a purely 'legal' account would be obscured, into the social construction of crime. What has been given here is inevitably superficial but provides an important background to a comprehension of attitudes to blame.

3. CAUSE AND BLAME

Cause underlies blame. To blame someone for an occurrence is to assert a causal relation, although the converse is not true. There is a deep tension between the needs of the legal system to name an individual, whether in a civil or criminal

---

[40] Robens 1972: para. 261.
[41] e.g. Ford's indictment over the Pinto deaths, Cullen *et al.* 1987.
[42] In 1987, 1989 and 1997 respectively.   [43] Taylor 1983: 107.

action, and the multiplicity of causes of any event. Causation illustrates well the argument that legal doctrine owes its existence to and is therefore dependent on a constellation of a wide range of factors. The inevitable result is that legal principles are blurred and often irreconcilable.

It is a trite point that in most cases imputing cause presents little difficulty. For those situations where there might be problems in choosing between a selection of immediate actors (the intervening event case for example), Hart and Honoré propose that legal liability attaches on the basis of the abnormality of the cause. In other words, certain things are taken for granted such as a reasonably competent, good-faith rescue and medical service. Where the result, the death, can be attributed to a break in that expectation (especially if the incompetence was gross) then the original but-for cause may be wiped out.[44] But a principle which depends on a criterion such as normal/abnormal runs into the problem that it involves a value-judgement. '[O]ne obvious way of fleshing our ideas of "abnormality" . . . is to do so in terms of degrees of responsibility or culpability.'[45] Causation then ceases to be determined from within but draws on other considerations such as intention, knowledge, or recklessness which are necessary anyway to a finding of culpability. 'Because attribution lies on the fault line between the law's abstract view of individual agency and the social contexts within which individual agency is rooted (and by which it can validly be said to be "caused" in the Hart and Honoré sense), the question of legal causation must always ultimately rely upon a closure of the issue brought about "from outside", by "policy" argument.'[46]

The classic intervening cause examples tend to divert attention from other circumstances in which multiplicity of cause also complicates the attempt to establish a clear line of causal attribution from an event to an individual. Norrie terms this the 'historically rooted contradiction between legal form and social context'.[47] Disasters provide a useful illustration of this. It will be helpful first to point up two different ways in which corporate wrongdoing might manifest itself. There is, on the one hand, systemic harm caused by workplace or more widespread exposure to toxic material.[48] On the other hand, there are specific incidents which cause specific injury or death. Because they usually attract detailed formal investigation in the form of public inquiries, publicized inquests, and so on, disasters provide useful material from which to draw when considering the complexity of factors which contribute to social perceptions of corporate activities. Although there are interesting questions about what makes a particular event a 'disaster', those are not my concern here. The insights which are gained need not be restricted to large-scale incidents and can be helpful in assisting our thinking about attribution of cause and blame in relation to corporations.

---

[44] Hart and Honoré 1985: 352 et seq.
[45] Lacey and Wells 1998: 35. See also similar arguments by Ashworth 1999: 126 and Norrie 1991.
[46] Norrie 1991: 689.   [47] Ibid. 688.
[48] For a useful account of developing group liability in US tort cases, see Bush 1986; for the UK see Hedley 1994.

The range of causal factors from which to select in our explanation or attribution of any accident includes at one end the individual operator's human error and at the other the accepted practices and operating procedures of particular industries. Two examples illustrate this: the *Herald of Free Enterprise* disaster in 1987 and the Southall rail crash in 1997.

The following extracts from the Sheen Report into the *Herald of Free Enterprise* disaster display an unusually explicit account of the different causal factors.

M.V. Herald of Free Enterprise Report of the Court No. 8074, Dept. of Transport[49]

Para 1.1

On the 6th March 1987 the Roll on/Roll off passenger and freight ferry HERALD OF FREE ENTERPRISE under the command of Captain David Lewry sailed from Number 12 berth in the inner harbour at Zeebrugge at 18.05 G.M.T. The HERALD was manned by a crew of 80 hands all told and was laden with 81 cars, 47 freight vehicles and three other vehicles.

Para 1.2

Approximately 459 passengers had embarked for the voyage to Dover, which they expected to be completed without incident in the prevailing good weather. There was a light easterly breeze and very little sea or swell. The HERALD passed the outer mole at 18.24. She capsized about 4 minutes later. During the final moments the HERALD turned rapidly to starboard and was prevented from sinking totally by reason only that her port side took the ground in shallow water. The HERALD came to rest on a heading of 136° with her starboard side above the surface. Water rapidly filled the ship below the surface level with the result that not less than 150 passengers and 38 members of the crew lost their lives. Many others were injured. The position in which the HERALD came to rest was less than 7 cables from the harbour entrance and was latitude 51°22′28.5″ North, longitude 3°11′26″ East.

The Immediate Cause of the Disaster

Para 10.1

The HERALD capsized because she went to sea with her inner and outer bow doors open. From the outset Mr Mark Victor Stanley, who was the assistant bosun, has accepted that it was his duty to close the bow doors at the time of departure from Zeebrugge and that he failed to carry out this duty. Mr Stanley had opened the bow doors on arrival in Zeebrugge. Therafter he was engaged in supervising members of the crew in maintenance and cleaning the ship until he was released from work by the bosun, Mr Ayling. Mr Stanley then went to his cabin, where he fell asleep and was not awakened by the call 'Harbour Stations', which was given over the Tannoy address sytem. He remained asleep on his bunk until he was thrown out of it when the HERALD began to capsize. Mr Stanley has frankly recognized his failure to turn up for duty and he will, no doubt, suffer remorse for a long time to come. If the Company regards it as appropriate or necessary to take disciplinary action against Mr Stanley it has power to do so under the Code of Conduct for the Merchant Navy. [The report then acknowledges Mr Stanley's bravery in assisting with the rescue operations.]

---

[49] Sheen 1987.

Para 10. 6

. . . Mr Leslie Sabel, the Chief Officer, relieved the second Officer as loading officer of G deck shortly before he instructed the quartermaster to call the crew to harbour stations. Accordingly, it then became the duty of Mr Sabel to ensure that the bow doors were closed. He does not dispute the fact that this was his duty. But he, too, interpreted the instruction laid down in July 1984 [that it was the duty of the officer loading G deck to ensure that the bow doors were 'secure when leaving port'] as a duty merely to ensure that the assistant bosun was at the controls. Mr Sabel had been working with Mr Stanley during the day of the disaster and he knew that it was Mr Stanley's duty to close the doors. Mr Sabel should have been able to recognize Mr Stanley.

Para 10.9

. . .Of all the many faults which combined to lead directly or indirectly to this tragic disaster that of Mr Leslie Sabel was the most immediate.

Pressure to Leave the Berth

Para 11.1

The Court found some difficulty in finding a clear answer to the question: Why could not the loading officer remain on G deck until the doors were closed before going to his harbour station on the bridge? That operation could be completed in less than three minutes. But the officers always felt under pressure to leave the berth immediately after the completion of loading . . .

Captain David Lewry

Para 12.1

Captain David Lewry was Master of the HERALD on the 6th March 1987. In that capacity he was responsible for the safety of his ship and every person on board. Captain Lewry took the HERALD to sea with the bow doors fully open, with the consequences which have been related. It follows that Captin Lewry must accept personal responsibility for the loss of his ship.

Para 12.5

In mitigation of Captain Lewry's failure to ensure that his ship was in all respects ready for sea a number of points were made on his behalf, of which the three principal ones were as follows. First, Captain Lewry merely followed a system which was operated by all the masters of the HERALD and approved by the Senior Master, Captain Kirby. Second, the court was reminded that the orders entitled 'Ship's standing orders' issued by the Company make no reference, as they should have done, to opening and closing the bow and stern doors. Third, before this disaster there had been no less than five occasions when one of the company's ships had proceeded to sea with bow or stern doors open. Some of those incidents were known to the management, who had not drawn them to the attention of the other Masters. Captain Lewry told the Court that if he had been made aware of any of those incidents he would have instituted a new system under which he would have required that the doors were closed. It is possible that he would have done so. But those Masters who were aware of the occasions when ships proceeded to sea with bow or stern doors open did not change their orders . . .

Captain John Michael Kirby

Para 13.1

Captain Kirby was one of the five masters who took it in turn to command the HERALD. He was the Senior Master as from May 1985. One of his functions as Senior Master was to act as a co-ordinator between all the masters and officers of the ship in order to achieve uniformity in the practices operated by the different crews.

Para 13.3

But not only did Captain Kirby fail to enforce such orders as had been promulgated, he also failed to issue clear and concise orders about the closing of the most important doors on G deck. He should have introduced a fail-safe system . . .

The Management

Para 14.1

At first sight the faults which led to this disaster were the aforesaid errors of omission on the part of the Master, the Chief Officer and the assistant bosun, and also the failure by Captain Kirby to issue and enforce clear orders. But a full investigation into the circumstances of the disaster leads inexorably to the conclusion that the underlying or cardinal faults lay higher up in the Company. The Board of Directors did not appreciate their responsibility for the safe management of their ships. They did not apply their minds to the question; What orders should be given for the safety of our ship? The directors did not have any proper comprehension of what their duties were. There appears to have been a lack of thought about the way in which the HERALD ought to have been organised for the Dover/Zeebrugge run. All concerned in management, from the members of the Board of Directors down to the junior superintendents, were guilty of fault in that all must be regarded as sharing responsibility for the failure of management. From top to bottom the body corporate was infected with the disease of sloppiness. . . . The failure on the part of the shore management to give proper and clear directions was a contributory cause of the disaster . . .

One of the reasons that traditional accounts of causation are unhelpful in these contexts is that their starting place is often that of an individual defendant facing a charge: did this person contribute causally to this result? That particular person's causal contribution is then all that matters; whether the result might additionally have been caused by someone else is not a relevant issue (unless it is one of the rare cases where a third party nullifies the causal effect).

The Southall rail crash in 1997 provides an example. The Automatic Warning System which would normally alert the driver if he passed a signal at danger was malfunctioning in one of the train's two power units. On its outward journey to Swansea the faulty unit was at the back of the train. The engineers were unable to fix it on arrival at Swansea. One solution would have been to reverse the train's configuration and place the functioning unit at the front of the train. This would have caused a delay. Instead the driver was authorized to operate the train without the warning system. When the train was in the last 10 miles of its journey to Paddington, its London terminus, the signals changed to red (stop). By the time the driver noticed the signal, it was too late to stop the train ploughing into a freight train which was crossing in front of his train. Seven people died. Was the precipitating factor in the train crash that the freight train was crossing later than usual? Or the driver's inattention? Or was it the decision not to swap over the power units? All of these were not normal. It was, however, normal to operate a train with one driver. There was no provision made by Great Western trains to prohibit a train operating without the warning system in place.

How is the decision to be made as to which or how many different causal actors are to be held responsible? Multiple causation is accepted implicitly when joint principals are charged or in complicity allegations. But it is less common, outside the joint enterprise example, for the notion that there may be a number of layers of causal responsibility to be explicitly acknowledged in criminal law. Feinberg notes that causal questions are likely to expand, 'Causal processes, of course, become much more complicated than simple models like stick rubbing suggests, and as our means for producing changes become more variegated and complex, our models for understanding causal talk shift and divagate.'[50]

The *Herald of Free Enterprise* case was exceptional for two reasons: to begin with the Sheen Report was very specific in its account of the distribution of causal factors and in addition, a point not unconnected with the first, sufficient pressure was brought to bear to induce the Director of Public Prosecutions to institute a corporate manslaughter prosecution. Once the decision was taken to prosecute P&O there seemed no question that all the employees named in the Sheen Report should also be prosecuted. It seemed to be assumed that if the company was to be charged then so also should each and every person however lowly their employment status. As well as P&O itself, included were the assistant Bosun, the Bosun, the Chief Officer, the two captains (Lewry and Kirby) as well as two representatives of senior management.[51] Assuming that a case could have been made against the company the implication was that they should all be convicted. Yet it is clear that the involvement of each was not only of a different magnitude but of a different order. The company's failure was the provision of a safe operating system. The Assistant Bosun's failure was to fall asleep on the job, in circumstances in which he was one member of a large team over whom he had no control. He would have found no refuge in the rules of causation or principles of culpability, although a jury might have rebelled at the inequity of convicting him of the same offence as the company. There was a nascent recognition of the qualified culpability of the operating officers in the decision to drop the charges once the case against the company had been declared unsustainable. It is instructive to think about ways in which the distribution and degree of culpability in the corporate context might be reflected.

As I suggest in Chapter 8.4 there may be good reasons for exonerating (partially at least) the immediate causal actor where their action was itself a product of management policies. This may seem a novel suggestion but if one reason for extending corporate liability is the realization that human action is a product of a complex web of relationships in which 'the individual' and 'society' are both

---

[50] Feinberg 1970: 159.
[51] The prosecutions arising from both the *Herald* and Southall disaster are discussed in detail in Ch. 6.

abstractions,[52] then it makes sense to apply that thinking to the employee. The Sheen Report emphasized the conflicting instructions which the Chief Officer had to work under and the extremely long hours which may have contributed to the Assistant Bosun's sleeping through the call for 'harbour stations'. If supervening 'abnormal' events can break the chain of causation, albeit only in the most exceptional cases, then it seems possible to mount an argument based on 'supervening employment requirements'. Another route to the same result would be to develop Feinberg's criticism of the view (espoused by Hart and Honoré)[53] that the concept of 'voluntary act' usually excludes an event caused by another person, on the ground that a person can be manipulated by another to act.[54] A similar argument could be used here. While this is open to the objection that it would be a haven for excuses of the 'I was only doing what I was told' variety, we cannot ignore the fact that prosecutorial discretion is continually being exercized in the making of choices as to which causal actor is prosecuted. It is argued in Chapter 8 that corporate liability should include an aggregation principle and that corporate fault should be drawn from a wider range of company employees than the identification rule presently permits. One implication of such a move would be that corporate liability would be more easily shown. Thus, in cases such as that in respect of P&O and Zeebrugge, a corporate prosecution could be separated from that against specific individuals. In some cases, of which Zeebrugge arguably is one, there might additionally be sufficient evidence to prosecute individual defendants also. It may be that a (partial) defence of 'employee necessity' should be available so that the individual's role is reduced either to that of an ancillary party or, possibly more appropriately, to an equivalent of inchoate liability. This would reflect the fact that the employee had been reckless but would prevent her being used as a scapegoat of the company's failure to devise and/or implement and/or enforce an adequate safety procedure.

It is clear therefore that legal determination of cause is relatively unsophisticated and often uncontentious. Many of the decisions which establish which causal actor to pursue are made at a broad cultural level. Since this is a process of selective reduction from a range of factors all of which satisfy the legal rules, the resulting decisions (producing a limited number of defendants) never come to be examined from a legal angle. This builds on Norrie's conclusion that 'Causal agency can only be artificially located in individuals in abstraction from their place in social relations, structures and belief systems, and therefore the work of location must ultimately be carried out by a fiat based upon non-individualistic, socio-political criteria.'[55] Cultural and psychological theories of blame attribution may help to identify some of those criteria. Deaths and serious injuries have an economic and political component as well as the more obvious emotional and religious connotations. There is a tendency for institutions to solve some of their organizational problems through public allocation of blame.[56] Cultural selection determines which dangers are recognized: the social institutions of public inquiry

---

[52] Williams 1965: ch. 3.   [53] Hart and Honoré 1959, 1st edn.   [54] Feinberg 1970: 159.
[55] Norrie 1991: 38.   [56] Douglas 1985: 56.

and punishment are ways in which this selection is translated into action.[57] Public moral judgements 'powerfully advertise certain risks' and thus a symbiotic relationship is produced between those risks and legitimating moral principles.[58] While all cultures share a basic repertoire of explanations for misfortune, argue Douglas and Wildavsky, which includes blaming the victim in a moralistic style, blaming unpopular groups or forces in an adversarial style or deflecting blame in a no-fault style, the choice is a function of the particular type of social organization in that society.[59] A hierarchical society will use a public inquiry to control the blaming process which can lead to a legitimating cover-up and avoidance of adversarial open dispute.[60] In relation to corporate harm the cultural shift which appears to be taking place can be seen perhaps as evidencing a move from a bonded, hierarchical society to one which sees confrontation as a condition of justice. In the next section I explore some of the formal manifestations of the blaming process; these are affected by, and themselves affect, public sentiment.

4. Institutional influences

The legal system's assumption that there is an easy distinction between establishing the cause of an event and attributing blame for it has been subjected to critical scrutiny above. This assumption and its associated problems are manifest in the institutional framework, not just at the criminal trial, which is but one stage in the criminal justice system. The process leading to trial in most cases is relatively simple and involves only one or two state agencies (the police, the Crown Prosecution Service and/or a regulatory body). But sometimes, as with deaths in disasters, other institutions play a significant role in determining the state response. The social and cultural responses to untoward events that have been described earlier in this chapter are first played out on the legal stage at coroner's inquests or public inquiries or both. Almost by definition disasters are out of the ordinary, and there is no agreed or consistent pattern of response. The causes (at whatever level) are rarely readily apparent as they would be if a multiply-stabbed body were discovered. The coroner (with or without an inquest) is the state's official certifier of cause of death. Additionally, a disaster usually prompts the calling of a public inquiry which generally is asked to give a causal account. There are different types of inquiry, some are judicial, some statutory, some both. What happens at the inquest and inquiry level will contribute to the eventual social and legal construction of the event.[61] Unlike a criminal trial there is no defendant on whom to focus, a choice can be made as to the range and depth of the causal search. Inquests and inquiries have ambiguous roles both in relation to each other and in terms of their role in determining or allocating blame. The ambiguity is inevitable given the reluctance to

---

[57] Ibid. 54. [58] Ibid. 60.
[59] Douglas and Wildavsky 1982: ch. VII; see also Sanders and Hamilton 1997.
[60] Douglas 1985: 64. [61] Wells 1999.

acknowledge that establishing cause can take place at a number of levels and that the level chosen will decide the extent to which blame is considered. In other words, when a person is tried for a homicide, it is necessary to establish whether their acts or omissions were *a* cause of the death, but not whether anyone else contributed. An inquest or inquiry can look at a whole range of causal factors. The inquest's role is more clearly laid down and I look at that first. The argument which I make is that both the inquest and inquiry play a role in the construction of corporate crime; and that, because of the ambiguity in their functions, the discretion vested in those who preside over them and their relationship with the prosecution mechanism, this role is exceptionally and perhaps intentionally difficult to unravel.

i. THE CORONER'S INQUEST

The office of coroner dates back to medieval times,[62] although its form and function have altered considerably. Originally established as a means of raising Crown revenue',[63] the office 'was at its zenith in the second half of the thirteenth century',[64] after which a combination of factors led to its decline.[65] Nonetheless, the coroner's role in respect of 'sudden' or 'unnatural' death was well established by the nineteenth century.[66] The inquest has been gradually subordinated first to the medical profession, and more recently to the police and to the Director of Public Prosecutions. Because many 'sudden' deaths turn out to be from 'natural' causes the Coroners Act 1926 allowed coroners to hold a *post mortem* without an inquest, unless the death was violent or unnatural.[67] The coroner has a discretion to hold an inquest in other cases in order to allay suspicion. About a third of all deaths are reported to the coroner, and of those only 12 per cent gives rise to an inquest; and very few of those are conducted with a jury (one in 25).[68] Deaths in a disaster are always followed by an inquest, because an inquest is mandatory where there is reasonable cause to suspect a violent or unnatural death. There has to be a jury where death is caused by an accident notifiable under the Health and Safety at Work Act 1974, or where the death occurred in circumstances the continuance or possible recurrence of which is prejudicial to the health and safety of the public or any section of the public.[69] Most disasters will satisfy one or both of

---

[62] The office was established in 1194, almost coinciding with the replacement of trial by ordeal by trial by jury in 1215, see Green 1985: 51. See generally on the early years, Hunnisett 1961 and for a general history, McKeogh 1983.

[63] Hunnisett 1961: ch 1. The coroner at this time could be called upon to perform almost any duties, including that of full-time official to present Crown pleas.

[64] Ibid. 190.

[65] Hunnisett notes the decrease in the number of appeals, the abolition of the *murdrum* fine, the cessation of the general eyre (a periodical circuit of justices which could hear all manner of pleas), and the rise of the local justices of the peace.

[66] Warwick Inquest Group 1985: 38.

[67] Now Coroners Act 1988, s. 19. Various other statutes provide for a mandatory inquest following deaths in particular circumstances.

[68] Tarling 1998.   [69] Coroners Act 1988.

these conditions. Inquests with juries occupy an important symbolic, declamatory role in the legal process.

An inquest's role is to determine who the deceased was and how, when, and where the deceased came by her death.[70] There is no prescribed list of inquest verdicts but the Coroners' Rules give a number of suggestions which include accident/misadventure, unlawful killing, or an open verdict.[71] In order to bring in a verdict of unlawful killing, a jury needs to be convinced on the criminal standard of proof that the deaths were caused unlawfully.[72] The official purpose of an inquest is not to determine criminal or civil liability. Yet disaster inquest juries have sometimes defied the coroner's instructions and returned verdicts of unlawful killing.[73] This could be regarded as unavoidable where a lay panel is allowed the final say in a legal forum. But it could also be explained as the result of a fundamental contradiction in the role of the inquest. Historically, determination of criminal liability was part of the inquest's formal remit. It was only in 1977 that coroners' juries lost the power to commit a named individual for trial.[74] Until this reform the inquest could function as an alternative to the normal procedure for bringing a person to trial on indictment. Perhaps it was anticipated that the abolition of the committal power would result in some change in the underlying function of inquests, but it is difficult to see how that could have been achieved given that the rest of the procedure was left unaltered. Inquest juries are told both that they are not concerned with criminal liability and that they are to reach a conclusion about how the deceased came to die.

This simple division between allocation of blame and establishing cause is not a distinction which is easy to maintain. The jurors at the inquest into the deaths of passengers on the *Herald of Free Enterprise* at Zeebrugge could go about their task of accounting how the victims came to die in a number of ways. They could select the from the following cumulative levels of causal specificity:

(*a*) the deaths were caused by drowning;

(*b*) the people drowned because the ferry capsized;

(*c*) the ferry capsized because the bow doors were left open;

(*d*) the bow doors were left open because the Assistant Bosun did not shut them;

(*e*) the doors were not shut because the Chief Officer did not check whether the AB had closed them;

(*f*) the ferry sailed with the doors open because the Captain did not check that the doors were shut;

[70] Coroners Act 1988, s. 11(3)(a).

[71] Coroners Rules 1984, Sched. 4, Form 22, note 4, S.I. 1984 No. 552.

[72] i.e. beyond reasonable doubt that the deaths were caused by another's gross negligence. *R v. West London Coroner, ex parte Gray* (1987).

[73] Zeebrugge inquest 9 Oct. 1987 (192 deaths from ferry capsize in 1987), Glanrhyd, 22 July 1988 (3 died after rail bridge collapsed), and Clapham, 13 Sept. 1990 (35 died after signalling failure, 1989). In the inquest into the King's Cross fire the coroner withdrew the unlawful killing option on the advice of the Lord Chief Justice, *Guardian*, 12 Oct. 1988.

[74] Criminal Law Act 1977, s. 56.

(g) the ferry sailed with the bow doors open because P&O failed to respond to requests by captains that door indicator lights be installed on the bridge)[75] . . . And so on.

These are all valid causal explanations. Is the inquest a forum for answering the causal question at the furthest level of generality or is the answer expected to be more specific?[76]

As the explanations become more specific, the causal explanations become more judgmental. It is not possible for a jury to eschew questions of liability in deciding how a person came to die while at the same time considering a verdict of 'unlawful killing' as one of their options.

ii. PUBLIC INQUIRIES

Public inquiries following disasters have a number of functions and purposes. As well as providing a forum in which those directly affected, whether bereaved or survivors, can transact their grief and anger or other emotions in a controlled and public manner, they can also furnish an opportunity for the event to be held up to public obloquy and to exert pressure for policy changes. The purposes of an inquiry are to establish the facts, survey causes, and identify any culpability. This Section looks first at the different types of public inquiry, and secondly at their powers and procedures.

We freely use the term 'public inquiry' as though everyone were clear about what was meant. This is far from the case. Not only is everyone not clear but it would be almost impossible to achieve any degree of clarity. Although major disasters are invariably followed by some form of inquiry, 'public inquiry' is a generic term which provides a useful cover for a labyrinthine substructure. Broadly, inquiries can be divided into two types: technical investigations and judicial inquiries. Technical investigations are those which have to be held following certain types of accident. For example, rail, air, and shipping accidents all have their own statutory systems of mandatory inquiry. Often these are conducted in private by an inspector, although in general a report is published. These technical inquiries generally attract little attention although in terms of avoiding future disasters their findings may be extremely valuable.

Judicial inquiries take a number of forms. Many statutes which provide for the mandatory technical inquiries described above also give discretion for a more formal investigation in the nature of a public inquiry to be set up. A disaster may often trigger the exercise of this discretionary power; for example, after the *Herald of Free Enterprise* capsized with the loss of 192 lives off Zeebrugge in 1987, the Minister of Transport ordered a Formal Investigation under Merchant

---

[75] As revealed in the company's manslaughter trial these requests were greeted with derision by its directors, *Guardian*, 15 Sept. 1990.

[76] The inquest into the deaths in the Aberfan disaster seems to conform to this type. The hearing lasted 4 minutes because the coroner directed that the conclusion of the Tribunal of Inquiry amounted to a finding of accidental death, *The Times*, 29 Sept. 1967.

Shipping legislation.[77] The King's Cross underground fire later that year gave rise to a formal investigation under the Regulation of Railways Act 1871.[78] These investigations are closer to the ad hoc judicial inquiry, than they are to the technical accident investigation (despite sharing the same legislative base as these latter). Ad hoc inquiries are set up where there is no specific provision for accident investigation. The football stadium disaster at Hillsborough prompted the Home Secretary to appoint Lord Justice Taylor to conduct an inquiry.[79] Lastly, there is a very special type of 'discretionary' or judicial inquiry—those set up under the Tribunals of Inquiry Act 1921. The Cullen Inquiry into the shootings at Dunblane in 1996 was the first Tribunal of Inquiry for 14 years, although it appears to have established a trend. It was closely followed by the establishment of that into child abuse in North Wales children's homes and was also chosen for the inquiry into the events leading to the conviction of Dr Harold Shipman.[80] Of the disasters studied here, only *Aberfan* gave rise to a 1921 Inquiry.[81] Tribunals of Inquiry carry great weight, and they require the authorization of both Houses of Parliament that the matter is 'of urgent public importance'. They are always chaired by a senior judge and exercise High Court powers.

The lack of uniformity between types of inquiry leaves a significant discretion in the hands of the Government in how to orchestrate the public response to a disaster. This discretion is increasingly under challenge. First, the long-running dissatisfaction with the handling of the *Marchioness* disaster, discussed below, gave rise to an inquiry into whether there should be a public inquiry.[82] This disclosed for the first time a number of government papers on the holding of an inquiry, in particular a memorandum (whose circulation was previously restricted) by the Lord Chancellor's Department in 1991. This outlined the order of priority between inquiry and criminal investigation following a disaster.[83] Secondly, the decision to hold a departmental rather than a public judicial inquiry into the Harold Shipman murders was successfully challenged in a judicial review.[84]

There are variations in the powers and procedures between the different types of inquiry. Predicting which type of inquiry will be used is an inexact science but the following indicators can be used: the more serious the incident, the more likely that a judge will chair it, and that a form of inquiry allowing witnesses to be compelled and to give evidence on oath will be used (thus pointing to an ad hoc judicial inquiry or Tribunal of Inquiry). Whichever form of inquiry is set up, it will be reported as 'a public inquiry'—the people who will know the difference will be the lawyers and those who have to give evidence.

---

[77] Sheen Report 1987. [78] Fennell Report 1988; Hidden Report 1989.
[79] Taylor Report 1990; and see Popplewell Report 1986 [Inquiry into the Bradford Stadium Fire].
[80] Waterhouse 1999 and Laming Inquiry appointed 2000.
[81] Edmund-Davies Report 1967.
[82] Clarke 2000 decided that there should be a public inquiry, see n. 91.
[83] Ibid. Appendix D.
[84] *R v. Secretary of State for Health, ex parte Wagstaffe, R v. Secretary of State for Health ex parte Associated Newspapers Ltd* (2000). Shipman was a general practitioner who is thought to have murdered up to 150 elderly patients.

As to powers and procedures, judicial inquiries share the following general characteristics: they become high-profile, are usually held in public, and will be chaired by a judge or, (1921 Tribunals excepted), senior Queen's Counsel. More specifically, the inquiry will have terms of reference; the Chair will probably appoint a Counsel to the inquiry, whose job will be to elicit and lay before the inquiry relevant evidence, and 'wing' members and/or expert assessors to assist. The Inquiry's powers will partly be determined by its terms of reference within which it must always act. However, these are generally very broad as exemplified by those of the Hillsborough Inquiry: 'to inquire into the events at Sheffield Wednesday football ground on 15 April 1989 and to make recommendations about the needs of crowd control and safety at sports events', or for Piper Alpha: 'an inquiry to establish the circumstances of the accident and its cause'.[85]

Tribunals of Inquiry under the 1921 Act, and many judicial inquiries set up under specific Acts of Parliament, provide powers to compel witnesses, to compel the production of documents, and to require evidence to be given on oath. Departmental inquiries do not. One reason why Ministers' thoughts turn to 1921 Act Tribunals of Inquiry rather than the discretionary inquiry is for the powers they bring. It can be difficult to predict the procedure which will be adopted since even the same type of inquiry may be conducted differently according to the circumstances, including the personal style of the Chair. This is a good moment to consider why judges are used for many inquiries. Judges bring a number of qualities. First, they impart what can be called 'borrowed authority'. It can be politically useful for government to have the shield of a senior judge. So it might be said that the greater the potential embarrassment to the Government, the more senior the judge. Secondly, judges import professional expertise in the conduct of hearings, in sifting evidence, and appraising the veracity of witnesses. Thirdly, they have 'lofty detachment' from the rough and tumble of party politics.[86] Of course, the very reasons that lead government to rely on judges (their authority, expertise and detachment), also mean that they are likely to exercise an independent attitude to procedure.

The procedure adopted will reflect the general purposes of inquiries: establishing facts, determining cause, and allocating blame. Many of the procedural difficulties arise not from the lack of a single model but from the nature of the inquiry process itself, which is inquisitorial rather than adversarial. Although individual reputations and public safety may be affected, inquiries do not give rights in relation to such matters as legal representation, cross-examination, or of appeal. One of the major difficulties (from a lawyer's point of view) presented by inquiries is how they fit into the legal scheme of things. Our court tradition is built on the adversarial model under which the judge acts as umpire between two sides, each of which presents facts and law. This adversarial model of procedural fairness depends, among other things, on notice and disclosure, confrontation and cross-examination, and a reasoned decision. An inquiry is clearly not like

---

[85] Cullen Inquiry 1990.   [86] Blom-Cooper 1996.

that. It is not a trial, with an allegation, or a statement of claim, with a burden of proof, and with a determination at the end that one side has made out the case. The inquiry itself is responsible for gathering evidence, questioning witnesses, and determining the progress and direction of the proceedings. On the other hand, as with so many attempts to divide up the world into neat categories, there is more of a continuum than this might suggest with some inquires having more adversarial elements than others, different groups of individuals having different sets of interests. Survivors and those bereaved clearly have agendas at variance with those of corporations, or the police.

A review commissioned by the Lord Chancellor's Department and published as advice by the Council on Tribunals in February 1996 recommended that inquiries should where possible be held in public; that there should be a preliminary public hearing at which the inquiry's procedural ground rules can be announced, explained, and discussed with 'the major interested parties'.[87] This covers all those likely to be called as principal witnesses. Witnesses would have advance notice of the inquiry's areas of concern and the extent to which they may be vulnerable to criticism. If damaging evidence emerges after the witness has given evidence, there should be an opportunity to respond. The document draws a distinction between legal advice (help in preparing for the inquiry) which should always be allowed, and representation (speaking through a lawyer) which should not be an absolute entitlement. This, along with other aspects of how the inquiry actually goes about its work, should be in the discretion of the inquiry Chair.

To summarize this section, there is no simple structure of public inquiry, neither the type of inquiry nor the procedural safeguards adopted is capable of prediction but in practice there are many areas of commonality. Difficulties arise because of the inquisitorial model and because of the relationship between inquiries and inquests, discussed below.

Inquest procedure is largely in the coroner's discretion and there is no legal aid for the family of the deceased to be represented. Coroners often say that the purpose of an inquest is not to determine civil or criminal liability and at one level that is right. The inquest cannot determine these matters, but on the other hand, in order to answer the questions an inquest is mandated to answer (in particular, how the deceased came to die), an answer in terms of civil or criminal liability may be unavoidable. The main mechanisms for avoiding this clash of purpose are that coroners are required to adjourn any inquest pending police investigation of any possible homicide charges, and that any inquest held after a trial cannot record a verdict inconsistent with the finding of the trial. Therefore, the sequence of events following the *Herald of Free Enterprise* disaster was most unusual. There the inquest jury returned unlawful killing verdicts before the question of prosecution had been considered. This demonstrates clearly the socio-cultural impact on legal proceedings: the idea that a company running a ferry service might be indictable for manslaughter did not apparently occur to the police and

---

[87] Council on Tribunals 1996.

no investigation was launched. The combination of an inquiry report in which Mr Justice Sheen condemned P&O's sloppy management and disregard for safety, and the inquest verdicts (facilitated by a legal challenge to the coroner brought by the Herald Families Association),[88] led to a belated examination of criminal proceedings. P&O were eventually prosecuted. The *Marchioness* Riverboat disaster in 1989 also gave rise to unusual proceedings. The inquests were delayed while the captain of the dredger was tried for an offence under the Merchant Shipping Act, a process which took some time. The coroner's decision in 1992 not to resume the inquests on the grounds that this would be an unnecessary formality was successfully challenged.[89] The inquests were eventually held six years after the tragedy when, defiantly, the jury returned verdicts of unlawful killing.

The relationship between inquiry and inquest can be difficult to predict but in general the inquest will usually await any inquiry. Part of the problem with the proceedings following *Marchioness* was that the inquiry (conducted by the Marine Accident Investigation Branch) was held in private and the report withheld until August 1991, nearly two years after disaster.[90] The eventual inquest revealed evidence which contradicted that of the official inquiry. All this contributed to the relatives' not unreasonable belief that they had been deprived of the opportunity of a public forum in which to transact their grief. A judicial inquiry was eventually instituted in 2000.[91] Broadly, inquiries might be seen as serving a public need to establish causes and recommend preventive measures. Inquests represent a more individually based investigation, which relatives seem to regard as very important for two main reasons: first, an inquest allows them to grieve over their own particular loss and to separate their relative from the disaster as a whole, and secondly, inquests through their juries are seen as a useful way of exerting pressure on authorities to consider criminal proceedings.

The Home Office conducted an interdepartmental investigation into the roles of the public inquiry and the inquest following disaster in 1990.[92] The duplication which currently occurs is thought to be both wasteful and also difficult for witnesses. Three options were considered, to subsume the inquiry into the inquest, to subsume the inquest into the inquiry, or to retain both with a limited role for the inquest. The first was thought to be problematic because coroners are not the sort of authority figures which would reassure the public. The second would require a number of statutory changes since inquests are mandatory in these circumstances while inquiries are not. Therefore, the third option found favour. Under this recommendation, not only—as now—would an inquest be adjourned pending any public inquiry, but coroners would only be able to resume for limited purposes after the inquiry. The resumed inquest would be without jury, would allow admission of documentary evidence (for example, the Inquiry

[88] R v. *HM Coroner for East Kent, ex parte Spooner* (1989).
[89] R v. *Inner West London Coroner, ex parte Dallaglio and others* (1994).
[90] Department of Transport 1990.   [91] Clarke Inquiry, appointed 2000.
[92] Home Office 1997.

Report) thus saving witnesses from having to rehearse oral evidence once more. Thus the inquest would effectively be subordinated to the inquiry. It is anticipated that these proposals would be controversial since the symbolic and instrumental pull of the jury is strong. Arising from this a requirement has been introduced that they must adjourn if the cause of death is likely to be investigated in a public inquiry.[93]

Thus the process whereby a disaster arguably caused by corporate recklessness comes to be considered as possibly giving rise to criminal liability is complex. The 'legal' questions such as 'identification' for the purposes of corporate liability and gross negligence for the purposes of establishing manslaughter play a small and insignificant role in this. The DPP, the public inquiry, and the inquest can each be considerably influenced by the timing, and the findings, of the others. The DPP and the police have powers which can ensure either that criminal proceedings are concluded or discounted before any inquest is held. This can have the effect of reducing inquests merely to a formality, unable to contradict previous findings, albeit those findings having emerged from an entirely different forum. The dangers to individuals of having their trial prejudiced by an inquest verdict have to be taken into account. Where there is only one possible suspect the dangers are far greater. But few cases are so clear cut. There is often room for doubt as to whether the right person was prosecuted or as to whether the evidence disclosed a criminal offence at all. With regard to the latter, the DPP is vested with enormous power. The decision that there should be no prosecution may effectively foreclose the issue. As the Clapham inquest showed inquest juries can, if they feel strongly enough (and if the coroner allows them),[94] defy that assessment. But inquest juries are largely at the mercy of outside institutional forces. The recommendation of the Fennell Report into the King's Cross fire that the requirement to hold an inquest should be abolished where there has been a Formal Investigation into an accident would confirm and exacerbate this.[95] The inquest occupies an important place in allowing, through the jury, a voice for public reproach of corporations for their neglect of safety. Any move to rationalize the institutional responses to disasters should take into account the role that a lay panel such as an inquest jury can play in voicing culturally changing attitudes and be wary of giving too much discretion to executive arms of the state with their tendency to regard corporate harms uncritically.

All deaths have an economic and a political component as well as the more obvious emotional and perhaps religious connotations. There is no simple account of a disaster. The inquest shares its place as a forum of public response and as a means of determining cause and allocating blame, with the media, public inquiries, and sometimes the criminal trial.[96]

---

[93] Access to Justice Act 1999, s. 71.

[94] Cf. the King's Cross inquest.

[95] Fennell 1989: para. 19.40. The Lord Advocate already has an equivalent discretion in Scotland but in any case the Fatal Accidents and Sudden Deaths Inquiry (Scotland) Act 1976 does not provide for juries.

[96] See Haines 1997: 221 and Wells: 1995*a*.

Any consideration of corporate liability which ignores the complex process of social construction will be arid and unproductive. There has been an extraordinary increase in the attention given to corporate responsibility both in the media and in scholarly literature in the past few years. It is undoubtedly the case that each has fed on the other and also that they form part of an elaborate pattern of cultural changes prompted by technological, political, economic, and social movements. None of these can be isolated, but nor can they all be examined simultaneously. My arguments about corporations and criminal responsibility are offered with that qualification or proviso.

4

Criminal Responsibility and the Corporate Entity

> If, for example, the invisible, intangible essence of air, which we term a corporation, can level mountains, fill up valleys, lay down iron tracks, and run railroad cars on them, it can intend to do it, and can act therein as well viciously as virtuously.[1]

The extent to which stereotypes of criminal behaviour rely on images of individual offenders is nowhere seen more clearly than in the doctrinal explanations of the criminal law. The literature of criminal law assumes that subject and object are individual. Indictments are brought in the name of the Queen (an individual, albeit a privileged one) and summonses carry the name of the individual law enforcer. Most people recognize that behind this façade is the state. When it comes to the defendant, however, individualism is ubiquitous. So, when a company is prosecuted, the incongruity of a case name like *Tesco Supermarkets* v. *Nattrass*[2] is more marked. This is both a trivial and a significant point. Trivial because we know in fact that individual law enforcers bear more power and responsibility than ordinary citizens, but significant because even at this public symbolic level the idea that criminal law concerns communities or groups rather than individuals is precluded.[3]

In order to understand the legal system's difficulties with making corporations criminally accountable we need to examine some of the instruments it employs to ascribe responsibility.[4] This is usually conducted at two (doctrinally) separate but (factually) interconnected levels. First, there is the 'who did what'/causation level, and, second, there is ascription of legal responsibility. Specific issues of causation were discussed in Chapter 3 along with a general examination of attribution theories. In this chapter I first give a critical account of the mechanisms through which criminal law ascribes individual culpability and secondly relate them to arguments about the nature of the corporate entity.

Both the structure and the language of responsibility colour the picture of criminal liability. The framework of offences slants perceptions and contributes

---

[1] *NY Railroad* v. *US* (1909) at 492–3.   [2] 1971.
[3] This derives no doubt from the paramountcy of liberalism and therefore of the individual, see Lacey 1988: ch. 7 and Fisse and Braithwaite 1993.
[4] Hart 1968.

to the individualist image. The most obvious example is regulatory crime; because it is written in an inchoate mode causing a result or outcome is not relevant. A reckless workplace death will be translated into the regulatory language of breach of statutory duty to ensure the health and safety of employees.[5] A larger proportion of traditional or non-regulatory offences are result-based, what is prohibited is the causing of a particular result. In these, the first step towards attributing blame will be the causal connection. There is a double significance here for notions of corporate liability. Regulatory language ensures that we are not accustomed to the official denunciation of the consequences of corporate negligence and, second, corporations confront the individualist assumptions which underlie blame attribution.

The use of a unified normative vocabulary that is oblivious to differences between individuals and organizations allows the law to deal with various organizations within an essentially individualistic framework, without confronting organizational realities and exploring their potential legal implications.[6]

Although part of the challenge is to accommodate organizations within the idioms of criminal law, the process is two-way. Traditional notions of criminal responsibility might be ill-suited for application to organizations, but from this it should not be assumed that they are immune from critical analysis in general. In the first section I consider the influence of moral philosophy on ideas of responsibility. Strict liability, which raises problems for traditional theories of culpability but which has particular relevance to corporate criminal liability, is then discussed. The third section is concerned with the way criminal law deals with groups and associations and in the final part the problems in assigning 'personality' to a corporate entity are considered.

1. NOTIONS OF CRIMINAL RESPONSIBILITY

The work of moral philosophers has exerted an extraordinary influence on the criminal lawyer's notion of criminal responsibility. There has at the same time been a historically specific cultural emphasis on the individual rather than on community or society. Both these have affected ideas about criminal responsibility in ways which have implications both for corporate and individual defendants. I discuss each of these.

The literature of criminal law is infused with ideas drawn from moral philosophy and philosophy of action.[7] Even if later they broaden to acknowledge assistance from cultural or psychological theories, most accounts of responsibility start from there.[8] Michael Moore, for example, asserts that moral ideas represent

---

[5] Health and Safety at Work Act 1974, s. 3.   [6] Dan-Cohen 1986: 5.

[7] Although it can lack a certain rigour and bear a strong relation to armchair philosophy. See Nelken 1987.

[8] Duff 1990.

one of the two main sources on which criminal law draws (metaphysical ideas being the other). The moral basis is found in the four principles under which fault is ascribed to persons for their behaviour: accountability; fair opportunity; answerability; and justification or excuse.[9] Corporations are lined up with animals, infants, and the insane as non-accountable. There is an underlying historical paralysis about this which would not be borne out on closer examination. In rather the same way as it is often asserted that criminal culpability has always rested on proof of some mental element, so it is implied that animals, children, and the insane have always been non-accountable. But this is not so. Even now, it is not descriptively accurate except in respect of animals.[10] Both children (over the age of 10) and 'the insane' are held accountable in England which suggests that the moral principle may be too broadly stated, or at least that there is a disjuncture between those principles and the practice of criminal law.[11]

The reason that corporations are excluded, according to Moore, is that the principles of fault ascription *presuppose* rationality and autonomy. Rationality implies that an agent acts for reasons; this is based on belief and desire (or perhaps desire and belief: I desire to be warm; I believe that closing the window will achieve that).[12] Reasons for action both *rationalize* the action and *causally* explain it.[13] As I show in section 4, applying this to corporations should not necessarily present problems. What is interesting is that the language of rationality and of autonomy assumes a human (usually male) body. Autonomy suggests an agent with causal power over her body. It is seen as an essential attribute by which we understand and evaluate ourselves as persons.[14] 'One of our fundamental ideas about persons is that they are beings who are (to paraphrase Locke) masters of themselves and proprietors of their own bodies, and thus, of the actions or labor of it.'[15] An inextricable link is presented between fault ascription, autonomy, and human bodies.[16]

Two different lines of attack can be made on this sort of analysis. First, even if the concepts of rationality and autonomy were to prove helpful in articulating the moral premises of criminal responsibility, it does not necessarily follow that corporations should thereby be excluded. Only if autonomy and rationality as understood above were both necessary and sufficient for criminal responsibility would corporations have to be excluded *ex necessitate*. There may be good reasons why corporate liability should neither flow from nor depend on the same arguments as those which serve for individuals.

Part of the reason why the account of rationality and autonomy appears to exclude corporations is that words such as 'person' are assumed to be

---

[9] Moore 1985: 11.

[10] A dog was sentenced to life imprisonment in Argentina for killing its owner's 3-year-old stepson, *Independent*, 15 Aug. 1991: 8.

[11] In the following senses: that insanity can result in compulsory detention; that the insanity defence sometimes draws in defendants who would otherwise have a clear defence, e.g. *Hennessy*, 1989; that the insanity defence covers only a narrow type of disorder such that the judiciary will talk of a defendant being mentally ill as a reason for reducing sentence *e.g. Jones, Independent*, 30 July 1991.

[12] Moore 1985: 23.   [13] Ibid.   [14] Ibid.   [15] Ibid.   [16] Ibid.

metaphysically limited. Why are there problems in applying this to corporations: partly it is because *the language* of rationality and autonomy reflects our understanding of the individual. A complex circle develops whereby individuals are the starting- and end-point for debate about something quite different, viz. corporations. It is important now to keep in mind that legal and moral concepts can be used both descriptively and prescriptively.[17] Concern about the consequences of using a particular term should not be used to conclude any substantive or prescriptive argument. If corporations are to be criminally responsible, this should be based on a normative argument not on a linguistic one.[18] The relationship between language, concept, and culture cannot be simply wished away; it can be doubted whether moral philosophy can be of any help unless it begins with the admission that people do not think as individuals but are subject to all kinds of institutional or cultural constraint.[19] In the same way as punishment can be seen both as a product of and an influence on culture,[20] so also notions of criminal responsibility cannot be separated from the social context in which they develop.[21] The uncritical use of individualistic and other frames of reference has to be exposed.

Secondly, we might cast doubt on the aptness of the underlying assumption of mentalism and autonomy in this analysis of individual responsibility.[22] This will then raise suspicion and scepticism about its utility as a method of excluding corporations. Subjective mental states have become associated with an account of culpability which best protects the defendant from oppression; they are aligned to or appropriate a liberal world view. But they are problematic in a number of ways.

A philosophical account might entertain doubts about the appropriateness of mentalism and autonomy in establishing responsibility; such doubts might be seen as having their origin in Wittgenstein's hermeneutic scepticism which asserts that behaviour gets its characteristics through the observer's interpretive stance.[23] Those who subscribe to this view resist mentalism on the ground that, because it is based on the notion of intentional and unintentional acts, to say an act is done intentionally merely rebuts someone else's claim that the act was non-standard or 'unintentional' with respect to the actor's control.[24] The anti-realist position about minds casts doubt on the central assumption about autonomy and rationality and denies that the actor's control is a mental matter at all.[25] A different line of attack on subjective states or mentalism comes from behavioural psychology which rejects their use on the grounds that they are private, internal, or inferred or, in the logical behaviourist school, accepts that their only use is to indicate a disposition to engage in certain types of activity.[26] Mental states either do not exist or are inaccessible. Attempting to divine a separate mental state from

[17] Ibid. 27.   [18] Foerschler 1991: n. 3 makes this point about *mens rea* generally.
[19] Douglas 1986: 124.
[20] This Garland describes as 'penality's role in the creation of culture', 1990: 249.
[21] Lacey 1988: ch. 8.   [22] Ibid. ch. 3.   [23] Moore 1985: 28.
[24] Ibid.   [25] Gross 1979 and Fletcher 1978.   [26] Moore 1985: 36.

a person's action is then a misconceived task. People's actions are more than bodily movements, but any additional ingredient cannot be reduced to some hidden mental ingredient.[27]

Considering mental states in this way, they look less like a guarantee from oppression and more as a potential for oppression. To argue that a person intended something is to draw a conclusion which cannot be challenged. It is for these and other reasons that Lacey advances the character conception of responsibility as an alternative to that of capacity which has underlain criminal jurisprudence for the past few decades.[28] Casting doubt on the wisdom and practicality of drawing a clear distinction between the subjective and objective features of person's conduct will facilitate the development of a theory of corporate fault. Further background can be found in the genesis of the individual as understood in contemporary legal thought and practice.

2. CULPABILITY AND STRICT LIABILITY

Criminal offences are greatly varied in their definitional requirements. For some, for example murder, it is necessary to prove subjective intention. For many, including most non-fatal offences against the person, the minimum culpability requirement is based on foresight of risk, so-called 'subjective' recklessness. The common law offence of manslaughter relies on the concept of gross negligence. Many other offences, including most regulatory offences, do not require proof of any of these mental elements and are known as offences of strict liability. Some of the problems associated with the underlying premise of subjective mental states have been discussed above. Bearing in mind those arguments, and avoiding the distraction which debates about the precise meanings to be accorded to terms such as intention, recklessness, and/or negligence entails, I shall concentrate on an issue central to corporate responsibility.

The numerous statutory and regulatory offences which do not require proof of recklessness or even negligence,[29] have attracted much criticism.[30] There is generally little attempt to relate the criticism to the specific framework of regulation nor to step outside the analytical compartments of act and mental element. Legal scholars make their own structures within which to contain, comment, and criticize material which they have selected. The Law Commission, for example, frequently uses the expression 'contrary to principle' which both forecloses and mystifies criticism.[31] The infrastructure of criminal law marginalizes not only statutory and regulatory offences but also 'defences' or exceptions to the 'golden principles'.[32] By this I mean that it is not only in the selection of material (common law, 'serious' offences such as homicide and rape) that the distortion occurs.

---

[27] Duff 1990: 129.   [28] Lacey 1988: 65 ff.
[29] The distinction is of minimal significance following the introduction of *Caldwell* recklessness.
[30] The most useful recent common law survey is by Singer 1989; see also Leigh 1982.
[31] Wells 1986.   [32] Wells 1982.

It is in the analysis, the abstraction of broad principle (all crimes have/must have a subjective mental element) that the corruption begins. A prescriptive aspiration (no person should be guilty without proof of a subjective mental element) is wrapped in a descriptive truth (criminal law is based on such a fundamental principle). While something of a caricature, the pervasiveness of such modes of writing should not be underestimated, and their seductiveness needs to be resisted.

The history of strict liability, for long accepted as a straightforward response to industrialization,[33] has recently been subjected to re-assessment. Singer makes a detailed argument that the 'seminal' case of *Woodrow*[34] and the early Sale of Food and Drugs Acts are not examples of strict criminal liability but represent enforcement against tax evasion and consumer fraud.[35] Strict liability, where it was used in the nineteenth century, was more commonly found in the areas of morals, minors, and drink.[36] The point is an interesting one for it demonstrates how the strength of an orthodoxy does not necessarily reflect the soundness of its origin.

Three approaches to strict liability can be discerned: one is based on deterrence; another is to admit its utility in relation to regulatory offences; while the third casts doubt on the premise that strict liability equals blamelessness.

The use and abuse of strict liability as a deterrent to careless corporate activity are arguments which have been well-rehearsed.[37] As with many deterrence arguments it is singularly difficult to arbitrate; the whole concept is an unattractive one to many and even those who regard it as an important goal of criminal law would find difficulty in empirically demonstrating its efficacy. Added to that, the further difficulty arises with strict liability that the empirical evidence points to the fact that law enforcers rarely prosecute unless they have evidence of fault. This adds fuel in two forms to the opponents of strict liability: it reinforces the argument that strict liability is not necessary to control the waywardness of the entrepreneurial capitalist and in addition it might suggest that the wilful lawbreaker is being treated as a luckless innocent.

It is unnecessary to dwell here on the argument from deterrence, other perhaps than to insert a note of surprise that deterrence can be presented in terms of a 'potentially inefficient or thoughtless member of society [who might] effectively mend his[sic] ways if he knows that no excuse will be allowed'.[38] This pathologizes the notion of deterrence in an unrealistic way. What on any account would be a complex, social, and (in the case of corporations) group psychology of risk awareness or aversion cannot be reduced to 'ordinary man in the street' musing. One approach is to adopt different standards for corporations, to accept the inevitability and even utility of strict liability for regulatory offences but to outlaw it for private individuals.[39]

---

[33] Sayre 1933.   [34] (1846).
[35] Singer 1989: 340–53.   [36] Ibid. 339.
[37] See Howard 1962; Kadish 1963 and Peiris 1983.   [38] Howard 1962: 24.
[39] Ashworth 1989: 52. He in fact contrasts private individuals and corporate crime, but it is clear that he intends that only to include regulatory offences.

Prosecution for corporate crime often results from the enforcement strategy of a regulatory agency that has been monitoring the company's operations for some time, that sees compliance with the law as its ultimate aim, and that regards criminal prosecution as the last resort. Such an approach, combined with strict liability when the law is enforced, may be defended as an effective crime prevention strategy . . .[40]

Ashworth goes on to make the point that many companies possess resources on such a scale that it may be justifiable to reverse the procedural balance in favour of the regulatory inspectorates.

Both this argument and that from deterrence suffer the flaw (as Ashworth acknowledges) that embracing strict liability for utilitarian reasons may be counter-productive, that strict liability 'downgrades the importance with which the targeted offences are regarded and that it is socially unjust to deploy the stigmatic process of police and conviction of "real" crime against individuals who commit ordinary offences of a non serious kind, while persisting in the corporate sphere with the often less stigmatic process of regulation and with crimes whose penalties inflict little hardship on convicted companies'.[41]

A third strand of argument pitches strict liability against the 'reality' of the criminal justice process. There is often an assumption that *mens rea* offences are proceeded against with full procedural safeguards, such as proof of fault. The reality in the bulk of prosecutions is of course entirely different. The inducements to plead guilty include removal of the immediate pressure of post-arrest detention, the reduction of potential charges (in quantity and quality), the hope of a lower sentence and so on.[42] When strict liability is discussed, there often lurks an implicit model of the criminal justice process which is based on an ideal rarely achieved. And to this procedural point has to be added, of course, the substantive argument already mentioned that much traditional criminal law departs from the 'golden rule' of subjective *mens rea*.[43]

Strict liability has been frequently assailed for being 'unjust', 'unfair', and therefore morally wrong.[44] It is regarded by some as dissonant with the basic premise of criminal liability—that only a morally blameworthy defendant should be stigmatized much less imprisoned.[45] It has also been criticized for possibly over-deterring socially beneficial behaviour.[46] Doubt, however, can be cast on the assumption that strict liability (if it were enforced literally) involves conviction of the 'blameless innocent'.[47] It is somewhat secondary to the main argument, but fascinating nonetheless, that the case over which many a first-year student has been asked to weep into their hankies, *Hobbs* v. *Winchester Corpn*[48] in sympathy with the innocent butcher convicted of selling unsound meat turns out, after all, not to have involved a criminal conviction at all. With some deft detective work, Singer uncovered the real story: local meat inspectors had confiscated and

---

[40] Ibid.   [41] Ibid.   [42] Baldwin and McConville 1977.
[43] Lacey and Wells 1998: 195–219 covers both procedural and substantive examples in the area of drugs and intoxication.
[44] Hart 1968: 152.   [45] Singer 1989: 407.   [46] Note, Harvard 1979: 1270.
[47] Smith and Hogan 1996: 120.   [48] 1910.

destroyed diseased meat sold by Hobbs, who then sought compensation which the Public Health Act 1875 allowed for a person who sustained damage 'to any matter as to which he is not himself in default'. Hobbs had previously been acquitted of criminal charges of selling unsound meat through lack of knowledge; the burden of proof was reversed on the compensation claim and thus it failed.[49]

What this helps to demonstrate is the necessity of looking behind the curtain of the textbook or case report. In a more radical way, the time-frame in which the moral acceptability of a strict liability principle can be re-examined. As Kelman argues, if we take a broader focus on business activities, the clarity which earlier disclosed an 'innocent' shopkeeper caught by the rigour of strict liability regulation, fades.[50] The choice of a narrow time-frame in which to assess culpability is symptomatic of the use of interpretive constructions in criminal law. A broader time-frame might well disclose that the defendant was aware of the risk of the harm occurring. A second point of significance is made with the use of another 'construct', the conscious legislative choice between rules and standards. Conceding that strict liability 'like all conclusive presumptions . . . is inaccurate in particular places', he argues that negligence is not very reliable either and suffers the further disadvantage that 'it may convict innocents for *bad* reasons (e.g. race prejudice in juries) rather than *no* reason (i.e. the accidental over-inclusiveness of the conclusive presumption'.[51] One response to this argument would be to abandon both strict liability and negligence standards; its importance, however, is in highlighting the implication in critics of strict liability that other standards avoid the conviction of the innocent.

The risk-taker concept has been used to reconcile strict liability with just deserts theories of punishment.[52] Davis proposes a variation based on social contract theory such that punishment for a strict liability offence is related to the unfair advantage gained by the offender.[53] The principle of just punishment requires us, Davis asserts, to measure punishment in accordance with the seriousness of the harm, but how is seriousness of harm to be measured? One suggested measure could be the unfair advantage the offender gains by doing what the law forbids. 'Thinking of the unfair advantage of breaking the law as a licence, the size of the unfair advantage can be measured by gauging the value of the corresponding market. Licences can be seen as "pardons-in-advance", "immunities" or a currency with which to pay one's debt to society.'[54] Without subscribing to just deserts, there are echoes of this sort of thinking in the extensive literature on strict liability.

3. Groups, Associations, and Corporations

As well as introducing scepticism about some of the traditional accounts, the analysis in this chapter opens the way to a rather different conception of criminal

[49] Singer 1989: 351.   [50] Kelman 1981.   [51] Ibid. 46.
[52] Gross 1979.   [53] Davis 1987.   [54] Ibid.

responsibility. Many of the discussions of corporate accountability fail to comprehend the broad nature of criminal culpability principles. Few crimes require proof of intention, many rely on 'objective' recklessness or partial strict liability. Some attempts have been made to address the issue of corporate liability through a re-examination of culpability in a way which recognizes and is responsive to some of the dissimilarities between corporate and other defendants. A number of writers have endorsed the view that the responsibility of corporations may need to be differently conceived.[55] 'Corporations exhibit their own special kind of intentionality, namely corporate policy.'[56]

But the argument may need to be put another way. Corporations are not human beings, but nor do human beings act and think according to the models of culpability on which criminal law is premised. Adherence to a dualist conception of human action is mistaken and misleading.[57] Under the subjectivist position on recklessness, responsibility is only properly attributed to a defendant when there is proof of that person's actual awareness of the risk she creates. While criminal law has abandoned this requirement for many offences (including manslaughter) it is important to demonstrate that the debate about subjective and objective recklessness misfires. The work of Duff is instructive here and, although not specifically so directed, has clear application to the corporate liability debate. Recklessness can be defined, not in terms of awareness of risk, but as indifference. 'The indifference which constitutes recklessness is a matter, not of feeling as distinct from action, but of the practical attitude which the action itself displays.'[58] Practical indifference is not 'objective' for two reasons: it draws on latent knowledge of risks in general and the attitudes which it represents (of indifference, of not caring for the victim's life, etc.) are themselves 'subjective'.[59] The crucial question is to determine what attitude the defendant's action displayed rather than to look for a hidden mental state or feeling.[60] Duff's practical indifference test of culpability occupies a middle ground between *Caldwell* recklessness and subjective recklessness, it demands a relationship between what the defendant intended to do and the risk which that involved. So someone who intended property damage but ended up endangering lives may not have displayed practical indifference, while someone whose intended assault escalated into homicide may have displayed a practical indifference to another's life.[61] Corporate activity is clearly susceptible to an approach to culpability such as this. Because it eschews the premise of mental or hidden states, it avoids many of the conceptual hurdles confronting corporate crime theorists.

Many commentators recognize that corporate harms demand different types of analysis but few are bold enough to suggest that the traditional basis for ascribing responsibility is inadequate. Those specific proposals for the introduction into criminal law of new types of corporate fault are discussed below in Chapter 8. Only by understanding criminal law and justice as they apply to individual citizens can a debate about corporate accountability begin to be soundly addressed.

---

[55] See Ch. 8.   [56] Fisse and Braithwaite 1988*b*: 483.   [57] See Duff 1990:116–35.
[58] Ibid. 162.   [59] Ibid. 163.   [60] Ibid. 164.   [61] Ibid.

But some issues which so far have been taken as read now have to be opened up for analysis.

Group solidarity leading to group liability has been common in the history of civilization.[62] The development of the concept of person in English law can be traced to the twelfth century, a time when the state was concerned to centralize its control over a conquered people.[63] The task was accomplished by the appointment of a small number of administrators, including coroners who were charged with tax collection.[64] Communities were required to pay a fine for any killing of a Norman of which discovery of a Norman body was conclusive evidence. This useful source of revenue continued in respect of all felonious killings until the thirteenth century.[65] Homicide had been punishable only when committed in secret and the notion that it should be punished gradually emerged with the threat to disorder which accompanied more public killings.

It can be seen that as Church doctrine, popular sermons and the use of some Roman concepts in legal literature converged, a climate of thought slowly developed in which the individual, and not the entire community, came to be seen as the irreducible unit of moral and social life, and hence a climate established within which distinctively English concepts of criminal liability and procedure could develop.[66]

By the early thirteenth century, this process spawned defences such as infancy, insanity and compulsion.[67]

The background to this cultural shift is that in medieval thinking 'individual' equated with 'inseparable' but gradually came to mean a member of a group. 'The crucial history of the modern description is a change in emphasis which enabled us to think of "the individual" as a kind of absolute, without immediate reference, by the very structure of the term, to the group of which he is a member.'[68] While now the word connotes an individual in her own right, then it indicated an example of the group of which she was a member. The individual has been abstracted from the complex of relationships, such as nationality, class, or occupation, by which she was previously defined. At the same time society became an abstraction, from its earlier meaning, 'the society of [her] fellows', in the late sixteenth century it began to develop as a thing itself 'the system of common life'.[69] The Victorians reinforced these changes with a firm commitment to individual responsibility as a method of achieving social progress. As Wiener writes,

A crucial supposition underlying early Victorian reform was that the most urgent need was to make people self governing and that the best way to do so was to hold them sternly and unblinkingly, responsible for the consequences of their actions. In this way, the more precise definitions and higher legal standards of personal liability declared a faith in the existence of individual freewill and made use of a promising instrument for developing such capabilities of will.[70]

---

[62] Feinberg 1970: 233.	[63] Rosen 1985.	[64] Hunnisett 1961.
[65] Keogh 1983: 202.	[66] Rosen 1985.	[67] Sayre 1932.
[68] Williams 1965: 90–1.	[69] Ibid. 93.	[70] Wiener 1991: 54.

And, of course, when this attempt failed, the next move was to pathologize, medicalize, and incarcerate the incorrigible deviant. Some doubt about individual responsibility also arose with the reluctance to apply its logic to the new industrial urban context of factories, roads, and railways.[71]

The significance of this is not merely historical; methodological individualism 'is unable to account for the corporateness of corporate action and corporate responsibility'.[72] Although the major tradition of subsequent social thinking has drawn on these new usages, the common starting point 'from Hobbes to the Utilitarians' has been man as a bare human being, this has been at the cost of acknowledging that people are born into relationships.[73] We show no surprise that psychology, ethics, politics, and law start with the individual; we forget that in 'other systems of thinking, the community would be the axiom, an individual man the derivative'.[74]

The importance of a society's concept of the individual should not be underestimated; it informs and cements its picture of the world: 'It is particularly in the concept of the person that many of the strands by which a society articulates its vision of reality are drawn together.'[75] But as individuals we act as part of a group, our actions derive meaning from their social and cultural contexts.[76] And so the interplay between the influence of moral philosophy and the particular meaning which 'individual' has acquired can be seen. In a Weberian analysis, our assessment of others including their mental state is a public process, 'taken from this angle, motives and intentions are neither wholly private nor independently causal: they are culturally characteristic ascriptions by means of which the situations in which people find themselves are made more or less comprehensible'.[77]

As Douglas comments on Fuller's Speluncean explorers, only individualists, 'bound by no ties to one another and imbued by no principles of solidarity, would hit upon the cannibal gamble as the proper course'.[78] (The emphasis here being on the lottery rather than the cannibalism.) One of the reasons why contemporary legal systems have difficulty with any concept other than that of the individual is the heritage of political liberalism. The dominance of liberalism which has celebrated the ultimate value of the individual person and correspondingly denounced collectivism or social welfarism has inevitably been reflected in legal accounts of responsibility. Corporate accountability can be seen as an example of the beginnings of a shift towards a mid-way theory of communitarianism, which undermines the liberal theory of self but is equally wary of social welfarism.[79]

Individuals are not only constituted within groups but are creations of specific culture(s). A critique which draws on a cultural or social institution perspective devastates the assumptions of mentalism and individual culpability with their failure to acknowledge that people belong to, act as part of, and are influenced by social institutions. A social institution can be defined in this context as a

---

[71] Ibid. 75.
[73] Williams 1965: 94.
[76] Weber 1949.
[79] Bush 1986: 1529 ff.

[72] See generally Fisse and Braithwaite 1988*b*: 476 ff.
[74] Ibid.
[77] Rosen 1985: 68.

[75] Rosen 1985: 69.
[78] Douglas 1986: 8.

legitimized social grouping.[80] This approach begins to help unravel why, for example, business corporations are today expected to provide compensation for injuries that in earlier times would have been attributed to individual fault or fate.[81] When as lawyers we speak of responsibility, of risk and of danger we are not speaking of a rational objectively neutral concept. The roles of responsibility and blame allocation do not begin and end with individual moral positions. Whether victims are blamed, whether misfortunes are regarded as natural rather than man-made and the types of official institutional response to them are functions of the type of social system in which they arise.[82] In the same way as rational choice theory was forced to acknowledge bounded rationality,[83] so also lawyers should recognize the cultural (and political) foundations of the concepts they use.[84] This is of particular relevance in a discussion of mental elements, which themselves turn on assessments of risk. An interminable debate about subjective and objective mental elements obscures the existence and undermines the importance of debates on different planes.

4. The Corporate Entity

While some of the major issues raised by a system of criminal justice in general and their implications for corporate enterprises in particular have already been addressed, what for some might seem the core question has yet to be considered. Does it make sense, philosophically or practically, to treat a corporation as a single and separate entity capable of committing a criminal offence? The traditional concern of social commentators in examining law has been with its effects on individual human beings; comparatively little thought has been given to whether or how law should respond to the organizations which occupy powerful positions in society.[85] And, as Stone points out, theorists from Durkheim onwards have analysed organizations but there has been little cross fertilization between these two streams of investigation. Two effects of the individualistic bias of criminal laws can be identified. One is that concepts about individual liability, responsibility, and accountability are applied unaltered to organizations such as corporations. Secondly, and following on from that, insufficient thought is given to how criminal law should address itself to the corporate offender in terms of liability and sanction. Law recognizes both individuals and corporations as persons but that neither means that they are (nor necessarily should be) subjected to the same legal treatment, nor that as a matter of social construction that corporations are perceived in the same way.

[80] Douglas 1986: 47.

[81] Douglas and Wildavsky, 1982. For the shift to group responsibility in mass tort actions in the States, see Bush 1986.

[82] Douglas 1985: 64 and Ch. 3 above.   [83] Simon 1955.

[84] The cultural reasons for the increased tendency in our society to blame technology and industry ...sed in Ch. 3 (in the context of attribution and the social perceptions of disasters). ...1975: p. xii. There are others: government, police, trade unions.

The factors contributing to the differential perceptions of corporate criminal activity were discussed in Chapter 3. In this section the notion of corporate responsibility is examined from a philosophical perspective. This provides the foundation for the account in the next two chapters of the legal development of corporate criminal liability and for the discussion in Chapter 8 of the form corporate legal liability might appropriately take in the future. Although there is clearly much interplay between all these approaches, the first question to address would seem to be whether the wrongs of organizations are attributable to an entity called the organization or whether they are only a function of the individuals within it, and their moral blameworthiness. A metaphysical approach would require us to ask what is the nature of an organization. Those who accept that a corporation does have distinct attributes quarrel over whether it can be morally blameworthy.

There is something of a paradox here. Criticism was made earlier of the over-reliance placed by criminal law commentators on notions derived from moral philosophy. The continuing and overriding emphasis on the individual rather than the group as an organizing feature of modern life and of criminal responsibility was partly attributed to that reliance. Yet lawyers have shown a remarkable reluctance to expose the notion of the corporate entity to any form of critical analysis. This may well be because the corporation's separate legal personality serves a number of purposes not least of which is to insulate those whose livelihood depends on investment in the financial markets. Subjecting it to philosophical scrutiny may not be uppermost in the lawyer's mind. Conjecture as to whether the corporation is 'fictitious' or 'real' clearly bored Holdsworth who regarded English law as having escaped 'very lightly touched by these speculations'.[86] He thought it understandable that lawyers in the Middle Ages should have indulged in 'crude and somewhat anthropomorphic' speculations 'to help themselves out of the difficulties which they were experiencing in distinguishing this new entity from the human persons who composed it',[87] but such doubts were unnecessary once the law was established. Perhaps Holdsworth would have had more interest if the question had been phrased differently: to pose it as a choice between fiction or reality may not be altogether helpful. To give some thought to the nature of the corporate entity and to the relationship between it and those who work for it is, however, important and rewarding. The basic choice is between the atomic (or nominalist) view, in which corporations are nothing more than a collection of individuals and the organic (or realist) view which sees the organization as a different entity than the sum of its parts.[88]

i. ARE CORPORATIONS PERSONS?

The individualistic notions implicit in discussions of criminal liability owe their origins to a broader individualist tradition characterizing Western moral

---

[86] Holdsworth, 3rd edn, 1944: ix. 70.   [87] Ibid.

[88] See generally, Hager 1989, for a comprehensive history of competing conceptions.

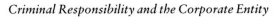

thought. This in turn is traced by French to 'Western religion's conception of personal salvation'.[89] Baron Thurlow's epithet that a corporation has 'no soul to damn, no body to kick' is certainly one of the most frequently quoted.[90] The starting point that corporations lack certain human characteristics can, however, lead to entirely different conclusions. For some, the clear difference between a human being (to which the status of person is accorded) and a corporation means that it is not possible to say that a corporation is itself a person. Others take a functional approach which admits and builds on the distinctiveness of corporations. Thus, Stone, for example, would not seek to deny, far from it, that corporations are different entities from individuals but would say that there are good reasons for treating corporations as legal persons.[91]

It is helpful initially to break down the notion of personhood, as French does, into three types: the metaphysical, the moral, and the legal.[92] Can a corporation be a person in a descriptive sense; can a corporation be a person in a moral sense; and can a corporation be a legal person? In many ways the first two are the most challenging while the latter question gives rise to a ready answer—law can and does accord to the corporation a separate status.

Since juristic personhood can be based on agency (as with vicarious liability), separate legal personality does not necessarily involve a moral personhood. The relationship between metaphysical and moral personhood is more difficult. Metaphysics describes the nature of things; morality is concerned with their rightness and wrongness. Moore argues that '[W]e all have a metaphysics, an implicit or explicit view of how the world is constructed.'[93] Lawyers are often sceptical about metaphysics because they are preoccupied with the consequences of using a term such as 'person' or 'intention'.[94] However, the use of such a term has both a descriptive and a prescriptive element. Metaphysics is concerned only with what Moore calls the 'factual questions . . . not empty labels for a moral or legal conclusion reached on other grounds; they are concepts having a descriptive and explanatory function, no matter what other expressive, prescriptive, or ascriptive functions they may serve in contexts such as those of responsibility assessment'.[95] It is one thing to say that a corporation has the legal status to own property, make contracts in its own name, even be sued in negligence in its own name, and another to say that it can be morally responsible. Deeming the corporation a *legal* person may facilitate the attribution of responsibility, but by itself that mechanism does not answer core questions about the nature of blame and its applicability to a non-human person. These are vital matters to resolve if corporations are to be held liable for breaches of law which require proof of fault, as do the majority of criminal laws.

Is it important whether a corporation is described as a person in any other (*non-juristic*) sense? Moore argues that a metaphysical theory is unavoidable

[89] French 1984: p. viii.

[90] Williams 1961 cites Wilberforce's *Life of Thurlow*, iii App., and adds 'Perhaps Lord Thurlow had in mind the *Case of Sutton's Hospital* (1612) at 32b: "they cannot be excommunicated, for they have no souls" ' (p. 856 n. 12).

[91] Stone 1975.   [92] French 1984: ch. 3; Metzger and Dalton 1996.

[93] Moore 1985: 23.   [94] Ibid.   [95] Ibid. 29.

despite its evasion by lawyers who concentrate on the consequences rather than the appropriateness of using the term. Modern philosophical thinking associates personhood with human beings. That does not necessarily preclude an organization from being regarded as a person, especially if the organization is regarded as nothing more than a group of human beings. The real question is whether that group can be regarded as an individual in the sense of an indivisible whole.

At the metaphysical level there is disagreement about whether a conglomerate, an organization (including a corporation), can, by its nature, be seen as a person. On one view, person equals human being, and therefore it is not possible to call a corporation a person.[96] This anthropocentric view is reflected in much modern philosophical thinking.[97] Other difficulties have arisen when terms become associated with what are perceived to be undesirable political positions. Vincent suggests that many of the criticisms of the notion 'group person' are actually directed at other ideas such as that the group is organic or that it is an individual.[98] A difficulty with seeing the group as organic is that it has unfortunate associations with anti-democratic, anti-libertarian movements; it echoes earlier political debates in which organic theories justified monarchism,[99] and in which organizations are granted a kind of autonomy.[100] The fears which the association engenders can be assuaged by distinguishing between individualism and individuals.[101] While individualism is 'a political and moral doctrine which extols the value of the individual human being'[102] the concept of the individual has wider connotation. To say that something is an individual is literally to say that it cannot be divided, that it is a whole, not necessarily that it is either equivalent to a human person nor that it is organic.[103] The term 'person' has itself acquired a narrower meaning; in earlier times it was used without difficulty to refer to a social role. The Latin word 'persona' initially meant the mask worn by actors in Roman theatre, although it later came to designate both actor and the role he played.[104] Separating the notion of individual from the political connotations it has acquired and by comprehending 'person' in a wider sense, it is possible to imagine both the co-existence of corporate persons and individual human persons. French has been the most articulate proponent of the view that 'corporations are not just organized crowds of people . . . they have a metaphysical-logical identity that does not reduce to a mere sum of human members'.[105]

The metaphysical debate does not end, nor is it the only way to approach, the matter. Not everyone is convinced that it is necessary to take on board a descriptive or metaphysical account of personhood when considering the question of corporate liability. Proponents of corporate liability are more likely to reject or ignore that angle and, unlike French, collapse the question into a prescriptive one of whether legal liability should attach to

---

[96] But is it gendered? See Corcoran 1997 and Gherardi 1995.　[97] French 1984: 33.
[98] Ibid. 695.　[99] Vincent 1989: 692.　[100] Wolf 1985: 271.
[101] Vincent 1989: 694.　[102] Ibid. 693.
[103] Ibid. 694. See also Dan-Cohen 1986: 15.　[104] Vincent 1989: 700.
[105] French 1984: 32.

corporations.[106] Thus moral personhood has tended to be the meeting place for theories of corporate accountability.

ii. CAN CORPORATIONS ACT MORALLY?

Even if we accept that (some) organizations have a separate existence, and are not merely aggregations of human beings, does that mean they are moral persons as well? Certainly, one step in the argument that organizations may be regarded as capable of moral decision-making and therefore susceptible to moral blame (and thus to criminal accountability), is acceptance of the proposition that they are not just collections of people. The next step involves consideration of ideas central to moral accountability, such as agency, rationality, and autonomy. Can they apply to an organization?

One of the main proponents of corporate moral personality, Peter French, seeks to compare organizational decision-making structures with the human mind, so that corporate intentionality is regarded as comparable with human intentionality. For others, this is seen as too restrictive and fails to exploit the potential of developing different criteria for ascribing organizational responsibility. These proponents of organizational accountability distinguish between different types of groups, between conglomerates which do attract such accountability and aggregates (mere collections of people) which do not. Corporations qualify as conglomerates since, amongst other things, they have internal decision procedures. For others, moral personhood is so closely dependent on human capacities for emotion and evil that it cannot, by definition, apply to an organization.

An alternative approach is to start from the opposite end altogether. Instead of asking whether the corporation is like a human being, we could question how far human beings fit into the assumed picture of isolated actors, divorced from their social context. This reflects a theory most closely associated with Hegel who 'tried in many different ways to show that the formation of what might appear to an individual to be his or her own particular intention or desire or belief already reflected a complex social inheritance that could itself be said to be evolving, even evolving progressively, with a "logic" of its own'.[107]

Personhood can be equated instead with moral responsibility. The starting point would then no longer be with human attributes but with the notions which are seen as central to moral accountability. Can ideas of accountability (which might include agency, rationality, and autonomy) be properly applied to a conglomerate? Are organizations ever morally blameworthy themselves or is the apparent blameworthiness always more properly regarded as a function of the blameworthiness of one or more of the individuals in it?[108]

Organizations are comprised of groups of people. But are they more? Statements about the behaviour of organizations cannot be translated into a set of statements about the behav-

---

[106] e.g. Stone 1975. See also Fisse and Braithwaite 1988*b*, who assert that wholes are always more than the sum of their parts, 479.

[107] Audi 1995: 314.   [108] Wolf 1985: 268.

iour of identifiable persons without remainder. If we eliminate all reference to the organization and its attributes, we lose something of significance in the translation—of significance both for legal guilt and moral blame.[109]

Against this, Wolf argues that all you have left when you put all the members of the organization on one side is merely 'a set of abstract relations . . . a conceptual flow chart'.[110] Since the idea of a flow chart being guilty is absurd, Wolf's argument can only be overcome by challenging her maths (suggesting that the remainder is more than a flow chart) or, as she does, by re-examining the concept of responsibility. It will be helpful to divide the ensuing argument in this way: first, the maths problem—does 2+2=5? and secondly, the responsibility question.

Not all types of collectivity should attract moral responsibility. French distinguishes different types of collectivity: the aggregate and the conglomerate.[111] An 'aggregate collectivity' is a mere collection of people such as a gang which, while it might be regarded as causally responsible of its actions, cannot be seen as a moral agent.[112] An aggregate's identity will change whenever there is a change in its membership. A conglomerate collectivity is an organization of individuals whose identity is not exhausted by the conjunction of the identities of the persons in the organization.[113] French proposes three significant different characteristics to distinguish a conglomerate from an aggregate:

a. conglomerates have internal organization and/or decision procedures by which courses of concerted action can be chosen.

b. the enforced standards of conduct for individuals associated in a conglomerate are different and more stringent than those applying in wider community.

c. members of a conglomerate fill differing defined roles by virtue of which they exercise powers over other members.

Why should a conglomerate be regarded as a moral person? French assumes, like Austin, that ascription of responsibility is based on intentionality. He needs to show that a conglomerate such as a corporation can be an intentional agent. 'Corporate intention' has to be something more than a shorthand way of attributing intentions to the biological persons that comprise the corporation. If intentions are taken broadly as reasons for acting, then this requires the identification of a corporation's reasons for acting, over and above the reasons of the individuals. These can be found in the Corporation's Internal Decision-Making Structure (CID),[114] which has three elements: an organizational or responsibility flowchart, procedural rules, and policies. Because these latter two amount to an organizational rule of recognition (in the Hart sense), it is possible to conclude that corporations have their own reasons for acting, or their own intentionality.[115] Thus, it is not the flow-chart which is responsible, but what the

[109] Stone 1985: 243. [110] Wolf 1985: 273. [111] French 1984: 8.
[112] Ibid. [113] Ibid.: 31.
[114] Ibid. 39. French himself has recently shifted his position somewhat, 1996.
[115] Supported by Field and Jorg 1991.

flow-chart represents, which is the corporate 'mind'. The policies, standard operating procedures (SOPs), regulations, and institutionalized practices are evidence of corporate aims, intentions, and knowledge. These are not reducible to individuals within the corporation: 'There is a strong argument for seeing such capacities for reasoning, understanding and control of conduct as the essence of moral personality.'[116]

Not everyone cares for the analogy used by French.[117] Efforts to show that corporations have decision-making structures and capacity for long-term planning does not mean that they have minds in the way that individuals do.[118] Since no one is arguing that corporations are humans we would not expect the analogy to be perfect. But as the discussion of corporate fault in Chapter 8 demonstrates, there are attractions in breaking away from the assumptions underlying individual responsibility. 'Since', says Thompson, 'the "minds" of organizations differ so fundamentally from the minds of persons, we should expect the criteria for ascribing organizational responsibility also to differ.'[119] It seems inconsistent then for him ultimately to incline against corporate liability on the ground that it could be used as the foundation on which to base an argument that corporations are entitled to the advantages as well as subject to the liabilities of their autonomous status.

A different argument against corporate blameworthiness is advanced by Wolf. Starting from the possibly self-defeating position that: 'It seems that either evil lurks in the hearts of men and women, or it lurks nowhere at all,'[120] she considers carefully the notion of a distinctive organizational responsibility. She recognizes that the organization could have subjected itself to moral constraints by incorporating moral considerations in its decision-making procedure. While the organization's ability to do otherwise depends on individuals its responsibility does not depend on an individual's responsibilities. This, however, does not make them irreducible moral agents because they do not possess the emotional capacity to be moved by moral concerns, they lack souls.[121]

Having drawn such a fine distinction between abilities and responsibility, Wolf follows by separating emotional capacities (which organizations lack) and cognitive capacities (which they do not). Because her conception of criminal responsibility is dependent on a notion of moral blame, she concludes that corporations cannot be appropriate subjects of criminal accountability. There is more attraction in the approaches of Thompson (corporations do not have 'minds') and Stone (whatever they appear to be like, why should corporations not be held responsible). There is no reason to remain tied to individualized moral blame as the keystone for criminal responsibility.

In conclusion it can be argued that the close analogy which French asserts between the human mind and corporate rationality, corporations are like people, may be inhibiting. More mileage can be obtained by acknowledging that the two

---

[116] Supported by Field and Jorg 1991. 159.   [117] Thompson 1985: 211.
[118] Ibid.   [119] Ibid. 212.   [120] Wolf 1985: 273.
[121] Ibid. 279.

are disanalogous so that different types of culpability criteria can be explored.[122] A position which views corporate organization structures as unlike human minds but which relies ultimately on moral blame is unconvincing. The criminal responsibility of corporations requires the development of notions of accountability which take account of their organizational and functional complexities. 'Moral' blame is perhaps too loaded a term to be of use in this area. The concept 'moral person' also has inappropriate connotations. So although these ideas might withstand a philosophical exercise in applying them to organizations, it may be safer to use more neutral terminology such as accountability. It is inescapable that any form of organizational accountability will in the end be brought to bear in some way on individuals. But that is not the same as saying that only individuals can be responsible.

iii. JURISTIC PERSONHOOD: THE CORPORATION IN LAW

At this stage, an exploration of legal or juristic personhood serves as a prelude to a discussion of the mechanics corporate liability might take. It is easy to forget, whilst immersed in the above debate about the metaphysical and moral aspects of personhood that lawyers have long adapted the terminology to give corporations the juristic status of person. In the Roman tradition persons are creations or artefacts of the law itself. Corporations can be subject to this fiction, like any other entity.[123] In historical terms, it may have been an understandable path given the 'passive' social function of many of the 'proto-corporations' such as universities, guilds, and the Church.[124] The problem of deciding who owned the Church once the power of the local landowners had dwindled was resolved in the twelfth century by saying that church property was owned by 'the Church' meaning the congregation.[125] This was a foretaste of the use of the legal fiction of person as a device for holding property through incorporation.

All human beings have legal personality although their responsibilities and rights may vary according their age and status.[126] A group of people—for example, a club, association, or partnership—does not generally have a legal existence separate from its individual members. Blackstone explains, in this passage, why this may cause problems and how they may be overcome:

As all personal rights die with the person; and, as the necessary forms of investing a series of individuals, one after another, with the same identical rights, would be very inconvenient, if not impracticable; it has been found necessary, when it is for the advantage of the public to have any particular rights kept on foot and continued, to constitute artificial persons, who may maintain a perpetual succession, and enjoy a kind of legal immortality. These artificial persons are called bodies politic, bodies corporate (*corpora corporata*), or corporations: of which there is a great variety subsisting, for the advancement of religion,

---

[122] Thompson 1984: 211.   [123] French 1984: 34.
[124] Stone 1975 ch. 2; Bernard 1984: 4.   [125] Bernard 1984: 4.
[126] And historically according to their sex. See generally Fredman 1997 ch. 1 and on the corporation, Corcoran 1997: 222.

of learning, and of commerce; in order to preserve entire and for ever those rights and immunities, which, if they were granted only to those individuals of which the body corporate is composed, would upon their death be utterly lost and extinct.[127]

The origins of both separate personality, and the connected development of limited liability, can be found in Roman law. However, it is ironic that limited liability emerged at that stage in order to protect the public property of municipalities, whereas its clear function now is to protect private investors from the claims of third parties.

The early corporations had little, if anything, in common with business corporations. They were more like guilds, functioning as a mechanism for controlling the right to engage in specific business activities.[128] The resolution of the East India Company in 1612 that thenceforth trading should only be carried on by the corporation is cast by Stone as the turning point in the development of the modern business corporation. '[T]he company, through its officers, was no longer merely laying down by-laws under which the members would engage among themselves, directly as entrepreneurs.'[129] The diffusion between capital and management was only then properly beginning. Until then membership in the company merely gave a right to exercise the exclusive trading privileges of the company. By the nineteenth century, investors were protected through limited liability, and corporations began to be sued in tort for some of the injuries they caused. Separate legal personality was cemented, save a few later exceptions, by the House of Lords in *Salomon* v. *Salomon*.[130] A competing model which also proved attractive is the legal aggregate theory under which the corporate name is no more than an umbrella for the individuals within it. One problem with this is that it tends to identify a corporation with its directors and shareholders and ignores employees.[131] The model is based, he suggests, on the primitive partnership. For example, the House of Lords in *Continental Tyre and Rubber* v. *Daimler*[132] held that an English company whose directors were all German was not a British subject. The context of the case may go some way towards explaining this departure from the corporation as a separate entity model. The company sought to establish its British citizenship so that it could overcome the problem of suing in the court of the enemy during a state of war. The third view of legal personality which French identifies is the Reality theory derived from the Germanic tradition. This does not accept that law can create its own subjects, it can only reflect pre-legal existing sociological persons.

Whether we regard a corporation as a metaphysical and/or moral person will have clear implications for the theory of legal liability adopted.[133] The fiction and aggregate theories of juristic personhood can exist without any commitment to the metaphysical or moral. It may be that, although broad in scope, the fiction theory will constrain the corporation's liability. If that liability is based on noth-

[127] Blackstone 1765: 455.   [128] Bernard 1984: 4.   [129] Stone 1975: 15.
[130] 1897. See Pennington 1990: ch. 2.   [131] French 1984: 34.   [132] 1916.
[133] Dan-Cohen 1986: 41.

ing more than an artificially constructed responsibility it is easier for it to evade the implications of that responsibility. The fiction theory can be an accomplice in the corporation's lack of accountability. Regarding a corporation as a moral person would allow the concepts of corporate recklessness or negligence to have a meaning beyond that of its merely being an agent of another's culpability. A different route is to abandon the metaphor of 'person' and replace it with something of more descriptive accuracy such as 'intelligent machine'.[134] Because they '[hover] between the abstract and the concrete', corporations are elusive legal subjects.[135] The machine metaphor has the merit, Dan-Cohen claims, of forcing us to confront the reality of the organization; it does not allow us to ignore it by absorbing and enveloping it in the prevailing individualistic framework.[136]

The Anglo-American common law systems have not shown a consistent or explicit commitment to one particular theory in their development of corporate criminal liability. Holdsworth claimed that the common law had only ever possessed one theory of corporate personality, that it was to be treated as far as possible like a natural man. Though 'a large and vague idea', this he claimed had the virtue of flexibility.[137] The legal system's failure to consider special structures which might take account of the 'special institutional natures'[138] of corporations is not altogether surprising given the common law tendency either to resist or to embrace as long-lost friends any new phenomena to which it is introduced. Nonetheless, although not expressed with criminal liability in mind, Friedmann's 'challenge to the contemporary lawyer . . . to translate the social transformation of [corporations] from private associations to public organisms into legal terms' has yet to be heeded.[139] The problem with large, vague, and flexible legal theories is that they are capable of manipulation in different directions. Lack of clarity in the legal objective in holding corporations criminally liable helps to explain the somewhat haphazard development outlined in the next chapter.

---

[134] Ibid. 43. [135] Ibid. [136] Ibid. 50.
[137] Holdsworth 1944: ix. 70. [138] Stone 1975: 28. [139] Friedmann 1972: 333.

5

Corporate Liability in England and Wales

Difficulty of attributing mens rea to a company [handwritten]

> It is well said that individuals suffer from the bounding of their rationality, and it is true that by making organizations they extend the limits of their capacity for handling information.[1]

There is no single broadly accepted theory of corporate blameworthiness which justifies the imposition of criminal penalties on corporations.[2] Individual liability is, it is claimed, grounded in a theory of culpability based on mental states. As we have seen, not everyone is convinced that corporations can be said to possess a mental state. This could be overcome either by reconsidering what corporate intentionality represents, or by accepting the earlier argument that mentalism is overvalued, or of course by being sceptical about the claim itself (that corporations cannot be mental actors). Even if it were accepted that a corporation can be a moral agent, there would still be some value in Stone's observation that law plays a different role in relation to corporations. Corporations may be likened to, or treated as individuals for some purposes, but should not be regarded as individuals. To do so would artificially limit the role of corporate liability and render sterile much of the argument about corporate structures, activities, and capacities to cause harm. For individuals law makes a contribution as one of a number of strategies of social control not all of which are of relevance to a corporation: school, religion, family, peer group, and so on.[3] This may give law a larger, or at least a different, role to play: it has to counter the 'ethical numbness' of corporate executives and managers and what Hills has called the corporation's 'pragmatic structural amorality'.[4]

Although corporations had been regarded as a kind of legal person for the purposes of property ownership since the seventeenth century, this did not necessarily mean that they were so regarded in other contexts, nor necessarily that they were thought to be capable of committing criminal offences. Despite this long history of endowing certain organizations with separate legal personality, there has been an increasingly lively debate as to its theoretical basis as we saw in the

---

[1] Douglas 1986: 55. [2] Note Harvard 1979: 1241.
[3] Stone 1975: 35; Elkins 1976: 7.
[4] Hills 1987: 190.

last chapter. Are corporations merely, and nothing more than, collections of individuals, as the 'nominalist' view would hold, or does the corporation have an existence and meaning as well as a legal personality of its own, as the 'realist' view contends?

The development of corporate criminal liability is woven from a number of interweaving strands and the resulting cloth is uneven.[5] Three different theories of corporate blameworthiness, broad agency, identification, and the holistic models, have competed for attention.[6] The first is based on the principle whereby a corporation is taken to be agent of all its employees.[7] United States federal law employs a principle of this type, *respondeat superior*, while English law limits the application of vicarious liability to certain regulatory offences. The second theory of blame attribution, which English law utilizes for all other offences identifies a limited layer of senior officers within the company as its 'brains' and renders the company liable for their culpable transgressions, not for those of other workers.[8] The third locates corporate blame in the procedures, operating systems, or culture of a company. Company culture theory is deployed for Commonwealth (federal) offences in Australia,[9] and has been proposed for corporate homicide in England.[10] The first two theories have in common that they seek in different ways to equate corporate culpability with that of an individual and both are therefore derivative forms of liability. Further, the second version adopts an anthropomorphic vision of company decision-making. The third theory, on the other hand, exploits the dissimilarities between individual human beings and group entities. English law draws on the first theory only in relation to strict liability offences;[11] for crimes requiring proof of a mental element, the much more restricted liability identified in the second theory has applied.[12] US federal courts broke away at the turn of the century to a more general reliance on the first theory. In neither jurisdiction has the history been straightforward.

The current law of corporate criminal liability owes its history to two parallel developments: one is that of vicarious liability which is not peculiar to corporations but can apply to unincorporated associations or sole traders. The other is the development of liability of the corporation for *mens rea* offences. In the US federal courts this has tended to run more closely to vicarious liability and be based on the tortious doctrine, *respondeat superior*. In England and Wales the gestation took longer and the infant which emerged was rather more benign.

---

[5] See generally Leigh 1969.   [6] Note Harvard 1979: 1243.
[7] This includes so-called 'personal' liability under duty-based legislation such as the Health and Safety at Work Act 1974.
[8] As I show in Ch. 7 the layer is narrower in some jurisdictions than in others.
[9] Criminal Code Act 1995, s. 12.   [10] Home Office 2000, draft Bill, cl. 4.
[11] 'English' is used here as a shorthand for English, Welsh, and Northern Irish. Scots law follows the same principles, although there is little authority outside the vicarious category, Mays, 2000. Canada and New Zealand both rely on a form of this theory as do some state jurisdictions in the US, see Ch. 7.2.
[12] The one exception being *Mousell Bros Ltd* v. *London and N.W. Rlwy* (1917), discussed below.

In this chapter I concentrate on the development of the law of corporate criminal liability in England and Wales. The following chapter discusses the rise of corporate manslaughter while Chapter 7 outlines the position in a selection of other jurisdictions, including the rapid movement for reform in the civil law systems of Europe. Since the current state of play in this area of law can best be understood through a historical account, I devote the first section of this chapter to a brief history before dealing in the second part with developments over the last decade, many of which challenge the orthodox account of this area of law.

1. Historical development

i. Conception

Although treated separately here, it is important to note that the recognition of the corporation as a legal person is not a fact whose provenance can be pinpointed, but rather it is a tidemark subject to the ebb and flow of many different factors. By the end of the nineteenth century courts were quite familiar with the idea that, for some purposes, the word 'person' in a criminal statute might include a corporation. This received endorsement in *Royal Mail Steam Packet Co v. Braham*[13] when the Privy Council advised that 'person' in a legal sense was an apt word to describe a corporation.

Whether the word 'person' in a statute can be treated as including a corporation was held to depend on a consideration of the object of the statute and of the enactments passed with a view to carrying that object into effect. A small body of persons had obtained registration under the Companies Acts 1862–7. One only of these persons was a qualified, certified, and registered chemist. His share in the company was small; he appeared in the shop and conducted sales and received a salary for his labour in dispensing drugs. It was held that the word 'person' in the Pharmacy Act 1868 did not apply so as to make this unincorporated company liable to a penalty for contravening the restrictions on sales by unqualified persons.[14] Certainly for Lord Blackburn, this turned more on the construction of that particular statute than on any conceptual obstacle as to whether a corporation could ever commit a crime. Although the Criminal Law Act 1827 had provided that, in the absence of contrary intention the word 'person' in statutes applied to corporations,[15] it was not until this was repeated in the Interpretation Act of 1889 that courts began to make extensive reference to it. Section 2(1) of the 1889 Act was as follows:

In the construction of every enactment relating to an offence punishable on indictment or on summary conviction, whether contained in an Act passed before or after the com-

---

[13] 1877.
[14] *Pharmaceutical Soc v. London and Provincial Supply Co* (1880). This was given a restrictive interpretation in *R v. Cory Bros* (1927).
[15] s. 14.

mencement of this Act, the expression 'person' shall, unless the contrary intention appears include a body corporate.[16]

Contrary statutory intention could be express or implied. In *Wills* v. *Tozer*, a case decided shortly after the Act, it was held that the word 'person' when used in a statute does not include a corporation where the statute contains expressions that are repugnant to that construction; so that a corporation was not a person under a statute providing that persons present at a meeting may vote.[17] Statutes referring to persons 'selling' began to be construed, however, as including corporations. Under the Sale of Food and Drugs Act 1875 it was an offence under section 6 for a person to 'sell to the prejudice of the purchaser any article of food or any drug which was not of the nature, substance and quality of the articles demanded by the purchaser'. This applied to a joint stock company incorporated under the Companies Act.[18] Corporate liability under this legislation was taken further when a corporation was convicted of the section 20 offence of giving a false warranty to the purchaser of food or drugs sold.[19] Since there was a defence if the seller proved that when he gave the warranty he had reason to believe that the statements or descriptions were true, its application to a company indicates that companies could not expect easily to evade liability on the 'person' ground. These provide an interesting contrast with cases such as *Pharmaceutical Soc* v. *London and Provincial Supply Co*[20] discussed above, in which the Pharmacy Act, whose object was to establish and maintain a professional restrictive practice were not extended to corporations despite also using the verb 'sell'.

ii. INFANCY: TO 1900

The industrial revolution and improved transportation resulted in changes in corporations and in the function they played in society. Many smaller enterprises came to need capital and many others became large enough to need the services of a full-time administrator. The development of corporate executive structures clearly challenged a legal response. The one-person entrepreneur was being replaced by more complex business arrangements, and in terms of activity, the development of the railways transformed the landscape, the economy, and mobility. Corporations began to cause damage and injury both to property and person. Plaintiffs discovered that the individual at fault might not be capable of being sued or worth suing. It emerged that what was the simplest for the injured party was also the safest for management: to treat the corporation as the actor. The emergence of civil claims against corporations provides only part of the

[16] See now Interpretation Act 1978, s. 5, sched 1, which extends to unincorporated associations also. The US equivalent, Title 1 US Code, s.1, states that in Acts of Congress, 'the words "person" and "whoever" include corporations, companies, associations, firms, partnerships, societies, and joint stock companies, as well as individuals'.

[17] 1904. Corporations cannot, for example, commit a 'driving' offence, *Richmond LBC* v. *Pinn and Wheeler* (1989).

[18] *Pearks, Dunston & Tee Ltd* v. *Ward* (1902).

[19] *Chuter* v. *Freeth and Pocock Ltd* (1911).   [20] 1880.

background to the development of corporate criminal liability. As the discussion below reveals the history of liability of local authorities and later railway companies for breaches of duty also played a significant role. There was also a move in the late eighteenth and early nineteenth centuries towards a broader notion of manslaughter; carelessness became less tolerated and the penalties and scope of manslaughter liability were extended.[21]

It is only later in the story that the problem of whether a corporation is capable of committing criminal offences really emerged. The first step, as Welsh pointed out, was to overcome the 'real difficulty' of how an individual could be vicariously liable to pay damages for the wrongful act or negligence of his servant.[22] When the problem of establishing liability for an injury which he had not authorized and might even have expressly forbidden was sidestepped, 'the difficulty of ascribing wrongful intention to an artificial person was in truth only a residue of anthropomorphic imagination'.[23] The emergence of the common law principle that masters had 'vicarious' liability for their servants facilitated the development both of civil and criminal liability of corporations. '[I]t was only a short step from the idea of a master as a human person to the master as a corporate person.'[24] This 'modern' vicarious liability of masters was itself a revival of an ancient principle, which had been eroded in the medieval period, of absolute liability for *all* the wrongful actions of servants.[25] By the time that the corporation began to appear as a significant social and economic force the liability of masters for their servants' criminal wrongs had almost completely vanished except where the master had given his command or consent.[26] This limitation on masters' liability of course protected corporations since it could be argued that they were incapable of giving such command or consent. But there were exceptions, such that masters *were* strictly (i.e. absent command or consent) liable for public nuisance: if any member of his household 'layeth or casteth anything out of his house into the street or common highway, to the damage of any individual or the common nuisance of his majesty's leige people'.[27]

Corporate liability was founded on a combination of this exception, extending an individual master's liability, and the parallel liability of municipalities to maintain roads and waterways running through their jurisdiction. Local authorities' liability for public nuisance provided a model for the application of the juristic person concept to the newly developing collective body, the corporation. The basis of local authority liability for nuisance was itself rooted in an analogy with the master/servant relationship. They were liable as 'masters' when their 'servants', the local officials, created a public nuisance in streets through failing to maintain them.

At the same time, many of the early large corporate bodies such as the railway companies were set up under special charters or private Acts which imposed

[21] Beattie 1986: 89–91; Wiener 1991: 78.   [22] Welsh 1946: 51; see also Hager 1989: 600 ff.
[23] Pollock 1911: 235.   [24] Bernard 1984: 5.
[25] Holdsworth 1944: iii. 46–7.   [26] Bernard 1984: 6.
[27] Ibid. See also Welsh 1946.

specific duties upon them, analogous to the municipal duties of local authorities.[28] Thus, it was not a huge step to hold them liable, at first for failing in those duties, non-feasance,[29] and later for misfeasance, as in the key decision of *R v. Gt North of England Railway Co* in 1846.[30] The company had unlawfully destroyed a highway in the construction of its own bridge. While those who voted to erect it and those who built it might be liable, Lord Denman said:

the public knows nothing of the former; and the latter, if they can be identified, are commonly persons of the lowest rank, wholly incompetent to make any reparation for the injury. There can be no effectual means for deterring from an oppressive exercise of power for the purpose of gain, except the remedy by an indictment against those who truly commit it, that is, by the corporation, acting by its majority.[31]

As Bernard comments, 'The point is that, according to the statutory provision, the obligation to construct the bridges lay with the corporation itself, rather than with any individual officers. In England, then, the initial criminal liability of a private corporation was at least partly attributable to prior legislative action, rather than solely to judicial interpretation.'[32]

The question became, how far was this liability to go; was it to follow closely the nuisance exception? To accept liability driven by specific statutory provision was one thing, even to translate master/servant vicarious liability to a corporate setting was not so daring. But the real problem came with traditional offences in general and *mens rea* in particular. In the *Great North of England Rlwy Case* Lord Denman had highlighted some *dicta* from old cases:

'A corporation cannot be guilty of treason or of felony.' It might be added 'of perjury, or offences against the person'. The Court of Common Pleas lately held that a corporation might be sued in trespass; but nobody has sought to fix them with acts of immorality. These plainly derive their character from the corrupted mind of the person committing them, and are violations of the social duties that belong to men and subjects. A corporation which has no such duties, cannot be guilty in these cases: but they may be guilty as body corporate of commanding acts to be done to the nuisance of the community at large.[33]

On the one hand, a conventional view emanated which said that capacity to commit crime 'presupposes an act of understanding and an exercise of will'[34] and that, as had been said repeatedly since the *Case of Sutton's Hospital* in 1612,[35] a corporation is incapable of an act of understanding and it has no will to exercise.[36] On the other hand, the implications of pushing the doctrine to its logical conclusion had been largely evaded in the English law of contract and tort through the use of wide principles of agency and vicarious liability. 'A corporation is not, in the eye of the law, so abstract, impalpable or metaphysical that it cannot be regarded as a principal or master.'[37] (Welsh is using the word

---

[28] Elkins 1976: 76; and see French 1984: 174. [29] *R v. Birm. and Glos. Rlwy* 1842.

[30] 1846.   [31] 1846 at 1298.   [32] Bernard 1984: 7.

[33] 1846 at 1298.   [34] Archbold 1943: 11.   [35] *Case of Sutton's Hospital* (1612).

[36] Welsh 1946: 347.   [37] Ibid.

metaphysical here in its restricted sense of intangible.) Vicarious liability was assumed to be confined to those offences which required no *mens rea*. There are numerous examples of statutory constructions of words such as 'use', 'cause', and 'permit'. In some of these, the word itself is taken to import vicarious liability whereas others ('permit', for example) are seen as 'personal' which precludes vicarious liability. (It is not proposed to deal in detail with these.)[38]

Procedural problems are often mentioned as a factor which obstructed steps towards a more general liability of corporations. Not only was it difficult to contemplate a corporation being immoral or corrupt (see Lord Denman, above) but most felonies attracted punishments such as imprisonment or death that could have no application to an inert body.[39] In addition, Welsh suggests that the procedural rule which required the personal appearance of defendants tried on indictment was an obstacle which had to be overcome.[40] Corporations were given immunity from the requirement to stand at the bar by section 33 of the Criminal Justice Act 1925 which provided that they could enter in writing, by their representative, a plea of Guilty or Not Guilty. If this were previously an obstacle it is not clear how to reconcile the trial of the Great North of England Railway Company at Durham Spring Assizes in 1845.[41]

iii. CHILDHOOD: 1900–40

The first indication that corporate liability might move beyond the confines of strict liability or nuisance came in *Mousell* v. *London and North Western Rlwy*.[42] The company was held vicariously liable for an offence which required *mens rea*, the act of its manager in giving a false account with intent to avoid payment of tolls.[43] Lord Atkin made little of the *mens rea* point: 'While prima facie a principal is not to be made criminally liable for the acts of his servants, yet the legislature may prohibit an act or enforce a duty in such words as to make the prohibition or the duty absolute; in which case the principal is liable if the act is in fact done by his servants.'[44] Atkin's test for establishing the existence of vicarious liability under statute was as follows:

Regard must be had to the object of the statute, the words used, the nature of the duty laid down, the person upon whom it is imposed, the person by whom in ordinary circumstances it would be performed, and the person upon whom the penalty is imposed.[45]

---

[38] A full account is found in Leigh 1982*a*. See also the discussion of strict liability in Ch. 4.2.

[39] Felonies were only finable if statute expressly provided, as with Offences Against the Person 1861, s. 5 for manslaughter. This presumption against fines was removed by Criminal Justice Act 1948, s. 13. This obstacle did not prevent the US federal court from upholding an indictment for an imprisonable only offence: *US* v. *Van Schaick* (1904).

[40] Welsh 1946: 346. This did not apply in the Kings Bench, Williams 1961: 853.

[41] *R* v. *Great North of England Rly Co* (1846). In *Birmingham and Gloucester Rlwy Co* 1842 the indictment was moved by *certiorari* into the Kings Bench in order to overcome this problem, 493.

[42] 1917.   [43] Contrary to Railway Clauses Consolidation Act 1845, s. 99.
[44] 1917 at 845.   [45] Ibid.

The emphasis then is on the offence being statutory and in this it echoes the 1902 decision of *Pearks Gunston and Tee Ltd*[46] which upheld corporate vicarious liability for a statutory offence (albeit one of strict liability) on the ground that there was no reason against its imposition, since the very object of the Legislature was to forbid the thing absolutely.[47] But Channell J. indicated that a corporation could be convicted under section 3 of the same Act which does involve criminal intent or at least knowledge. His inclination was followed by the Divisional Court in *Chuter* v. *Freeth and Pocock Ltd* in 1911.[48] So it does not seem that it was an oversight which led to vicarious liability for statutory offences being imposed beyond the realm of strict liability in *Mousell Bros.*

Williams, however, regarded that case as belonging to an intermediate stage in the development of corporate criminal responsibility, that is, between vicarious liability for strict liability offences and the restrictive identification doctrine for *mens rea* offences.[49] It is certainly true in retrospect: that is the role it has been assigned. But that is not quite the same as saying that the case could not have led somewhere different. It was only later that *Mousell* became confined to its position as an exception, it could just as easily have provided a springboard for an entirely different development.

An early opportunity presented itself when a private mining company was prosecuted for manslaughter.[50] During the miners' strike of 1926, the directors of Cory Bros., the defendant company, decided to erect a fence around a power house belonging to the company 'for the purpose of protecting the bunkers against pilfering'. The fence was electrified. Shortly after an unemployed miner stumbled against it during a ratting expedition and was electrocuted. Private prosecutions were brought against the company and three of its engineers for manslaughter and setting a mantrap.[51] Despite, or perhaps because of, suggestions by defence counsel that a 'scheme of propaganda' lay behind the prosecutions which were brought by the deceased's brother through the South Wales Miners' Federation, the committal proceedings were successful.[52] At the Assizes, however, Finlay J. was persuaded otherwise and felt himself 'bound by authorities which show quite clearly that as the law stands an indictment will not lie against a corporation either for a felony or for a misdemeanour of the nature set out in the second count of this indictment'.[53] The charges against three

---

[46] 1902.   [47] The offence was under the Food and Drugs Act 1875, s. 6.
[48] 1911.   [49] 1961: 274.
[50] *R* v. *Cory Bros* 1927. A full report of the committal proceedings is given in the *Western Mail*, 11 and 12 Feb. 1927.
[51] Offences Against the Person Act 1861, s. 31.
[52] *Western Mail*, 12 Jan. 1927. The prosecutions were taken seriously it seems with the defence led by Edward Marshall-Hall KC. He died before the trial and his place was taken by Norman Birkett KC.
[53] 1927: 817 (citing *R* v. *Bham and Glos Rlwy* 1842, *R* v. *Gt North of England Rlwy* (1846), *Pharmaceutical Soc* v. *London and Provincial Supply Co* (1880) and *R* v. *Tyler & International Commercial Co* (1891). The second count was setting up an engine calculated to destroy human life, etc., under Offences Against the Person Act 1861, s. 31.

individual engineers were prosecuted but resulted in acquittals.[54] The decision
was not without criticism at the time,[55] and, given the major strides taken
towards corporate liability in the railway cases, the food and drug cases, and the
potential opportunity of using *Mousell Bros.* as the stepping stone, it would not
have been inconceivable for the corporate charges to be allowed.[56]

Procedural objections either no longer obtained (there was no need for the
company to appear in person)[57] or were irrelevant (the offences were punishable
with a fine), but what was different was that the prosecution was for a common
law offence and an offence against the person, both of which required some form
of *mens rea*. The emphasis in the case, however, was much more on the
significance of its concerning an offence against the person. Finlay J. was reluctant to enter into debate about whether *dicta* in earlier cases that indictments
would not lie for such offences reflected procedural restrictions or suggested a
substantive objection. Thus he said, after relaying *dicta* from cases such as *R v.
Birmingham and Gloucester Railway*: 'Now, in that state of the authorities, the
less I say about this matter the better.' And while acknowledging that it might be
tempting to agree that the common law should keep pace with modern developments, all he could say to that argument was '[I]t may well be that the law ought
to be altered; on the other hand it may be that these authorities ought still to govern the law.'[58] By the mid-1940s a different view was being taken of corporate liability for *mens rea* offences, although the specific question of manslaughter was
not directly raised again for another 50 years.[59] But a judicial willingness to contemplate that corporations might be capable of committing offences of violence
was evident much earlier. 'If the matter came before the Court today,' Stable J.
said in 1944, 'the result [in *R v. Cory Bros.*] might well be different . . . This is a
branch of the law to which the attitude of the Courts has in the passage of time
undergone a process of development.'[60]

Corporate liability for strict liability was established in the United States at
roughly the same time as in England,[61] but the development of liability for crimes
of intent was much accelerated. The discussion above of the development of corporate liability in England prompts some speculation as to when the idea that a
corporation might be responsible not only for the acts but also for the intentions
of its agents came to be regarded as such a conceptual hurdle. It is fairly clear that
much of the early opposition to corporate liability came from, or at least hid
behind, obstacles of a procedural nature that dictated that corporations were

---

[54] *The Times,* 4 Mar. 1927, *Western Mail,* 4 Mar. 1927.   [55] Winn 1929.

[56] Convictions for contempt of court and libel had already been obtained: *Hammond & Co Ltd*
(1914) and *Triplex Safety Glass Co v. Lancegay Safety Glass Co* (1939).

[57] Committal of corporations is now governed by Magistrates Court Act 1980, s. 46 and Schedule
3. See *R v. Nelson Group Services* (1998).

[58] 1927 at 817.

[59] *R v. HM Coroner for East Kent, ex parte Spooner* (1989).

[60] *R v. ICR Haulage* (1944) at 36. The prediction was borne out when no question was raised at a
corporate manslaughter prosecution brought in 1965, *R v. Northern Strip Mining Co., The Times,* 2,
4, and 5 Feb. 1965.

[61] *Commonwealth v. Proprietors of New Bedford Bridge* (1854).

untouched by certain crimes. When the procedural difficulties were removed the substantive conclusions which had been drawn from them were retained. In other words, procedure bound courts in the mid-nineteenth century to the conclusion that corporations could not be guilty of a felony. Once those bonds were removed, courts then quoted the previous cases as precedent for the conclusion that corporations could not be guilty of felony.

iv. ADOLESCENCE: 1940–90

A trio of cases in the 1940s established the corporate liability principle for *mens rea* offences which is known in English law today. This is seen as a different species from vicarious liability. As Welsh commented at the time of this development, if a corporation is to be liable outside the accepted categories (of public nuisance, vicarious and specific statutory provision), 'it can only be on the ground that the acts (including the states of mind) of its human agents may in certain circumstances be regarded in law as the acts of the corporation itself'.[62] Thus corporate liability bifurcated: the vicarious type, which was largely associated with strict liability and direct or imputed liability, based on the identification or *alter ego* theory. Before discussing the latter development below, it is important to emphasize that the holy alliance between vicarious and strict liability, and therefore between corporate vicarious liability and strict liability, was not inevitable.[63] It is often thought that because, with the exceptions of the statutory examples discussed above and the delegation cases,[64] vicarious liability is based on strict liability, therefore the only avenue for corporate liability in *mens rea* crimes was via an alternative route. As we will see in Chapter 7, the history of corporate liability in the United States shows that running the division between vicarious and identification liability along the fault line of the distinction between strict liability and *mens rea* is historically contingent and jurisdictionally specific.

The seeds of corporate liability sown in the railway company cases only fully germinated a century later. In the meantime, as we have seen, a rather different conception had emerged, one which tied their liability closely to the master/servant notion of vicarious responsibility. Before the 1940s one or two isolated weeds competed, unsuccessfully, for attention. A certain amount of crop rotation was in evidence too, such that the key idea behind the identification theory was transplanted from another field, that of tort. This key concept is the notion that there are times when a company is not merely responsible for the acts of its servants, but on its own account for its own acts. The legal battle can be related to discussions about the metaphysics of the corporation and its status as a moral person. Once given its own patch in which to grow, this particular plant did not

---

[62] Welsh 1946: 347.
[63] As was accepted without argument in *NCB* v. *Gamble* (1959). Cf. implication in Law Commission 1989, paras. 10.4 and 10.5.
[64] See the account below.

meet much competition, although it has never been fed much encouragement nor been allowed to spread.

Described as 'revolutionary'[65] the harvest of cases which marked this new crop were *DPP* v. *Kent and Sussex Contractors, R* v. *ICR Haulage,* and *Moore* v. *Bresler.*[66] They all concerned frauds of one kind or another, two statutory and one common law. The first, *DPP* v. *Kent and Sussex Contractors* went from the Glamorgan Justices to the Divisional Court, whose decision was later confirmed in *R* v. *ICR Haulage* by the Court of Criminal Appeal. The company had been charged under the Defence (General) Regulations 1939 in that 'with intent to deceive' they made use of a document which was false in a material particular and 'they made a statement which they knew to be false in a material particular'. This company's transport manager had sent in false returns to obtain petrol coupons. The justices dismissed the informations on the ground that a body corporate could not be guilty of offences requiring proof of a dishonest state of mind. Viscount Caldecote, LCJ based his judgment on the following argument:

> The offences created by the regulation are those of doing something with intent to deceive or of making a statement known to be false in a material particular. There was ample evidence, on the facts as stated in the special case, that the company, by the only people who could act or speak or think for it, had done both these things, and I can see nothing in the authorities to which we have been referred which requires us to say that a company is incapable of being found guilty of the offences with which the respondent company was charged.[67]

Acknowledging that any *mens rea* would have to be imputed to the company, Macnaghten J. gave the following explanation:

> If the responsible agent of a company, acting within the scope of his authority, puts forward on its behalf a document which he knows to be false and by which he intends to deceive, I apprehend that according to the authorities . . . his knowledge and intention must be imputed to the company.[68]

In applying this reasoning to the common law offence of conspiracy to defraud, the Court of Criminal Appeal in *R* v. *ICR Haulage*[69] took the identification or *alter ego* theory a step further. ICR Haulage had contracted to supply hard core and ballast to public works contractors, Rice and Son Ltd, the goods to be paid per cubic yard. It was alleged that the defendants who included the company's managing director, two of their lorry drivers, and two of Rice and Sons' employees, in addition to ICR, had agreed to charge Rice & Sons for more hard core than was actually delivered. They were all found guilty of conspiring to defraud. In dismissing their appeals the Court of Criminal Appeal held that there was no reason in law why such an indictment should not lie. On the facts, there was clearly no question that, if corporate liability were to attach in any circumstances, that the dishonesty of the managing director of a two-director private family company would be imputable to the company. The court's reserved judgment gave

---

[65] Welsh 1946: 346.   [66] All reported in 1944.

[67] 1944 at 155.   [68] 1944 at 156.   [69] 1944.

remarkably little guidance as to where the appropriate limits of this liability should lie.

Whether in any particular case there is evidence to go to a jury that the criminal act of an agent, including his state of mind, intention, knowledge or belief is the act of the company, ... must depend on the nature of the charge, the relative position of the officer or agent and the other relevant facts and circumstances of the case.[70]

ICR Haulage is important because, alone amongst the three landmark cases at that time, it dealt with a non-statutory offence. The third decision, *Moore v. Bresler*, served to confirm that there was indeed a growing movement towards a novel type of corporate liability. Together with two of its officials, the company was prosecuted under the Finance No. 2 Act 1940, s. 35(2) of which provided that it was an offence for any person for the purposes of the Act to make use of a document which was false in a material particular with intent to deceive. The secretary of the company (who was also general manager of the Nottingham branch and had sole responsibility for keeping the books) and the sales manager had sold certain goods belonging to the company, fraudulently intending to keep the proceeds of the sale for themselves. They then made certain documents which were false because they certified less than the true amount of transactions which had been entered into so as to make the company liable to pay less purchase tax. Thus they embezzled the company and at the same time evaded its tax liability. They were personally convicted of contravening s. 35(2), and the Divisional Court reversed the Recorder's finding that the sales were not made by them as the agents or with the authority of the company. There is a certain oddity about this decision since the secretary and sales manager were deceiving not only the tax authorities but defrauding the company itself. But in so far as the offence charged was concerned with the tax aspect, this should not cause concern.

What is clear is that none of these cases gave any clear idea as to how far this doctrine whereby the *mens rea* of certain company officers could be imputed to the company should extend. The contemporary criticism of *Moore v. Bresler* that it confused *respondeat superior* (or vicarious liability) and the doctrine of identification[71] is taken as valid by Williams,[72] who conflates two separate criticisms of the case, neither of which seems cogent. One draws on the point mentioned above which is that it could appear that the company was being held liable for an act of its officer which was not done in order to advance the company's business (far from it, since the company was embezzled). This is disposed of by the point that the prosecution here was based on the defrauding of the revenue which the embezzlement incidentally involved. Whether a company should be liable in the absence of an intention to advance its purpose and where it is the only victim of the illegality has been considered in the US federal courts, and is discussed further in Chapter 7.2.iv. The other criticism is in the implication that the two officials were rather lowly; Williams describes the decision as 'identifying

---

[70] 1944 at 39 and 40 *per* Stable J.   [71] Welsh 1946: 360.   [72] 1961: 859.

the company with the acts of the general and sales managers at a branch of the company'.[73] This seems misleading as one of them was the company secretary and, arguably, a general sales manager is a policy-making officer.

It is in earlier civil cases that the background both to the identification or *alter ego* concept and its later judicial refinement can be found. Welsh makes an ingenious argument based on the common employment principle in tort.[74] This comprised two complementary rules:

First, a master was not responsible for negligent harm done by one of his servants to a fellow-servant engaged in a common employment with him; and

secondly, a master was responsible for harm caused by his own personal negligence to his servants.

'If it were true', Welsh comments, 'that directors are merely its agents or servants then a corporation would always be exempted at common law by the rule of common employment from liability to its own servants . . . Under the first rule it has been held that the directors by whom a corporation fulfils its functions are not the fellow-servants of the inferior servants of the corporation.'[75] It was also settled law that a corporation could have personal negligence imputed to it. As Greer LJ said in *Fanton* v. *Denville* 'a general manager of the business is deemed to be the *alter ego* of the company, and it would be responsible for his personal negligence',[76] and, in a later case it was said that the same applied to managing directors 'or other person having authority from the board of directors to conduct the company's business'.[77] There is an irony in the origin of criminal liability of corporations being found in the oppressive and management-serving doctrine of common employment.

Further evidence of the tortious connection and origin of the *alter ego* idea is found in the speech of Viscount Haldane in *Lennards Carrying Co* v. *Asiatic Petroleum*.[78] The question raised was whether the plaintiff's loss occurred 'without actual fault or privity' of the defendant company, within the meaning of s. 502 of Merchant Shipping Act 1894:

A corporation is an abstraction. It has no mind of its own any more than it has a body of its own; its active and directing will must consequently be sought in the person of somebody who for some purposes may be called an agent, but who is really the directing mind and will of the corporation; the very ego and centre of the personality of the corporation. That person may be under the direction of the shareholders in general meeting; that person may be the board of directors itself . . . It must be upon the true construction of that section in such a case as the present one that the fault or privity is the fault or privity of somebody who is not merely a servant or agent for whom the company is liable upon the footing respondeat superior, but somebody for whom the company is liable because his action is the very action of the company itself.[79]

---

[73] 1961: 858.

[74] Welsh 1946: 353. The rule was abolished by Law Reform (Personal Injuries) Act 1948 s. 1(1).

[75] Welsh 1946: 353.   [76] Ibid.

[77] Per Lawrence LJ in *Rudd* v. *Elder Dempster & Co* (1933) 594.

[78] 1915.   [79] 1915: 713.

Although this case was not specifically mentioned in the three 1944 cases from which modern doctrine originates, it seems clear that they were impliedly based on Haldane's view that certain officers *are* the company and not merely agents of it.[80]

It was not until 1971 that any clear guidance emerged as to who for the purposes of criminal liability might be regarded as a company's *alter ego*.[81] And when the House of Lords came to consider the issue in *Tesco Supermarkets Ltd* v. *Nattrass*[82] the question was not whether the company was guilty of an offence because of the acts of its store manager, but whether it could evade liability through a due diligence defence. The company was charged under s. 11(2) of the Trade Descriptions Act 1968 with indicating that goods would be sold at a lower price than in fact they were sold. A defence of due diligence was provided by s. 24(1) if, *inter alia*, the defendant could show that the offence was due to the act or default of 'another person'. The company claimed that the misleading price arose through the default of the manager at the particular branch where the offence was committed.

The case suggests a strong aversion to regulatory strict liability offences. The House of Lords rejected two possible avenues by which the company might be convicted. One, which is not the main concern here, would have been on broad principles of statutory interpretation: section 24(1) required the company to prove that the offence was caused by 'the act or default of some other person, an accident, or some other cause beyond his control'. This suggests that the legislation aimed at giving a defence where some quite extraneous factor had intervened to cause the offence, not as here, to exonerate them for the acts of their employees. The other avenue would have been to define more extensively the 'controlling' officers or 'directing minds'[83] of a company. The decision came at a time when there was little judicial sympathy for strict liability offences, and the nature of the issue inevitably made the case a poor vehicle for a proper discussion of the ambit of corporate liability.

Lord Reid epitomized the House's response when he 'considered the nature of the personality which by a fiction the law attributes to a corporation'. A corporation has none of the features which characterize a living person, 'a mind which can have knowledge or intention or be negligent and he has hands to carry out his intentions'.[84] This observation does not of course answer the question as to where corporate liability begins. What elevates someone who works in and for a company to the position of acting 'as the company'? For the House of Lords in *Tesco* v. *Nattrass* the answer clearly derived from a conception of the company in which there existed a nerve-centre of command. Only the transgressions of those who belong to this nerve-centre could be imputed to the company. Some assistance with this came from Lord Pearson:

[80] Gower 1979: 208.

[81] Although, of course, it was only in 1960 that the House of Lords became more generally available as a final appellate level in criminal matters, Administration of Justice Act 1960.

[82] 1971.

[83] From Denning LJ in *H. L. Bolton (Engineering) Co Ltd* v. *T. J. Graham and Sons* (1957) at 172.

[84] 1971: 1177.

There are some officers of a company who may for some purposes be identified with it, as being or having its directing mind and will, its centre or ego, and its brains . . . The reference in section 20 of the Trade Descriptions Act 1968 to 'any director, manager, secretary or other similar officer of the body corporate' affords a useful indication of the grades of officers who may for some purposes be identifiable with the company, although in any particular case the constitution of the company concerned should be taken into account.[85]

The potential usefulness of the phrase Lord Pearson quoted was somewhat undermined by his following remark that the word 'manager' only refers to someone in the position of managing the affairs of the company, and would not cover the manager of a store.

Lord Reid recognized the difficulty of drawing the line between the acts of those who were the 'directing mind' of the company and those who were its mere servants. He also acknowledged that the board of directors may have delegated its responsibilities and functions to a layer of management, 'But here the board never delegated any part of their functions. They set up a chain of command through regional and district supervisors, but they remained in control.' The commission of the offence in the first place indicates that the control was ineffective. This approach only holds by resting on an unexamined and unanalysed premise: the company cannot be liable, the argument goes, because its board of directors remained in control. If the board had left all the control and management to someone else, then the company might be liable for that other's acts or defaults. If the board has not delegated its powers, the company will only be liable if the board itself acts criminally. But between these two positions of, on the one hand, a board which has delegated nothing and controls all, and one which has delegated all, comes the common situation, exemplified by the *Tesco* case, where the company is diffuse in its operations with the result that a good deal of day-to-day management has to be delegated.[86] The premise, then, is that the only type of control which is considered relevant is the type which a board of directors traditionally maintains.

The impact of *Tesco* v. *Nattrass* has been diluted in part, as explained in the section below, by decisions in the 1990s removing its application in some reverse-onus regulatory offences. To complete this account of the historical foundations of corporate liability, mention should be made of the so-called 'delegation' exception. This is an exception to the rule that an employer (corporate or otherwise) is not to be held vicariously responsible for her employees' *mens rea* offences. Although it has little relevance to corporate liability per se, it helps to reinforce the point that conceptually it is possible to combine vicarious and *mens rea* liability. It may also have influenced the reasoning in *Tesco* v. *Nattrass*. The delegation principle imposes vicarious liability when a public licence holder delegates to another the management of the business in respect of which the licence is granted. Most commonly it applies to publicans who delegate the running of licensed premises to managers.[87] Apart from the fact that this was probably a practical necessity since the Licensing Acts impose liability specifically on

---

[85]   1971: 1196.   [86] Field and Jorg 1991.
[87] See, for example, *Allen* v. *Whitehead* (1930).

licensees, the rationale behind the principle can be explained on the ground that a system of licensing individuals on the basis of their good repute would be pointless if they could evade responsibility by getting someone else to do their work. For some reason, despite cases such as *Mousell Bros* and *dicta* in *Chuter* v. *Freeth*, this type of vicarious liability is represented as the *only* example of vicarious liability for *mens rea* offences. And since it was described as anomalous by the House of Lords in *Vane* v. *Yiannopoulos*[88] the Law Commission's draft Criminal Code went so far as to abolish it for future offences.[89] It is entirely possible that it appeared to the House of Lords to be anomalous because it had been rendered such by a generation of criminal law scholars who had taken the development of corporate liability for any *mens rea* offences as having begun only in the 1940s. If, as the above argument suggests, parallel with the delegation cases (which clearly did not have relevance for corporations), were other cases in which vicarious liability for *mens rea* offences was acknowledged, then the move towards a broader conception of vicarious, and therefore eventually corporate, liability might have emerged. The significance of all this is that the identification theory of 'direct' liability has been allowed only an extremely restricted ambit.

2. CORPORATE LIABILITY—A MATURING IDEA

In truth, then, there is no easy history of corporate criminal liability. Master/servant liability, municipal liability in public nuisance, and the specific statutory origin of the early railway companies all played a role, which was followed by particular judicial responses to new forms of statutory liability, dubbed 'public welfare', culminating in the identification or *alter ego* model. Two different accounts can be given of the relationship between the earlier vicarious liability and the new identification doctrine: the rationalistic and the historical accounts. Under the rationalistic explanation, two main categories of offence are recognized, the quasi-criminal and the 'ordinary' criminal. The quasi-criminal consists entirely of statutory offences and subdivides into offences of strict liability and offences that require proof of some form of *mens rea*. Vicarious liability can be imposed for either subdivision of quasi-criminal offences, depending on statutory construction, although it is easier to do so where the offence is one of strict liability.[90] For all other other offences (that is, 'ordinary', non-public-welfare offences, whether common law or statutory) the only possible corporate liability is the post 1944 *alter ego* or identification type.[91]

Under the historical account, however, which is preferred here, there is less analytic purity. The *alter ego* development is of symbolic importance in that it opened up the possibility of liability for non-statutory and therefore non-quasi-

---

[88] 1965.   [89] Law Commission 1989: cl. 29(3).
[90] Leigh 1969: 78. An exception to the imposition of vicarious and thus corporate liability for an SL offence being offences such as that in *Pharmaceutical Soc* v. *London Prov.* (1880).
[91] See, for example, *John Henshall (Quarries) Ltd* v. *Harvey* (1965).

crimes, as with *ICR Haulage*.[92] But the direct corporate liability which *alter ego* heralded effectively replaced any earlier liability for *mens rea* offences of the quasi kind. The subsequent outcome was that, even for offences that pre-1944 would have been characterized as imposing vicarious liability, the narrow *alter ego* doctrine applied. The leading case on the *alter ego* notion and the case that gives guidance on identification, *Tesco* v. *Nattrass*,[93] exemplifies this since it concerned an offence which was clearly 'quasi-criminal'.[94] Thus, the pre-1944 cases which imposed vicarious liability outside the bounds of strict liability, such as *Chuter* v. *Freeth*,[95] have been rendered aberrational, and partly subsumed, by the late emergence of the identification doctrine. Identification does not, of course, merely replace the vicarious principle as a route to liability for these *mens rea* offences because it applies only where the offence has been committed by a 'directing' mind in the company. Thus it has ensured both that the tentative steps towards the wider vicarious-type liability which had been imposed in some statutory offences have been halted. The new but restricted identification liability can however be imposed for the full range of offences.

The simple model of company structure, reinforced by the House of Lords in *Tesco* v. *Nattrass,* utilizes a restrictive concept of delegation, trapped in the specifics of the delegation principle as it applies in vicarious liability, which operates only in the narrow confines of the licensing cases. The idea that only certain people act *as* the company presents a problem over and above the difficulties attending any such line-drawing exercise. While the company is regarded as a fiction, it is nonetheless real. Whatever the managing director does as an individual will be entirely different in its scope and effect from anything a managing director does within the company. The same goes for other workers. It is true that they could engage in a fight in the canteen which would be no different in its impact than a fight in the local pub. But once the individual in the company does anything that is part of the greater enterprise of which she is a part, then she contributes to the corporate effect. Whatever the branch manager of Tesco did with special offers (the subject of this prosecution) he was only able to do because the company had invested and maintained the shop, the supplies to it, the posters advertising the offer and so on. The idea that some people within a corporation act as that corporation while others do not is fundamentally flawed.

The limitations of the doctrine are summed up by James Gobert: 'One of the prime ironies of *Nattrass* is that it propounds a theory of corporate liability which works best in cases where it is needed least and works least in cases where it is needed most.'[96]

At the beginning of the 1990s it was possible to state the position on corporate liability for criminal offences in the following way. In terms of numbers of prosecutions the vast majority of cases occured in the regulatory field. Unlike laws against murder, assault, and theft, for example, which apply universally to all

---

[92] 1944. The offence charged was conspiracy to defraud.   [93] 1972.
[94] There are exceptions, such as *Wings Ltd* v. *Ellis* (1985).   [95] 1911.
[96] 1994a: 401.

persons of sound mind, there are schemes created specifically to regulate areas of business activity. Trading standards laws, health and safety laws, and environmental protection laws all fit this category. Only two mechanisms for attributing fault to a corporate body were recognized—the vicarious principle and the doctrine of identification. Whether a criminal prohibition could be applied to a corporation was a matter of interpreting the object of the statute. In the past, corporate liability was imposed mainly for offences which did not require proof of *mens rea* or a mental element. By the mid-1940s a different view of *mens rea* offences emerged, although it was another 30 years before the doctrine was considered in the House of Lords and another 50 before the specific question of corporate manslaughter was settled. The introduction of identification theory marked the first recognition of corporations as capable of committing serious non-regulatory offences.

The relatively narrow doctrine developed via the leading House of Lords case of *Tesco v. Nattrass*[97] had as its governing principle that only those who control or manage the affairs of a company are regarded as embodying the company itself. The underlying theory is that company employees can be divided into those who act as the 'hands' and those who represent the 'brains' of the company, the so-called anthropomorphic approach. The identification principle essentially meant that a company would be liable for a serious criminal offence (only) where one of its most senior officers had acted with the requisite fault.

Corporate criminal liability had been a subject undeveloped in theory and little explored in practice. This changed in the 1990s after which developments fell into two broad categories: judicial or legal changes in corporate liability generally and proposals for the reform of corporate manslaughter.[98] The judicial changes themselves fall into two divisions: those concerning the 'classification' of offences, and moves to extend identification liability.

i. STRICT LIABILITY AND HYBRID OFFENCES

As I have explained, two quite different models of attribution apply in England and Wales, the extensive vicarious model and the restrictive identification model. Clearly, the categorization of any particular offence between these two types of liability is critical: identification liability stops at the boardroom, vicarious extends to the company liability for all employees. Yet this important element in considering corporate responsibility has until recently remained largely hidden. Most accounts of the subject seemed to assume that there were only two types of offence. Only if the offence were one of strict liability (that is, no mental element was required) would the corporation's liability be determined on the vicarious route. If the offence required proof of a mental element such as intention, or recklessness, then the identification principle applied. However, this left a large number of offences out of consideration. Many regulatory offences have a hybrid nature. They are similar to strict liability offences in the sense that the prosecutor

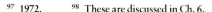

---

[97] 1972.   [98] These are discussed in Ch. 6.

does not have to prove knowledge, intention, or recklessness. But for the purposes of corporate liability they have been treated as *mens rea* offences because they contain a reverse onus of proof defence which allows the defendant to prove that she exercised all due diligence in avoiding the offence, or took all reasonable precautions or some similar formulation. An additional characteristic of some offences, for example those under the Health and Safety at Work Act 1974, is that they are duty-based. For example, section 3 of the Act provides:

It shall be the duty of every employer to conduct his undertaking in such a way as to ensure, so far as is reasonably practicable, that persons not in his employment who may be affected thereby are not thereby exposed to risks to their health and safety.

Until 1995 no one seemed to question that *Tesco* v. *Nattrass* was the appropriate route to liability where corporate employers were concerned, However, in *R* v. *British Steel*,[99] the Court of Appeal held that section 3 imposed a strict, or vicarious, liability. The company could not escape liability by showing that, at a senior level, it had taken steps to ensure safety if, at the operating level, all reasonably practicable steps had not been taken. The company, in other words, falls to be judged not on its words but its actions, including the actions of all its employees.

A number of other cases have taken a similar line.[100] There is some debate about the appropriateness of the term 'vicarious liability' for the liability is a personal one owed by the employer. However, this is largely a distinction without a difference. Whether it is a personal or a vicarious liability (that is, whether the company is liable because it has breached its duty personally or because an employee has done a wrongful act), the breach has to come about through human agency. 'The difference seems highly formalistic: one did not impute liability from agent to principal; rather, one decided that agent and principal were the same person.'[101] Courts have not been consistent in their interpretation of the extent of the duty imposed on employers but they have been consistent in rejecting *Tesco* v. *Nattrass* as the governing principle.[102] The law was summarized in 1998 thus:

If the person not in the employment of the employer are exposed to risks to their health or safety by the conduct of the employer's undertaking, the employer will be in breach of s 3 (1) . . . unless the employer can prove on a balance of probabilities that all that was reasonably practicable had been done by the employer *or on the employer's behalf* to ensure that such persons were not exposed to such risks.[103]

These cases all point in the direction of the appellate courts taking a far stricter approach than was evidenced in the years following *Tesco* v *Nattrass*. How do we explain this outbreak of purposive construction? Offences like this have been

    [99] 1995.
    [100] *R* v. *Associated Octel* (1996); *R* v. *Gateway Foodmarkets* (1997) (a case under Health and Safety at Work Act 1974, s. 2) and *Tesco Stores Ltd* v. *London Borough of Brent* (a case under the Video Recordings Act 1984).
    [101] Coffee 1999: 15.   [102] See, for example, *R* v. *Nelson Group Services* 1998.
    [103] Ibid. per Roch LJ at 351 (emphasis added).

on the statute book for decades. Indeed, *Tesco* v. *Nattrass* itself concerned an offence with a due diligence type defence. One explanation is that *Tesco* v. *Nattrass* was a category mistake in the first place. It was as though the opening of the new route of liability for *mens rea* offences led to a diversion of offences which would have fallen under the vicarious umbrella. That diversion appears now to be in the process of coming to an end.

No one argued at the time that the liability should be vicarious. Of the many reasons why the issue came to the fore twenty-five years later, the most prominent include the trend towards blaming of corporations, consequent increased levels of enforcement, and higher maximum penalties. All this promotes a culture in which lawyers are more critical and in which corporations wish to defend health and safety prosecutions more vigorously. Both regulators and the regulated have a heightened interest in the form that liability takes in an increasingly deterrence orientated enforcement culture. In defending themselves rigorously corporate employers have in fact subjected themselves to broader liability principles. While British Steel may have rued the day it appealed a conviction for a negligently caused workplace death which had attracted a meagre £100 fine, the fact that they did appeal perhaps tells us something about the impact of a criminal record on a corporate offender as well as about corporate arrogance.

ii. MENS REA OFFENCES

It seemed at one stage that there was likely to be a broadening of identification liability itself. A decision of the Privy Council, *Meridian Global Funds Management Asia Ltd* v. *Securities Commission*[104] appeared to herald a more modern, organizational, concept of liability. An alleged breach of the securities legislation turned on whether the company had knowledge of the activities of its investment managers. Lord Hoffmann showed an appreciation of the need for a more sophisticated and flexible approach to the problem of attributing knowledge (or other *mens rea*) to a corporate body. Admitting that attribution of knowledge raised difficult philosophical questions, he suggested that the directing mind model was not always appropriate. It was relevant to examine the language of the particular statute, its content and policy. Since, in this case, the policy was to compel disclosure of a substantial security holder, the relevant knowledge should be that of the person who acquired the relevant interest.

After referring to a company's primary rules of attribution (generally found in its constitution) and the general principles of agency, he said:

> The company's primary rules of attribution together with the general principles of agency, vicarious liability and so forth are usually sufficient to enable one to determine its rights and obligations. In exceptional cases, however, they will not provide an answer. This will be the case when a rule of law, either expressly or by implication, excludes attribution on the basis of the general principles of agency or vicarious liability. For example, a rule may

[104] 1995.

be stated in language primarily applicable to a natural person and require some act or state of mind on the part of that person 'himself', as opposed to his servants or agents. This is generally true of rules of the criminal law which ordinarily impose liability only for the *actus reus* and *mens rea* of the defendant himself. How is such a rule to be applied to a company? . . . there will be many cases . . . in which the court considers the law was intended to apply to companies and that, although it excludes ordinary vicarious liability, insistence on the primary rules of attribution would in practice defeat that intention. In such a case, the court must fashion a special rule of attribution for the particular substantive rule. This is always a matter of interpretation: given that it was intended to apply to a company, how was it intended to apply? Whose act (or knowledge, or state of mind) was for this purpose intended to count as the act etc. of the company? One finds the answer to this question by applying the usual canons of interpretation, taking into account the language of the rule (if it is a statute) and its content and policy.[105]

The Court of Appeal has recently held that this statement of principle is of general application and applied it to assist in determining when perjured evidence will be attributed to the company on whose behalf it is given.[106] Lord Hoffmann's approach was combined with the status and authority test in *Andrews-Weatherfoil Ltd*: 'It is necessary to establish whether the natural person or persons in question have the status and authority which in law makes their acts in the matter under consideration the acts of the company so that the natural person is to be treated as the company itself.'[107] However, it was rejected in the manslaughter case against GWT, discussed in the following chapter.

Meridian suggested a promising line of reasoning. If the question to be considered is who in the company is actually in charge of x, y, or z matters, then their knowledge may be attributed to the company even though they may fall well outside the 'gang of four' (or five or six) directors whom *Tesco v. Nattrass* recognizes as the nerve-centre of command. It seemed clear that *Meridian,* in acknowledging the need for a more sensitive test of corporate attribution, was stretching the identification model, rather than taking the offence into the vicarious category. As one commentator states: 'Organisation theory and practice have certainly moved away from the simple vertical command-and-control model of how a company functions. In an age of flatter corporate hierarchies, "empowered" front-line employees and devolved decision-making, Lord Hoffmann's decision has considerable resonance in the real commercial world.'[108] There remains a lack of clarity and certainty, however, with both the company's own rules of attribution and the particular statute competing for attention in deciding whose acts can be said to be those of the company.

Thus there is undoubtedly a judicial mood of strict interpretation of health and safety, consumer protection, and other regulatory offences. There is undoubtedly a judicial move away from *Tesco v. Nattrass* in terms of when it will apply to hybrid offences (less often) but more ambivalence in terms of the identification

[105] Ibid. 507.
[106] *Odyssey and Alexander Howden Holdings v. OIC Run-Off Ltd* (2000).
[107] *R v Andrews-Weatherfoil Ltd* (1972) per Eveleigh J. at 124.
[108] Gray 1996: 299.

principle (widening, sometimes disappearing in a generic 'attribution'). In yet another of those ironies afflicting this area, the broader *Meridian* rule now determines corporate liability in New Zealand, while in England it has been firmly rejected by the Court of Appeal in *R* v. *Great Western Trains*.[109] What the *GWT* case demonstrates is that corporate criminal law is far easier to apply when there is an identified individual's act to be attributed rather than a negligent failure to take appropriate safety measures. As we will see in Chapter 7, other common law jurisdictions have drawn away from a strict interpretation of the identification doctrine as espoused in *Tesco* v. *Nattras*.[110]

Running parallel to the developments described here have been the widely publicized campaigns following major disasters to persuade the authorities to bring a manslaughter prosecution against a corporate body, and corporate manslaughter is the subject of the following chapter.

[109] The company's acquittal led to *Attorney-General's Reference (No.2 of 1999)*, 2000.
[110] e.g. *Canadian Dredge and Dock v. R* (1985).

Maybe look at corporate manslaughter in other countries?

6

Corporate Manslaughter

The cultural coding of responsibility is also the coding for perceiving risks.[1]

The literature of criminal law abounds with examples of non-organizational defendants exposed to the criminal justice process. Appellate cases give only a glimpse of the full extent of their interaction with the agencies of criminal justice. Reading the reports tells only a small part of any individual tale. Nonetheless, criminal law at least affords many examples of these partial peeks at the social practice of criminal justice. Each doctrinal citation is a chance to reinforce that partial picture. Corporations present a different problem. It is not that the portrait is half-finished. It has rarely been commissioned let alone begun. The appeal courts in this country have had very few opportunities to think about corporate manslaughter or even about corporate liability more generally. The trial of P&O on charges of manslaughter following the *Herald of Free Enterprise* disaster was a landmark in this bare picture. Although the prosecution of P&O was ultimately unsuccessful, as was that of Great Western Trains almost a decade later, *the idea* of corporate manslaughter now has a clear place in popular vocabulary. This cultural recognition was reflected in the Law Commission's 1996 Report on Involuntary Manslaughter almost half of which is occupied with this issue.[2]

1. KEY DEVELOPMENTS

The indictment against P&O was not the first attempt to prosecute a company for manslaughter. Cory Brothers had been indicted in 1927,[3] and there was an isolated trial in 1965 which attracted little publicity.[4] Apart from these, corporate liability for manslaughter was not properly considered in modern times until the *Herald* capsize. When the company was tried in 1991 a judge ruled for the first time that a charge of manslaughter against a corporation was recognized in law.[5] In confirming this Turner J. followed an earlier Queens Bench Division ruling arising from the inquests into the *Herald* deaths.[6] P&O were indicted for

---

[1] Douglas 1985: 72. [2] Law Commission 1996.
[3] *Cory Bros.* (1927).
[4] R v. *Northern Strip Mining* (1965). Presumably, a conviction would have attracted more notice.
[5] *P&O European Ferries (Dover) Ltd* (1991).
[6] R v. *Coroner for East Kent ex. parte Spooner* (1989).

manslaughter after 192 people were drowned when their ferry capsized as a result of leaving Zeebrugge harbour with its bow doors open. As the detailed discussion of the case below discloses, the case ended when the judge directed acquittals. Since there is no appeal from acquittal in the Crown Court, the only possible avenue for further action would have been a reference by the Attorney-General to the Court of Appeal on a point of law.[7] When Great Western Trains were prosecuted in 1999 for the manslaughter of seven passengers in the Southall rail crash the case also resulted in directed acquittals. This time, however, the Attorney-General did refer the legal issues to the Court of Appeal, making history as the first time that an appellate court had considered the law relating to corporate manslaughter.[8] Shortly after the reference was determined, the Government accepted the Law Commission's recommendation of a corporate killing offence. In the period between these two highly publicized cases, two companies were convicted for manslaughter. Each, however, concerned a small 'one-person' company and therefore did not provide the challenge that the large modern corporation brings to criminal law.[9]

The first two sections of this chapter are devoted to an analysis of the P&O and GWT cases and of the conceptions of risk underlying legal principles in this area. Unlawful act manslaughter is discussed in the third section, while the chapter concludes with a critical analysis of the proposed corporate killing offence.

i. P&O

The *Herald of Free Enterprise* roll-on roll-off car ferry capsized in March 1987 just outside Zeebrugge harbour after leaving the port of with its bow doors open. The assistant bosun who was responsible for shutting the doors had fallen asleep and the Chief Officer whose responsibility was to ensure the doors were shut had failed to do so. There were no means by which the Captain could confirm from the bridge whether or not the doors had been shut. The official shipping inquiry was extremely critical of the company's safety policy. There was evidence of crews' working long shifts, and of captains' having previously drawn to the attention of management the need for door indicator lights on the bridge.[10] The inquiry found that no reference was made in the company's 'Ship's Standing Orders' to the closing of the doors and that this was not the first occasion on which the company's ships had gone to sea with doors open.[11]

The investigation report not only criticized several of the ship's crew for failing to ensure the doors were shut but also reproached the company:

At first sight the faults which led to this disaster were the aforeseaid errors of omission on the part of the Master, the Chief Officer and the assistant bosun, and also the failure by

---

[7] Criminal Justice Act 1972, s. 36.
[8] *Attorney-General's Reference (no. 2 of 1999) (2000)*.
[9] *R v. Kite and others* (1994); *R v. Jackson Transport (Ossett) Ltd* (1996).
[10] Sheen Report 1987. See Ch. 3 for extracts and discussion in relation to causation.
[11] Ibid: para 10.9, and see Law Commission 1996: paras 8.45–8.

Captain Kirby to issue and enforce clear orders. But a full investigation into the circumstances of the disaster leads inexorably to the conclusion that the underlying or cardinal faults lay higher up in the company. All concerned in management, from the members of the Board of Directors down to the junior superintendents, were guilty of fault in that all must be regarded as sharing responsibility for the failure of management.[12]

The legal issues arose in two court actions. Initially, judicial review was sought to challenge the coroner's rulings at the inquest into the deaths.[13] The coroner had told the inquest jury that they could not return verdicts of unlawful killing, an instruction which he based on two reasons. He concluded that there was no arguable case of manslaughter against any of the named individuals, and that a company cannot in law be indicted for manslaughter. Although the Divisional Court was not persuaded that the coroner had erred in his conclusion that there was insufficient evidence to support a finding of unlawful killing, it proceeded on the assumption that a corporation was indictable for manslaughter. Lending weight to the argument, Bingham J. said: '[T]he question has not been fully argued and I have not found it necessary to reach a final conclusion. I am, however, tentatively of the opinion that on appropriate facts the *mens rea* required for manslaughter can be established against a corporation. I see no reason in principle why such a charge should not be established.'[14] However, in supporting the coroner's conclusion, if not all his reasoning, the Court endorsed the coroner's dismissal of aggregation as a possible route to corporate manslaughter. It had been suggested by bereaved relatives that evidence of the company's culpability could be collated from a number of individual instances of neglect or negligence. For example, one director might have known that ferries had previously sailed with open doors. Another might have known that a request for warning lights on the bridge had been made. But Bingham J. said he did not think that 'the aggregation argument assists the applicants', although he advanced no reasons for this opinion. He restated the conclusion in different terms: 'A case against a personal defendant cannot be fortified by evidence against another defendant. The case against a corporation can only be made by evidence properly addressed to showing guilt on the part of the corporation as such.'[15] This last phrase begs the fundamental question underlying the thesis of this book.

On the resumption of the inquest, the jury nevertheless returned verdicts of unlawful killing. Since the jury had been told that there was insufficient evidence against any of the named individuals, and since aggregation had been discounted, their verdicts can be seen as technically 'perverse'. Their significance can be seen in the subsequent decision to prosecute P&O and seven individuals for manslaughter. Without the unlawful killing verdicts it is unlikely that the police would have referred the evidence to the Crown Prosecution Service.

[12] Sheen Report 1987: para. 14.1.
[13] *R v. HM Coroner for East Kent, ex parte Spooner* (1989).
[14] *Ex parte Spooner* at 16.
[15] Ibid. As Field and Jorg point out the argument here is circular, 1991: 161.

Manslaughter, a less serious form of unlawful homicide than murder, can be committed in a number of different ways. Gross negligence manslaughter is of direct relevance here but unlawful act manslaughter merits later discussion. Unlike murder, neither requires proof that the defendant subjectively intended to cause death or grievous bodily harm. At the time of the P&O case, negligence manslaughter was going through a phase when it was known as 'reckless' manslaughter. There were some differences between the test for recklessness and that for negligence but they had in common that they were based on an objective assessment of the defendant's conduct. Reckless manslaughter had two elements:

a person is reckless if

a). she does an act which in fact creates an obvious (and serious[16] risk of causing physical injury and

b). has either failed to give any thought to the possibility of there being any such risk or has recognized that there was some risk involved and has nonetheless gone on to do it.[17]

Under the identification theory of corporate criminal liability, a corporation can be liable for an offence such as manslaughter only if a senior manager of the company, and probably a director, was individually criminally culpable.[18] In addition to P&O, there were seven defendants in the trial, two of whom were sufficiently senior to be 'identified' with the company for the purposes of criminal liability. Aggregation was again removed by a sidewind. Turner J. said in his direction to the jury that to allow aggregation would run counter to several recent House of Lords' decisions.[19] It is difficult to know which cases he had in mind since the only significant case on corporate criminal liability ever to have reached the House of Lords is *Tesco* v. *Nattrass*.[20] It does seem clear, however, that the aggregation argument is unlikely to take root in the common law and that statutory intervention would be necessary for it to become a part of the English law of corporate liability. Whether that would be desirable is considered in Chapter 8.

This ruling contributed to the judge's decision to halt proceedings and direct acquittals before the prosecution had finished presenting its case. None of the defendants had been reckless as to the drownings, he said. None had ignored an 'obvious and serious risk that the vessel would sail with her bow doors open, when trimmed by the head, and capsize'. There was apparently no evidence forthcoming that 'any one of the defendants . . . would themselves, or should themselves, have perceived the risk of an open-door sailing was either obvious and/or serious' (*sic*).[21] At first sight this conclusion is surprising given the finding of the Sheen Inquiry that 'from top to bottom the body corporate was infected with the disease of sloppiness',[22] and also the descriptions by marine engineers of the well-known design problems of roll-on roll-off ferries.[23] An

---

[16] The 'serious' was added to the *Caldwell* test in *Lawrence* (1982).
[17] *Seymour* (1983); *Kong Cheuk Kwan* (1986).
[18] *Tesco Supermarkets* v. *Nattrass* (1972); discussed in Ch. 5
[19] *R* v. *Stanley and others* (1990).   [20] 1972.
[21] *R* v. *Stanley and others* (1990).   [22] Sheen Report 1987: para. 14.1.
[23] See the references in Hamer 1990: 45.

explanation emerges only from a closer examination of the judge's approach to recklessness. In this section, I demonstrate that his conclusion that recklessness could not be established was misplaced. The reason that it is important to consider these arguments despite their apparently having been rendered obsolete by the reintroduction of 'gross negligence' is that many of the same misconceptions and wrong turnings could have arisen under that test as well. In other words, the difficulties are not specific to 'recklessness'. What is disclosed is that the underlying concept of risk on which recklessness and negligence tests rest is poorly articulated.[24]

Three points can be raised about Turner J.'s interpretation of recklessness: the obvious risk question; the prudent person question; and the prior knowledge question. The prosecution had not alleged that the defendants had foreseen the risk themselves. The question then was whether they had failed to realize an obvious and/or serious risk of physical injury. There was evidence of previous open-door sailings known to management and that the cost of indicator lights was both relatively insignificant and they were indeed fitted on P&O's ferries shortly after the tragedy.[25] One commentator explains the trial judge's approach in these terms: 'Evidence that the ships had, in the past, sailed safely was the main reason for the failure of the prosecution. The system "had worked without mishap for over seven years" during which there had been "upwards of over 50,000 sailings".'[26] This approach demonstrates a clear failure to consider what might be meant by risk. It is reminiscent of the small child who, having survived crossing a road without looking, disputes the risk involved in such a strategy with the statement 'But it was safe: I didn't get run over'.

The judge's unsophisticated approach is not entirely surprising since little thought is given in legal literature to the problematic nature of the concept of risk. Since P&O could be expected to know more than most about ferry operations it was entirely appropriate that Turner J. should ask whether the risk of sailing with the doors open would have occurred to a *prudent ferry operator*. What was, however, problematic was the course that the trial judge took in order to establish whether the defendant company had failed to realize that which a prudent ferry company should have realized. To begin with he appeared to have heard evidence only from witnesses who were at the time or had been in the past employed by P&O itself. It is difficult to see how such witnesses could have represented the foresight of a prudent ferry company, since the company for which they worked was on trial for this very failure of foresight. One of the clear lessons of risk perception surveys is that people who benefit from a risky activity underestimate the risks, while those who are its potential victims overestimate them.[27] (While it is less easy to categorize the passengers in terms of benefit or victim, it is clear that the company was a beneficiary which would suggest that the risk foresight of its employees would not be particularly helpful.)

---

[24] Rather than negligence, the preferred phrase in the draft Bill is 'gross carelessness' clause 2.

[25] Sheen Report 1987: paras 18.4 and 18.8.   [26] Bergman 1991: 19.

[27] Douglas 1985: 21.

It is possible that the selection of witnesses was due to a failure on the part of the prosecution to trawl a sufficiently deep sea in search of marine witnesses. There was no hint from the judge, however, that he would have expected different evidence had there been such witnesses. Furthermore, he did refer to some evidence yet to be heard, in which Chief Officers would have described the problems of being required both to supervise the bow doors and to be on the bridge when the ferry sailed. The judge apparently did not regard this as sufficient to raise a case to answer. The judge's insistence on witness evidence was itself unusual, and the sidelining of this evidence was particularly strange. It might have assisted the jury in deciding whether the company had failed to realize that which a prudent operator would have seen: that one person cannot both ensure that doors have been shut and be out of sight of them on the bridge. The problem appeared to be that he required actual evidence that *a particular person* had indeed had such foresight prior to the accident before a jury could consider whether a prudent ferry company would have realized the risk of open-door sailing. This involves some slippage from the way juries are usually asked to apply a recklessness (or negligence) test. Although this is rarely articulated, a test of this type generally operates *ex post facto* so that the question to be asked is whether a prudent person would, on thinking about it, have realized that the system which P&O operated could lead to this disaster. This is very different from requiring proof that *a particular person* did so realize before the accident. That would be like requiring in a reckless driving case evidence that a prudent motorist had realized that driving at 70 mph round the particular bend would cause the car to skid. If the prosecution had been able to find a witness who could assert prior foresight of this particular risk, that would have strengthened the case considerably. But their failure to find such a witness should not have led to the case being regarded as fatally flawed or inadequate. Conversely, the defence might well have been helped by witnesses who testified that no one in the shipping industry had ever heard of such an occurrence.

Throughout the direction to the jury to acquit there is an assumption not only that there must be evidence that someone realized the risk before it happened but that that could only come from witnesses, and by implication only from witnesses within the company itself. Juries usually draw inferences about recklessness from the evidence given of the incident which has given rise to the prosecution in the first place. The point is made more clearly when it is considered that the prosecution was only concerned to prove an objective recklessness. One of the criticisms made of the concept of subjective recklessness is that it is inappropriate to require that the defendant had actual (as opposed to latent) knowledge of the risk taken. 'It is absurd to suggest that that knowledge can be actual only if it is made . . . explicit.' [28] To base objective recklessness on the actual foresight of someone other than the defendant is another contortion in the twisted recklessness tale.

[28] Duff 1990: 160.

ii. GREAT WESTERN TRAINS

The Southall rail crash in 1997 provided the next opportunity to test the tracks of corporate manslaughter; a Great Western train en route from Swansea to London ran through red lights and collided with a goods unit on the last leg of its journey, while the driver was allegedly packing his bag ready for arrival at Paddington.[29] GWT's procedures had allowed a high-speed train with a malfunctioning Automatic Warning System to be driven by one man. The new Automatic Train Protection system, promised after earlier rail crashes,[30] was not in use because this particular driver had not been trained to operate it. Seven passengers were killed. The company pleaded guilty to a charge under section 3(1) of the Health and Safety at Work Act 1974. The evidence disclosed that the company encouraged drivers to depart on time even if safety devices were not working. The company was fined a record £1.5 million. But the manslaughter prosecution proved to be much more difficult.

In the period between these two transport disasters, there had been some indication of a 'quiet revolution' in corporate liability.[31] As described in the previous chapter, the first stage was the side-lining of the *Tesco* v. *Nattrass* identification doctrine in relation to some regulatory offences.[32] Secondly, the Privy Council in *Meridian* laid the foundations for a broader conception of the 'directing mind' in offences still subject to the identification rules.[33] In their case against GWT, the prosecution sought to exploit these changes arguing that it was unnecessary to pursue an individual director of GWT. Instead, the company's liability should be established by proving that the company's management policies had resulted in the failure to have a proper warning system which led directly to the crash. This attempt to forge a route to liability independent of an individual director's negligence was rejected by the trial judge who ruled that a non-human defendant could only be convicted via the guilt of a human being with whom it could be identified; it was a condition precedent to a conviction for manslaughter by gross negligence for a guilty (human) mind to be proved. The case therefore collapsed. The Attorney General referred the question to the Court of Appeal for a ruling on whether this was correct. This would not have affected the outcome in this particular case but would have clarified the law.

It did indeed clarify the law but only to tell us that the narrow identification doctrine of *Tesco* v. *Nattrass* still applied. The quiet revolution was in reverse. The questions referred to the Court of Appeal were these:

1. Whether a defendant could properly be convicted of manslaughter by gross negligence in the absence of evidence as to that defendant's state of mind and
2. Whether a non-human defendant could be convicted of the crime of manslaughter in

---

[29] Cullen Inquiry 2000.

[30] Specifically after the Inquiry into the Clapham Junction crash in 1988, Hidden Report 1989.

[31] Wells 1995c.   [32] Following cases such as *British Steel* (1995), see Ch. 5.2.i.

[33] *Meridian Global Management* (1995).

the absence of evidence establishing the guilt of an identified human individual for the same crime.

The first question was answered with a straightforward 'yes' by Rose LJ on behalf of the court. The definition of gross negligence is relatively simple: 'The jury will have to decide whether the extent to which the defendant's conduct departed from the proper standard of care incumbent upon him . . . was such that it should be judged criminal.'[34] The prosecution argued that the company should be convicted if it was proved that the deaths occurred by reason of a gross breach by the defendant of its personal duty to have a safe system of train operation in place. The court responded that the identification theory, which attributed to the company the mind and will of senior directors, was developed in order to avoid the injustice of imputing to the blameless company every act and state of mind of individual employees. Unfortunately this does not address the converse question of justice, that of ensuring that companies which are not blameless in relation to matters of safety are held accountable. It is this latter question which led directly to the Court of Appeal's earlier decision in *R* v. *British Steel* to disapply identification theory to health and safety offences. In the GWT reference, the Court of Appeal dealt with this argument by saying that 'There is . . . no sound basis for suggesting that, by their recent decisions, the courts have started a process of moving from identification to personal liability as a basis for corporate liability for manslaughter.'[35] The court added, somewhat gratuitously, that when the House of Lords adopted gross negligence as the standard for manslaughter in *Adomako* 'corporate liability was not mentioned anywhere in the submissions of counsel or their lordships' speeches'.[36] It would have been surprising if they had. The conclusion was that 'unless an identified individual's conduct, characterisable as gross criminal negligence, can be attributed to the company is not, in the present state of the common law, liable for manslaughter'.[37] Given that few directors are involved in operational roles (they do not actually drive trains), the suggestion that this includes the *actus reus*[38] would add an additional burden in a corporate prosecution. Despite corporate liability and corporate manslaughter being relatively new creatures of the common law, they seem destined to be treated as an important historic species, to be preserved in their embryonic form, never allowed to develop a bite.

Thus an opportunity was lost to establish the law of corporate manslaughter on a sound basis. Instead, a series of cases ranging from the prosecution of a supermarket for misadvertising a sales offer (*Tesco* v. *Nattrass*), the conviction of a company for failing to ensure the health (and life) of one of its workers (*British Steel*), the conviction of a company for failing to notify a shares acquisition (*Meridian*), to the conviction of an anaesthetist for the manslaughter of a patient (*Adomako*), was used to divine the common law on corporate manslaughter, a subject central to none of them. The court showed no inclination

[34] *R* v. *Adomako* (1995) per Lord Mackay of Clashfern, Lord Chancellor at 157.
[35] *Attorney-General's Reference (No 2 of 1999)* (2000) per Rose LJ at 191.
[36] Ibid.   [37] Ibid.   [38] Ibid.

at all to consider the issue from a point of first principle. As we saw in the last chapter *Tesco v. Nattrass* relies on an outdated and shallow theory of organizational behaviour in assuming that only directors make decisions. It also fails to see companies as an organic whole or to capture the 'corporateness' of their conduct. Given that *Tesco v. Nattrass* was 30 years old, had no direct bearing on manslaughter, and had been diluted by a number of decisions since, and given the development of theories in relation to corporate attribution in the ensuing period, this was a disappointingly blinkered decision.

iii. THE AFTERMATH

Why did the prosecutions against P&O and GWT fail? The following letter was published in *The Times* shortly after the GWT case:

The fifth report of the Cardwell committee contained the desire to extend culpable negligence in the case of railway accidents to cases where there were no fatalities. If it be right, as doubtless it is, that the culpable negligence of railway managers resulting in death to a traveller should be manslaughter, there seems no good reason why the same negligence resulting in serious injury or risk of life or limb, should not constitute a crime.

Also, recognising the difficulty in identifying a responsible individual, the committee suggested that in every case some one managing director should be held responsible for the safe conduct of the traffic, and similarly individual engineers should be named as in charge of the track and the rolling stock, in order that in case of accident from culpable negligence the person in whose immediate department that negligence has occurred might be known. The date of the Cardwell committee? 1853.[39]

In terms of corporate behaviour it is as well to bear in mind that 'the negotiation of meaning is biased in favour of structurally powerful groups'.[40] Corporations often have far greater access to resources than the jurisdictions under whose laws they operate; the income of General Motors and Exxon, for example, is larger than that of most countries.[41] Not only did the prosecution of P&O following the *Herald of Free Enterprise* tragedy cost an estimated one million pounds but the various corporate and individual defendants were able to employ the combined services of fourteen defence counsel. These facts alone demonstrate some of the difficulties and differences which corporate liability presents for the criminal justice system. Corporations are also able to manipulate the media to influence public opinion in their favour, both generally and in relation to specific disasters. The further removed the harms they cause are from the public experience, the easier this is. It was relatively straightforward for Union Carbide to give the impression to the American public that the Bhopal chemical explosion was caused by the local Indian workforce. The process can be a subtle and long-term one which involves not only corporate attempts to recover their reputation after a disaster but in more general ways to give the impression that safety is their foremost concern.

[39] Roderick Smith, *The Times*, 23 Feb. 2000.   [40] Nelken 1983: 211.
[41] Clinard and Yeager 1980: 1–2.

Since the P&O case, two companies *have* been convicted of manslaughter. Both, however, were small, effectively one-person companies, in which the identification doctrine for attributing fault to a company can work very easily. There was no problem in saying that the documented disregard for safety of Peter Kite, the managing director of the leisure company responsible for the deaths of three teenagers in the Lyme Bay canoeing tragedy, could be imputed to OLL Ltd.[42] On the other hand, it is difficult to argue that the company's conviction added much to that of Mr Kite. After all, no one had heard of OLL Ltd before the tragedy and it is unlikely that it continued trading after it. Precisely the big corporate names which people may want to blame are those which are most difficult to target under the identification rule (or possibly any other).

I want to make a further argument, however, which is that the legal discussions of the concept of negligence have ignored the problematic in the concept of risk itself.

2. CULPABILITY AND RISK

A critical examination of the P&O and GWT trials raises some awkward questions about the concept of risk, the foundation stone of recklessness and negligence. The nature of the legal debate with its preoccupation with the pros and cons of cognitive awareness has meant that the nature of risk itself has been sidestepped. There are two types of risk, one based on probability and one which includes a utility calculus.[43] Legal discussions do not dwell on what 'obvious or serious risk' or 'falling below the expected standard' might actually mean, but it seems likely that it is expected to imply a utility test. We tolerate different degrees of risk according to the nature of the activity, its social utility, any future benefits it might bring, the type of harm threatened and the cost of its avoidance. The risks taken in open-heart surgery, for example, might be high but the pay-off is too, while the prospects if the operation is not done are limited. Transport systems also have social utility. In the case of both surgery and transport we neither expect that all risks can be eliminated nor that 'clear' risks will be ignored by those who have the specialized knowledge and skill with which to assess them.

The calculation is not simple, social utility has to be measured against the cost and/or practicality of eliminating or reducing that risk and the interest threatened (property, life, etc.). To apply this to the P&O case would mean a calculation of the relative probability that the ferry might leave port with the doors open against the cost of providing foolproof information to the Captain that the doors had been shut, plus the knowledge that both life and property are vulnerable in a capsize.

This is not the only dimension of risk. A sophisticated analysis will confront also the cultural significance of risk. Culture in the sense of 'actively invoked conventional wisdom', is seen by Douglas as the coding principle by which

---

[42] *Kite and OLL Ltd* (1994).
[43] i.e. probability times harm. Douglas 1985: 20 and Irwin, Smith, and Griffiths 1982: 13.

hazards are recognized.[44] The assignment of responsibility takes place through the emergence of cultural standards of what is to constitute a proper risk.[45] So, rather than an objective probability being the means by which a decision as to culpability is reached, it is the other way round. Communities use their shared experiences to determine acceptable risk taking.[46]

Legal accounts of recklessness assume that while some risks are justifiable, others are not, without any attempt being made to calibrate them. The lack of attention paid to this adds credence to the type of cultural analysis outlined above. A phrase such as 'obvious risk' is left to carry the burden of determining the acceptable levels of risk in any particular activity.[47] Reaching agreement on what are 'fair risks' is never going to be easy. There is probably no such thing as an intrinsically 'fair or acceptable risk', only risks which are judged acceptable by specific groups of individuals in specific circumstances.[48] People tend to ignore high probabilities such as road and domestic accidents and concentrate their attention on the middle range probabilities.[49]

Risk assessment requires the selection of an acceptance standard, such as risk criteria.[50] Tolerability of risk can be represented in pyramid form; at the top is an area representing intolerable risk on which action must be taken and at the bottom an area of negligible risk which requires no action. In-between is an area which demands that the risk should be reduced to 'as low as reasonably practicable' (ALARP).[51] The Cullen Report on the *Piper Alpha* disaster, for example, recognized that this involved a cost-benefit exercise and that due regard should be had, when formulating risk criteria to 'risk aversion, the aversion which society has to major accidents'.[52] It could be argued that variables such as ease of elimination and the nature of the harm threatened could enter the equation through the words 'obvious/and serious' and 'gross' negligence. The emphasis in legal discourse on the significance of cognitive awareness is misdirected. If some of these questions of justifiability, in other words, the utility calculus, are inherent in the phrase 'obvious/and serious risk' then the question should not just be whether that person would have *foreseen* the risk but also whether they would have *taken* that risk. This can be illustrated by the following psychological insight.

Phenomenological and behaviouristic psychology both recognize that two opposite forces contribute to any one piece of behaviour.[53] Approach factors induce it and avoidance factors discourage it. Ruimschotel uses premeditation to describe a desired result. A premeditated murder would, in psychological terms, be one in which a positive value was attached to the death. With any other mental state, such as intention or recklessness, the outcome would not be positively valued. A person who intends the result in the sense of having full knowledge that it will occur raises no particular problem; they may attach negative value to the

---

[44] Douglas 1985: 67–8.   [45] Ibid.   [46] Ibid. 69.
[47] See, for example, Birch 1988: 4.   [48] Irwin, Smith, and Griffiths 1982: 262.
[49] Douglas 1985: 60.   [50] Cullen 1990: para. 17.55.
[51] HSE discussion document on tolerability, referred to in Cullen, ibid.
[52] Ibid   [53] Ruimschotel 1988: 85.

result but they are not restrained by that. However, Ruimschotel points to an ambivalence wherever the outcome is known to the actor as anything less than certain. This arises because in those cases we do not know what adjustments the actor would have made had she known what the result would be.[54] If she would have acted in the same way, it can be said that there is a value deficit: she no more values life than the intentional (with full knowledge) or premeditative actor. The knowledge/value deficit type of argument could be helpful in applying the conventional prudent person test for recklessness, negligence, or carelessness. No account is taken of the defendant's knowledge deficit, but where the person has a surplus of knowledge compared with a reasonable person that is regarded as relevant. Applying this analysis to the P&O case then the most important question would be to ask how much how much of a risk an open-door sailing would be before a prudent ferry operator would ignore it: 1 in a 1,000, 1 in a 1 million, or what? And, having asked that, to examine the state of the defendant's knowledge (actual or expected as a prudent operator) on this.

This discussion of risk is relevant whether recklessness or negligence are conceived in objective or subjective terms. The P&O case was of course based on an objective conception of recklessness which many commentators regard in general as an unacceptable, and atypical, test of culpability. It is clear, however, not only that English criminal law relies on an objective formulation of recklessness for many offences, but that in many other respects its devotion to subjectivism is less than complete.[55] Manslaughter is, however, the major example of a serious offence relying on a negligence standard. Despite its previous adherence to subjective fault terms, the Law Commission did not depart from this approach in the reform recommendations in their 1996 report on involuntary manslaughter.

3. Unlawful act manslaughter—the forgotten question

The relationship between constructive (unlawful act) manslaughter and corporate liability is significant. The case of *Andrews* in 1937 was pivotal in ensuring that those causing death by driving or while acting professionally would not be drawn into the full depths of the manslaughter net.[56] In addition to the gross negligence head of manslaughter is that known as 'unlawful act' or constructive manslaughter. A good indication both of its earlier draconian formulation and its less severe replacement can be seen in the judgment of Edmund-Davies J. in *R* v. *Church*:

An unlawful act causing the death of another cannot, simply because it is an unlawful act, render a manslaughter verdict inevitable. For such a verdict inexorably to follow, the unlawful act must be such as all sober and reasonable people would inevitably recognize must subject the other person to, at least, the risk of some harm resulting therefrom, albeit not serious harm.[57]

It can be seen that such a test might implicate corporate defendants following transport disasters. British Rail, for example, was prosecuted for failing to ensure

---

[54] Ibid. 88.   [55] Wells 1982.   [56] 1937.   [57] 1966 at 69.

passenger safety following the Clapham Rail crash in 1988 as was GWT after Southall.[58] Each case would seem to satisfy the *Church* unlawful act criteria. One explanation for the DPP's reaching the conclusion that there was insufficient evidence to bring a manslaughter charge after Clapham is the qualification to unlawful act introduced in *Andrews*. A bus company employee was charged with manslaughter following a hit-and-run accident while driving a van to rescue a broken-down bus. The House of Lords accepted that a conviction could be based on (the then equivalent of) reckless manslaughter, but Lord Atkin specified that it could not be assumed that conviction would necessarily follow merely because there had been careless or reckless driving contrary to the Road Traffic Acts:

[The Road Traffic Acts] have provisions which regulate the degree of care to be taken in driving motor vehicles. They have no direct reference to causing death by negligence. . . . s.11 imposes a penalty for driving recklessly or at a speed or in a manner which is dangerous to the public. There can be no doubt that this section covers driving with such a high degree of negligence as that if death were caused the offender would have committed manslaughter. But the converse is not true, and it is perfectly possible that a man may drive at a speed or in a manner dangerous to the public and cause death and yet not be guilty of manslaughter.[59]

This meant that the unlawful act head would not apply. 'There is an obvious difference in the law of manslaughter between doing an unlawful act and doing a lawful act with a degree of carelessness which the Legislature makes criminal. If it were otherwise a man who killed another while driving without due care and attention would *ex necessitate* commit manslaughter.'[60]

This case has not only privileged the careless, drunken, and dangerous driver from the full application of the law of manslaughter, but has also secured a firmer immunity from prosecution for corporate defendants since the unlawful act which led to the death will frequently fall within Atkin's exception. Health and safety breaches for example can be seen not as 'unlawful' but as 'doing a lawful act with a degree of carelessness . . .'. But a moment's reflection might reveal the potential vacuity of this distinction. It seems to have at its base a class assumption about the types of person who commit crimes of violence reinforced by a proposition that legislative offences are different from 'real' crime. Taking that point first, dangerous drivers are not committing an offence, they are infringing a statutory provision while acting lawfully. This echoes the distinction between *mala prohibita* and *mala in se* discussed in Chapter I. One of the implicit features of *mala prohibita* offences is that because they are of statutory origin the harms they proscribe are less serious. The criminal stereotyping involved in the *Andrews* doctrine conjures the image of a classic unlawful act manslaughter occurring when a pub brawl goes wrong. Is there a sense in which this can be described as an intrinsically 'unlawful' activity, unlike careless, reckless, or dangerous driving which is at base 'lawful'.[61] It is true that

---

[58] Following a guilty plea, British Rail was fined £250,000 which at the time equalled the record for a safety conviction in England, *Guardian*, 15 June 1991. GWT were fined £1.5 million after Southall.

[59] *Andrews* (1937) per Lord Atkin at 583.   [60] Ibid. 584.

[61] The alternative 'dangerous' was removed in 1972; the Road Traffic Act 1991, s. 1, revived and elevated it by replacing the offence of reckless driving with that of dangerous driving.

brawling, unlike driving, is an activity with little if any social utility. But it is also true that going to pubs is a lawful social activity. Neither brawling nor careless, reckless, or dangerous driving have social utility. The timeframe of criminal activity needs critically to be addressed;[62] at what point does a pub visit turn into an unlawful activity? If it is only at the point at which an assault or battery is committed then this does not seem very different from the point at which lawful driving becomes careless. Thus it is not driving with which brawling should be compared but careless, reckless, or dangerous driving.

Andrews epitomized a general reluctance to see road users as part of the criminal fraternity. It proved difficult to convict even where deaths resulted from blatantly reckless driving (and therefore came within the other head of manslaughter). A statutory offence of causing death by dangerous driving with a maximum sentence of five years' imprisonment was introduced.[63] The conviction of *Robert Millar (Contractors) Ltd* for causing death by dangerous driving illustrates the dissonance between the statutory offence and manslaughter. Had the same events given rise to a manslaughter prosecution, the case would undoubtedly have attracted a great deal more contemporary comment and would have secured a firm place in the history of corporate criminal liability. The managing director of a Scottish haulage company knew that a tyre on one of its lorries was seriously defective. The driver had complained about the tyre to his employers on more than one occasion. On the return part of a trip to the English midlands, the tyre burst, causing the lorry to cross the central reservation of the M6 motorway in Lancashire and crash into an oncoming car, killing all six occupants. The charges of death by dangerous driving brought against the company and its managing director were based on complicity. The Court of Appeal accepted the argument that the company had counselled and procured the offence. 'In our view,' Fenton Atkinson LJ said,

if a driver is sent out by his employer to drive a heavy vehicle on a trip extending over some hundreds of miles carrying heavy loads with a dangerously defective front offside tyre, by an employer who knows that the tyre is dangerous, and that there is a serious risk of harm resulting to other road-users, then if that tyre does burst and thereby causes an accident killing somebody, the employer is guilty of counselling and procuring death by dangerous driving.[64]

The court confirmed a fine of £750 on the company and a sentence of nine months' imprisonment for the managing director.[65] Because the prosecution was brought for the (then)[66] morally somewhat innocuous statutory offence, an opportunity was lost to portray it as corporate homicide.

---

[62] Kelman 1981.

[63] Road Traffic Act 1956; now Road traffic Act 1991, s. 1.

[64] *R v. Robert Millar (Contractors) Ltd and Robert Millar* (1970) at 579.

[65] The driver, who did not appeal, was disqualified and given a 'modest fine', 'the trial judge taking the view (as we think rightly) that the real responsibility for the disaster lay elsewhere'. Ibid. 578.

[66] There is some evidence that dangerous driving, particularly drink-driving, is now taken more seriously. The decrease in numbers of deaths on UK roads could be accounted for by a number of factors (better vehicle design, road lighting, etc.) but may well also be a sign of safer driving.

The idea of unlawful act (constructive) manslaughter is itself unappealing.[67] It could be argued that the *Andrews* doctrine, by removing its application from some situations of 'socially acceptable' lawbreaking has ensured its survival. Equally, while it remains part of our jurisprudence it is inappropriate to exclude killings from its ambit on the basis of the barren *Andrews* distinction. Many workplace accidents could be considered as negligent killings in themselves, but there is no reason why they should not also be open to prosecution on the easier to prove unlawful act head. The Robert Millar case also raises the interesting, but separate, question of whether the P&O prosecution could have been based on complicity in the reckless manslaughter arguably committed by the Assistant Bosun. The point here is that, as with the driver in the Millar case, the Assistant Bosun could not act *as* the company for the purposes of direct corporate liability.

4. Corporate killing—a proposed offence

i. The background

The prosecutions of P&O and GWT arose from high-profile public transport disasters. There were several other well-publicized disasters in the 1980s and 1990s which cumulatively gave rise to demands for corporate manslaughter prosecutions. At the same time, there was pressure from some campaign groups for workplace deaths to be taken more seriously in the criminal justice system. These parallel developments reflect changing perceptions of risk and blame. This is an interesting reversal of the more usual relation between civil and criminal processes. Where the prosecuting authorities are reluctant to pursue a particular individual, civil law, with its lower standard of proof, has sometimes been used as an alternative. Disasters have presented the converse—the use of criminal law where previously civil law has been seen as the appropriate forum. Different explanations have been suggested for this trend. Campaigning for criminal liability is sometimes thought to be used as a means of applying pressure to the civil process, but evidence from the aftermath of disasters such as those of *Piper Alpha*, *Marchioness*, and Hillsborough suggests otherwise.[68] Settlements after *Piper Alpha* were prompt and generous and predated the pursuit of criminal proceedings against Occidental.[69] The campaign represented something other than a means of obtaining leverage for compensation. One reason for the persistence of the private prosecutions after *Marchioness* and Hillsborough was that there was little scope for argument in the claim for damages. As mostly young adults with no dependants, the victims' deaths resulted in bereavement damages which are of limited value.[70] The bereaved relatives may well have felt that these payments were inadequate and also that the fixed limit deprived them of any oppor-

---

[67] The Government differed from the Law Commission (1996) on this and proposed an offence of causing death intending or reckless as to some injury, Home Office 2000 para. 2.11.
[68] Wells 1995*a*: Ch. 2.   [69] Ibid.   [70] Fatal Accidents Act 1976, s. 1A.

tunity of a public outlet for their outrage at the safety failures of both the Department of Transport and the *Bowbelle*'s owners. There was no public inquiry until 11 years later and the inquests were adjourned many times.[71] But trying to establish what people do 'want' from the legal system involves examining a deep, challenging, and elusive seam of human psychology and cultural preference. It would appear that bereaved relatives use law for a number of different purposes, including venting anger or frustration or both, seeking revenge, demanding compensation and wanting to prevent future tragedies.[72] A variety of legal institutions and different types of legal process can be invoked in the search for satisfaction which appears to go beyond mere compensation in the quest for something like 'truth' or 'justice'. Amidst this diversity clear patterns emerge which affect and reflect broader cultural attitudes. One such pattern is the increased use of criminal in addition to civil proceedings following disasters causing multiple deaths.

Between 1996 and 1998, 510 people died and 47,803 suffered major injuries from work-related accidents.[73] In some industrial sectors the number of major injuries has increased in the last two decades.[74] A total of 3,555 people have lost their lives at work in the last ten years.[75] Many of these deaths were preventable according to the Health and Safety Executive which concluded that 75 per cent of maintenance accidents in the chemical industry were either partly or wholly the result of site management's failure to take reasonably practicable precautions.[76] Studies of other industries reveal similar startlingly high rates of both regulatory violations and reckless endangerment of workers' lives.[77] '[I]n at least two out of three fatal accidents, managements were in violation of the Health and Safety at Work Act 1974 . . . Popular definitions of an "accident" are called into question by such data.'[78] Between 1981 and 1985 there were 739 deaths in the construction industry 70 per cent of which (over 500) could have been avoided by 'positive action by management'.[79] Yet there have been only a handful of prosecutions of company directors for manslaughter following a workplace death and these resulted in only two convictions.[80] Prosecutions of companies are also rare. Workplace deaths are automatically investigated by the HSE who do not have the power to bring manslaughter prosecutions and have only since 1998 agreed a protocol with the police and the Crown Prosecution Service for co-ordinating

[71] See Ch. 3.4.i.

[72] Harris *et al.* suggest that in general personal injury claimants are noticeable for a diversity of desires, and that what most people want is a by-product of what they believe it is permissible to want, 1984: Ch. 4.

[73] Centre for Corporate Accountability: 1999.

[74] HSE 1985*a* and Pearce and Tombs 1990: 426.

[75] Centre for Corporate Accountability 1999.

[76] HSE 1987*a*.

[77] Carson 1970; HSE 1983, 1985*b*, 1986, 1988.

[78] Pearce and Tombs 1990: 426.

[79] HSE 1988*b*.

[80] Slapper 1991, Centre for Corporate Accountability 1999. Brothers, David and Norman Holt, directors of David Holt Plastics, were charged with manslaughter. Norman Holt pleaded guilty and received a 1-year suspended prison sentence; the CPS accepted David Holt's not guilty plea, see Bergman 1990*a*.

investigations in such cases. As noted in Chapter 1, of fifty-nine cases referred to the CPS by the HSE in the period 1992–8, only eighteen prosecutions for manslaughter were brought, most against individuals. Prosecutions under the Health and Safety at Work Act are brought in only 20 per cent of workplace deaths and after 1 per cent of reported major injuries.[81]

The Home Office comments that these low numbers 'do not reflect any unwillingness on the part of the health and safety enforcing authorities to refer such cases to the CPS and the police but result principally from shortcomings in the existing law on corporate manslaughter'.[82] However, this explanation hardly fits with the *Akhter* case. In April 2000 the High Court ordered the HSE to undertake an investigation into the death of a worker killed in August 1997.[83] Akhter was killed when a forklift truck struck the car he was driving. After the death the HSE, although it was the enforcing authority, refused to investigate the conduct of the forklift driver's employer to determine whether any health and safety offences had been committed by the company or one of its company officers. The HSE's refusal also meant that there could be no manslaughter investigation since, at the time, the police would only carry out such an investigation if the case was referred onto them by the HSE. The HSE had been informed of the death by Trafford Borough Council within forty minutes of the death taking place. Yet in its evidence to the Select Committee on Environment Transport and the Regions, the HSE had said that it 'investigated all deaths'. The only investigation into this death was undertaken by the Road Traffic Police. As a result, the driver of the forklift truck and his employer were convicted for failing to have a driving licence. They both received a six-month conditional discharge.

ii. Law Commission Report 237

In 1996 the Law Commission recommended that a separate offence of corporate killing be introduced. A large part of its report on reforming involuntary homicide law was devoted to the issue of corporate, as opposed to individual, manslaughter. Two possible explanations for this outbreak of interest in corporate homicide are suggested. The first is that pressure to enforce more rigorously regulatory provisions on safety at work and on environmental matters has greatly increased. This is a reflection of changing attitudes to safety and risk, and to differing perceptions of transport and other disasters, leading to the now familiar history of calls for corporations to be prosecuted for manslaughter. Despite these significant shifts in attitudes, their translation into legal form has as we have witnessed been slow. The Commission's proposals testify to the contemporary social and symbolic importance of corporate accountability. The second is that, until this Report, the Law Commission believed that responsibility could be properly reflected only in subjective principles of fault. The

---

[81] Centre for Corporate Accountability 1999.   [82] Home Office 2000: 13, n. 4.
[83] *R* v. *CPS, ex parte Akhter*, 2000 unreported. See also *R* v. *DPP and others, ex parte Timothy Jones*, 24 Mar. 2000, unreported.

Commission articulated in this Report some of the arguments in favour of culpable inadvertence.[84] This departure allowed the possibility of extending corporate liability for serious offences to be less incongruous or doctrinally challenging than it would have been earlier.

Shortly after the Southall rail crash in 1997, in which seven passengers died, the Government announced its intention to legislate the Law Commission's proposed offence of corporate killing. A consultation paper was not, however, published until May 2000; this coincided with the failure of the manslaughter charges against Great Western Trains. The Paddington (Ladbroke Grove) crash in October 1999, in which thirty-one people died served as an additional reminder that the promise to legislate had not been fulfilled.[85]

The Law Commission proposed three offences to replace the current single offence of manslaughter. For individual offenders two offences were proposed: reckless killing and killing by gross carelessness (which would replace manslaughter by the gross negligence route). It is envisaged that a corporation could also be indicted for these offences through the existing identification rules. In addition, however, the Report proposed a separate offence of corporate killing which could only be committed by a corporation. The offence is intended to be the corporate equivalent of killing by gross carelessness, but the Report sought to overcome the problems of the identification principle by introducing a tailor-made test of corporate culpability based on 'management failure'.[86]

The key to the Law Commission's thinking lay in the collapse of the prosecution for manslaughter of P&O Ferries. The law applicable at the time presented three potential hurdles to a successful prosecution of P&O (the judge directed an acquittal before the prosecution had presented all its evidence). First, could a corporation commit manslaughter? That question was resolved as an initial point of law.[87] Secondly, the restrictive, anthropomorphic identification doctrine of corporate liability meant that the company could be liable only through its directing mind, in this case represented by some of its directors. Thirdly, the substantive law of manslaughter which relied on a test of whether the defendant (here one or more of the directors) had realized that there was an 'obvious and serious risk' of such an event occurring gave rise to problems. Before the Report was published the last difficulty was removed by the re-introduction of 'gross negligence' as the legal test for manslaughter: 'The jury will have to decide whether the extent to which the defendant's conduct departed from the proper standard of care incumbent upon him, . . ., was such that it should be judged criminal.'[88]

The Law Commission's version of this test is 'gross carelessness':

(1) A person who by his conduct causes the death of another is guilty of killing by gross carelessness if—

(a) a risk that his conduct will cause death or serious injury would be obvious to a reasonable person in his position;

[84] 1996: Part IV; see discussion below in Ch. 7.2.   [85] See also Wells 2000.
[86] 1996: Part VIII.   [87] *P&O European Ferries (Dover) Ltd* 1991.
[88] *R v. Adomako* [1995] 1 AC 171, 187, per Lord Mackay of Clashfern, LC.

(*b*) he is capable of appreciating that risk at the material time; and

(*c*) either—

(i) his conduct falls far below what can reasonably be expected of him in the circumstances; or

(ii) he intends by his conduct to cause some injury or is aware of, and unreasonably takes, the risk that it may do so.

A corporation would be liable for this offence as before under the existing identification rule. The Law Commission recognized that it is difficult to apply the identification principle especially to large corporations with diffuse management structures. Rather than recommend any change to that rule, a separate offence of corporate killing was proposed. This offence adopts a 'holistic' theory of attribution, that is a theory that does not derive from the actions of one individual in the company. The Commission argued that it would be difficult to apply a holistic theory of attribution to the offence of killing by gross carelessness. It would be clumsy to speak of a 'company' failing to realize that a risk was 'obvious'. Therefore the Commission proposed a specially styled offence—with both a different definition of culpability and a new route to attribution.

Under clause 4 of the draft Bill:

(1) A corporation is guilty of corporate killing if—

(a) a management failure by the corporation is the cause or one of the causes of a person's death; and

(b) that failure constitutes conduct falling far below what can reasonably be expected of the corporation in the circumstances.

(2) For the purposes of subsection (1) above—

(a) There is a management failure by the company if the way in which its activities are managed or organised fails to ensure the health and safety of persons employed in or affected by those activities; and

(b) Such a failure may be regarded as a cause of a person's death notwithstanding that the immediate cause is the act or omission of an individual.

Apart from being somewhat circular, a major weakness in the Commission's formulation is that 'management' is not defined. It could either lead to an exceptionally broad test or to one which is interpreted very narrowly. John Coffee, the leading US commentator on corporate liability, puts it well:

This standard if adopted could make the corporation a virtual insurer for any accidental killing. In any event, this . . . proposal suggests a high degree of cognitive dissonance within the British legal community; on the one hand, the prevailing legal rule on corporate criminal liability is understood to be very narrow and, on the other hand, the appropriate legal standard proposed by the leading law reform group is extremely broad.[89]

Given the judicial aversion to corporate liability evidenced in the GWT and P&O trials it is possible that the cognitive dissonance will be resolved in favour of a narrow interpretation. The judge in the aborted P&O trial gave as his reason for

---

[89] 1999: 18.

directing an acquittal that evidence had been heard from P&O's own employees that no one had thought that there might be a risk of the ferry sailing with an open door:

> I do not understand that the statements of any of these witnesses condescend to criticism of the system employed by the defendants in this case as one which created an obvious and serious risk, *except to the extent that any legitimate deduction may be made from the fact that they took precautions other than those employed by any of these defendants.*[90]

Yet the official shipping inquiry into the disaster had concluded that all concerned in the company's management shared responsibility for the failure in their safety system.[91] The Law Commission argued that its new culpability test based on management failure would allow a jury to conclude that

> even if the immediate cause of the deaths was the conduct of the assistant bosun, the Chief Officer or both, another of the causes was the failure of the company to devise a safe system for the operation of the ferries; and that that failure fell far below what could reasonably have been expected.[92]

Is there not a difficulty here? The reasons given for the failure of the prosecution (that there was no obvious and serious risk perceptible to a prudent master that the ferry might sail with its doors open), suggests that we cannot regard it as a management failure that no system was devised to avoid it. Are not the two tests (obvious and serious risk and management failure to ensure safety) very similar ways of putting the same question? We can either say 'the company's failure to provide a safe system fell far below what was reasonably expected' or 'the company' [the management] failed to realise that there was an obvious risk that a ship might sail with its doors open'. If the risk were not obvious, as the judge concluded, why should we expect the company to devise a safe system to prevent it?

A test based on 'management failure' begins to address some of the shortcomings. However, the belief that the new test would entirely solve the problems inherent in corporate manslaughter cases may be misplaced. The major difference between these two tests is that the new test allows us to speak of 'management' rather than having to look to individual directors. In some cases, looking to 'management' may well involve a more effective method of capturing the essence of a company's decision-making framework than the identification theory allows. The conundrums which corporate liability presents still remain, in particular that tricky question 'who is the company?' It would be churlish not to concede that speaking of management and failures of systems is an advance on the identification doctrine. It will undoubtedly be easier in many cases to address corporate culpability through 'management failure' than through the directing mind notion. But it is not enough to speak of 'management' or 'the way its activities are managed or organised' without resurrecting the same old problems: which employees and which systems can be said to be those of the company? If

---

[90] *Stanley and others*, 10 Oct. 1990 (CCC) transcript, p. 17 D–F, quoted in the Report, para. 6.54, emphasis added.
[91] Sheen Report 1987: para. 14.1.   [92] 1996: para. 8.50.

there is one lesson from the P&O and other corporate killing sagas, it is that corporate defendants are highly motivated and well-placed to exploit the metaphysical gap between 'the company' and its members.

In endorsing the Law Commission's proposals, the Government proposes to extend the application of the new offence beyond incorporated bodies to cover 'undertakings'. It is usually assumed that corporate liability will extend at least to incorporated business enterprises, local authorities, charities, and incorporated clubs. It does not cover unincorporated associations such as partnerships, trusts, registered Friendly societies, and registered trade unions. Since many unincorporated bodies are in practice indistinguishable from corporations the Government would extend the application of corporate killing to cover 'undertakings', that is 'any trade or business or other activity providing employment'.[93] This [would] mean that three and a half million enterprises now subject to the Health and Safety at Work Act 1974 would additionally be potentially liable for corporate killing.[94]

Aside from the definitional shortcomings to which I have alluded, a separate offence may lead to more marginalization of corporate killing rather than less. In addition, the question of individual liability of directors and senior managers requires further attention. Many commentators on corporate regulation recognize that enforcement against corporations is most effective when accompanied also by action against high-level managers at the same time.[95] These broader questions relating to the reform of corporate liability principles and their proper relationship with individual liability are discussed in detail in the final chapter.

[93] Home Office 2000: para. 3.2.2. This relies on the term used in Health and Safety at Work Act 1974 as defined in Local Employment Act 1960.

[94] Home Office 2000: para. 3.2.5. Hospital Trusts are bodies corporate, National Health and Community Care Act 1990, s. 5(5).

[95] See, for example, Smith 1995: 14.

7

\

Comparative and International Solutions

The last two chapters have concentrated on the development of corporate liability for criminal offences in England and Wales. Now it is time to reflect the
view of the cathedral through a number of different angles and lights.[1] Legal
systems throughout the world appear to be asking similar questions about corporate responsibility for harms caused by their negligent, corrupt, or fraudulent operations. Corporate liability for crime has appeared on the agenda in
many jurisdictions over the last 10 years, including Germany, France, Italy, and
Spain. The Council of Europe reached a consensus that it was desirable in
1988;[2] corporate liability was the subject of the International Congress of
Comparative Law in Athens 1994,[3] and of an international colloquium spon-
sored by the Ministry of Justice in Germany in 1998.[4] Common law jurisdictions have embraced corporate criminal liability for over 150 years but
unsurprisingly there are differences in the approach each has taken. It can be
said that in general the federal rules in the United States and in Australia are
much the broadest[5] while England has the narrowest. Many civil law jurisdictions in Europe, on the other hand, have only recently begun to introduce corporate liability into their Penal Codes. As Legrand puts it they are 'experiencing
a comparative moment'.[6] National legal systems increasingly subject themselves to international conventions (such as those emanating from their membership of the Council of Europe or the OECD), or supranational bodies (such
as the EU). These bodies exert pressures to harmonize or approximate
responses to phenomena such as environmental offences, corruption and
bribery, and other economic offences. Concerns about the reach and power of
global corporations, about fraud, corruption, occupational safety, and environmental depredations have brought the question to the fore of our collective
attention. From a wide diversity of legal cultures and traditions emerges therefore a debate on shared terms.

---

[1] Monet Rouen Cathedral (1892–4), Hamilton (1960).
[2] Recommendation No. R (88) 18, see s. 4 below.
[3] de Doelder and Tiedemann 1996.   [4] Eser, Heine, and Huber 1999.
[5] However, in both those countries, much of what we would recognize as traditional criminal law
is conducted at the state not the federal level. There different rules apply.
[6] Legrand 1996: 232. And see Cadoppi 1998.

This chapter serves as an introduction to these various legal responses before placing them in the context of a normative debate about the most appropriate mechanisms for the control of corporate wrongdoing in Chapter 8. It is divided into four sections: comparative cautions; common law variations; civil law changes; and convergence.

1. COMPARATIVE CAUTIONS

Some preliminary comments about the nature of comparative studies of this kind are necessary. Before we make comparisons with other jurisdictions it is important to recognize that the constitutional, administrative, and procedural differences are as significant as those of substantive law. There are many other problems, too, those of translation, of theoretical boundary (what is law and what is not), and of culture: '[T]here is much of the utmost relevance to a deep understanding of a legal order, of an experience of law, that is simply not found in legislative texts and in judicial decisions.'[7] Even in England and Wales where corporate bodies have long been subject to both regulatory and 'classic' criminal law, corporate liability has been a Cinderella topic, largely ignored by the major writers and theorists, and rarely appearing for discussion at the appellate level.[8]

In practical terms most corporate liability in England and Wales as I have shown is seen in the regulatory field and thus comparable with administrative regulation in some other jurisdictions. Many European jurisdictions have until recently made no provision for the criminal liability of non-human agents in their Penal Codes but may instead have administrative sanctions which are not dissimilar in effect. In addition, discretion in respect of investigation and prosecution on the part of regulatory agencies, the police, and the Crown Prosecution Service reduces the number of instances of corporate wrongdoing which are formally pursued. These discretions shield both companies and their directors from prosecution or other official action. Corporate liability for offences is not always translated into practical enforcement. In those countries which have used administrative penalties for corporate wrongdoing, non-human liability under the penal law has either been historically or constitutionally unacceptable.[9] Criminal law in these jurisdictions addresses individual people. Nonetheless, it is not uncommon for individual directors of corporations to be charged with manslaughter following negligently caused deaths for example. And, indeed, in some systems prosecution is mandatory.

Additionally, as I argued in Chapter 3, whichever of these models—the criminal/penal (the criminal *character*), the quasi-criminal/regulatory (the criminal *silhouette*), or the administrative sanction (the criminal *shadow*)—is adopted it will also form part of a larger legal institutional structure. We should not for-

---

[7] Legrand 1996: 235.
[8] The lack of appellate decisions is both a cause and effect of scholarly marginalization.
[9] Italy, for example.

get, in examining the finer detail, that claims about one area of law may make little sense when the landscape is viewed at more of a distance. Marc Galanter outlines four different types of institutional and legal response to the risks inherent in our increasing reliance on technology.[10] First, there are controls intrinsic to technology: the initial design, safety procedures, worker training, and so on. While many are not specifically legal they are nonetheless regulated through scientific and technological practice. Unlike some legal regulation, this transfers fairly easily with the technology across national boundaries. Secondly, there is a layer of administrative controls by government including health and safety regulatory regimes as well as specific legislative provisions (for example, those dealing with the 'Millennium Bug'). This second type inevitably varies depending on the jurisdiction and, like after the event forum-shopping, these differences form part of business considerations in determining the best location for manufacturing and production of goods. The same is true of the third layer which consists of the public institutions for absorbing and spreading losses, health care systems and services, and welfare institutions. Private law compensation, through tort for example, comprises the fourth layer. It is surprising that neither criminal law, nor what we might call the public institutions of investigation such as public inquiries, inquests or fatal accident inquiries, make an appearance in this conceptualization. This under-emphasis on public law institutions including criminal law mirrors the mistake we sometimes make of seeing the legal world *only* through the keyhole of the criminal justice system. This distribution of work between the different layers of institutional responses affects the balance between prospective and preventive mechanisms as against retrospective and remedial controls. However, in all systems there is a mix and we should not conceive of them as separate, unrelated alternatives, nor assume that it is possible to pull out one section of a criminal code and compare it with that in another jurisdiction on the assumption that everything else in the way of legal institutional and cultural arrangements will remain conveniently static.

2. COMMON LAW VARIATIONS

This section deals with legal principles in the common law jurisdictions of England and Wales,[11] the United States, Australia, Canada, and New Zealand. The United States and Australia have both federal and state criminal laws. Different corporate liability rules apply at the federal and state levels.

Some common law jurisdictions do not have a code of criminal law or procedure but general principles, in relation both to the minimum fault element in criminal offences, and to corporate liability, have developed. These may be overridden by particular statutes. As explained in Chapter 5, determining the type of

---

[10] Galanter 1994.
[11] Which for ease of exposition I will refer to (inaccurately) as the UK.

offence and the type of fault element in any particular offence is a crucial factor in establishing the standard of corporate liability for criminal offences in the UK.

Three different theories for attributing blame to corporations were outlined in Chapter 5. The agency principle, *respondeat superior,* whereby the company is liable for the wrongful acts of all its employees, is deployed in the United States federal law. A full-scale vicarious liability principle is also endorsed in South Africa thus confirming that there is no conceptual difficulty in applying the vicarious principle to offences both of strict liability and of subjective knowledge.[12] English law limits the application of vicarious liability to certain regulatory offences. Vicarious liability, a doctrine transplanted from civil law which grew out of the development of the liability of a master (employer) for his servant (employee), facilitated the development of both the civil and criminal liability of corporations. The vicarious principle applied only to some statutory offences in the regulatory field and, by 1900, a number of regulatory provisions were construed as applying to corporations. Whether a criminal prohibition could be applied to a corporation in this way was a matter of interpreting the object of the statute. In general, the process of judicial interpretation of the statutory object led to corporate liability being imposed only for regulatory offences, especially those offences which did not require proof of *mens rea* or a mental element. While the general principle that a company can be prosecuted for a criminal offence has long been accepted, the question whether a *particular* statute imposes such liability and whether the vicarious or identification doctrine will apply, is rarely if ever spelled out, and the process of interpretation is thus on-going.

The second theory of blame attribution, utilized in English law for all other offences, renders the company liable only for their culpable transgressions, not for those of other workers. Identification theory forms the basis of corporate liability, although often interpreted more generously, in many American states, in Canada, New Zealand, and the state jurisdictions in Australia. The third theory locates corporate blame in the procedures, operating systems, or culture of a company. Company culture theory is deployed in the Australian Criminal Code Act, and in the proposed corporate homicide offence in the United Kingdom.[13]

With this common law framework in mind it is now possible to gain an understanding of some of the approaches to the criminal liability of corporations that have been adopted in other common law jurisdictions.

i. CANADA

The Canadian Supreme Court has expanded identification liability, recognizing that companies may have more than one directing mind.[14] The essence of the test is whether the identity of the directing mind and the company coincide when the 'directing mind' is operating in his/her assigned field of operations. The field of

---

[12] van Oosten 1999: 195.

[13] Clause 4, draft Involuntary Homicide Bill, Law Commission Report 1996.

[14] See Ferguson 1999 for a full account.

operations may be geographic or functional or embrace the entire operations of the company.[15] The Canadian Law Reform Commission in 1987 proposed that persons whose conduct could create corporate liability were those 'with authority over the formulation or implementation of corporate policy'.[16]

ii. NEW ZEALAND

Although New Zealand adopts the English identification doctrine it has recently moved to a more flexible attribution principle.[17] The *Meridian* case allows the court to look with an open mind at the attribution rules. The Privy Council has returned the law to first principles and advised that there is no general rule requiring a court to isolate the 'controlling mind' of a company. In determining who amongst the employees acts as the company itself depends on a number of factors: the structure of the company; the functions performed by the company and who performs them in practice and the policy underpinning the law being enforced. The person or persons whose actions are attributable to the company will be determined so as to give effect to the purpose of the law.

iii. UNITED STATES—STATE JURISDICTIONS

It is vital to distinguish between state and federal jurisdictions. States enforce most conventional crimes. Twenty-eight states have adopted corporate liability principles and many have gradually adopted legislation along the lines of the Model Penal Code formulation which takes as its model the English approach.[18] The Model Penal Code retains three different systems of liability.[19] For crimes of intent, where no 'legislative purpose to impose liability on corporations plainly appears' the English identification model is adopted.[20] Under this a corporation would only be liable for crimes usually committed by individuals if 'the commission of the offence was requested, commanded, performed, or recklessly tolerated by the board of directors or a high managerial agent'.[21] A 'high managerial agent' is defined as an officer or agent of the corporation 'having duties of such responsibility that his conduct may fairly be assumed to represent the policy of the corporation'.[22] The agent need not direct or command—it is enough that he or the board 'recklessly tolerated' the offence.

However, many states have adapted the code so that liability is closer to that of the federal *respondeat superior*.[23] The second category of liability in the MPC is for crimes of intent where the legislature clearly does intend to impose liability on

---

[15] *Canadian Dredge and Dock Co Ltd* v. *The Queen* (1985).
[16] Law Reform Commission of Canada 1987: 26.
[17] *Meridian Global Funds Management Asia Ltd* v. *Securities Commission* (1995).
[18] American Law Institute 1962: para. 2.07.
[19] Discussed by Tigar 1990: 226; Note, Harvard 1979: 1251; and Foerschler 1990: 295.
[20] 207 (1) a–c.   [21] 207 (1) (c).
[22] 207 (4) (c); for an example see NY Penal Law para. 20.20 (1994).
[23] Brickey 1988: 633–4.

corporations. It suggests a liability similar to vicarious liability but with a defence available if the corporation can prove on a balance of probabilities (preponderance of evidence) that the high managerial agent with supervisory responsibility over the subject-matter of the offence acted with 'due diligence'. This was added in the belief that '[T]he primary purpose of holding corporations accountable for the acts of lower-level employees is to encourage diligent supervision by managerial officials.'[24] And lastly, for strict liability offences, the MPC reflects the vicarious principle and assumes a legislative purpose to impose liability on corporations 'unless the contrary plainly appears'.[25]

Provisions in other states echo the broad federal attribution rules whereby a corporation is liable for the acts committed by its agents acting within the scope of their authority. Corporations have been held liable for manslaughter or reckless homicide in states ranging from California to Texas.[26] As in England and Wales it has often proved easier to obtain convictions against smaller companies than against nationals and multinationals operating across a number of sites. This underlines the need for the common law to tailor a rule of attribution for manslaughter which is responsive both to small and large enterprises.

iv. UNITED STATES—FEDERAL JURISDICTION

US federal courts have taken a broad approach. Now backed by a legislative sentencing structure, the agency/vicarious doctrine applies to all offences. Conceptual problems presented by the need in some offences to prove knowledge within a company have been overcome with imaginative use of existing principle. Federal offences include those concerned with occupational safety and health, interstate commerce and corruption. Although homicide is a state concern, there is for example an offence under the Occupational Safety and Health Act providing for criminal penalties for wilful violations of the Act causing death.[27] Although rare, the United States has brought prosecutions against corporations under this statute. Such prosecutions will be governed by the federal principles outlined below.

In reaching a position on corporate liability which is based far more closely on the agency model, US federal law has not been disturbed by the difficulties of imputing intent to a corporation. The point of departure was, paradoxically, a case not dissimilar from *Mousell Bros.*[28] but which had an extraordinarily different effect on future developments.[29] The object of the Federal Courts has been

[24] Note Harvard 1979: 1252.   [25] 207 (2).

[26] California (*Sea Horse Ranch Inc* v. *San Mateo County Superior Court* (1994); *Granite Construction Co* v. *Superior Court* (1983); Illinois (*People of State of Illinois* v. *O'Neil, et al., and Film Recovery Systems* (1990); Indiana (*People* v. *General Dynamics Land Sys Inc.*; Pennsylvania (*Commonwealth of Pennsylvania* v. *Penn Valley Resorts Inc.* (1985); New York (*People of State of New York* v. *Warner-Lambert Co.* (1979); Wisconsin (*State of Wisconsin* v. *Knutson* (1995), *State of Wisconsin* v. *SA Healy Co.* 1990; see Hamilton 1992, and Texas (*Sabine Consolidated Inc.* v. *State* (1991).

[27] OSHA 29 USC 666 (e).   [28] 1917.   [29] Bernard 1984: 9.

'to ensure compliance with regulatory legislation much of which affects the oper-
ation of large loosely-organized corporations engaged in interstate commerce'.[30]
In 1903, as part of a system of regulating interstate shipment, congress passed the
Elkins Act prohibiting the payment of rebates to shippers.[31] The New York and
Hudson River Railroad was prosecuted not long after.[32] The Act contained a
specific provision that deemed a corporation responsible for its employees.

In construing and enforcing the provisions of this section, the act, omission or failure of
any officer, agent, or other person acting for or employed by any common carrier, acting
within the scope of his employment, shall in every case be also deemed to be the act, omission, or failure of such carrier, as well as of that person.

The constitutionality of the statute was upheld; the court was impressed by
arguments both about the need for such liability on grounds of effective enforcement and the difficulty of saying that a corporation could act, but not intend,
through its agents.[33] The court was going 'only a step farther' than the principles
of civil liability.[34] The principle of *respondeat superior* in the law of tort attributed to the corporation all acts of agents within the scope of their employment,
even where the agent acts 'wantonly or recklessly or against the express orders of
the principal. In such cases, liability is not imputed because the principal actually
participates in the malice or fraud, but because the act is done for the benefit of
the principal'.[35] The decision in this case has held a powerful influence over federal corporate liability ever since. It is probably significant, Stone suggests, that it
concerned the sort of crime that a corporation is 'far more apt to commit than the
old common-law crimes about which some doubts lingered, for example, larceny
and manslaughter'.[36]

These doubts aside, the statutory definition of manslaughter was itself an
obstacle because it referred to 'another person', one which was exacerbated by
the phasing out of federal responsibility for homicide. At a stage when unlawful
killing was still a federal concern, a district court had approved an indictment
against a corporation following the deaths of 900 passengers in a shipping accident.[37] Similarly, an early state response was not inhibited by any conceptual
difficulties from supporting the notion that a corporation might be capable of
committing manslaughter.[38] State responses were limited, however, by statutory
wording in which manslaughter was defined as 'the killing of one human being
... by another'.[39] The manslaughter prosecution brought against the Rochester
Railroad & Light Company after it had caused the death of a householder
through its negligent installation of a gas appliance in a Rochester residence
failed because 'another' naturally meant another human person. The court itself

---

[30] Leigh 1969: 114.   [31] Elkins Act, ch. 708, 32 Stat. 847.
[32] *NY Railroad v. US* (1909). Often referred to as the *Central Railroad* or *New York Central* case.
[33] Bernard 1984: 9.   [34] At 494.   [35] Ibid. at 493.
[36] Stone 1975: 25.   [37] *US v. Van Schaik* 1904.
[38] *State v. Lehigh Valley RR Co* (1917).
[39] *People v. Rochester Ry and Light Co.* (1909). A similar objection was taken in *New Zealand in
R v. Murray Wright* (1970).

suggested, and the legislature responded some 65 years later, that the resolution to this would be to add 'person' after 'another'.[40] In many ways the surprise is that corporate liability for intent crimes in general, and for homicide in particular, had taken hold of the imagination of prosecutors and in some cases judges in both jurisdictions.

Under the federal doctrine of *respondeat superior* a corporation may be held criminally liable for the acts of any of its agents if an agent commits a crime within the scope of his employment and with intent to benefit the corporation.[41] The position of the agent in the corporate hierarchy is not important. Corporations have been recognized as aggregate bodies such that it is not necessary to prove either which employee had the intent,[42] or, indeed, whether any particular employee did so. Collective knowledge is based on the idea that information known in part to multiple actors within the corporation but not known fully to one actor be aggregated and imputed to the corporation. Collective knowledge was used to convict in a case brought under an ICC regulation which forbade lorry drivers from driving when ill.[43] One employee knew that the driver concerned had telephoned to say that he could not work and then, when learning the company's new absentee policy (which required him to obtain a doctor's note), had changed his mind. Since corporate officers knew that the policy would encourage drivers to work even when they were ill, the corporation could be found to have 'knowingly and wilfully violated the regulation'. Since this theory of 'collective knowledge' has been frequently quoted in later cases and clearly marks out US federal corporate liability from any species recognized in England, it is instructive to quote:

[K]nowledge acquired by employees within the scope of their employment is imputed to the corporation. In consequence, a corporation cannot plead innocence by asserting that the information obtained by several employees was not acquired by any one individual employee who then should have comprehended its full import. Rather, the corporation is considered to have acquired the collective knowledge of its employees and is held responsible for their failure to act accordingly.[44]

In a later case the Court of Appeal affirmed a bank's conviction of thirty-one felony charges of failing to file reports of bank customer currency transactions of $10,000 or more as part of pattern of such law violations.[45] The statute required proof that the violations were done 'wilfully', that is with knowledge of the reporting requirements and specific intent to commit the crime. A single bank teller knew that each transaction was worth more than $10,000. The bank's conviction was based on instructions that permitted aggregating the knowledge of several employees to equal specific intent. This arguably goes further than the

---

[40] Maakestad, 1990: n.11.
[41] The separate ingredients are discussed exhaustively in Note, Harvard 1979.
[42] *US* v. *American Stevedores Inc.* (1962).   [43] *US* v. *T.I.M.E.-D.C., Inc.* (1974).
[44] At 738–9.
[45] *US* v. *Bank of New England* (1987); see also *US* v. *Shortt Accountancy Corp.* (1986); aggregation was rejected in *First Equity Corp.* v. *Standard and Poor's Corp.* (1988). See Foerschler 1990: 1304–6.

earlier case since that only required knowledge of the driver's physical condition as opposed to an intent to commit the crime.[46] *US* v. *Bank of New England* takes us beyond traditional theories and into a new realm of organizational liability.[47]

The court said that collective knowledge is appropriate in this context since 'corporations compartmentalize knowledge, subdividing the elements of specific duties and operations into smaller components'.[48] Rejecting the corporation's argument that it was effectively being punished for having a poor communications network, the court said that the aggregate of those components constitutes the corporation's knowledge of a particular operation and it is irrelevant whether employees administering one component of an operation know the specific activities of employees administering another.

As well as proving the ingredients of the crime the prosecution in a case against a corporation must show that the offence was committed within the scope of the agent's employment. This has been given a wide ambit, despite the traditional limits of the agency doctrine such that the conduct should either be authorized, explicitly or implicitly, by the principal or should be similar or incidental to authorised conduct. Even if the activity was specifically forbidden the courts will find conduct to be within the scope of employment.[49] Although this can be defended on the ground that otherwise a corporation could avoid liability by provisions prohibiting any illegal conduct,[50] it does make the phrase of restricted meaning. 'Thus, scope of employment in practice means little more than that the act occurred while the offending employee was carrying out a job-related activity.'[51]

The requirement of intent to benefit the corporation attracts only brief report by some commentators.[52] But it does appear that if the agent is acting in violation of the fiduciary duty owed to the corporation, in order to gain personal profit for example, the corporation will not be liable.[53] The decisive factor in the leading case of *Standard Oil* v. *US* was less that the company in fact obtained no benefit but that none was intended. In an earlier case benefit was described as at most 'an evidential, not an operative fact' in establishing liability.[54] Presumably if the company does benefit, even though it is not the purpose or intention of the employee, liability will also obtain. This perhaps indicates that any objection to the Divisional Court's stance in *Moore* v. *Bresler*,[55] should be founded on a distinction between the embezzlement of the company and any subsequent benefit which the company thereby obtained.

This very broad liability regime is softened by its relationship with prosecution and sentencing policies. The Department of Justice's prosecution guidelines emphasize the benefits of rigorous enforcement based on both general and specific deterrence, especially when combined with prosecutions of individual

---

[46] Tigar 1990: 223. It also concerned a felony rather than a misdemeanour as in *US* v. *T.I.M.E.*
[47] Coffee 1999.
[48] 1987 at 856.
[49] *US* v. *Hilton Hotels Corp* (1972).
[50] Note Harvard 1979: 1250.
[51] Ibid.
[52] Ibid.
[53] *Standard Oil Co. of Texas* v. *US* (1962).
[54] *Old Monastery Co.* v. *US* (1945).
[55] 1944, discussed in Ch. 5.1.iv.

directors and employees. The main thrust of the guidelines is that the same considerations should apply to corporations as to individuals in exercising the discretion to bring criminal charges. In addition, special factors relevant to corporate prosecution include: the corporation's past history; co-operation and voluntary disclosure.[56] In addition, the existence of a generally effective compliance programme is a counter indication for prosecution where the offence is committed by a 'rogue' employee. Prosecution discretion thus fits with the philosophy of the federal sentencing guidelines for corporate offenders which reward prevention and compliance.[57] Sentencing credit is given for effective compliance plans and for self-reporting. The latter entails reporting before the authorities have begun to track down the miscreant corporation. It is argued that in practical effect something close to an affirmative due diligence defence is introduced, by creating a strong incentive for monitoring by gearing the fine to whether there has been such monitoring. An effective compliance plan will reduce sentence by as much as 90 per cent. The seven-factor test for an effective program to prevent and detect violations of law has become in reality the operative definition in the United States of organisational negligence. This credit is not available if a member of the corporation's senior management has participated in or tolerated the criminal behaviour bringing liability closer to identification theory. Critics of the regime argue that this does not overcome the perverse effects of imposing liability for they believe that it creates a disincentive for the corporation to detect past wrongdoing.[58]

v. AUSTRALIA

The Australian Criminal Code Act 1995 appears to provide the most detailed consideration of organizational liability of the common law jurisdictions. The Act, which has been in force since 1999 for federal offences legislates general principles of criminal responsibility. The individual states, which enforce the vast majority of traditional criminal laws, are expected to adopt it in due course. The section dealing with corporate liability provides that for offences of intention, knowledge, or recklessness 'that fault element must be attributed to a body corporate that expressly, tacitly or impliedly authorised or permitted the commission of the offence'.[59] Authorization or permission can be shown in one of three ways—the first echoes the *Tesco* v. *Nattrass* version of identification liability, and the second extends the net wider to 'high managerial agents'. It is the third which represents a clear endorsement of an organizational or systems model, based on the idea of 'corporate culture'. This is defined in much more detail than is the Law Commission's 'management failure' provision for corpo-

---

[56] Federal Principles of Prosecution of Corporations, Department of Justice 1999.

[57] US Sentencing Guidelines Manual ch. 8, discussed in Ch. 2. See also Note 1996.

[58] Khanna 1996; Coffee 1999.

[59] Criminal Code Act 1995 (Cth), s. 12.3. Note that the provision for negligence offences is even less corporation friendly.

rate killing. 'Corporate culture' can be found in an attitude, policy, rule, course of conduct or practice within the corporate body generally or in the part of the body corporate where the offence occurred. Evidence may be led that the company's unwritten rules tacitly authorized non-compliance or failed to create a culture of compliance. The President of the Australian Law Reform Commission summarized the proposals thus:

This approach quite clearly seeks to address the significant criticisms of the 1972 *Tesco* decision, which restricted corporate criminal liability to the conduct or fault of high-level managers or a delegate with full discretion to act independently of in-house instructions, an approach ironically appropriate to the small and medium-sized business, with which large national and multi-national corporation [*sic*] have almost nothing in common.[60]

It is useful to examine section 12 in detail. It begins by attributing the physical conduct of an agent, employee, or officer to the corporation.[61] The fault requirement is deemed to be proved if the corporation 'expressly, tacitly or impliedly authorized or permitted the commission of the offence'.[62] Authorization or permission can be shown by:

(*a*) proving that the body corporate body's board of directors intentionally, knowingly or recklessly carried out the relevant conduct, or expressly, tacitly or impliedly authorized or permitted the commission of the offence; or

(*b*) proving that a high managerial agent of the body corporate intentionally, knowingly or recklessly engaged in the relevant conduct, or expressly, tacitly or impliedly authorized or permitted the commission of the offence; or

(*c*) proving that a corporate culture existed within the body corporate that directed, encouraged, tolerated or led to non-compliance with the relevant provision; or

(*d*) proving that the body corporate failed to create and maintain a corporate culture that requires compliance with the relevant provision.[63]

These paragraphs have to be read alongside s. 12.3.4 which states that the

Factors relevant to the application of paragraph 2(*c*) or (*d*) include:

(*a*) whether authority to commit an offence of the same or a similar character had been given by a high managerial agent of the body corporate; and

(*b*) whether the employee, agent, or officer of the body corporate who committed the offence believed on reasonable grounds, or entertained a reasonable expectation, that a high managerial agent of the body corporate would have authorized or permitted the commission of the offence.

As Coffee notes this amounts to saying that '[E]ven if a low-level agent was not authorized to commit the crime, it is sufficient that he had a "reasonable expectation" that he would have been permitted to engage in the crime by a superior who is a "high managerial agent".'[64] This permits the imposition of criminal liability on the corporation when the agent acted without *mens rea*, thus

---

[60] Rose 1995.   [61] Criminal Code Act 1995 (Cth) s.12.2.
[62] s. 12.3 (1).   [63] s. 12.3(2).
[64] Coffee 1999: 20. I have relied on Coffee's helpful analysis of these provisions. See also Woolf 1997.

introducing a negligence standard. The question would then be whether the corporation took appropriate precautions to minimize the risk of the crime. 'Thus the corporation would not be strictly liable (as it is in the United States) for the agent's misconduct, but it could have liability for negligent or non-knowing conduct by the agent (whereas it might not have such liability in the United States.),[65] While these provisions take a broader conception of corporate responsibility than any other common law models, the practical effect is to rein in the more extreme aspects of the strict *respondeat* doctrine operating in the United States. However, there is an 'inherent ambiguity' in the concept of corporate culture[66] and the precise scope of these provisions will not be revealed until courts begin to interpret them in the light of specific offences. This echoes the criticism of the concept of management failure in the proposed English corporate homicide offence.

3. CIVIL LAW CHANGES

Until recently, most civil law systems eschewed corporate liability.[67] The nature of their law-making discouraged the kind of piecemeal development which has characterized the Anglo-American progression in this field. The aversion is fast being eroded and the subject is under active debate in many jurisdictions. The debate is no longer whether to have corporate liability but what form it should take.[68] Not that the aversion was ever shared by all European jurisdictions; it was strongest amongst Germany, Italy, and Spain. Jurisdictions across Northern Europe such as the Netherlands and Denmark have adopted a pragmatic approach for some considerable time, with Denmark having a history that dates back to 1926.[69]

It is neither feasible nor desirable to conduct an extensive comparative survey particularly bearing in mind the cautionary comments made earlier about the pitfalls of the comparative exercise. The discussion of the US and Australian federal provisions already demonstrates the need to consider substantive principles in the context of prosecution and sentencing regimes.

A specific example comes from the Netherlands where parliament amended its Code in 1976 to overcome the restriction of corporate liability to strict liability offences against public welfare.[70] The Netherlands Criminal Code which had provided merely that offences can be committed by 'human beings and corporations' was reformulated with the addition of an explanatory memorandum which mentions specifically offences such as battery and involuntary manslaughter.[71] The Supreme Court in 1982 adopted the following criteria for liability: did

---

[65] Ibid. 21.   [66] Ibid. 20.   [67] See e.g. Mueller 1957.
[68] Coffee 1999: 9.
[69] The best general comparative collection is Eser, Heine, and Huber 1999; on Europe see Heine 1998.
[70] Penal Code, Art. 51; Field and Jorg 1991, 157; Vervaele 1997.
[71] Art. 51, Criminal Code, Netherlands, 1976.

the defendant company have power to determine whether the employee did or did not do the act in question and did the corporation usually 'accept' such acts.[72] Using this power and acceptance theory and the new encouragement in the Code to apply liability to corporations to a wider range of offences, a hospital was convicted of negligent homicide in 1987.[73] The charge arose after old, redundant anaesthetic equipment which had not been maintained was used in an operation. The hospital was grossly negligent in failing to remove it completely or render it unusable.

The Dutch system is clearly not as broad as the *respondeat superior* doctrine, nor is it as narrow as identification theory. Power and acceptance 'encompass the routinely tolerated as well as the explicitly sanctioned'.[74] This means that there is some reliance on the distinction between those who have managerial power and those who merely carry out the mundane operations of the corporate enterprise. But, on the other hand, the idea of aggregation does apply. It was not necessary in the hospital case to identify 'any individual as responsible for the sloppy supervision: it could be seen simply as a collective failure by management'.[75]

In the 1980s and 1990s Norway, France, and Finland all incorporated criminal punishments against enterprises in their new penal codes, and Denmark consolidated its existing provision which is based on a negligence standard.[76] The French Penal Code was amended in 1991 to remove the general principle that liability could not attach to *personnes morales* (i.e. non-human entities).[77] All sorts of exceptions to the presumption against liability had developed in the context of individual (non-penal code) statutes and, as in England, strict liability offences were enforced vicariously against corporations. A comprehensive scheme for establishing the liability of supervisory personnel for the crimes of their subordinates had been developed (*responsabilite du fait d'autrui*), while paying 'mere lip-service to the adequacy of the proof of criminal guilt'.[78] Under Art. 121-1 of the Code legal entities may be liable but there are two important qualifications. Corporations are only liable if the offence provision specifically declares that they should be, and secondly it is necessary to show that an employee or officer has acted on the corporation's behalf. The actions of 'rogue' employees would not be imputed to the corporate entity. Sanctions under the new provisions include fines, dissolution, and probation although only fines can be applied to private *personnes morales* (which are roughly equivalent to bodies incorporated under charter and some unincorporated associations). Fines may be up to three times higher than those imposed on a natural person.

In Germany (and countries such as Italy, Spain, Portugal, Greece, and Poland inspired by German doctrines) the principle *societas delinquere non potest* has dominated legal theory. Imposing criminal liability on legal entities was 'unthinkable' until very recently: '[I]t appeared to be an incontrovertible maxim that an enterprise had not the capacity to act nor could guilt (understood as a

---

[72] Field and Jorg 1991: 164. [73] Ibid. 158. [74] Ibid. 166.
[75] Ibid. 167. [76] See Heine 1998. [77] Jeandidier 1991: 341.
[78] Heine 1998: 177.

personal reproach) be imputed to it ... [and indeed this prohibition] was included in the Italian Constitution.'[79] However, this is a matter under active debate in many countries and Portugal, for example, introduced a limited exception to it in the new Penal Code of 1983.[80] The traditional objection to penal responsibility of legal persons in German criminal law culture has also begun to crumble.[81] Fewer theorists now subscribe to the view that the social and ethical disapproval inherent in criminal punishment makes no sense when applied to a corporation.[82]

Already most European jurisdictions have introduced sanctions in a variety of forms, particularly against those actions which could be called 'infractions' or violations of administrative regulations, similar to regulatory 'public welfare' offences in England or the United States. While they do not have the status of criminal sanctions an appeal lies, in Germany, in a criminal court. A non-criminal monetary penalty up to a maximum of one million German marks can be imposed on enterprises. The fines also include forfeiture of any profits of the illegal activity and thus, in certain areas such as antitrust, could exceed the limit and result in a penalty of several millions of marks.[83] These are not regarded as anything more than quasi-crimes, however, and do not satisfy the need to demonstrate that enterprises are subject to the penal law.

In most jurisdictions these administrative sanctions are gradually being replaced by direct criminal (penal) provisions. These European civil law developments display then a new willingness to move towards corporate liability and reflect cultural shifts in jurisdictions which have until recently been extremely reluctant to contemplate group liability because of its historical association with repressive regimes. There have also arguably been cultural changes in perceptions of corporate responsibility (in the broader sense), and of risk and safety. Because of differences in legal and political background, these have had disparate impacts in individual jurisdictions. Because these jurisdictions have come late to corporate liability they are in a position to develop principles that are less hidebound than those in the common law countries.

4. CONVERGENCE

The power of transnational corporate actors has been enhanced by their ability to conduct business across state boundaries, an ability that has been facilitated by the crumbling of those barriers as individual regimes themselves undergo seismic political changes.[84] Transnational interactions have intensified, from the globalization of production systems and financial transfers, 'to the world wide dissemination of information and images through mass media and communication technologies, and through the mass translocation of people either as tourists or as

---

[79] Ibid.   [80] Penal Code 1983, Art. 11, Portugal.
[81] Eser 1999, 2.   [82] Heine 1998.
[83] Non-criminal monetary sanctions or confiscation provisions are found widely including Scandinavian countries, and Austria.
[84] This section is taken, with permission, from Morgan 2001, ch. 2. See also Arthurs 1997.

migrant workers or refugees.'[85] The 'globalization process' has according to de Sousa Santos three main components; a new international division of labour, changes in the inter-state system, the political form of the modern world system and the debate over whether or not there has emerged a global culture.[86]

Transnationalism in law is not new. Indeed, a transnational legal culture can be illustrated in the reception of Roman law in the twelfth century and beyond. National sovereignty is not an insuperable obstacle to the creation of transnational regimes, as states can, and do, subordinate their domestic legal regimes to international standards when it suits them to do so, what de Sousa Santos calls 'sovereignty pooling'.[87] Thus they sign and respect international treaties, amend laws to conform to international commitments and expectations, harmonize regulatory practices and policies with trading partners to facilitate trade, and permit the development and expansion of private legal regimes to accommodate needs of transnational corporate movements.[88]

So far as the EU is concerned, despite the divergent national developments described above, there has been no move towards standardization. The EU institutions do not have authority to legislate in the area of criminal law, but there is a well-developed system of administrative sanctions for antitrust violations, imposing non-criminal monetary penalties against both legal entities and individuals. A monetary penalty can amount to millions of pounds and can also include forfeiture of illegally acquired profits.[89] The convention on the protection of the European Communities' financial interests requires member states to provide for various forms of liability on the part of legal persons, including liability for active corruption involving the financial interests of the Community.[90] This leaves the signatory states with no discretion, members of the EU would have to introduce criminal liability for enterprises in cases of government fraud concerning subsidies and similar crimes. A similar provision is incorporated in the recent OECD Convention, discussed below. The EU's own convention on corruption does not, however, deal directly with the liability of legal persons.[91]

The Council of Europe, which of course is a different kind of international organization from, and has a larger membership than, the EU, appointed a select committee in 1983 to examine the possibility and advisability of introducing the principle of criminal liability of corporate bodies in the legislation of member states.[92] The Council accepted in 1988 the recommendation that member states consider the promotion of corporate liability.[93] The principles by which they should be guided include:

(*a*) enterprises should be able to be made liable for offences committed in the exercise of their activities, even where the offence is alien to the purposes of the enterprise;

[85] de Sousa Santos 1995: 252. [86] Ibid. 253–8.
[87] Ibid. 254. [88] Arthurs, 1997.
[89] Heine 1998. [90] Art. 3 of the Second Protocol.
[91] Convention on the fight against corruption involving officials of the European Communities or officials of member states of the European Union (text approved by the Council on 3 Dec. 1998) (98/C 391/01).
[92] Decision CDPC/68/070582. [93] Recommendation No. R (88) 18.

(*b*) liability should attach irrespective of whether a natural person can be identified;

(*c*) the enterprise should be exonerated where its management is not implicated and has taken all necessary steps to avoid the offence;

(*d*) enterprise liability should be additional to any individual managerial liability.

Two Council of Europe treaties have since included corporate criminal liability, one dealing with environmental crimes and the second with corruption. Each recommends the introduction of corporate criminal liability, but leaves up to the signatory states to decide whether criminal penalties or other effective measures against legal entities should be imposed. Under the first Article 9 states:

1   Each Party shall adopt such appropriate measures as may be necessary to enable it to impose criminal or administrative sanctions or measures on legal persons on whose behalf an offence referred to in Articles 2 or 3 has been committed by their organs or by members thereof or by another representative.

2   Corporate liability under paragraph 1 of this article shall not exclude criminal proceedings against a natural person.

3   Any State may, at the time of signature or when depositing its instrument of ratification, acceptance, approval or accession, by a declaration addressed to the Secretary General of the Council of Europe, declare that it reserves the right not to apply paragraph 1 of this article or any part thereof or that it applies only to offences specified in such declaration.[94]

The Corruption treaty is more specific. It provides in Article 18 that :

1   Each Party shall adopt such legislative and other measures as may be necessary to ensure that legal persons can be held liable for the criminal offences of active bribery, trading in influence and money laundering established in accordance with this Convention, committed for their benefit by any natural person, acting either individually or as part of an organ of the legal person, who has a leading position within the legal person, based on:
—a power of representation of the legal person; or
—an authority to take decisions on behalf of the legal person; or
—an authority to exercise control within the legal person;
as well as for involvement of such a natural person as accessory or instigator in the above-mentioned offences.

2   Apart from the cases already provided for in paragraph 1, each Party shall take the necessary measures to ensure that a legal person can be held liable where the lack of supervision or control by a natural person referred to in paragraph 1 has made possible the commission of the criminal offences mentioned in paragraph 1 for the benefit of that legal person by a natural person under its authority.

3   Liability of a legal person under paragraphs 1 and 2 shall not exclude criminal proceedings against natural persons who are perpetrators, instigators of, or accessories to, the criminal offences mentioned in paragraph 1.[95]

The OECD Convention on Bribery and Corruption, signed by twenty-nine members and a further five non-members, has a wider reach than the EU or the Council of Europe treaties, although it lacks the supra-national legislative or persuasive

[94] Convention on the protection of the environment through criminal law Strasbourg, 4.XI.1998.
[95] Council of Europe Criminal law convention on corruption Strasbourg, 1999.

effects of the former. Article 2 requires each party 'to take such measures as may be necessary, in accordance with its legal principles, to establish the liability of legal persons for the bribery of a foreign public official'. Although this does not require signatories to legislate for corporate criminal liability as such, Article 3 obliges them to introduce effective, proportionate, and dissuasive criminal penalties for those who bribe foreign public officials. Under subsection 2 those countries where criminal responsibility does not apply to legal persons 'shall ensure that they are subject to effective, proportionate and dissuasive non-criminal sanctions, including monetary sanctions'.[96] In combination these international instruments will exercise a powerful pressure on states to introduce or refine existing corporate liability provisions. The OECD is actively monitoring the implementation of the Convention in member states and considering adding more specificity to Article 2.[97] The UK, for example, may have to consider its conformity. Corruption is an intention-based offence subject to the identification doctrine. It is unlikely that this narrow approach will be regarded as an ideal model.

If a wider model becomes the norm in the EU and OECD states, then the Law Commission's 1989 proposal will appear out of line. In the commentary on the draft Code the Commission noted that corporate liability was both a controversial and undeveloped subject: 'Although its essentials are reasonably clear, the Code team expressed surprise at the number of points at which, in drafting their suggested clause, they had to fill in gaps in the law for want of authority.'[98] This surprise reflects the traditional lawyers' reliance on case law as the source of legal construction and meaning attached to social phenomena. If the Commission had reflected on the infrequency with which corporations are prosecuted for conventional offences, they may have been less bewildered by the paucity of authority. Clause 29 deals with vicarious liability and clause 30 with direct or imputed liability.

Clause 29

(1) Subject to subsection (3), an element of an offence (other than a fault element) may be attributed to a person by reason of an act done by another only if that other is—
(a) specified in the definition of the offence as a person whose act may be so attributed; or
(b) acting within the scope of his employment or authority and definition of the offence specifies the element in terms which apply to both persons.

(2) Subject to ss. (3), a fault element of an offence may be attributed to a person by reason of the fault of another only if the terms of the enactment so provide.

(3) This section does not affect the application in relation to any pre-Code offence . . . of any existing rule whereby a person who has delegated to another the management of premises or of a business or activity may, in consequence of the acts and fault of the other, have the elements of the offence attributed to him.

Clause 30

(1) A corporation may be guilty as a principal of an offence not involving a fault element by reason of—

---

[96] OECD Convention on combating bribery of foreign public officials in international transactions, 1997 (in force 1999).
[97] See Laufer 1999.   [98] Law Commission 1989 Commentary: para. 10.4.

(a) an act done by its employee or agent, as provided by section 29; or

(b) an omission, state of affairs or occurrence that is an element of the offence.

(2) A corporation may be guilty

(a) as a principal, of an offence involving a fault element; or

(b) as an accessory, of any offenceonly if one of its controlling officers, acting within the scope of his office and with the fault required, is concerned in the offence.

(3) (a) 'controlling officer' of a corporation means a person participating in the control of the corporation in the capacity of a director, manager, secretary or other similar officer (whether or not he was, or was validly, appointed to such office). . . .

(c) Whether a person acting in a particular capacity is a controlling officer is a question of law.

Clause 29 sets out the basis of vicarious liability which, by clause 30(1), applies to corporations as well as individual employers. It is in subsection (2) that the commission's restatement of the alter ego principle is to be found with the concept of the 'controlling officer' defined in subsection (3). The phrase 'participating in the control of the corporation in the capacity of a director . . .' is, the Commentary explains, 'intended to capture the meaning of "directing mind and will" as explained in the . . . *Tesco* case'.[99]

In two specific respects this definition of liability cements the restrictive character of the identification doctrine, despite some ambivalence or ambiguity in the common law. The first concerns the use of the term 'officer' which is clearly intended only to include directors and those functioning as directors (clause 30(3)(a)), but not 'shadow directors' who are defined in the Companies Act 1985 as persons 'in accordance with whose instructions the directors of a company are accustomed to act'.[100] The Commission has some sympathy with the argument that shadow directors should be accounted 'controlling officers' but, in the absence of 'detailed consideration and appropriate consultation', felt debarred from adopting it.[101] Such reticence underlines a problem with the Commission's approach to the Code in general for, by incorporating some reform suggestions, it gives the impression of being a considered statement of the law on basic matters of liability. Yet, if there has been no official reform proposal (the reasons for which might be completely unrelated to whether the relevant law is in a satisfactory state), then all the Code gives is a strict restatement of the common law, with all the limitations of a case-based jurisprudence that implies.[102] This is further highlighted by the second example. The draft Code seals the fate of the aggregation approach to the mental element by providing in clause 30(2) that 'A corporation may be guilty . . . only if one of its controlling officers . . . with the fault required is concerned in the offence'. This, the Commentary explains, gives effect to the provisional view of the Working Party that 'a corporation should not be taken as having any required mental element unless at least one of its controlling officers has the whole element required for the offence'.[103] The aggregation point

---

[99] Law Commission 1989, Commentary: para. 10.6. [100] Companies Act 1985, s. 74(2).
[101] Law Commission 1989, Commentary: para. 10.8. [102] Wells 1986.
[103] Law Commission 1989, Commentary: para. 10.10, quoting Law Commission 1972: para. 39.d.

was one of those issues on which there was a surprising lack of authority, and it seems unfortunate that the Code should specifically exclude it on the basis of such a tentative argument. The only argument which the Working Party itself gave for its 'provisional view' was that such aggregation was 'thought to be undesirable' and contrary to the principles espoused by the Commission in its Working Paper on the mental element in crime.[104] All these conclusions (they hardly seem to merit the term 'debate') were reached before the aggregation argument was ever given judicial consideration following the *Herald of Free Enterprise* drownings.[105] It would seem that neither law reform nor judicial bodies are at all keen to consider aggregation as a serious principle of fault in relation to corporate liability, nor that governments are keen to legislate on this matter at all.[106]

This brief consideration of the draft Code is a useful point of departure from this chapter and entry to the next. Here I have discussed the range of solutions to the problem of holding corporations criminally liable in common law, civil law, and international jurisdictions. In the next chapter the emphasis moves to the normative debate. Which of these many solutions is the most appropriate given the diversity and reach of the modern corporation?

[104] Law Commission 1970.
[105] *R* v. *HM Coroner for East Kent* (1989) the proposed, and *R* v. *Stanley and others* (1990) discussed in Ch. 6.
[106] Other than piecemeal fashion as with corporate killing offence, see Ch. 6.3.

8

The Responsible Corporation

Suppose that the imposition of corporate liability can in some circumstances be legitimate, desirable, or justifiable. The major question then arises—what form should it take? Clearly, the answer will reflect the objectives which criminal liability seeks to achieve, either generally or in the specific context of the corporation. If the only purpose of sanctions through criminal law is the symbolic and ideological function, then critical analysis of types of liability may seem less important. The approach I have taken to the role of criminal law has emphasized the following features: its diversity of purpose; the interlocking relationship between the different institutions of criminal law; and the significance of the temporal, legal, political, and cultural contexts in which it operates. Eser identifies three basic approaches to the problem that corporate crime presents for criminal law: the pragmatic; the principled; and the evasive. The 'pragmatic' takes an inductive approach seeking to solve the social problem in a just and simple way. A deductive 'school of theorism' starts from first principles. Those first principles in criminal justice are of course generally based on the human individual. This school 'would not possibly function in real life due to its being paralysed in a Procrustes bed of theories and principles'.[1] The 'evasive' school seeks to resolve specific issues such as economic crime without addressing offences more broadly. In this book I have questioned the assumption that the principles of criminal law should exclusively address human agents. And, from the common law point of view, it is clear that criminal law does indeed address non-human agents, albeit in a somewhat reluctant and sometimes obscure way.

1. THE CORPORATE ORGANIZATION

Before attempting a critical assessment of the various approaches to legal liability disclosed in this and the previous chapters it is, however, necessary to add a further dimension. Some of the philosophical ideas associated with the corporate entity were introduced earlier.[2] The value of distinguishing between the contract or aggregate theory and the real entity theory is sometimes doubted,[3] yet in terms of business ethics and responsibility it is difficult to avoid. An aggregate theory, which views the corporation as simply the sum of its human parts and nothing else, has dominated much legal theorizing. It is underpinned by a view of human behav-

---

[1] Eser 1999: 363.　　　　[2] Ch. 4.4.　　　　[3] Metzger and Dalton 1996.

iour—methodological individualism—in which 'human beings are the basic unit of social reality and social explanation'.[4] But, as Phillips points out, methodological individualism is under intense pressure from holistic theorists who contend 'that the most important social actors are not human beings, but rather social wholes such as society itself and its component groups'.[5] What are the implications of this debate for a regime of corporate liability? It is useful to remember that, while real entity theory may assist in establishing corporate criminal liability, it was that very same theory which originally legitimized the growth of management-dominated businesses. And if we agree that it is philosophically respectable, if not universally accepted, to view a corporation as an entity in itself, we still need some assistance to determine what kind of real entity a corporation is. It is important to know whether it is morally responsible and whether a specific regime for corporate responsibility might assist in the control of business behaviour.[6] For this we can gain helpful insights through theories of the organization outlined below.

The role of the individual moral agent should also be kept in mind. Collective fault may not be an alternative to individual fault. The underlying individualistic bias of much jurisprudence has been a persistent theme. Corporations, whatever they are, are not individuals and do not act as unitary individuals. If we examine some theories about groups and organizations, and base our assessment of types of liability on them, it could be said that we are ignoring theories about individuals. In other words, we should not take for granted our understanding of ourselves and our behaviour as individuals any more than as members of groups. The fact that people act in groups and organizations is not an exception to the norm of individualism. Our membership of and participation in groups is inescapable.[7] 'Institutions are constituted by individuals and individuals are socially constituted by institutions.'[8] Since so much of our philosophical and legal thinking assumes that we operate only as atomistic individuals there is reason to redress the balance, particularly where the very subject under discussion is a type of group.

Organization theory is a term with broad and narrow meanings.[9] In its broad sense, it refers to studies of all kinds of formal organizations, while its narrow meaning refers only to decision-making in an organizational context. Decision-making theory emphasizes the rational aspect of the organization, attention is given to organizational processes such as information-processing, communications, and problem-solving.[10] Mouzelis identifies three stages or types of theorizing, ranging from scientific management through social psychology to decision-making. Initially, under the scientific management school of Taylorism, the individual worker was seen as 'a tool which can be manipulated for the purpose of increased productivity'.[11] The model is one that assumes that members of

---

[4] Phillips 1996: 240.   [5] Ibid.   [6] Phillips 1996.
[7] Ermann and Lundman 1996: introduction.   [8] Fisse and Braithwaite 1988*b*: 478.
[9] Mouzelis 1975: 120. I have relied heavily on this accessible but authoritative overview in the following discussion. See also Kreisburg 1976, for an early attempt to relate decision-making models and corporate crime control.
[10] Mouzelis 1975: 136.   [11] Ibid. 167.

organizations can be exploited as instruments of organizational goals. The human relations school introduced social psychology to this somewhat arid landscape, raising the possibility that individuals might resist their use as puppets of organizational strategy. The individual is recognized as possessing feelings and private goals which may conflict with those of the group.[12] Following the emphasis on the individual's motivations and aspirations, decision-making theory, or narrow organization theory, reintroduces the organization, with an attempt to integrate the management approach with the human relations perspective.[13] Theories of gendered organizations have recently come to the fore.[14]

In the business context, the narrow, decision-making sense of the term 'organization theory' is most often implied. Both management consultants and theorists conceive firms operationally as organic unities.[15] Orthodox theory acknowledges that companies may have a diffuse structure but that management's task is to ensure that the separate parts contribute to a dominant objective. This has been likened to a military organization, where 'all the sub-units or elements are commanded with respect to a coherent and unambiguous aim'.[16] Even where the goal is not achieved, there is an assumption that the rhetoric of the organization will be directed towards a common goal. Although such theories do have useful messages in a consideration of corporate liability, it would be a mistake to ignore the broader sociological context from which they have grown. The stress on decision-making can be criticized on account of its neglect of the whole organization and for distracting from the problems of social power and conflict which become more apparent when a broader scope is adopted.[17] Organization theory is often ahistorical, based on generalizations which fail to take seriously that organizational behaviour is inextricably linked with a historically specific social structure and culture.[18] The narrowness of the decision-making perspective might blind us to an understanding of organizational reality with unequal access to and control over resources resulting in the formation of interest groups competing to preserve or change their positions. Dalton showed how organizational members and groups may primarily be interested in the rational pursuit of their narrow interests and the consolidation and improvement of their own power position, even at the expense of wider organizational interests. This intense political activity is camouflaged so that the resulting policies appear to be in harmony.[19]

Organizational theory can, then, be seen as the filling in a sandwich whose crust is provided by Marx and Parsons. Marx started with a societal perspective emphasizing problems of power, alienation, and freedom. The shift to the level of the organization, described above, needs to be countered by a broader perspective which Parsons's theory of social systems provides. Organizations are seen as social systems comprising a series of sub-systems which interlock with

---

[12] Crozier 1964, and see generally Brown 1988.   [13] See Pugh and Hickson 1989.
[14] Gherardi 1995; Alvesson and Due Billing 1997; Buzzanell 2000.
[15] Thompson 1982: 234.   [16] Ibid. 235.   [17] Mouzelis 1975: 168.
[18] e.g. Brown 1988.   [19] Dalton 1959.

each other but which are also connected to a wider social system of values emanating from community and society. Parsons stressed the way in which a social system's core values and their institutionalization into norms and roles shape an individual's activities through socialization, internalization, and social control. Social reality is characterized as a complex of interlocking systems ranging from the individual personality and small groups to whole societies. The societal value-system can operate as a restraint on the 'self-orientation tendencies' of organizational units.[20] But the sandwich could be turned over and Marx re-examined. Societal values, rather than being seen 'as a kind of divine providence caring for the welfare of all sub-systems', could, Mouzelis suggests, be viewed 'as the dominant ideology which might in fact legitimise and impose as general interest the narrow interests of certain groups'.[21]

Phenomenologists seek to reverse the analytical direction and would discard the sandwich altogether. What is common, and they argue wrong, about all its components is the assumption that the process goes from the organization to the individual, that the social values insinuate themselves to the individual, or that organizations determine an individual's role. Phenomenology stresses the interaction, the construction involved in each encounter, the constant renegotiation of meanings.[22]

Both organization theory and legal doctrine largely assume that there are such things as organizational goals (with differences revolving around how those are achieved, and the competing or supporting roles of individuals and socio-political forces). Even that assumption can be challenged. One result of the conflicting and competing forces within the corporate structure is that there will not be just one locus within the firm where its agents operate. 'Management, or the agency of direction, is always faced with a series of obstacles and constraints against which it sets its own tasks and objectives.'[23] It will then try to reconcile conflicting conceptions and interests, it will continually negotiate, and the outcome will be alliances and compromises. 'If this is the case there can be no over-archingly unambiguous or fully coherent "meta-objective" for the firm, but rather a shifting series of conflicting, contradictory and contingent partial "objectives" organized with respect to particular knowledges and "interests".'[24]

Traditional theories of the firm assume that profit maximization and sales maximization will be the main objectives, but these will inevitably (if the above account represents a typical firm) be less than transparent either in conception or operation. Thompson notes that at least twenty different concepts of profit are employed in the world of business and commerce.[25] For some firms profit is an objective which is closely controlled, while for others it is more of a residual item when all else has been accounted for. Quite different things would be going on under this heading, even if it were the case that all firms actually did try to maximize it. At the management level there may be more concern with stability,

---

[20] Mouzelis 1975: 157.   [21] Ibid. 158.
[22] Ibid. xiii.   [23] Thompson 1982: 236.
[24] Ibid. 237.   [25] Ibid. 240, referring to Department of Trade 1975.

continuity, or empire-building than profit. The legal picture of a company owned and controlled by its shareholders is blind to the reality that management is the locus of power in a large company with numerous small investors.[26]

Thompson suggests that instead of the enterprise being conceived as a relatively homogeneous, organic, functioning unity typified by a universal calculating subject ('management'), it should be seen as a heterogeneous, non-unitary, dispersed, and fractured entity or social agency: there is no 'one thing' called the firm.[27] Although the message of diversity, dissimilarity, and dis-aggregation is always a useful one to consider, it is important not to lose sight of some of the framework within which such diversity operates. But when it is said that an organization has goals or strategies, rather than implying 'a mystical entity' it can simply amount to 'a short-hand way of referring to a set of empirically identifiable social processes'.[28]

Of course, these theorists were not addressing the issue of corporate wrongdoing. A few points about management control will be helpful before examining these ideas further. Corporate liability is partly about control of managers, while the key issue in management theory is control.[29] The essential elements of control are said to be planning objectives, establishing standards of performance, monitoring actual performance, comparing achievements with targets, and taking corrective action.[30] Reeves and Woodward suggest that the spectrum of control ranges from the completely personal and hierarchical to the completely mechanical.[31] Few large companies conform to the personal or charismatic end of the scale, although many may have begun life there. 'Completely mechanical' implies formal standardized procedures, production planning, and cost control. A further variable is whether the system is unitary or fragmented. Reeves and Woodward's thesis is that companies tend to progress from hierarchical and unitary (with a single integrated system of control) to mechanical (or impersonal) and unitary.[32] There is some empirical support for this. In many large-scale firms the decentralization of control is accompanied by an increase in formal structure with regard to organizational roles and activities.[33] As more authority is delegated to the periphery, there is reinforcement of formal procedural rules.

This overview of organization theories, both narrow and broad, serves as a salutary reminder that a consideration of types of criminal liability can draw upon and receive inspiration from a bewildering variety of perspectives. Business corporations wield vast economic, social, and political power. Beyond that generalization, numerous specifics compete. These insights have clear implications for the form and type of legal accountability that might be appropriate for corporations. Indeed, one message is that corporations are diverse both between themselves and in themselves. They may metamorphose from a humble beginning with one or two key players to a huge multinational with an economy larger

[26] Glasbeek 1988: 373.
[28] Mouzelis 1975.
[30] Ibid. 307.
[32] Woodward 1980: xxi.

[27] Thompson 1982: 286.
[29] Mullins 1985.
[31] Reeves and Woodward 1970.
[33] Pugh and Hickson 1989: 9–16.

than that of many countries.[34] Or a large company may spawn subsidiaries leading to difficult questions of legal relationship between them and the parent company.[35] The overall pattern of corporations has also changed. There has been a doubling in the number of small firms in the United Kingdom between 1979 and 1993 with the result that 99 per cent of all firms employ fewer that fifty people.[36] New management techniques have had an impact on organizational accountability in large firms as well. Total quality management, quality assurance, and just-in-time lean production have the capacity for improving internal compliance programmes but in other respects lead to fragmentation with less central control.[37] Further, organizations occupy a different position with respect to timescale. As Dan-Cohen puts it: 'The permanence of organizations renders them temporally independent: they operate on a different time-scale, in terms of both their memory and their planning, from that of any particular individual.'[38]

To summarize, theories of the organization tend to confirm that it is right to think of the corporation as a real entity; they tell us something about how decisions are made and the relationship between the individual, the organization, and wider social structures. It does not make sense to imagine a one-way traffic from the organization's goals or objectives to the individual's actions; nor should the relevance of temporal and developmental factors in analysing corporations be forgotten.

It is helpful now to isolate two basic models from the wide range of theories so far elucidated.[39] These will provide the basis for the argument that there is little to be gained from the either/or conception of corporate liability which has dominated Anglo-American jurisprudence: viz. either the corporation is to be treated holistically as if it were an individual or it is to be seen as atomized and consisting of nothing more than an aggregation of its constituent human parts.[40] The first model is that of organizational process, founded on specialization of tasks within an organization.[41] Responsibility is diffuse and corporate behaviour is 'not traceable or reducible to any one fully responsible individual'.[42] This has clear implications for a scheme of liability. Decisions reached under this model are decisions of the corporation as a group or organization, and attempting to track them from one individual misses the way. For different reasons, the second model, that of bureaucratic politics, also casts doubt on a view of corporate decision-making which comes from the decisions of specific individuals. Corporate decision-making is seen as 'a bargaining process among individuals', so that decisions will often be a compromise from a number of starting positions, although sometimes one individual may get her own way.[43] It is clear that these two models find

---

[34] According to one source, global corporations comprise 51 of the world's largest economies, and countries only 49, www.corporations.org.

[35] Grantham 1997. [36] Gunningham and Johnstone 1999, 3. See Ch. 2.3.i.

[37] Ibid. 41–8. [38] Dan-Cohen 1986: 38.

[39] Foerschler 1990: 1300.

[40] Dan-Cohen 1986: 15; Foerschler 1990: 1298; and see the argument against dualism in Thompson, Ellis, and Wildavsky 1990: 21.

[41] Foerschler 1990: 1300. [42] Ibid. 1301. [43] Ibid. 1302.

support in the theories of organizational structure outlined above and that they should alert those who design and work to implement the solutions in legal systems to the need to rethink the basis of liability. Although Stone argues that people in groups act more recklessly,[44] the 'risky shift' hypothesis has largely been replaced by emphasis on group choice shifts or group polarizations. People, in other words, draw their decisions and attitudes to risk from their cultural surroundings.[45] This would indicate that a culture of safety consciousness, for example, could lead to group decisions which were risk-averse.

An optimal theory of corporate criminal liability needs to address a number of issues of efficiency and effectiveness. It needs to take account of modern organizational forms and to consider how to relate the requirements of criminal law (matters such as causation, intention, knowledge, and recklessness). It needs also to be aware of so-called 'perverse effects' whereby strict enforcement may lead to less attention to corporate compliance with imposed standards than more.[46] In the next section I consider the debate between the protagonists of strict liability and due diligence; this is followed by a discussion first of systems and culture theories and secondly of the relationship between corporate and individual liability.

2. Strict (vicarious) liability versus due diligence

'U.S. commentators often assert that the role of corporate criminal liability is chiefly to induce the corporation, as principal, to monitor its agents.'[47] Drawing on the American federal experience, some writers regard a strict vicarious regime as the best way to induce corporations to consider the full social costs of their action.[48] Under this kind of scheme, compliance and due diligence can be rewarded at the sentencing stage but not in terms of liability. Not only does this save in transaction costs for the criminal justice system, it is argued that an affirmative due diligence regime may under-deter; firms might avoid the full costs of employees' actions simply by acting 'reasonably' or taking 'due care'. It can certainly be said that the judicial reception of due diligence reverse-onus defences in English regulatory law for many years supports this view. It was only in the 1990s that courts seemed to wake up to the idea that a restrictive liability regime frustrated the purpose of many regulatory schemes.[49] However, a duty-based system may produce fewer perverse effects for the compliant corporation. Arlen and Kraakman draw a distinction between preventive measures that deter without affecting future sanctioning (such as monitoring and record-keeping) and policing measures that investigate the agent's misconduct after the event, increasing the probability of sanctioning. Under strict vicarious liability, in detecting and sanctioning the agent the corporation renders itself liable as well. They conclude therefore that a duty-based scheme provides better incentives to the company to detect past misconduct, for in so doing the company demonstrates that it

---

[44] Stone 1975: 243.   [45] Douglas 1985: 66.   [46] Khanna 1996.
[47] Coffee 1999: 10.   [48] Arlen and Kraakman 1997.   [49] See Ch. 5.2.i.

has a strong monitoring programme. Coffee doubts that the suspected perverse effects are as severe as Arlen and Kraakman allege: 'Given that strict liability creates a greater incentive to expend corporate funds on preventive measures (in order to actually prevent crime, rather than simply to have tried earnestly), the loss from reduced "policing" measures under a strict liability regime would have to be significant in order to make a duty-based system preferable.' [50]

Vicarious liability has been criticized for including too little—in demanding that liability flow through an individual, however great the fault of the corporation—and for including too much—in blaming the corporation whenever the individual employee is at fault, even in the absence of corporate fault. This summary of the drawbacks of vicarious liability neatly encapsulates one of the major problems in any discussion of corporate responsibility—how to conceptualize 'corporate' fault. Should corporations be liable because of their own wrongdoing or because they are in a better position to control (or to be seen as responsible for) the wrongdoing of others? Vicarious liability attracts criticism as a mechanism for attributing fault because it is felt that there is some other way of measuring 'corporate culpability'. The key question is to establish what that way might be. Few would recommend the 'identification' theory as it has developed in England since the 1940s for serious offences such as fraud, theft, and manslaughter. One element in the debate should be dealt with first. It is often assumed that there is a primary distinction between vicarious 'agency' liability and identification liability. Because this has justified the perpetuation of the latter, it needs to be demystified.

As a label 'vicarious' usually connotes liability for offences of strict liability committed by a person's agent or employee; 'direct' connotes liability of a corporation for offences committed by someone within the company who is a 'directing mind'. There are three possibilities: the first two would deny that the categories which the labels describe represent a conceptual distinction. All corporate liability could be conceptually vicarious; all corporate liability could be conceptually direct; or the categories could be seen as reflecting a conceptual difference.

The first argument would suggest that whenever a corporation is held criminally liable, even under the identification doctrine, the underlying basis is vicarious, that the corporation is liable for the wrongs of its directors. The standard definition of 'vicarious' assumes that one person is substituted for another. The *Shorter OED* gives three meanings:

that takes or supplies the place of another thing or person; substituted instead of the proper thing or person; of punishment etc. endured or suffered by one person in place of another; performed or achieved by means of another, on behalf of another.[51]

Corporate liability does not fit happily with these meanings since both categories ('vicarious' and 'direct') assume that an individual may be found guilty as well. The corporation is not usually seen as a substitute or stand-in, except perhaps in

[50] 1999: 29. [51] *Shorter OED* 1970.

the moral sense of standing-in for (that is, behind) its agents. This contrasts with the civil field, where some take a pragmatic approach: 'If all those who committed torts were adequately insured there would be no need for a doctrine of vicarious liability.'[52] In other words, 'vicarious' liability in tort is seen in one sense as a way of shifting accountability from the impecunious to those with resources. In the criminal context corporate liability is usually seen as an additional liability, not one which removes or replaces that of the individual; a company has not, however, been regarded as so separate from its managing director that it can agree with him for the purposes of conspiracy.[53]

However, there has been a long-running debate as to whose liability is actually being impugned. Does vicarious liability mean that the master is responsible for the servant or that the servant's acts are those of the master?[54] In other words, is the liability imposed because whatever the employee does is in fact the act of the employer, or because that is the best way to recover compensation or deter?[55] The fact that corporate liability is not a substituted liability would tend to support the second approach, that conceptually both forms amount to a direct liability. This would be further supported by the type of statutory construction which leads to 'vicarious' liability. Employers (and therefore corporations) are not held vicariously liable for *any* strict liability offence which their employees commit. There has to be a statutory word such as 'sell' or 'use' which can be applied. If the liability were truly vicarious then no distinction would be drawn when a statute uses a personal word such as 'drive'.[56]

There seems little in favour of the argument that the two forms are conceptually distinct. It relies on an outdated 'hands and brains' view of the corporation in which employees act for and managers act as the organization. We should be suspicious of this device. The division of tasks into those for hands and brain has been used to justify the class structure, educational inequalities, and the division of labour between manual and intellectual worker. 'The shared analogy is a device for legitimizing a set of fragile institutions.'[57]

3. PEOPLE, SYSTEMS, AND CULTURE

In the arguments about the appropriate basis for corporate criminal liability two distinct strands emerge. One line seeks to equate the corporate entity with the individual, to tease out those characteristics of corporations which can be correlated with the essence of individual responsibility.[58] The other exploits the

---

[52] Hepple and Matthews 1991: 806.   [53] *McDonnell* (1966).

[54] Williams 1956 and Ferguson 1999: 166–7.

[55] Fisse 1967: 206–7 discusses these issues but appears to conflate the linguistic and conceptual applications of the terms.

[56] *Richmond LBC* v. *Pinn and Wheeler* (1989), and see extensive discussion in Williams 1961: 273 ff. In *Robert Millar and Sons* (1970), the conviction for causing death by reckless driving was founded on accessorial liability.

[57] Douglas 1986: 49.   [58] French 1984.

dissimilarities between individuals and the group entity. Corporations are different from human beings, their activities are not merely on a grander scale, their whole existence, function, and formation marks them apart. The contours of their culpability should reflect those differences.[59] Although either route can lead to corporate liability, the second has more potential. Any argument which seeks to equiparate corporate with individual liability has to confront the group difference at some point; efforts to bring out corporate intentionality from corporate policy need to face the complexities of group structures with their lines of authority and internal power distributions. At the same time, the idea that humans are atomistic individuals acting without reference to the groups of which they are a part is unhelpful.

With the concentration on the group/individual comparison, it is easy to lose sight of the culpability criterion itself. Much of the corporate crime literature makes false assumptions about the nature of criminal fault requirements; commentators use 'intention' without acknowledging the alternative of recklessness. Debate about how best to capture corporate responsibility is often hampered by a failure to distinguish between culpability criteria such as intention and recklessness. This applies as much to discussions of aggregation as to other proposals introduced below. Aggregation is often conceived as a collective 'knowledge'. An attitudinal rather than a cognitive version of recklessness facilitates the attribution of blame to the corporate entity. Recklessness can be found in the practical indifference, the attitude, which an action manifests.[60] A corporate action can be said to display such an indifference when it results from the decisions of its responsible officers. It is necessary then to adjust perceptions not only of groups and of individuals but also of culpability criteria; by so doing it is possible to emerge with a strengthened theory of corporate 'intentionality'. A theory which makes the corporation responsible for itself is also required. The two organizational models of organizational process and bureaucratic process lead to the recognition that responsibility can be found either in the individual corporate worker *or* in the corporate structure itself. The latter can have a number of forms, ranging from aggregate knowledge to full-blown corporate culture liability. It can also embrace compliance.

i. EXTENDING IDENTIFICATION

Since it is proposed that this second holistic type of liability should be additional and not a substitute for derivative forms, it is necessary first to consider whether the current form of identification liability for *mens rea* offences is broad enough in scope. Many commentators regard the *respondeat superior* doctrine which has developed in the US federal courts as too wide for *mens rea* offences; conversely, the UK direct liability scheme is seen as too narrow. There are strong arguments in favour of extending identification so that the corporation is liable for the

---

[59] Dan-Cohen 1986, Fisse and Braithwaite 1993.   [60] Duff 1990: 162.

crimes of those with responsibility for particular spheres. Under the 'responsible officer' theory regional managers, for example, would be included. This is already reflected in Canadian law; as Schroeder J. put it in one case: 'He may have been but a satellite to a major planet, but his position in the galaxy was not an inferior one.'[61] French proposes a test that at least includes anyone with a 'significant degree of autonomy with regard to making corporate decisions and instigating corporate actions'.[62] The identification rule should reflect actual responsibility rather than formal duty.

ii. Aggregation

The aggregation of employees' knowledge means that corporate culpability does not have to be contingent on one individual employee's satisfying the relevant culpability criterion. Aggregation straddles agency and holistic forms of liability. It is used in the United States[63] but has been rejected in English corporate manslaughter cases.[64] Conceptually or epistemologically the notion of aggregation is problematic if it is taken to mean that the fragmented knowledge of a number of individuals is fitted together to make one culpable whole. This is less of a problem in offences based on recklessness where recklessness is conceived in terms of practical indifference. But even if the knowledge-of-risk model of recklessness were adopted, the difficulties could be overcome. Aggregation needs to be seen as a recognition that individuals within a company contribute to the whole machine; it is the whole which is judged, not the parts. So the question would not be whether employee X's knowledge plus employee Y's knowledge *added up to* recklessness or whatever, but whether, given the information held amongst a number of 'responsible officers', it can be said that the corporation itself was reckless. This is no more demanding a feat of the imagination than that required by so-called subjective mental states when the court determines by what can only be a matter of guesswork whether a defendant actually foresaw a risk or actually intended a result.

iii. Going holistic

The images of the organization emerging from the discussion in section 1 suggest that a pure form of holistic liability is appropriate. Corporations can be seen as diverse and heterogeneous both within and amongst themselves, but with a core structure through which management exerts or attempts to exert control both over objectives and over attainment.[65] The anthropomorphic image infusing much legal discourse is unhelpful if it is taken to imply that the mind cannot be responsible for the body. But in other ways the physiological metaphor could be

---

[61] In *St Lawrence Corp. Ltd.* (1969), at 279.   [62] French 1984: 183.
[63] See Ch. 7.2.iv.   [64] See Ch. 6.1.
[65] Coffee 1977: 1147 ff. argues that the board of directors is the proper locus for reform. It is clear that management is not always aware of what is carried on in its name, Kagan and Scholz 1984: 83.

used as the basis for a form of liability which better reflects the reality of the corporate organization. Corporate liability in the United Kingdom assumes that only a select few officers exert control or have any managerial autonomy over aspects of the enterprise for which they work. This does not seem borne out by theories of organizations. Thus a widening of primary liability would be indicated. We do not imagine that we are transacting with the managing director of Marks and Spencer when we shop there, nor that when a plane takes off the airline's board of directors has specific knowledge of its activities, route, or condition that day. We do, however, expect that large companies operate according to a set of rules and procedures and that these, particularly in relation to public transport systems, have addressed the potential risks and developed safety procedures to ensure that those risks are minimized.

The two organizational models referred to earlier, those of organizational process and bureaucratic process, suggest that a scheme of corporate liability should recognize that responsibility can both flow from the individual to the corporation and be found in the corporation's structures themselves. Current liability reflects the first: the corporation can be vicariously or directly liable for the wrongdoing of individuals within it. The second goes further and demands that liability be placed on the corporation in some instances even though no identifiable individual has committed an offence. This rejects the conventional analysis of identification liability as the only way in which a corporation can be said to act directly and knowingly, supplementing it with the notion that *the corporation* can be responsible for *the corporation's activities*.

Tigar advances the following arguments for a broader starting point.[66] The first is the familiar one that identification is based on unwarranted assumptions about corporate managerial behaviour. Rules of liability should encourage management to have a preventive system: 'Broad rules of corporate criminal liability shape [the corporation's internal culture] towards law-abiding behaviour at all levels of the structure.'[67] Secondly, a point which was mentioned in Chapter 2, the operation of collateral estoppel: corporate liability is a means of promoting, encouraging, and facilitating civil recovery which would otherwise be inaccessible. And lastly, if the only route to criminal liability is through the complicity or acquiescence of top management, then every corporate guilty plea puts management at serious risk of suit by shareholders. Another point can be added, which is that the narrower the system of liability, the more it favours larger enterprises: smaller companies have fewer bureaucratic layers and differentiate less between managerial and operational roles.[68] Reliance on an identification model, even with a lower threshold of 'responsible officer', is insufficient. Concentration on the misdeeds of managerial officers ignores the reality of corporate decision-making. It is clear from what we know of the way large corporations organize themselves that power is both dispersed (within a clear structure) and that this is mediated by informal rules and rivalries. The identification doctrine applied to

---

[66] Tigar 1990: 216-18.   [67] Ibid. 217.   [68] Note, Harvard 1979: 1254.

diffuse corporate structures can result in no one being liable,[69] or improperly reflect the limits of moral responsibility. Management priorities set from above 'determine the social context within which a corporation's shop-floor workers make decisions about working practices'.[70]

French has provided a philosophical model through which to justify the imposition of liability on a company for the actions of its subordinate members. A corporation's internal decision structures, its CIDs, are seen as incorporating recognition rules.[71] A CID structure has three elements: an organizational flow-chart, procedural rules, and policies. The first provides the 'grammar' of the corporation, while the last two are 'corporate decision recognition rules'.[72] Corporations then are mini-jurisdictions and their operating policies are broad, general principles. Where the corporate CID structure has contributed to the realization of a risk, an appropriate legal mechanism should be found in response. Again, organization theories reinforce the argument by showing that corporations usually have detailed configurations which place responsibility for specific aspects on different departments. Internal structure and culture affect a company's actions. While some corporate harms are caused by senior management (individually or collectively) engaging knowingly in fraudulent activity or acting recklessly in the sense described above, many occur through a system failure.[73] The relevant question would then be whether the corporation can be blamed because its system, its operating policies, displayed a reckless attitude to safety. P&O's culpability in relation to the Zeebrugge tragedy provides an instructive example. In that case, the relevant issue was the company's failure to develop a safety policy, which was both a cause of the capsize and a large contributory factor in the failure of the prosecution. The very failures which caused the accident allowed the company to slip through the net of responsibility.[74]

Once the idea that a corporation's fault can be approached through its policies is established, refinements such as compliance or reactive fault can be introduced. CIDs can be used both to lead a corporation towards liability but also to give it the opportunity to escape. The corporation should be able to rebut the attribution of corporate responsibility to any act of its high managerial staff on the grounds that it is against established internal policy.[75] Such a defence will not be easy to mount because it will need evidence of the policy plus a lack of any previous examples whereby it has condoned similar failures: in other words, evidence that the illegal conduct was clearly and convincingly forbidden and of the development and implementation of reasonable safeguards designed to prevent corporate crime.[76] Providing the equivalent of a due diligence defence may also counter those who oppose an extension of identification liability beyond the

---

[69] Wells 1988, and Field and Jorg 1991: 158.   [70] Ibid. 159.

[71] French 1984: ch. 4. Although French has rethought his views on the meaning of intentionality, he still subscribes to this model of the way corporations plan their actions, French 1996: 150–2.

[72] Ibid. 48.   [73] See the discussion in Ch. 2.1

[74] Field and Jorg 1991: 162. It is also arguable that the company escaped through a misreading of recklessness, rather than through the limitations of corporate liability, see Ch. 6.2.

[75] French 1984: 184.   [76] Note Harvard 1979: 1257.

higher directorial echelons. Liability based either, as just discussed, on the company's structures, or on the wrongdoings of any of its employees, could be rebutted by proving that, as an organization, it exercised due diligence to prevent the crime.[77] If the acts of top officials represent the practices and procedures of the corporation, their involvement in corporate criminal activity should almost always defeat a due diligence defence. This could amount to an effective deterrent, since the affirmative defence of due diligence would have to be preceded by the adoption of stringent procedures to combat illegal activity.

This would be a clear recognition that an act is corporate not only because of its form, but because of the policy it instantiates, displays, or manifests.[78] A variation on this is Fisse's concept of reactive fault, that is: 'unreasonable corporate failure to devise and undertake satisfactory preventive or corrective measures in response to the commission of the *actus reus* of the offence.'[79] Focusing on the corporation's reactions would mean unlocking the time-frame of *actus reus/mens rea*; it would also counter the argument that broadening the liability base could have an undesirable effect on the range of penalties by 'undercutting' the justification for imposing sanctions more severe than a fine or other monetary penalty. The concept of reactive fault approaches corporate blameworthiness through its CIDs, but extends the enquiry to allow for the situation, one which is probably common, where a corporation fails to adapt its policies in the light of past errors. This could be particularly useful in the areas of health and safety of workers, product safety, and pollution regulation, where it is easy to refute an allegation of recklessness if each 'offence' is considered in isolation.

As I suggested earlier,[80] an advantage claimed for starting with a broad notion of liability based effectively on the actions of any corporate employee, which is then limited by proof of reasonable preventive strategies, is that it avoids the extremely difficult line-drawing exercise of deciding where in the corporation the threshold for liability should begin. Some clear models have now emerged. There is agency in one form or another—the strict *respondeat superior* version or the responsible officer version—or there is organizational liability which does not depend on the misdeeds of a specified individual. Each of these can be qualified by a compliance or due diligence component in the form of a positive liability requirement, an affirmative defence, or a sentencing discount.[81] Lastly, liability can in some circumstances be imposed on the individual employee or manager as well. A combination of these models is probably optimal, none is sufficient in all conditions and circumstances. The Australian Criminal Code Act discussed in Chapter 7 remains the main example of legislation aiming to achieve such a combination. John Coffee's somewhat tighter version emphasises the relevance of preventive compliance programmes:

---

[77] Ibid.
[79] Field and Jorg 1991: 253.
[78] French 1984: 184.
[80] In section 2.
[81] Under the US sentencing guidelines the discount is not available if a member of corporation's senior management participated in or tolerated the criminal behaviour.

A legal entity, including a corporation, partnership, union, or other form of business association, may be convicted of an offence if:

a. the offence is an offence (i) for which a legislative purpose to impose liability on such entity is plainly evident or (ii) in absence of such liability, there is significant risk that the legislature's purpose would be frustrated;

b. the commission of the offence was performed, authorised, requested, commanded, or recklessly tolerated by a senior managerial agent of the entity acting on behalf of the entity within the normal or foreseeable scope of such agent's authority and with an intent to benefit the entity; or

c. the offence was a proximate and foreseeable consequence of the entity's failure to devise and implement reasonable preventive, monitoring, or safety controls or precautions, or to adopt and maintain a reasonable compliance programme, which failure under the circumstances constituted a serious departure from the standards and procedures then observed by similarly situated entities or that should have been observed by any such entity.[82]

Provision should be made to counter the ability of organizations to disappear or to be absorbed into a different enterprise. An important contributory factor cited by relatives of those killed in the *Piper Alpha* oil rig explosion when they eventually abandoned their efforts to mount a private prosecution was the sale of the rig company by its parent company, Occidental.[83] This distinctive capacity of the company to disaggregate, dissolve, or reconstitute itself presents a challenge which is not peculiar to the enforcement of criminal law; plaintiffs in civil actions have this problem too. The range of possible devices which might be used to stay any such corporate escape moves have not been elaborated here. Where such devices fail, then of course the individual directors might be the only appropriate target. An additional, although related, problem is that identified by Collins as 'complex patterns of economic integration'.[84] A construction site, for example, will often be worked by a number of separate capital units, different contractors working together but legally distinct. This creates problems, particularly with regard to recovery for economic loss in tort, but it has wider implications. 'Firms enjoy considerable freedom both in law and in practice to determine the limits of their boundaries.'[85] Any adjustment of legal principles to reflect vertical integration will have clear implications for criminal liability, but it is not a matter to which I have devoted detailed attention here.

4. INDIVIDUAL LIABILITY

Corporate liability proposals range, then, from extending the identification doctrine, aggregating knowledge, recognizing corporate culture, to qualifying *respondeat superior* with a due diligence defence. Most proceed from the belief that in general, corporate criminal acts are not the result of the isolated activity of

---

[82] Coffee 1999: 33. There is also a draft provision dealing with intention or knowledge.

[83] The company's name was changed in this process, *Guardian,* 27 Jan. 1992.

[84] Collins 1990.   [85] Ibid.

a single employee, but arise 'from the complex interactions of many agents in a bureaucratic setting'.[86] It is the corporation itself which will be regarded as having committed the offence. This may additionally involve individual liability. Since much of the thrust of the argument of this book has been with corporate liability for non-regulatory crime, it is important to consider the relationship between the individual employee and the corporation's failures. Two points from opposite ends of the compass need now to be brought together. On the one hand, the courts have been reluctant to make a company liable for the activities of many of its employees. On the other hand, individual managers have been able to hide behind the corporation.

The argument is that corporate sanctions are necessary because 'it is often the complex interplay between managers, standard operating procedures, corporate priorities, market demands and various other forces at work within corporations, rather than simply the influence of a particular individual, which is the ultimate cause of criminal behaviour'.[87] It has further been argued that directors and officers of the corporation should also be vulnerable to prosecution where they have consented or connived in dangerous practices. Many commentators assert to the deterrent effect of the fear of prosecution on such people,[88] but the argument can be founded on retributive grounds as well.

Subject to the argument below about a defence of 'employee necessity', there is no reason why there should not normally be prosecutions of both.[89] It is increasingly argued that general deterrence as well as retributive arguments demand the prosecution of directors and managers as well as of the corporation itself.[90]

The use of individual managerial liability to penetrate the corporate shield has attracted attention in the United States.[91] In *US* v. *Park*, the president of Acme Corporation knew that his Philadelphia warehouses had been found inadequate by the Food and Drug Administration but failed to remove those responsible for sanitation. When the company's Baltimore warehouse was also so found he ordered the Philadelphia employees to clean it up. Two requirements for liability were suggested: that the superior must occupy a position of 'responsibility and authority' with regard to the act or transaction that constitutes the crime,[92] and that the defendant must have had the power to prevent it through the exercise of the 'highest standard of foresight and vigilance'.[93] Although this case is often presented as the Supreme Court imposing strict liability, a more careful reading shows that it either imposes liability for recklessness or at least allows a defence of impossibility if the defendant can show that, despite his exercise of extraordinary care, he was unable to prevent the violation.[94] In one sense, these cases might not be regarded as remarkable, since the essence of vicarious liability has always been to hold the 'master' responsible.

---

[86] Ibid. 1243.   [87] Bonner and Forman 1993: 20.

[88] Gunningham and Johnstone 1999: 219.   [89] French 1984: 114.

[90] Gunningham and Johnstone 1999: 215.

[91] *US* v. *Dotterweich* (1943); *US* v. *Park* (1975).   [92] *US* v. *Park* (1975), at 673–4.

[93] Ibid. at 672–3.   [94] Singer 1989: 401.

The question is whether, once the enterprise is incorporated, the 'master' is only to be found in the company itself.

Similar developments can be seen in England, such as the imposition of directorial liability for the company's acts through 'consent and connivance' provisions.[95] For example the Health and Safety at Work Act 1974 provides in section 37 that a director or corporate officer may be liable when an offence has been committed with their consent or connivance . . . or is attributable to any neglect on their part. However, the evidence is that regulators in the United Kingdom only rarely use the powers to prosecute individuals that they have at their disposal.[96] There were no prosecutions under section 37 in relation to any of the 510 workplace deaths between 1996 and 1998.[97]

The Health and Safety Executive has itself argued that legal action against individual managers would be more of a deterrent than against the company.[98] However, it is not clear how willing they are actually to implement individual prosecutions.[99] When they are used they often target directors in small companies, which, as Gunningham and Johnstone point out, raises issues of double jeopardy.[100] Prosecutions of directors for traditional criminal offences appear to be increasing but there has hardly been the opening of a floodgate. The first sentence of imprisonment for a health and safety offence was imposed on the director of a demolition company in 1995.[101] Four directors have been convicted of manslaughter for example, although this is more a by-product of the identification doctrine.[102] A company's conviction can only be established on the back of an individual director's guilt (though at least in theory not necessarily a conviction); where a corporation is prosecuted there must be evidence proving a director's guilt.[103]

The Law Commission argued that punitive sanctions on company directors would not be appropriate in relation to the special offence of corporate killing. The Government showed more concern that this would dilute the deterrent effect of the offence especially in larger businesses. It was also concerned to prevent culpable officers from setting up new businesses. This resulted in the recommendation that individual directors could be disqualified if they were shown to have had some influence or responsibility for the management failure in a corporate killing prosecution.[104] However, this seems a fairly minor penalty and furnishes another reason for supposing that the introduction of the corporate

---

[95] See generally Finch 1994.   [96] Wright 1997: 140–3.
[97] Centre for Corporate Accountability 1999. Slapper and Tombs report one in 1996, resulting in an imprisonment of two directors, 1999: 221.
[98] HSE 1988. They clearly have this power under the Health and Safety at Work Act 1974, s. 37.
[99] Where the employer is an individual and not a company, of necessity the prosecution will be against an individual. But this is different from the prosecution of individual directors or employees of a corporate employer.
[100] 1999: 247, n. 162.   [101] Slapper and Tombs 1999: 220.
[102] These include *R* v. *David and Norman Holt* (1990); Peter Kite and Alan Jackson were both imprisoned for 12 months *R* v. *Kite and OLL Ltd.* (1994) and *R* v. *Jackson and Jackson Transport* (1996); see Wright 1997: 148.
[103] *Attorney-General's Reference (no. 2 of 1999)* (2000).
[104] Home Office 2000, para 4.4.9.

killing offence might actually reduce the overall threat of conviction on companies and their directors following negligently caused deaths. Directors can be disqualified for, *inter alia*, conviction of an indictable offence connected with the promotion, formation, management, or liquidation of a company.[105] Although this can be interpreted to cover management of health and safety,[106] in 1998–9 the vast majority of disqualifications (1,284), were for unfitness shown by conduct while director of a company which became insolvent, with a further 198 under all other provisions.[107]

When individual liability versus corporate liability is raised it is important to distinguish between the situation where the individual worker might be seen as the scapegoat and where, as with health and safety enforcement, higher management shelters behind the company. In both cases, it could be said that the management level is the beneficiary. Supervisory liability as espoused in *US* v. *Park* is one way of removing that opportunity to evade responsibility; it could be seen either as a form of vicarious liability (which would only be appropriate for strict liability offences) or as a type of complicity.

But what, on the other hand, should be the liability of more lowly employees who (like the Assistant Bosun of the *Herald of Free Enterprise*, for example) recklessly cause deaths while employed by a company with hopelessly inadequate company safety procedures. It is usually argued that corporate liability should not supplant individual responsibility where that exists. But there may be circumstances in which the individual should not be regarded as a scapegoat for a system failure. This can occur even though the corporation is found liable. Again, the *Herald of Free Enterprise* capsize may provide an example. Assuming that P&O were convicted, could the Captain and/or the Assistant Bosun be regarded as responsible if they had done all they could to inform management of the inherent dangers of the system or, in the case of the Assistant Bosun, had been required to work an unreasonable roster which contributed to his being asleep? Few would suggest that employees can seek alternative employment if they are concerned about their employer's response to safety suggestions. If it is regarded as acceptable for corporations to invoke a due diligence defence is there any reason why an individual could not do the same as regards an offence committed in the course of employment? The sinking of the *Marchioness* Thames cruiser gave rise to a prosecution of the Captain of the dredger *Bowbelle* for failing to keep a lookout.[108] If the dredger had no effective means by which that lookout could be kept,[109] should the responsibility not only shift to its owners, but also from its employee?[110]

---

[105] Directors (Disqualification) Act 1986, s. 2.　　　[106] Slapper and Tombs 1999: 222.

[107] Mayson, French, and Ryan 2000: 720.

[108] The *Marchioness* sank in Aug. 1989. The charges were dropped after two juries failed to agree, *Independent*, 1 Aug. 1991.

[109] Marriott, 1991.

[110] Fletcher 1978: 834 refers to a German case which allowed such a defence. See also Brownlee 1989.

5. The responsible corporation

In this final section I summarize arguments that have been built on a number of different starting points. I should, perhaps belatedly, acknowledge my underlying sympathy with the notion of corporate liability. It would be difficult to write a book of this kind without having a view, opinion, intuition, prejudice about the issue. There have been times when I have wondered how far my initial conviction that corporate liability was not only defensible but also desirable could withstand the counter-arguments. The two most challenging arguments are, first, why extend criminal penalties at all and, secondly, why punish a fictional legal entity?

The social institution of criminal justice confronts individuals and groups with messages of denunciation, threats of punishment, and pre-emptive authority. Affluent, white, middle-class males experience criminal justice differently from poor, black males.[111] Women experience criminal justice differently from men.[112] Young people experience it differently from old.[113] The same laws, the same procedures apply; they are exercised differently. Business corporations also have a different encounter with criminal justice, which is attributable in part to the discretionary exercise of powers of surveillance, investigation, and enforcement. But the system treats them differently in a more fundamental sense. They are subject to separate systems with their own procedure and substance and their encounter with criminal justice diverges. This book attempts to provide an explanation for those differences and to consider whether there are any justifications for them.

Of course, it can be said that the explanation is simple. Corporations are not individual human beings, law primarily addresses individual human beings and therefore no surprise should be expressed at the different reception they receive. I have tried to indicate that perceptions of criminal law are historically, politically, and socially contingent, that law has never addressed only individuals and that the concept of the individual is itself a cultural–political construct. Business corporations, although varying in size and influence, and of relatively recent origin, are a distinct and powerful force at global, national, and local levels. They wield enormous economic power, collectively and in the case of transnationals singly; they are producers, service providers, media manipulators, political campaigners, advertisers, employers, consumers, polluters, . . . and criminals. The legal structure within which they operate largely serves their interests, corporate personality protects their owners from the full consequences of failure; the regulation to which they are subject assumes their benificence. At the same time the social practice of criminal law is complex and fragmentary. Much crime is unreported, undetected, or unenforced. Conviction and sentencing rates vary; moral panics erupt and subside. One question which has to be asked is whether current concern with the harmful effects of much business practice is itself a type of moral panic. If so, that

[111] Box 1987; Smith 1997.   [112] Heidensohn 1997.   [113] Ashworth 1999: 8.

lends support to the thesis that there has been a cultural shift towards blaming corporations for the injurious effects of modern, technological systems. Is criminal law and justice the servant or the mistress of such movements? Moral panics, like volcanoes, tell us something about underlying structures. Criminal law and regulation represent but one stratum in an elaborate, interactive maze. Perceptions of individuals and perceptions of crime are not neatly and separately packaged. It may be that ecological or industrial harm will come to be recognized as a greater collective threat and traditional offences such as burglary as less, with the result that their place in the system of enforcement and punishment is reversed.[114]

So whatever is said about corporations and crime has to be heard as one part in a larger score. A number of themes have emerged. Before embarking on a search for a set of principles of 'corporate' criminal responsibility or for inspiration about 'corporate' sanctions, it was necessary to give thought to the ideas underlying notions of individual culpability and individual punishment.[115] As to punishment the picture was fragmentary and diverse; as to responsibility the picture was obscured by overemphasis on mental states and the underplaying of the cultural significance of risk.[116] This laid the foundation for an exploration of the corporate entity; it seems that corporations, whatever their metaphysical nature, can be regarded as morally responsible 'persons'.[117]

It is clear that there is much scope for the development of a liability regime better tailored to the organizational facts of corporate existence. The key to opening up these possibilities is the move away from liability derivative on one specific individual. The relationship between the individuals and the group is in need of further exploration. There is, on the one hand, a danger that an individual may become the scapegoat for an organizational failure. There is conversely a danger that corporate liability will shield culpable individuals. A distinction has to be drawn between ordinary employees, shop-floor workers, operatives, and so on, and responsible officers. With regard to the former, there may be good reasons either not to prosecute or to provide a partial defence of employee necessity. The responsible officer presents a different problem. Here, experience with enforcement of health and safety legislation suggests that individual directors shelter behind the firm and are not sufficiently deterred by a prosecution of the company. The appropriate policy would then be to prosecute both.

Where there is sufficient evidence to prosecute individual defendants, it would be necessary to give consideration to a (partial) defence of 'employee necessity'. The effect would be to reduce the individual's role either to that of an ancillary party or, possibly more appropriately, to the equivalent of inchoate liability. This would reflect the fact that the employee had been reckless, but would prevent her being used as a scapegoat of the company's failure to devise and/or implement and/or enforce an adequate safety procedure.

Even though the conceptual problems can be overcome, awkward questions will be asked about the efficacy of corporate punishment. Fines are ineffective, it

---

[114] Nelken 1990: 834.   [115] Ch. 2.   [116] Chs. 3 and 6.   [117] Ch. 4.4.

is said. And corporate prosecutions allow guilty individuals to escape penalty and the target is misdirected because 'innocent' shareholders, employees, and so on bear the real costs. One simple answer to the suggestion that corporate liability is ineffective is to point to the extraordinary efforts corporations frequently employ to avoid conviction.[118] To the objection that corporate liability can shield individual miscreants, the answer is that this is not inevitable and that the structure of liability and its practical execution should ensure that individuals and corporations are appropriately dealt with. Of course, it is not so easy to say what that entails, and undoubtedly the strongest argument against corporate sanctions is that they eventually land on some individual(s). But once it is accepted that both individuals and groups are constructed, culturally constituted, and thus abstract, the issue becomes differently focused. For an individual to be found guilty of an offence and have a penalty imposed on her involves an entirely different proposition and experience from holding a collectivity liable and imposing a penalty which then has a fall-out on a number of individuals. A distinction has then to be drawn between intended and unintended fall-out. Shareholders are often introduced into the discussion as 'innocent', but this emotive terminology obscures the very role which brings them into the net in the first place: their financial involvement and thus their intimate 'interest' in the company cannot be written out of the account. When it comes to unintended effects, then the argument against corporate sanctions gains strength. It is again important to remember that the rhetoric of individual responsibility is not borne out in reality; the families of offenders (often women and children in particular) are the hidden victims of individual punishment. This is not, of course, an argument to defend the infliction of misery, it is merely to point out that what is raised as an objection to corporate punishment applies more generally. In each case the question which is raised is whether those indirect, secondary costs are outweighed by the benefits (however they are calibrated) of the primary criminal sanction.

First, then, the question is whether the activities of corporations concern us sufficiently to justify our imposing upon them criminal penalties. The real problem is that if a deterrent effect is sought, the size of the penalty might have to be so great that the unintended side-effects would indeed be intolerable. The almost exclusive reliance on fines has contributed to this sense of powerlessness. However, it is fair to say that there is little evidence within the criminal justice system of imagination or commitment to overcome the limitations of financial penalties. Equity fines, corporate probation, adverse publicity, and community service are all options as yet untested in the United Kingdom. The argument that there is no point in bringing corporations within the criminal justice net is often predicated on the unarticulated premiss that fines are the only conceivable penalty.

On the other hand, one of the conventions of a work of this kind is that certain assumptions are made. It has been assumed that there is a body of criminal law,

---

[118] *US* v. *Hilton Hotels Corp.* (1972), per Browning, Circ. J.

that there are institutions of enforcement, that there are systems of sanction, that there are in existence corporate bodies, and so on. Within a framework bounded by those assumptions, I have argued for the recognition of corporate criminal responsibility, for an altered perception of culpability, and for a wider basis of liability. Sanctions have been seen as potentially deterrent as well as denunciatory. Corporate harm should, it has been suggested, give rise to liability not only for regulatory offences but for traditional crimes such as manslaughter. But there are aspects of that framework which are open to challenge. Why should criminal law be strictly enforced with punitive sanction? Why impose on corporations that which is imposed on individuals? The second question is somewhat easier to answer. Assuming that individuals are subject to the coercion of a system of criminal justice, there is a strong argument grounded in fairness for making it apply also to corporations and/or other organizations. It is not so easy to make a convincing argument for punitive criminal enforcement.

A radical shift in emphasis utilizes communitarian ideas to bring conventional criminal justice policies more in line with regulatory compliance strategies. This turns the argument round; corporations and individuals would be treated similarly but the system would correspond with the negotiated bargaining strategy rather than with strict enforcement and punitive penalties.[119] Braithwaite and Pettit's republican criminology seeks a solution which is both principled and pragmatic.[120] Their theory is premised on four presumptions: parsimony, power-checking, reprobation, and reintegration of victims and offenders. As a constructive response to the arguments in favour of just deserts in sentencing, this republican theory aims to be comprehensive but above all practical. Given the extent of corporate crime it would be impossible, without bankrupting governments, to apply just deserts. In addition, corporate defendants possess the resources to challenge and deflect allegations of liability. Conventional criminal enforcement results, Braithwaite and Pettit assert, in the greatest punishment of those with the least desert.

While there is much to commend a theory which aspires to reparation rather than punishment, to the maximization of dominion ('freedom, holistically conceived . . . constituted by the enjoyment of certain rights and by the infrastructure of capacity and power which this involves'),[121] it leaves unanswered a number of important questions. One query is how this comprehensive republican criminology relates to the broader socio-political framework. Another is how to deal with those offenders who have no interest in reparation and who resist community disapproval. The theory favours property rather than incarcerative punishments, but offenders who are willing may lack the means to repair while those with the means may have no interest in altering their behaviour. In terms of the criminal justice response to individual offenders, the theory is attractive, although open to accusations of idealism. With corporate crime, where in any case the rigours of just deserts theories have had little impact,[122] it is even less easy

---

[119] Braithwaite 1989.   [120] 1990.   [121] Ibid. 9.
[122] The US sentencing guidelines for corporate offenders are explicitly deterrent in character, see Levitske 1991, and Coffee 1999.

to see it working. While some of the unacceptability of the system of criminal punishment takes on a less objectionable hue when applied to corporations, the harm which corporate crime inflicts can be far greater. Whether corporate or not, much crime is undiscovered, unrecognized, unreported, and unenforced. This threatens just deserts theories but does not necessarily lead to conversion to the republican faith. In her critique of republican criminology, Haines concludes that safety can be enhanced when virtue and profitability coincide, for example where new, safer machinery also leads to long-term profit.[123] An analysis based on the interaction between structure and culture shows that small businesses reap success in a capitalist economy by '' "exploit[ing] the margins" of the economic space left by larger players'.[124] In other words, the political and economic context ultimately dictates the potential success of regulating corporations into responsible behaviour.

Here I have attempted to develop a framework for debate about the criminal responsibility of corporations. I have questioned the inevitability of the connection between regulation and corporate crime and undermined some of the assumptions made about individual responsibility. Previous debates about corporate criminal liability have been hampered by an unwillingness to question some of these premisses. The criminality of corporations has been a neglected topic in England despite the contemporary concern about technological hazards. By incorporating and adapting ideas developed in other jurisdictions and in non-legal literature that debate is furthered. There will still be many questions to be faced, such as whether a new offence of corporate violence would better capture those concerns, or whether safety should be a mandatory duty on all company directors. At the very minimum it is vital that discussions about corporate responsibility are conducted at a level which recognizes the contingent and chance nature of the structure of current rules of liability as well as the potential for a more imaginative range of sanctions tailored to the task in hand. The last thing I want to suggest is that this is easy. There is no magic answer to corporate power, to issues of personal safety and their interrelationship with criminal law and justice. For, in truth, this debate tells us more about ourselves as human beings and citizens, with our fears and insecurities, than it does about criminal law.

[123] 1997: 234.   [124] Ibid.

Bibliography

ADAMS, S. (1984), *Roche versus Adams* (London: Jonathan Cape).

ALLDRIDGE, P. (1990), 'Rules for Courts and Rules for Citizens', *Oxford Journal of Legal Studies*, 10: 487.

ALVESSON, M., and DUE BILILNG, Y. (1997), *Understanding Gender and Organizations* (London: Sage).

AMERICAN LAW INSTITUTE (1962), *Model Penal Code* (Philadelphia: ALI).

ARCHBOLD, L. J. *Criminal Pleading and Practice*, 31st edn. (1943), eds. T. R. F. Butler and M. Garsia (London: Sweet & Maxwell).

ARLEN, J. (1994), 'The Potentially Perverse Effects of Corporate Criminal Liability', *J. Leg. Stud.* 23: 833.

—— and KRAAKMAN, R. (1997), 'Controlling Corporate Misconduct: An Analysis of Corporate Liability Regimes', *New York University Law Rev.*, 72: 687.

ARTHURS, H. (1997), 'Globalization of the Mind: Canadian Elites and the Restructuring of Legal Fields', *Canadian J. of Law & Society*, 12: 219.

ASHWORTH, A. (1987), 'Defining Offences Without Harm', in *Criminal Law: Essays in Honour of J. C. Smith*, ed. P. Smith (London: Butterworths).

—— (1989), 'Towards a Theory of Criminal Legislation', *Criminal Law Forum*, 1: 41.

—— (1999), *Principles of Criminal Law*, 3rd edn. (Oxford: Oxford University Press).

—— (2000), *Sentencing and Criminal Justice*, 3rd edn. (London: Butterworths).

AUDI R., ed. (1995), *Cambridge Dictionary of Philosophy* (Cambridge: Cambridge University Press).

AYRES, I., and BRAITHWAITE, J. (1991), *Responsive Regulation: Transcending the Deregulation Debate* (New York: Oxford University Press).

BALDWIN, J., and MCCONVILLE, M. (1977), *Negotiated Justice* (Oxford: Martin Robertson).

BALDWIN, R. (1987) 'Health and Safety at Work: Consensus and Self-Regulation', in Baldwin and McCrudden eds.

—— and MCCRUDDEN, C., eds. (1987), *Regulation and Public Law* (London: Weidenfeld & Nicolson).

BAUM A., FLEMING, R., and DAVIDSON, L. (1983), 'Natural Disaster and Technological Catastrophe', *Environment and Behaviour*, 3: 333.

BEATTIE, J. (1986), *Crime and the Courts in England, 1660–1800* (Oxford: Clarendon Press).

BECK, U. (1992), *Risk Society: Towards a New Modernity* (London: Sage).

BENN, S., and PETERS, R. (1965), *The Principles of Political Thought* (New York: Free Press).

BENSON, M., and CULLEN, F. (1998), *Combating Corporate Crime: Local Prosecutors at Work* (London: North Eastern University Press).

BERGMAN, D. (1990), 'Manslaughter in the Boardroom', *New Law Journal*, 140: 1496.

—— (1990), 'A Killing in the Boardroom', *New Statesman and Society*, 3 (5 June), 15.

BERNARD, T. (1984), 'The Historical Development of Corporate Criminal Liability', *Criminology*, 22: 3.

BERWICK, D. (1989), 'Continuous Improvement as an ideal in health care', *New England Journal of Medicine*, 320: 53.

BIRCH, D. (1988), 'The Foresight Saga: the Biggest Mistake of All', *Criminal Law Review*, 4.

BLACKMAN, D. (1981), 'On the Mental Element in Crime and Behaviourism', in Lloyd-Bostock, ed., *Law and Psychology* (Oxford: Centre for Socio-Legal Studies), 113.

BLACKSTONE (1765), *Commentary on the Laws of England*, 1.

BLOM-COOPER, L. (1996), 'Advice to Public Inquiries', *Public Law*, 560–1.

BONNER, J., and FORMAN, B. (1993), 'Bridging the Deterrence Gap: Imposing Criminal Penalties on Corporations and their Executives for Producing Hazaardous Products', *San Diego Justice Journal*, 1: 1.

BOX, S. (1983), *Power, Crime and Mystification* (London: Tavistock).

—— (1987), *Recession, Crime and Punishment* (London: MacMillan Education).

BRAITHWAITE, J. (1984), *Corporate Crime in the Pharmaceutical Industry* (London: Routledge).

—— (1991), 'Shame and Modernity', 33 *Brit. J. of Criminology*, 1.

—— and DRAHOS, P. (2000), *Global Business Regulation* (Cambridge: Cambridge University Press).

BRANDT, R. (1985), 'A Motivational Theory of Excuses in the Criminal Law', in Pennock and Chapman, eds., 1985: 165.

BRETT, P. (1974), 'Strict Responsibility; Possible Solutions', *Modern Law Review*, 37: 418–20.

BRICKEY, K. (1987), 'Death in the Workplace: Corporate Liability for Criminal Homicide', *Notre Dame J. of Law, Ethics and Public Policy*, 2: 753.

—— (1988), 'Rethinking Corporate Liability Under the Model Penal Code', *Rutgers Law Journal*, 19: 593.

BRITISH MEDICAL ASSOCIATION (1987), *Living with Risk* (London: John Wiley and Sons).

BROWN, R. (1988), *Group Processes* (Oxford: Blackwell).

—— and RANKIN, M. (1990), 'Persuasion, Penalties and Prosecution: Administrative v. Criminal Sanctions', in Friedland, M., ed., *Securing Compliance* (Toronto: University of Toronto Press).

BURGER, J. M. (1981), 'Motivational Biases in the Attribution of Responsibility for an Accident: A Meta-Analysis of the Defensive-Attribution Hypothesis', *Psychological Bulletin*, 90: 496–512.

BUSH, R. (1986), 'Between Two Worlds: the Shift from Individual to Group Responsibility in the Law of Causation', *University of California Law Review*, 33: 1473.

BUZZANELL, P., ed. (1997), *Rethinking Organizational and Managerial Communication from Feminist Perspectives* (London: Sage).

CADOPPI, A. (1998), 'Towards a European Criminal Code?', in Watkin, T., ed., *The Europeanization of Law* (London: United Kingdom National Committee of Comparative Law) 143.

CALAVITA, K., *et al.* (1991), 'Dam Disasters and Durkheim: An Analysis of the Theme of Repressive and Restitutive Law', *International Journal of Sociology of Law*, 19: 407.

CAMPBELL, D. (1996), 'Note: What is Wrong with Insider Dealing?', *Legal Studies*, 16: 185.

CARSON, W. (1979), 'The Conventionalization of Early Factory Crime', *Int. Jnl. of Sociology of Law*, 1: 37.

—— (1982), *The Other Price of Britain's Oil* (Oxford: Martin Robertson).

CATHCART, B. (1997), 'We're all tabloids now: the broadsheet press and the culture of hysteria', *CUSP Review*.

CENTRE FOR CORPORATE ACCOUNTABILLITY (1999), Written Evidence to the Environment Sub-Committee of the Select Committee on Environment, Transport and the Regions.

CHILDS, M. (1999), 'Medical Manslaughter and Corporate Liability', *Legal Studies*, 19: 316.

CLARK, G. (1979), 'Corporate Homicide: A New Assault on Corporate Decision-Making', *Notre Dame Lawyer*, 54: 911.

CLARKE, LORD JUSTICE (2000), *Thames Safety Inquiry: Final Report*, Cmnd 4558 (London: HMSO).

CLARKSON, C. (1996), 'Kicking Corporate Bodies and damning their Souls', *Mod. Law Review*, 59: 557.

CLINARD, M., and YEAGER, P. (1980), *Corporate Crime* (New York: Free Press).

—— (1983), *Corporate Ethics and Crime: The Role of Management* (London: Sage).

COFFEE, J. C. (1977), 'Beyond the Shut-Eyed Sentry: Toward a Theoretical View of Corporate Misconduct', *Virginia Law Review*, 63: 1099–1278.

—— (1981), ' "No Soul to Damn: No Body to Kick": An Unscandalized Inquiry into the Problems of Corporate Punishment', *Michigan Law Review*, 79: 397–400.

—— (1999), 'Corporate Criminal liability: An Introduction and Comparative Survey', in Eser, Heine, and Huber, eds., 1.

COHEN, M. (1989), 'Corporate Crime and Punishment: A Study of Social Harm and Sentencing Practice in the Federal Courts, 1984–1987', *American Criminal Law Review*, 26: 605.

COLEMAN, B. (1975), 'Is Corporate Criminal Liability Really Necessary?', *Southwestern Law Journal*, 29: 908.

COLEMAN, J. (1986), *Individual Interests and Collective Actions* (Cambridge: Cambridge University Press).

COLLINS, H. (1990), 'Ascription of Legal Responsibility to Groups in Complex Patterns of Economic Integration', *Modern Law Review*, 53: 731.

COLVIN, E. (1995), 'Corporate Personality and Criminal Liability', *Criminal Law Forum*, 6(1): 8–25.

COOK, D. (1989), *Rich Law, Poor Law* (London: Open University Press).

COOKE, J. (1999), *Cannibals, Cows and Catastrophe* (Sydney: Random House).

CORCORAN, S. (1997), 'Does a Corporation have a Sex? Corporations as Legal Persons', in Naffine, N., and Owens, R., eds, *Sexing the Subject of Law* (Sydney: Law Book Co. Ltd), 215.

CORNS, C. (1991), 'The Liability of Corporations for Homicide in Victoria', *Criminal Law Journal*, 15: 351.

COTTA, S. (1985), *Why Violence?* (Gainesville: University Presses of Florida).

COUNCIL ON TRIBUNALS (1996), *Advice to the Lord Chancellor on the Procedural Issues Arising in the Conduct of Public Inquiries Set up by Ministers* (London: HMSO).

CRESSEY, D. R. (1988), 'The Poverty of Theory in Corporate Crime Research', *Advances in Theoretical Criminology*, 1: 31.

CROZIER, M. (1964), *The Bureaucratic Phenomenon* (London: Tavistock).

CULLEN, F., LINK, B., and POLANZI, C. (1982), 'The Seriousness of Crime Revisited', *Criminology*, 20: 83–102.

—— MAAKESTAD, W., and CAVENDER, G. (1987), *Corporate Crime Under Attack: The Ford Pinto Case and Beyond* (Cincinatti: Anderson).

CULLEN, LORD (1990), *The Public Inquiry into the Piper Alpha Disaster*, Cm 1310 (London: HMSO).

CULLEN, LORD (2001), *Inquiry into Rail Accidents at Southall and Ladbroke Grove* (London: HMSO).

DALTON, M. (1959), *Men Who Manage* (New York: Wiley).

DAN-COHEN, M. (1986), *Rights, Persons, and Organizations: A Legal Theory for Bureaucratic Society* (London: University of California Press).

DANDURAND, Y. (1999), 'Entertaining Realistic Expectations about the Effect of Criminal Sanctions Imposed on Corporate Entities: Canada', in Eser, Heine, and Huber, eds., 267.

DAVIS, M. (1985), 'How To Make the Punishment Fit the Crime?', in Pennock and Chapman, 1985: 119.

—— (1986), 'Harm and Retribution', *Philosophy and Public Affairs*, 15: 236.

DE DOELDER, HANS, and TIEDEMANN, KLAUS, eds. (1995), *Criminal Liability of Corporations* (Kluwer Law International: Dordrecht).

DE HAAN, W. (1990), *The Politics of Redress: Crime, Punishment and Penal Abolition* (London: Unwin Hyman).

DE SOUSA SANTOS, B. (1995), *Towards a New Common Sense: Law, Science and Politics in the Paradigmatic Transition* (London: Routledge).

DELMAS-MARTY, M. (1988), *Projet de Nouveau Code Penal* (Dalloz: Paris).

DEPARTMENT OF JUSTICE, *Federal Principles of Prosecution of Corporations* (1999) (Washington).

DEVLIN, P. (1968), *The Enforcement of Morals* (Oxford: Oxford University Press).

DOUGLAS, M. (1985), *How Institutions Think* (New York: Syracuse University Press).

—— (1986), *Risk: Perceptions According to the Social Sciences* (London: Routledge).

—— (1990), 'Risk as a Forensic Resource', *Daedalus*, 119: 10.

—— (1992), *Risk and Blame* (London: Routledge).

—— and WILDAVSKY, A. (1982), *Risk and Culture* (London: University of California Press).

DRABECK, T., and QARANTELLI, E. (1967), 'Scapegoats, Villains and Disasters', *Transaction*, 4: 12.

DUFF, A. (1990), *Intention, Agency and Criminal Liability* (Oxford: Basil Blackwell).

DUNFORD, L., and RIDLEY, A. (1996), ' "No Soul to be Damned, No Body to be Kicked": Responsibility, Blame and Corporate Punishment', *International Journal of Sociology of Law*, 24: 1.

DURKHEIM, E. (1951), *Suicide* (New York: Free Press) (first published 1898).

EDMUND DAVIES, LORD JUSTICE (1967), *Report of the Tribunal into the Disaster at Aberfan*, HC Paper No. 553.

ELKINS, J. (1976), 'Corporations and Criminal Law', *Kentucky Law Journal*, 65: 73.

ERICSON, R., and HAGGERTY, K. (1997), *Policing the Risk Society* (Oxford: Clarendon Press).

ERIKSON, K. (1966), *Wayward Puritans* (New York: John Wiley).

ERMANN, D., and LUNDMAN, R., eds. (1996), *Corporate and Governmental Deviance*, 5th edn (Oxford: Oxford University Press).

ESER, A. (1999), 'Comparative observations', in Eser, A. Heine, G. and Huber, B., eds., 363.

—— HEINE, G., and HUBER, B., eds. (1999), *Criminal Responsibility of Legal and Collective Entities* (Freiburg: Ius crim).

FEINBERG, J. (1970), *Doing and Deserving* (Princeton: Princeton University Press).

—— (1984), *The Moral Limits of Criminal Law, Offense to Others* (Oxford: Oxford University Press).

FELSTINER, W., ABEL, R., and SARAT, A. (1980–1), 'The Emergence and Transformation of Disputes: Naming, Blaming, Claiming', *Law and Society Review*, 15: 63–94.

FENNELL REPORT, (1988), *Investigation into the King's Cross Underground Fire*, Cm 499 (London: HMSO).

FERGUSON, G. (1999), 'The Basis for Criminal Responsibility of Collective Entities in Canada', in Eser, Heine, Huber, eds., 153.

FIELD, S. (1990), 'Without the Law? Professor Arthurs and the Early Factory Inspectorate', *Journal of Law and Society*, 17: 445.

—— and JORG, N. (1991), 'Corporate Liability and Manslaughter: Should we be Going Dutch?', *Criminal Law Review*, 156.

FINCH, V. (1994), 'Personal Accountability and Corporate Control: The Role of Directors' and Officers' Liability Insurance', *Mod. Law Review*, 57: 880.

FINN, CYNTHIA (1996), 'The Responsible Corporate Officer, Criminal Liability, and Mens Rea: Limitations on the RCO Doctrine', *American University Law Review*, 46: 543.

FISSE, B. (1967), 'The Distinction Between Primary and Vicarious Corporate Criminal Liability', *Australian Law Journal*, 41: 203.

—— (1978), 'The Social Policy of Corporate Criminal Liability', *Adelaide Law Review*, 6: 361.

—— (1983), 'Reconstructing Corporate Criminal Law', *S. Ca. Law Review*, 56: 1141.

—— (1985), 'Sanctions Against Corporations: The Limitations of Fines and the Enterprise of Creating Alternatives', in Fisse and French, eds, *Corrigible Corporations and Unruly Law* (San Antonio: Trinity University Press).

—— (1990), 'Sentencing Options against Corporations', *Criminal Law Forum*, 1: 211.

—— and BRAITHWAITE, J. (1988), 'The Allocation of Responsibility for Corporate Crime: Individualism, Collectivism and Accountability', *Sydney Law Review*, 11: 468.

—— —— (1988), 'Accountability and the Control of Corporate Crime: Making the Buck Stop', in Findlay and Hogg, *Understanding Crime and Criminal Justice* (Sydney: Law Book Co. Ltd), 93.

—— —— (1993), *Corporations, Crime and Accountability* (Cambridge: Cambridge University Press).

FLETCHER, G. (1978), *Rethinking Criminal Law* (Boston: Little, Brown).

FOERSCHLER, A. (1990), 'Corporate Criminal Intent: Toward a Better Understanding of Corporate Misconduct', *California Law Review*, 78: 1287.

FRANK, N., and LOMBNESS, M. (1988), *Controlling Corporate Illegality: The Regulatory Justice System* (Cincinnati: Anderson Publishing Co.).

FREDMAN, S. (1997), *Women and the Law* (Oxford: Oxford University Press).

FRENCH, Peter (1979), 'The Corporation as a Moral Person', *American Philosophical Quarterly*, 16: 207.

—— (1984), *Collective and Corporate Responsibility* (Columbia University Press, New York).

—— (1996), 'Integrity, Intentions and Corporations', *American Business Law Journal*, 34: 141.

FRIEDMAN, H. (1979), 'Some Reflections on the Corporation as Criminal Defendant', *Notre Dame Lawyer*, 55: 173.

FRIEDMANN, WOLFGANG (1967), *Legal Theory*, 5th edn (London: Stevens & Sons).

—— (1972), *Law in a Changing Society*, 2nd edn (Harmondsworth: Stevens & Sons and Penguin).

FRIEDRICHS, D. (1996), *Trusted Criminals: White Collar Crime in Contemporary Society* (Belmont: Wadsworth).

GAINER, R. A. (1999), 'Caution Concerning Runaway Criminalisation of Corporate Activities', in Eser, Heine, and Huber, eds. (1999), 333.

GALANTER, M. (1994), 'The Transnational Traffic in Legal Remedies', in Jasanoff, S., ed., *Learning from Disaster* (University of Pennsylvania Press), 133–57.

GEIS, G. (1972), 'Criminal Penalties for Corporate Criminals', *Criminal Law Bulletin*, 8: 377.

GEORGE, B., LACEY, K., and BIRMELE, J. (2000), 'The 1998 OECD Convention: an Impetus for Worldwide Changes in Attitudes Toward Corruption in Business Transactions', *Am. Bus. Law Journal*, 37: 485.

GHERARDI, S. (1995), *Gender, Symbolism and Organizational Cultures* (London: Sage).

GIDDENS, T. (1991), *Modernity and Self-identity* (Cambridge: Polity Press).

—— (1999), 'Risk and Responsibility', *Modern Law Review*, 62: 1.

GLASBEEK, H. J. (1988), 'The Corporate Social Reponsibility Movement—The Latest in Maginot Lines to Save Capitalism', *Dalhousie Law Journal*, 11: 363–402.

GOBERT, J. (1994*a*), 'Corporate Criminality: four models of fault', *Legal Studies*, 14: 393.

—— (1994*b*), 'Corporate Criminality: New Crimes for the Times', *Crim. Law Review*, 722.

—— (1998), 'Controlling Corporate Criminality: Penal Sanctions and Beyond', *Web Journal of Current Legal Issues* Vol. 2.

GORDON, G. (1978), *The Criminal Law of Scotland* (Edinburgh: W. Green & Sons).

GOWER, L. (1979), *Company Law*, 4th edn (London: Butterworths).

GRANTHAM, R. (1997), 'Parent Company Liability for Directors of Subsidiaries', *The Company Lawyer*, 18: 138.

GRAY, J. (1996), 'Company Directors and Ignorance of the Law', *The Company Lawyer*, 17: 2296.

GREEN, T. (1985), *Verdict According to Conscience* (Chicago: University of Chicago Press).

GROSS, H. (1979), *A Theory of Criminal Justice* (Oxford: Oxford University Press).

GUNNINGHAM, N. (1987), 'Negotiated Non-Compliance: A Case Study of Regulatory Failure', *Law and Policy*, 9: 69.

—— and JOHNSTONE, R. (1999), *Regulating Workplace Safety: System and Sanctions* (Oxford: Oxford University Press).

GUSFIELD, J. (1981), *The Culture of Public Problems: Drinking, Driving and the Symbolic Order* (Chicago: University of Chicago Press).

HADDEN, T. (1977), *Company Law and Capitalism* (London: Weidenfeld & Nicolson).

HAGAN, J. (1988), *Structural Criminology* (Cambridge: Polity Press).

HAGEMANN, T., and GRINSTEIN, J. (1997), 'The Mythology of Aggregate Corporate Knowledge: A Deconstruction', *Geo. Wash. Law Review*, 65: 210.

HAGER, M. (1989), 'Bodies Politic: The Progressive History of Organizational "Real Entity" Theory', *U. Pitt. Law Review*, 50: 575.

HAINES, F. (1994), 'The Use and Effectiveness of Prosecution in the Industrial Safety Context: Interrogating the Punish/Persuade Debate', in Johnstone, R., ed., *Occupational Health and Safety Prosecutions in Australia* (Melbourne: Centre for Employment and Labour Relations Law), 39–52.

—— (1997), *Corporate Regulation: Beyond 'Punish or Persuade'* (Oxford: Clarendon Press).

HAMER, M. (1990), 'The Risks Of Ferry Travel', *New Scientist*, 18 Aug.

HAMILTON, P. (1992), 'Corporate Criminal Liability for Injuries and Death', *U. Kan. Law Review*, 40: 1091.

HANS, V., and LOFQUIST, W. (1987), 'Lay Perceptions of Business Responsibility for Harm', paper at Law and Society Conference, Amsterdam.

HARRIS, D., *et al.* (1984), *Compensation and Support for Illness and Injury* (Oxford: Oxford University Press).

HARRIS, R. (1987), *Power and Powerlessness in Industry* (London: Tavistock).

HART, H. (1968), *Law, Liberty and Morality* (Oxford: Oxford University Press).

—— and HONORÉ, T. (1985), *Causation in the Law*, 2nd edn (Oxford: Clarendon Press).

HAWKINS, K. (1984*a*), *Environment and Enforcement; Regulation and the Social Definition of Polllution* (Oxford: Oxford University Press).

—— (1984*b*), 'Creating Cases in a Regulatory Agency', *Urban Life*, 12: 371.

—— (1989), ' "FATCATS" and Prosecution in a Regulatory Agency: A Footnote on the Social Construction of Risk', *Law and Policy*, 11: 370.

—— (1990), 'Compliance Strategy, Prosecution Policy, and Aunt Sally', *Brit. Jnl of Criminology*, 30: 444.

—— and THOMAS, J., eds (1984), *Enforcing Regulation* (Boston: Kluwer: Nihjoff).

—— —— (1984), 'The Enforcement Process in Regulatory Bureaucracies', in Hawkins and Thomas, eds.

HAZLITT, W. (1901), *Table Talk* (Worlds Classics, first published 1821–2).

HEALTH AND SAFETY EXECUTIVE (1988), *Deadly Maintenance* (London: HMSO).

HSE (1991), *Fatal Accidents* (London: HMSO).

HSE (1994), *Review of Health and Safety Legislation* (London: HMSO).

HSE (1995), *Health and Safety in Small Firms* (London: HMSO).

HSE *Annual Report 1995/6* (1996) (HSE Books).

HEDLEY, S. (1994), 'Group Personal Injury Litigation and Public Opinion', *Legal Studies*, 14: 70.

HEIDENSOHN, F., (1997), 'Gender and Crime', in Maguire, M., Morgan, R., Reiner, R., eds., *Oxford Handbook of Criminology* (Oxford: Oxford University Press), 761.

HEINE, G. (1995), 'Criminal Liability of Enterprises and New Risks, International Developments—National Consequences', *Maastricht Jnl*, 2: 107.

—— (1998), 'New Developments in Corporate Criminal Liability in Europe: Can Europeans Learn from the American Experience—or Vice Versa?', *St Louis–Warsaw Transatlantic Law Journal*, 173.

—— (1999), 'Sanctions in the Field of Corporate Criminal Liability', in Eser, Heine, Huber, eds., 237.

HIDDEN, B. (1989), *Investigation into the Clapham Junction Railway Accident*, Cm 820 (London: HMSO).

HILL, J., and HARMER, S. (1995), 'Criminal Liability of Corporations—Australia', in de Doelder and Tiedemann, eds.

HILLS, S. L., ed. (1987), *Corporate Violence: Injury and Death for Profit* (New Jersey: Rowman and Littlefield).

HIRSCH, A. VON (1986), *Past or Future Crimes* (Manchester: Manchester University Press).

—— (1990), 'Proportionality in the Philosophy of Punishment', *Criminal Law Forum*, 1: 259.

HMSO (1975), *Inflation Accounting*, Cmnd 6225 (London: HMSO).

HOLDSWORTH, W. (1944), *A History of English Law*, 3rd edn (London: Sweet & Maxwell).

HOME OFFICE (1997), *Report of the Disasters and Inquests Working Group* (London: HMSO).

HOME OFFICE (2000), *Reforming the Law of Involuntary Manslaughter: the Government's Proposals* (London: HMSO).

HONORÉ, A. M. (1973), 'Groups, Laws and Obedience', in Simpson, A. W. B., *Oxford Essays in Jurisprudence* (Oxford: Oxford University Press).

HOOD, C., and JONES, D., eds (1996), *Accident and Design* (London: UCL Press).

HORDER, J. (1990), 'Cognition, Emotion and Criminal Culpability', *Law Quarterly Review*, 106: 469.

HOWARD, C. (1963), *Strict Responsibility* (London: Sweet & Maxwell).

HUGHES, E. (1958), *Men and Their Work* (Westport, Connecticut: Greenwood Press).

HUNNISETT, R. F. (1961), *The Medieval Coroner* (Cambridge: Cambridge University Press).

IRWIN, A., SMITH, D., and GRIFFITHS, R. (1982), 'Risk Analysis and Public Policy in Major Hazards', *Physical Technology*, p. 13.

IVES, JANE (1985), *The Export of Hazard* (London: Routledge).

JAMES, P. (1992), 'Reforming Britsh Health and Safety Law: a Framework for Discussion', *Industrial Law Journal*, 21 (2): 87.

JANOFF-BULMAN, R. (1979), 'Characteroligical versus behavioural self-blame: Inquiries into Depression and Rape', *Journal of Personality and Social Psychology*, 37: 1798.

—— and WORTMAN, C. B. (1977), 'Attributions of Blame and Coping in the "Real World": Severe Accident Victims React to their Lot', *Journal of Personality and Social Psychology*, 35: 351–63.

JOHNSTONE, R., ed. (1994), *Occupational Health and Safety Prosecutions in Australia*, Centre for Employment and Labour Relations Law (Melbourne: University of Melbourne).

—— (1996), *New Directions in Occupational Health and Safety Prosecutions: The Individual Liability of Corporate Officers, and Prosecutions for Industrial Manslaughter and Related Offences*, Centre for Employment and Labour Relations Law (Melbourne: University of Melbourne).

JONES, KELVIN (1982), *Law and Economy: The Legal Regulation of Corporate Capital* (London: Academic Press).

KADISH, S. (1963), 'Some Observations on the Use of Criminal Sanctions in Enforcing Economic Regulations', *University of Chicago Law Review*, 30: 423.

KAGAN, R. (1984), 'On Regulatory Inspectorates and Police', in Hawkins and Thomas, eds.

—— and SCHOLZ, J. (1984), 'The "Criminology" of the Corporation and Regulatory Enforcement Strategies', in Hawkins and Thomas, eds.

KASPERSON, R. (1992), 'The Social Amplification of Risk: Progress in Developing an Integrative Framework', in Krimsky, S., and Golding, D., eds, *Theories of Risk* (New York: Praeger) 153.

KATZ, LEO (1987), *Bad Acts and Guilty Minds: Conundrums of the Criminal Law* (London: University of Chicago Press).

KATZMAN, M. (1986), 'Chemical Catastrophes and the Courts', *The Public Interest*, 91.

KELLEY, H. (1971), *Attribution in Social Interaction* (Morriston NJ.: General learning Corp.).

—— and MICHAELA, J. (1980), 'Attribution Theory and Research', *Ann. Rev Psychol.*, 31: 457–501.

KELMAN, M. (1981), 'Interpretive Construction in the Substantive Criminal Law', *Stanford Law Review*, 33: 591.

KEOGH, J. (1983), 'Origins of Coronial Jurisdiction', *University of New South Wales Law Journal*, 6: 191.

KHANNA, V. (1996), 'Corporate Criminal Liability: What Purpose Does it Serve?', 109 *Harv Law Review*, 1477.

—— (1999), 'Is the Notion of Corporate Fault a Faulty Notion?: The Case of Corporate Mens Rea', *Boston University Law Review*, 79: 355.

KRAMER, RONALD, C. (1989), 'Criminologists and the Social Movement Against Corporate Crime', *Social Justice*, 16: 146.

KREISBERG, S. M. (1976), 'Decision-Making Models and the Control of Corporate Crime', *Yale Law Journal*, 85: 1091.

LACEY, N. (1984), 'Punishment, Justice and Consequentialism', in Duff, A., and Simmonds, N., *Philosophy and the Criminal Law* (Wiesbaden, Franz Steiner Verlag).

—— (1988), *State Punishment* (London: Routledge).

—— (1995), 'Law, Politics and Criminalisation', in Loveland, ed., *Frontiers of Criminality* (London: Sweet & Maxwell).

—— and WELLS, C. (1998), *Reconstructing Criminal Law*, 2nd edn (London: Butterworths).

LASKI, H. (1917), 'The Early History of the Corporation in England', *Harv. Law Review*, 30: 561.

LAUFER, WILLIAM, S. (1999), 'Corporate Liability, Risk Shifting, and the Paradox of Compliance', *Vand. Law Review*, 52: 1343.

LAW COMMISSION (1970), *The Mental Element in Crime*, Working Paper no. 31 (London: HMSO).

—— (1972), *The Criminal Liability of Corporations*, Working Paper No. 44 (London: HMSO).

—— (1989), *A Criminal Code for England and Wales*, Report. No. 177 (London: HMSO).

—— (1996), *Legislating the Criminal Code: Involuntary Manslaughter,* Report No. 237 (London: HMSO).

LAW REFORM COMMISSION OF CANADA, (1987), *Recodifying Criminal Law,* Report No. 31 (Ottawa).

LEDERMAN, E. (1985), 'Criminal Law, Perpetrator and Corporations: Rethinking a Complex Triangle', *Journal of Criminal Law and Criminology*, 76: 285.

LEE, T. (1981), 'The Public's Perception of Risk and the Question of Irrationality', in Warner, ed., *The Assessment and Perception of Risk* (London: The Royal Society) 12.

LEGRAND, P. (1996), 'How to compare now', *Legal Studies*, 16: 232.

LEIGH, L. H. (1969), *The Criminal Liability of Corporations in English Law* (London: Weidenfeld & Nicolson).

—— (1982*a*), *Strict and Vicarious Liability* (London: Sweet & Maxwell).

—— (1982*b*), *The Control of Commercial Faud* (London: Heinemann).

—— (1982*c*), 'The Criminal Liability of Corporations and Other Groups: A Comparative View', *Michigan Law Review*, 80: 1508.

LERNER, M. J., and SIMMONS, C. H. (1966), 'Observer's Reaction to the "innocent victim": Compassion or Rejection?', *Journal of Personality and Social Psychology*, 4: 203.

LEVI, M. (1987*a*), *Regulating Fraud: White-Collar Crime and the Criminal Process* (London: Tavistock).

—— (1987*b*), 'Attitudes to Crime: A Critical Overview', *Violence, Aggression and Terrorism*, 1: 99–108.

—— (1991), 'Developments in Business Crime Control in Europe', in Heidensohn, F., and Farrell, M., eds, *Crime in Europe* (London: Routledge) 172.

—— and JONES, S. (1985), 'Public and Police Perceptions of Crime Seriousness in England and Wales', *The British Journal of Criminology*, 25: 234–50.

LIND, E. A., and TYLER, T. R. (1988), *The Social Psychology of Procedural Justice* (New York and London: Plenum Press).

LYNCH, M., NALLA, M., and MILLER, K. (1989), 'Cross-Cultural Perspectives of Deviance: the Case of Bhopal', *Journal of Research in Crime and Delinquency*, 267.

MCLEAN, I., and JOHNES, M. (2000), *Aberfan: Government and Disasters* (Cardiff: Welsh Academic Press).

MAAKESTAD, W. (1981), 'A Historical Survey of Corporate Homicide in the United States: Could It Be Prosecuted in Illinois?', *Illinois Bar Journal*, 69: 772.

—— (1990), 'Corporate Homicide', *New Law Journal*, 140: 356.

MAITLAND, F. W. (1911), 'Moral Personality and Legal Personality', in Fisher, H. A. L., ed, *The Collected Papers*, vol. 3 (Cambridge: Cambridge University Press).

MANCHESTER, C. (1977), 'The Origins of Strict Criminal Liability', *Anglo-American L. Rev.*, 6: 277.

MARRIOTT, J. (1991), *Report of the Chief Inspector of Marine Accidents into the Collision between the Passenger Launch Marchioness and MV Bowbelle with the loss of life on the River Thames on 20 August 1989* (London: Department of Transport, HMSO).

MAUGHAN, B., and COPP, S. (1998), 'Piercing the Corporate Veil', *New Law Journal*, 148: 938.

MAYS, R., 'The Criminal Liability of Corporations and Scots Law: Learning the Lessons of Anglo-American Jurisprudence' (2000) 4 *Edin. Law Review* 46.

MAYSON, S., FRENCH, D., and RYAN, C. (2000), *Company Law, 2000–2001*, 17th edn. (London: Blackstone).

MEIR, R. F., ed. (1984), *Major Forms of Crime* (London: Sage).

METZGER, M., and DALTON, D. (1996), 'Seeing the Elephant: An Organizational Perspective on Corporate Moral Agency', *Am Bus. Law Journal*, 33: 554.

MILL, J. (1974), *On Liberty* (Harmondsworth: Penguin) (first published 1859).

MOORE, M. (1985), 'The Moral and Mataphysical Sources of the Criminal Law', in Pennock and Chapman, eds., 1985: 11.

MORGAN, D. (1994), 'Relatively Late Payments: Damages Beyond Death and Bereavement', in Morgan, D., and Lee, R., eds, *Death Rites* (London: Routledge).

—— (2001), *Medical Examinations* (London: Cavendish).

MORRIS, A. (1987), *Women, Crime and Criminal Justice* (Oxford: Blackwell).

MOUZELIS, N. (1975), *Organisation and Bureaucracy* (London: Routledge).

MUCHLINSKI, P. T. (1987), 'The Bhopal Case: Controlling Ultrahazardous Industrial Activities Undertaken by Foreign Investors', *Modern Law Review*, 50: 545.

MUELLER, G. (1957), 'Mens Rea and the Corporation', *University of Pittsburgh Law Review*, 19: 21.

MULLINS, L. J. (1985), *Management and Organisational Behaviour* (London: Pitman).

MURPHY, J. (1985), 'Retributivism and the State's Interest in Punishment', in Pennock and Chapman, eds, 1985: 156.

NELKEN, D. (1983), *The Limits of the Legal Process: A Study of Landlords, Law and Crime* (London: Academic Press).

—— (1987), 'Criminal Law and Criminal Justice: Some Notes on their Irrelation', in Dennis, I., ed., *Criminal Law and Justice* (London: Sweet & Maxwell).

—— (1990), 'Why Punish?', *Modern Law Review*, 53: 829.

NEMERSON, S. (1975), Note: 'Criminal Liability Without Fault, A Philosophical Perspective', *Columbia Law Review*, 75: 517.

NIJBOER, H. (1999), 'A Plea for a Systematic Approach in Developing Criminal Procedural Law Concerning the Investigation, Prosecution and Adjudication of Corporate Entities', in Eser, Heine, and Huber, eds., 1999: 303.

NORRIE, A. (1991), 'A Critique of Criminal Causation', *Modern Law Review*, 54: 685.

NOTE, COLUMBIA (1996), 'The Role of Corporate Compliance Program in Determining Corporate Liability: A Suggested Approach', *Colum. Law Review*, 96: 1252.

NOTE, HARVARD (1979), 'Corporate Crime: Regulating Corporate Behaviour Through Criminal Sanctions', *Harvard Law Review*, 92: 1227.

NOTE, YALE (1979), 'Structural Crime and Institutional Rehabilitation: A New Approach to Sentencing', *Yale Law Journal*, 89: 353.

O'DONOVAN, K. (1985), *Sexual Divisions in Law* (London: Weidenfeld & Nicolson).

OGUS, A. (1994), *Regulation: Legal Form and Economic History* (Oxford: Clarendon Press).

—— (1998), 'Corrective Taxes and Financial Impositions as Regulatory Instruments', *Modern Law Review*, 98: 767.

OOSTEN, F. VAN (1999), 'Theoretical Bases for the Criminal Liability of Legal Persona in South Africa', in Eser, Heine, and Huber, eds., 1999: 195.

ORLAND, L. (1980), 'Reflections on Corp. Crime', 17 *Am. Crim. Law Review*, 501.

—— and CACHERA, C. (1995), 'Corporate Crime and Punishment in France: Criminal Responsibility of Legal Entitles (*Personnes Morales*) Under the New French Criminal Code (*Nouveau Penal Code*)', *Cnn J. Int'l L* 11: 111.

P.A. MANAGEMENT CONSULTANTS LTD (1969), *Company Organization: Theory and Practice* (London: George Allen & Unwin).

PARKER, J. (1989), 'Criminal Sentencing Policy for Organizations: The Unifying Approach of Optimal Penalties', *American Criminal Law Review*, 26: 513.

—— (1996), 'Doctrine for Destruction: The Case of Corporate Criminal Liability', *Managerial and Decision Economics*, 17: 381.

PARKER, T. (1990), *Life After Life* (London: Secker & Warburg).

PARKINSON, J. (1993), *Corporate Power and Responsibility: Issues in the Theory of Company Law* (Oxford: Oxford University Press).

PAULUS, I. (1974), *The Search for Pure Food* (Oxford: Martin Robertson).

PEARCE, F. (1987), 'Corporate Crime', *Critical Social Policy*, 19.

—— and SNIDER, L., eds (1995), *Corporate Crime: Contemporary Debates* (Toronto: University of Toronto Press).

—— and TOMBS, S. (1989), 'Bhopal: Union Carbide and the Hubris of the Capitalist Technocracy', *Social Justice*, 16: 116–45.

—— and TOMBS, S. (1990) 'Ideology, Hegemony, and Empiricism, Compliance Theories of regulation', *Brit. Jnl of Criminology*, 30: 423.

PENNOCK, J. R., and CHAPMAN, J. M. (1985), *Criminal Justice* (New York and London: New York University Press).

PERKINS, C. (1952), 'The Civil Offense', *U. Pa. Law Review*, 100: 832.

—— (1964), 'Alignment of Sanction with culpable Conduct', *Iowa L. Rev.*, 49: 325.

PERROW, C. (1984), *Normal Accidents: Living with High Risk Technologies* (New York: Basic Books).

PHILLIPS, M. (1996), 'How Much Does Corporate Theory Matter?', *Am. Bus. Law Journal*, 34: 239.

PHILLIPS, LORD (2000), Report of the Inquiry into the Emergency and Identification of Bovine Spongiform Encephalopathy and variant Creutzfeldt-Jakob Disease and the action taken in Reponse to it (London: HMSO).

Polk, K., Haines, F., and Perrone, S. (1995), 'Work Death in Victoria 1987–90: An Overview', *Australian and NZ Journal of Criminology*, 28: 178–92.

Pollock, F. (1911), 'Has the Common Law Received the Fiction Theory of Corporations?', *Law Quarterly Review*, 27: 219.

Popplewell Mr Justice (1986), *Final Report of the Committee of Inquiry into Crowd Safety and Control at Sports Grounds*, Cmnd 9710 (London: HMSO).

Prefontaine, D. (1999), 'Effective Criminal Sanctions against Corporate Entities: Canada', in Eser, Heine, Huber, eds, 1999: 276.

Pugh, D. S., and Hickson, D. J. (1989), *Writers on Organisations* (Harmondsworth: Penguin).

Punch, M. (1996), *Dirty Business Exploring Corporate Misconduct* (London: Sage).

Quaid, J. A. (1998), 'The Assessment of Corporate Criminal Liability on the Basis of Corporate Identity: An Analysis', *McGill Law Journal*, 43: 67.

Quinney, R. (1970), *The Social Reality of Crime* (Boston: Little, Brown).

Rayner, S. (1992), 'Cultural Theory and Risk Analysis', in Krimsky and Golding, eds., *Theories of Risk* (New York: Praeger), 1992: 83.

Reason, J. (1997), *Managing the Risks of Organizational Accidents* (Aldershot: Ashgate).

Reeves, D., and Woodward, J. (1970), 'The Study of Managerial Control', in Woodward ed., *Industrial Organisations: Behaviour and Control* (Oxford: Oxford University Press).

Reiner, I., and Chatten-Brown, J. (1989), 'Deterring Death in the Workplace: The Prosecutor's Perspective', *Law Medicine and Health Care*, 17: 23–31.

—— —— (1989a), 'When it is not an Accident but a Crime; Prosecutors Get Tough with OSHA Violations', *Northern Kentucky Law Review*, 17: 83–103.

Reiss, A. (1984), 'Selecting Strategies of Social Control over Organizational Life', in Hawkins and Thomas, eds, *Enforcing Regulation*, 1984.

Richardson, G. (1987), 'Strict Liability for Regulatory Crime', *Criminal Law Review*, 295.

Rider, B. (1989), 'Insider-Trading—A Crime of Our Time?', *Current Legal Problems*, 63.

Rifkin, J. (2000), *The Age of Access* (Harmondsworth: Penguin).

Rimington, J. (1991), 'Reply to David Bergman', *Safety Management*, Dec. 6.

Robens, Lord (1972), *Safety and Health at Work*, Report of the Committee, 1970–2, Cmnd 5034 (London: HMSO).

Rose, A. (1995), '1995 Australian Criminal Code Act: Corporate Criminal Provisions', *Criminal Law Forum*, 6: 129.

Rosen, L. (1985), 'Intentionality and the Concept of the Person', in Pennock and Chapman, eds, 1985: 52.

Rowan-Robinson J., Watchman, P., and Barker, C. (1988), 'Crime and Regulation', *Criminal Law Review*, 211.

—— —— —— (1990), *Crime and Regulation: A Study of the Enforcement of Statutory Codes* (Edinburgh: T. & T. Clark).

Ruimschotel, D. (1988), 'The Psychological Reality of Intentional and Negligent Criminal Acts', in Van Koppen, Hessing, and van den Heuvel, eds, *Lawyers on Psychology and Psychologists on Law* (Amsterdam: Swets & Zeitlinger), 1988.

Ryan, P. (1990), 'Regulation by Osmosis', *Criminal Law Forum*, 1: 357.

Sanders, J., and Hamilton, V. (1997), 'Distributing Responsibility for Wrongdoing Inside Corporate Hierarchies: Public Judgments in Three Societies', *Law and Social Inquiry*, 815.

SAYRE, F. (1932), 'Mens Rea', *Harvard Law Review*, 45: 974.

—— (1933), 'Public Welfare Offenses', *Columbia Law Review*, 33: 55.

SCHLEGEL, K. (1990), *Just Deserts for Corporate Criminals* (Boston: North Eastern University Press).

SCHRAGER, L., and SHORT, J. (1980), 'How Serious a Crime? Perceptions of Organizational and Ordinary Crimes', in Geis, G., and Stotland, E., eds., *White Collar Crime: Theory and Research* (Beverly Hills: Sage), 1980.

SCHUR, E. (1981), *The Politics of Deviance* (Englewood Cliffs: Prentice-Hall).

SCWENK, E. H. (1943), 'The Administrative Crime, its Creation and Punishment by Aministrative Agencies', *Michigan Law Review*, 42: 51.

SHAVER, K. G. (1970), 'Defensive Attribution: Effects of Severity and Relevance on the Responsibility Assigned for an Accident', *Journal of Personality and Social Psychology*, 14: 101.

SHEEN REPORT, (1987), *M.V. Herald of Free Enterprise Report of the Court No. 8074, Dept of Transport* (London: HMSO).

Shorter Oxford English Dictionary (1970), (Oxford: Clarendon Press).

SIGLER, J., and MURPHY, J. (1988), *Interactive Corporate Compliance: An Alternative to Regulatory Compulsion* (New York: Quorum Books).

SIMON, H. (1957), *Models of Man* (New York: Wiley).

SIMPSON, A. (1984), 'Legal Liability for Bursting Reservoirs: The Historical Context of *Rylands v Fletcher*', *Journal of Legal Studies*, xiii: 209.

SINGER, R. G. (1989), 'The Resurgence of *Mens Rea*: III—The Rise and Fall of Strict Criminal Liability', *Boston College Law Review*, 30: 337–408.

SKOLNICK, J. (1968), 'Coercion to Virtue: The Enforcement of Morals', *Southern California Law Review*, 41: 588.

SLAPPER, G. (1993), 'Corporate Manslaughter: An Examination of the Determinants of Prosecutorial Policy', *Social and Legal Studies*, 2: 423.

—— (1994), 'A Corporate Killing', *New Law Journal*, 144: 1735.

—— (1999), *Blood in the Bank: Social and Legal Aspects of Deaths at Work* (Aldershot: Ashgate).

—— and TOMBS, S. (1999), *Corporate Crime* (Harlow: Longman).

SMITH, D. (1997), 'Ethnic Origins, Crime, and Criminal Justice', in Maguire, M., Morgan, R., and Reiner, R., eds., *Oxford Handbook of Criminology* (Oxford: Oxford University Press), 703.

SMITH, J., and HOGAN, B. (1996), *Criminal Law*, 8th edn (London: Butterworths).

SMITH, M. A., ed, (1987), *The Chemical Industry After Bhopal: An International Symposium in London* (London: IBC Technical Services Ltd).

SMITH, S. (1995), 'An Iron Fist in the Velvet Glove: Redefining the Role of Criminal Prosecution in Creating an Effective Environmental Enforcement System', *Crim. Law Journal*, 19: 12.

SNIDER, L. (1991), 'The Regulatory Dance: Understanding Reform Processes in Corporate Crime', *International Journal of Sociology of Law*, 19: 209.

SPARKS, R., GENN, H., and DODD, D. (1977), *Surveying Victims* (Chichester: John Wiley & Sons).

SPINDLER, G. (1999), 'Alternatives to Criminal Responsibility of Corporations: Considerations of a Corporate Lawyer', in Eser, Heine, and Huber, eds., 1999: 341.

SPURGEON, W. and FAGAN, T. (1981), 'Criminal Liability for Life Endangering Corporate Conduct', *Journal of Criminal Law and Criminology*, 72: 400.

STESSENS, G. (1994), 'Corporate Criminal Liability: A Comparative Perspective', *International and Comparative Law Quarterly*, 43: 493.

STONE, C. (1975), *Where the Law Ends: The Social Control of Corporate Behaviour* (New York: Harper & Row).

—— (1977), 'Controlling Corporate Misconduct', *Public Interest*, 48: 55.

—— (1985), 'A Comment on Criminal Responsibility in Government', in Pennock and Chapman, 1985: 241.

STUART, D. (1995), 'Punishing Corporate Criminals with Restraint', *Criminal Law Forum*, 6: 219.

SULLIVAN, G. (1996), 'The Attribution of Culpability to Limited Companies', *Cambridge Law Journal*, 515.

SUTHERLAND, E. (1937), *The Professional Thief* (Chicago: University of Chicago Press).

—— (1983), *White Collar Crime* (New York: Holt, Rhinehart & Wilson, first published 1949).

SWIGERT, V. L., and FARRELL, R. A. (1976), *Murder, Inequality and the Law* (Lexington: Lexington Books).

TARLING, R. (1998), *Coroner Service Survey*, Home Office Research Study 181 (London: Home Office).

TAYLOR, I. (1983), *Crime, Capitalism and Community* (Toronto: Butterworths).

TAYLOR, I. (1997), 'The Political Economy of Crime', in Maguire, M., Morgan, R., and Reiner, R., eds., *Oxford Handbook of Criminology* (Oxford: Oxford University Press), 265.

TAYLOR, LORD JUSTICE (1990), *Hillsborough Stadium Disaster*, Cm 962 (London: HMSO).

THOMAS, K. (1973), *Religion and the Decline of Magic* (Harmondsworth: Penguin).

THOMPSON, DENNIS (1985), 'Criminal Responsibility in Government', in Pennock and Chapman, eds., 1985: 200.

THOMPSON, GRAHAME (1982), 'The Enterprise as a Dispersed Agency', *Economy and Society*, 11: 233.

THOMPSON, M., ELLIS, R., and WILDAVSKY, A. (1990), *Cultural Theory* (Oxford: Westview Press).

TIGAR, MICHAEL (1990), 'It Does the Crime But Not the Time: Corporate Criminal Liability in Federal Law', *American Journal of Criminal Law*, 17: 211.

TUCKER, E. (1995), 'The Westray Mine Disaster and its Aftermath: The Politics of Causation', *Cdn Jnl of Law and Society*, 10: 91.

TURNER, B., and TOFT, B. (1987), 'The Schematic report analysis diagram: a Simple aid to Learning from Large-Scale Failures', *International CIS Journal*, 1: 12–23.

—— —— (1988), 'Organisational Learning from Disaster', in Gow, H., and Kay, R., eds., *Emergency Planning for Industrial Hazards* (London: Elsevier) 1988: 297–313.

—— and PIDGEON, NICK (1997), *Man-Made Disasters*, 2nd edn (London: Butterworth Heinemann).

UGLOW, S. (1988), *Policing Liberal Society* (Oxford: Oxford University Press).

VAUGHAN, DIANE (1985), *Controlling Unlawful Organizational Behaviour* (London: University of Chicago Press).

—— (1990), 'Autonomy, Interdependence and Social Control', *Ad. Sci. Q.*, 35: 225–57.

—— (1999), 'The Dark Side of Organisations: Mistake, Misconduct and Disaster', *Ann. Rev. Sociology*, 25: 271–305.

VELJANOWSKI, C. (1984), 'The Economics of Regulatory Enforcement', in Hawkins, K., and Thomas, J., 1984.

VERVAELE, J. A. (1997), 'La responsabilité pénale de et au sein de la personne morale aux Pays-Bas. Mariage entre pragmatisme et dogmatisme juridique', *Revue de Science criminelle et de droit pénal comparé*, 2: 325–46.

VINCENT, A. (1989), 'Can Groups Be Persons?', *Review of Metaphysics*, 42: 687–715.

WALKER, N. (1985), *Sentencing: Theory Law and Practice* (London: Butterworths).

WALSTER, E. (1966), 'Assignment of Responsibility for an Accident', *Journal of Personality and Social Psychology*, 3: 73.

WALTON, C. C., and CLEVELAND, F. W. (1964), *Corporations on Trial: The Electric Cases* (New York: Wadsworth).

WARWICK INQUEST GROUP (1985), 'The Inquest as a Theatre for Police Tragedy: The Davey Case', *Jnl of Law and Society*, 12: 35.

WASSERSTROM, R. (1960), 'Strict Liability in the Criminal Law', *Stanford Law Review*, 12: 731.

WATERHOUSE, J. (2000), *Report of the Tribunal into the Abuse of Children in Care in the former county areas of Gwynedd and Clwyd since 1974*, HC 201 (London: HMSO).

WEAIT, M. (1996), 'Problems of Generating and Sustaining Compliance with Law in Complex Organisations', *Comparative Social Research Supplement*, 2: 69–90.

WEBER, M. (1949), *On the Methodology of the Social Sciences* (Glencoe: Free Press).

WECHSLER, H. (1955), 'The Criteria of Criminal Reponsibility', *University of Chicago Law Review*, 22: 374.

WEINFELD, S. (1982), 'Criminal Liability of Corporate Managers for Deaths of Their Employees: *People v Warner-Lambert Co.*', *Albany Law Review*, 46: 655.

WELLS, C. (1982), 'Swatting the Subjectivist Bug', *Criminal Law Review*, 209.

—— (1986), 'Restatement or Reform', *Criminal Law Review*, 314.

—— (1988), 'The Decline and Rise of English Murder: Corporate Crime and Individual Responsibility', *Criminal Law Review*, 788.

—— (1991), 'Inquests, Inquiries and Indictments: The Official Reception of Death by Disaster', *Legal Studies*, 11: 71.

—— (1994), 'Corporate Liability and Consumer Protection: *Tesco v Nattrass* Revisited', *Modern Law Review*, 57: 817–23.

—— (1995*a*), *Negotiating Tragedy: Law and Disasters* (London: Sweet & Maxwell).

—— (1995*b*), 'Corporate Manslaughter: A Cultural and Legal Form', *Criminal Law Forum*, 6: 45.

—— (1995*c*), 'Cry in the Dark: Corporate Manslaughter and Cultural Meaning', in Loveland, I., ed, *Frontiers of Criminality* (London: Sweet & Maxwell).

—— (1995*d*), 'A Quiet Revolution in Corporate Liability for Crime', *New Law Journal*, 145: 1326.

—— (1997), 'Health and Safety Laws take Corporate Liability for a Ride', *Archbold News*, issue 5.

—— (1998), 'Corporate Responsibility', in Chadwick, ed., *Encyclopedia of Applied Ethics* (San Diego: Academic Press), 653.

—— (1999*a*), 'Inquiring into Disasters: Law, Politics and Blame', *Risk Management*, 2: 7–19.

—— (1999*b*) 'The Millennium Bug and Corporate Criminal Liability', *The Journal of Information, Law and Technology* vol. 2.

—— (1999*c*), 'A New Offence of Corporate Killing—The English Law Commission's Proposals', in Eser, Heine, Huber, eds, 1999: 119.

—— (1999*d*), 'Developments in Corporate Liability in England and Wales', in Eser, Heine, Huber, eds, 1999: 217.

WELLS, C. (2000), 'Prosecuting Safety—A Cautionary Tale', *New Law Journal*, 150: 1648.

—— MORGAN, D., and QUICK, O. (2000), 'Disasters—A Challenge for the Law', *Washburn Law Journal*, 39: 496.

WELSH, R. S. (1946), 'Criminal Liability of Corporations', *Law Quarterly Review*, 62: 345.

WHEEN, F. (1999), *Karl Marx* (London: Fourth Estate).

WIENER, M. (1991), *Reconstructing the Criminal* (Cambridge: Cambridge University Press).

WILLIAMS, G. (1956), 'Vicarious Liability: Tort of the Master or of the Servant?', *Law Quarterly Review*, 72: 522.

—— *Criminal Law, The General Part*, 2nd edn (London, 1961) Stevens.

WILLIAMS, R. (1965) *The Long Revolution* (Harmondsworth: Penguin).

—— (1981), *Culture* (London: Fontana).

WILSON, J. (1985), *The Politics of Health and Safety* (Oxford: Oxford University Press).

WINN, C. (1929), 'The Criminal Responsibility of Corporations', *Cambridge Law Journal*, 3: 398.

WOLF, S. (1985), 'The Legal and Moral Reponsibility of Organisations', in Pennock and Chapman, eds, 1985: 267.

WOODWARD, J. (1980), *Industrial Organization: Theory and Practice* (Oxford: Oxford University Press).

WOOLF, T. (1997), 'The Criminal Code Act 1995 (cth)—Towards a Realist Vision of Corporate Criminal Liability', 21 *Crim. Law Journal*, 257.

WOOTTON, B. (1982), *Crime and the Criminal Law*, 2nd edn (London: Stevens).

WRIGHT, F. (1997), *Law of Health and Safety at Work* (London: Sweet & Maxwell).

YOUNG, M. (1991), *An Inside Job* (Oxford: Oxford University Press).

ZEDNER, L. (1994), 'Reparation and Retribution: Are They Reconcilable?', *Modern Law Review*, 57: 228.

Index

Index compiled by Frank Pert

Printed in the United Kingdom
by Lightning Source UK Ltd.
108403UKS00001B/161

aloud in 'their' presence. He draws this methodological

and subtle modes and relationships were in themselves devel-
social practice, and are fundamentally connected with the
in dramatic form, of new and altered social relationships,
of self and others, complex alternatives of private and public
is true then that what has been discovered, and can later be
the form can be shown to be relatively associated with a
area of social practice and social change. New conceptions of
mous or relatively autonomous individual, new senses of the
tween such an individual and an assigned or expected social
at in other kinds of contemporary discourse but evident also
history of the major social changes of this precise period, are
r relation with the 'device'.

necessary to explain the device as their consequence, taking
ciology and then the form. This may often appear to be the
ents, but it is often also clear that the formal innovation is a
tegral element of the changes themselves: an articulation, by
iscovery, of changes in consciousness which are themselves
onsciousness of change. Thus to analyse the soliloquy in
aissance drama is necessarily, first, a matter of formal analysis,
way of denying or making irrelevant a social analysis; rather as
echnically rigorous kind of social analysis of *this* social practice.

n see the point at which formal analysis necessarily challenges
limited or displaced kinds of social analysis. For while social
confined to the society which, as it were, *already* exists, in
ways, before the cultural practice begins, it is not only that
ade elsewhere are simply applied to actual works, imposing on
the most general considerations and missing or neglecting
ents of their composition. It is also that actual evidence of the
io-cultural process, in one of its significant practices, is not
d for, though it is in fact abundant. This is the point of transition
ogy of culture, to include, as a major emphasis, the *sociology*
OC, pp. 142–3)

to 'displaced' social analysis clarifies the 'limit' Williams
his endorsement of that technique in *Marxism and Literature*.[115]
rns to the case of the soliloquy later in the same chapter,
ally suggests a formal-comparative exercise of drawing up two
listing formal characteristics of the soliloquy, the other listing
changes in self-conceptions of the individual and in relations
iduals in this new sense and their assigned or expected social

aesthetic forms' (1992, p. 64). Nonetheless, Genette is prepared to concede that 'a certain number of thematic, modal and formal determinations . . . are *relatively constant and transhistorical*' (1992, p. 78). It was these that he characterized in his earlier work as fundamental.

Genette's clarifications highlight the key difference between a genre analysis and a 'structuralist analysis of narrative': the restoration of diachrony to the synchronic bias of a 'sentential' analysis. The relation between a genre's 'history' and contemporary composition is more than the product of the intersection of syntagmatic 'choices' from a paradigmatic axis, as the sentential model necessitates.

It is in a similar context that Williams valued genetic structuralism's potential to encompass 'the full emphasis of the social process'. For Williams then, the tasks of social formalism include a recognition of the 'transhistorical' dimensions of genres. He so supplants the role of the formalist/structuralist self-reproducing synchronic system by, crucially, the provision of a means of socio-historically accounting for the generic innovations of 'devices', and more major formal/conventional innovations. In terms of the production paradigm (especially for Adorno), this constitutes a recognition of the *cumulative* determinacy of cultural forms as a *productive force*.[108]

Yet this recognition in turn raises in a different manner those complexities of social and historical correspondence discussed in previous chapters. Williams's key step is to provide his own typology of cultural forms specifically designed to recognize *differing* modes of correspondence of conjunctural cultural forms, including that determinacy exercised by 'trans-epochal' cultural forms.

As noted in Section 2.5, Williams too works with a conception of mode, but this is not derived directly from any Aristotelian schema. Williams would thus appear to escape Genette's major criticism of most other theorists who conflate the concepts of mode and genre. Williams's reassessment of genre theory had begun in the 'Base and Superstructure' essay. There he made it plain that analysis of cultural forms was crucial to his adoption of the notion of 'practice' instead of 'art object', but that the genre analysis of 'orthodox criticism' was inadequate, and that there need be no coincidence of 'collective modes' and genres.[109] *Marxism and Literature* provided Williams's own criticism of neo-classical and Romantic genre theories.[110] By *The Sociology of Culture* this position had gelled into the development of the typology in Table 4.1.[111]

For Williams, as we have seen, Goldmann's genetic structuralism was flawed by its confinement of correspondence to an 'epochal' frame. Williams's delineation of the varying levels of correspondence and conditions of reproducibility of the different subtypes of cultural forms is clearly designed to prevent the collapse of such analysis into 'epochal' reductivism. Moving down column 1, we can see that each sub-type brings us closer to specificity – not of 'the present' but rather to an abstract-historical specificity – by introducing

Table 4.1 Williams's typology of cultural forms

Form	Immanent formal properties	Correspondence (if any)	Examples
Mode	'Properly collective forms' constituted by highly complex external and internal *signals* capable of elaboration into contemporary genres	Relatively independent of specific social orders	Drama Lyric Narrative utopia[a] 'New mode' of cinema
Genre (Kind)	Specific activations and elaborations of 'modes' within definite social orders	Have *some definite dependence* on changes in epochal orders	Tragedy Comedy Epic Romance 'Fiction'
Type	Radical distributions, redistributions and innovations operating over relatively long periods within an epoch	*Correspondence* with 'specific and changed social character of an epoch'	'Bourgeois' drama Realist novel Landscape painting
Form	Radical distributions, redistributions and innovations linked to the smaller-scale social contradictions within an epoch; often tied to alterations of the typical	Subject to forms of organization of cultural producers/formation, cultural institutions and level of development of means of cultural production; major formal *innovations* have a further set of determinants	Breaks to naturalist drama and subjective expressionism in television; Soliloquy

[a] Williams (1978g). Cf. discussion in Chapter 7.

more and more external-social and *internal-cultural-formal* determinants. In effect, Williams has added what he sees as further necessary levels of mediation. Only with the confusingly named 'form' do we reach a 'sub-epochal' arena of formal change.

With concrete formal analysis, however, Williams is otherwise quite close to Goldmann (at his best). As we saw in Section 3.2, Goldmann's analysis of Racine's tragedies in *The Hidden God*, for example, did not attempt to establish an homology between world views and the 'content' of artworks understood as anything as crude as expressed politico-social statements. More specifically, the formal component of his analysis sought homologous relations between certain events, and changes in Racine's usage of formal 'devices' from play to play, culminating in the role of two Aristotelian features

of tragedy, 'peripeteia' (unexpected reve Racine's *Phèdre*.[112] As we saw in Section forms placed a similar emphasis on form *conventions*.

As can also be seen in Table 4.1, Will the Vološinovian conception of signal (level, as 'highly developed and complex effect, the formalist conception of dev while at all others it is replaced by soci tions (understood at their formation as this that marks Williams's social form opposed to Genette's structuralist delin phenomenon. Indeed, Williams's typolo makes it evident that the 'external sig (non-linguistic) means of cultural produ Williams can 'modernize' genre theory's set of practices.

Williams's emphasis on the social prod much with Goldmann's genetic structura in the 1978 assessment:

> This position is then distinguished from on the presence of such *subjects* (the f social embodiment); by a consequent forms, in the actual relations and str them; and by a final emphasis on histe forms – their formation, maintenance a of the changing totality of social life. (

The 'genesis', crucially, is not simply a ma on a separate and discrete cultural form. formal innovation at key historical mome 'way of seeing' changed social relations.

There is no question that the paradig which, as he makes it perfectly plain, is pa interest but also, fortuitously, one of the b trans-epochal endurance of a (modal) cul forms in *The Sociology of Culture* is devotec of dramatic forms that Williams had pr lications.[114] Two case studies he provides useful here.

The first is a case study of the solilo gence and acceptance by audiences of the

would reflect conclusion:

These new opments i discovery, perception thought. I analysed, much wide the autonc tensions b role, evide in analytic then in cle

But it is nc first the sc order of ev true and ir technical forms of English Re but not as a new and

We can th previously analysis is completec analyses r them only other eler general so even looke for a socic *of forms.* (

The referenc would place c When he re Williams cas columns: on 'general soci between ind roles' (*SOC*, p. 145). Such correspondences are found, but Williams insists this is an insufficient means of abstract recognition of the sociality *embedded in* the form that he argues for in the above. The case he has chosen is one of dynamic change. It is precisely such innovative experimentation with different combinations of univocality and multivocality that demonstrates the socially exploratory character of these conventions. Williams quickly makes another homological correlation at this level too, but his point at this stage of his exposition is that not all such correlations can be as neat as formalist or sociological reductivists might have it.[116]

In his second case study Williams spends considerable time filling out the mutations of 'bourgeois drama' (Table 4.1, row 3) in discussing his favourite case, the crisis of naturalism. This account too is socially formal-comparative, and traces mutations in that form in the *formational* context of the crisis of the 'fractions' who produced 'late high naturalism' (the classic example being Ibsen's *The Wild Duck*).[117] Williams insists that the development of the famous theatrical convention of the three-walled room should not be seen as merely another 'device'. Rather, the naturalists could be seen to have dramatized the recognition, by an enlightened fraction of their class, of a fundamental contradiction of bourgeois existence – that the private world of the bourgeois living room was entirely dependent on a set of social relations outside it. Yet the form nonetheless prevented direct dramatization of this external world despite the socially expansive impetus of naturalism.

These two examples fill out what Hall might call the decoding and encoding moments respectively of Williams's social formalist conception of cultural forms. To take the second case first, we have an example of Williams's formational analysis. Here, however *the formal innovation* – not the structuring limits of overt 'content', as implied in the petty bourgeois case of *The Brumaire* 'solution' – is seen to be in a homologous relationship with a fractional class perspective. The homology is still one set by contradictory limits, *pace* (revised) Goldmann and *Brumaire*. With the formal properties of the cultural form recognized, this mode of analysis escapes the usual formalist critiques of Marxian 'sociological reductivism'. Moreover, this case also demonstrates that the correspondence concerning bourgeois drama in Table 4.1 is only a preliminary indication, an '1859 Preface'-style summary, subject to the minutiae of a *Brumaire*-like concrete analysis.

The first example demonstrates the manner in which Williams, at least in historical cases of literature, regards an 'accepted' formal innovation like the soliloquy (or indeed naturalism's three-walled room) as a 'common property . . . of writers and audiences or readers, before any communicative composition can occur' (*M&L*, pp. 187–8). Although in principle this 'property' is as historically specifiable as his formational analyses, Williams tends to be more presumptuously formalist about the formal embeddedness of receptivity than about the 'intentions' of authors and other cultural producers.

As Andrew Milner has recently observed, where many poststructuralists have sought to 'narrativize history', so rejecting a sociology of genres, Williams's typology of cultural forms and its attendant analytic practice is clearly designed to historicize 'literature'.[118] Indeed, we might add, it is not insignificant that Genette's discussion of the mode/genre distinction is a prime point of critical departure for one of the 'classics' of poststructuralism, Derrida's 'Law of Genre'.[119]

However, Williams's typology implies the historicization of more than literature. In *The Sociology of Culture* Table 4.1's typology is presented within a broader discussion of cultural reproduction. Similarly, Williams's social formalism did not disqualify *The Long Revolution*'s historicist method examined in Section 1.2. His heuristic characterization of that method was after all, 'historical criticism', but plainly included more than overtly literary cultural forms.

So the problematic culture/not-culture distinction resurfaces. It shall be addressed in the next chapter together with other implications of Williams's social formalism for his sociology of culture.

5
Towards a Sociology of Culture

5.1 Williams's (re)mapping of the sociological field

The Sociology of Culture was published in 1981, exactly twenty years after *The Long Revolution*. It provides a revisitation of most of the themes of that earlier book. This revisitation is conducted from the vantage point of Williams's theoretical reworkings undertaken in the interim. Missing from this revisitation, however, is the explicitly normative dimension of *The Long Revolution*. That was to be provided two years later, in *Towards 2000*, and was to continue in the planned work, *The Politics of Modernism: against the new conformists*.

Together, those works and some related late publications constitute a culmination of Williams's methodological and political reflections of the previous two decades. This chapter and the next outline this position largely as it was presented in *The Sociology of Culture*. However, even by Williams's own standards, this book is notoriously eccentric in its forms of self-presentation. This may be one reason why it has largely eluded scholarly discussion since its publication.[1] Williams brings together here the fruits of his reflections on both the production paradigm and the social formalism he developed for the analysis of cultural forms. The production paradigm is largely taken as a given but, as we began to see in Chapter 4, Williams spends a considerable section of *The Sociology of Culture* advocating his social formalism.

As we also saw, Williams's advocacy of a social formalism featured in his 1977 critique of work from the Birmingham CCCS. Indeed, one common strand in these late writings is Williams's repositioning of his relationship with the cultural studies project. It is not that Williams 'abandons' cultural studies for sociology. Rather, he sharply corrects certain tendencies in cultural studies that constitute illegitimate *projections* of social theory, broadly corresponding to formalism (among others). Yet he also challenges sociology with his reflections on the implications of a body of work – including developments within cultural studies – that no longer marginalizes 'communications, media and arts' as he believed orthodox sociology had done (*SOC*, pp. 9–10). Further, as we shall see, he argues that *both* fields should heed the lessons of 'social formalism'.

Like Stuart Hall, Williams assumes that contemporary sociological orthodoxy is dominated by the conservative and somewhat moribund legacy
of (Parsonian) functionalism.[2] However, unlike Hall, Williams consistently
acknowledges the strengths of sociology and does not reduce sociology to
that functionalist legacy.[3] Nonetheless, his '(re)mapping' of the sociological
field is somewhat unusual. Figure 5.1 is designed to aid comprehension
of this (re)mapping. Williams provides a number of mutually compatible
variants of this mapping process: one in *Television* (1974), two in articles
first published in 1974 and 1976, one in *Marxism and Literature*, and, finally,
the opening chapter of *The Sociology of Culture* itself.[4] The last is the most
elaborated in its historical account and so forms the basis of Figure 5.1.

The Sociology of Culture's account resembles *The Long Revolution*'s delibera-
tions on the relation between the meanings of 'culture' and related methods
(Table 1.1). Here, however, the previously advocated 'reconciliations' of the
different meanings are taken as an historical given, that is, Williams asserts
that there have been many 'convergences' between different meanings of
culture. He traces these to two distinct variants of the notion of 'whole way
of life', each of which 'implies a broad method'. These are contrasted with
'a new kind of convergence' (Table 5.1).

Table 5.1   The 'convergences' in meanings of culture presented in *The Sociology of Culture*

Convergences of 'culture'	Manifestation	Implied method
(a) 'Informing spirit of a whole way of life'	A specifiable culture, in styles of art and kinds of intellectual work, is seen as the direct or indirect product of an order primarily constituted by other social activities	Illustration and clarification of 'informing spirit'
(b) Whole social order	Styles of art and kinds of intellectual work seen as direct or indirect product of an order constituted by other social activities	Explorations from the character of a social order to the specific forms taken by its cultural manifestations
(c) The contemporary convergence: signifying system;[a] convergence between 'whole way of life' sense and a broadened 'aesthetic' sense	Constitutive 'system through which a social order is communicated, reproduced, experienced and explored'	Dominated by theoretical work and studies of ideology. But 'signifying system' seen as involved in all forms of social activity and conception of 'artistic and intellectual activities' broadened to include 'popular culture'

[a] See Section 5.2 for further elaboration of this row.

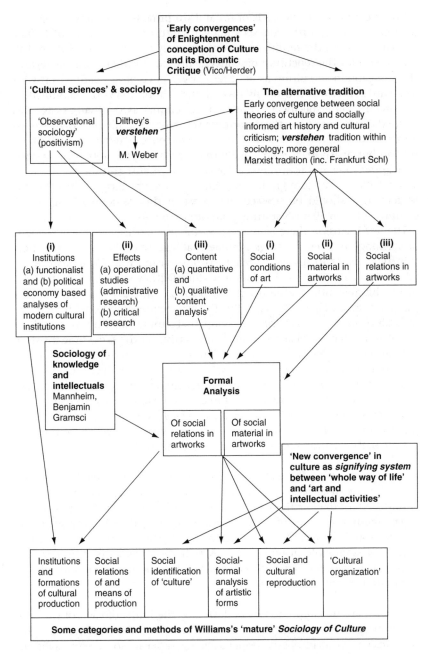

Figure 5.1   Williams's (re)mapping of the sociological field.

The meanings and methods of (a) and (b) provide, Williams argues, the parameters of the orthodox sociology of culture. *The Sociology of Culture* is 'written within the terms of the contemporary convergence' (*SOC*, p. 13). The reason for the repetition of 'convergence' here is that Williams regards this conception of culture as another convergence of a redefined (a) with (b). This is a clear echo of his own strategy from 1958–61 (examined in Chapter 1). More specifically, the model of culture as signifying system, as defined above, supplants the 'informing spirit' of (a). Williams's own elaboration of the implications of this new convergence is detailed in the next section but, in short, it seems likely that he was deliberately seeking both to acknowledge and to influence the rise of formalist cultural theory with a conception of culture grounded primarily in his reading of Mukařovský. Moreover, it should be stressed that most of the elements of Figure 5.1 comprise only Williams's starting point for discussion.

The key inclusion there is 'modern sociology'. But the acknowledgement of sociology in these writings is somewhat selective, since the 'tendency' Williams wishes to discuss at length is positivism or, as Williams calls it, 'observational sociology'. He does introduce Dilthey's *verstehen* as the basis of the hermeneutic tradition within sociology and the 'cultural sciences (*Geisteswissenschaften*)': 'Specifically, Dilthey defined method through the difficult concept of "*verstehen*" – a "sympathetic understanding" or "intuitive grasp" of human social and cultural forms – while at the same time insisting that all such studies must be historical' (*SOC*, p. 15). Interestingly, Williams does not make the obvious connection between *verstehen* and his own historicist programme for a structure of feeling in *The Long Revolution*. But then he sets *verstehen* aside as an influence on Max Weber and thus 'one tendency in modern sociology' (*SOC*, p. 15). Before discussing positivism (the traditional opponent of hermeneutic sociology), however, he provides a comparative methodological assessment of the two:

> There were strengths and weaknesses in each of these tendencies. The method of "*verstehen*" could be quite insufficiently explanatory, or could fall back for explanation on a (theoretically circular) "informing spirit". The method of objective observation, while accumulating indispensable empirical data, was often insufficiently conscious of the nature of some of the less tangible cultural processes, of these as elements of history and, crucially, of the effects on observation of the specific social and cultural situation of the observer. (*SOC*, p. 16)

In effect these two approaches are flawed by the limits of each of the earlier 'convergences', *verstehen* by idealism and positivism by reductivism. Yet Williams's interest in observational sociology appears to be more substantive than methodological. He wishes to prioritize studies of modern culture that expand the sociology of culture beyond its traditional institutional foci of religion and education. Accordingly, his account of observational sociology's contribution is dominated by the role of the US functionalist tradition in sociology of the media, as manifested in the subcategories contained in boxes (i) institutions, (ii) effects and (iii) content on the left of Figure 5.1.

Williams had already provided a surprisingly explicit critique of such functionalism in 1974 – in *Television* – that relied on the hermeneutic tradition within sociology:

> Cultural science, when it emerged as a method in early classical socio-logy, was concerned with the necessary differentiation of its proced-ures from those of natural science. In its central concept of "understanding", and in its sensitivity to the problems of judgement and value and of the participation and involvement of the investigator, it was radically different from the assumptions and methods of the "sociology of mass communications" which is now orthodox and which at times even claims the authority of just this classical sociology. (*TV1*, pp. 119–20)

Williams points to the legacy of Harold Lasswell's famous methodological question, 'who says what, how, to whom with what effect' and comments: 'what this question has excluded is *intention*, and therefore all real social and cultural process' (*TV1*, p. 120).[5] *Television* was published only a year after the 'Base and Superstructure' essay, so it is not surprising to see the appeal to 'intention' here as well.[6] But this time the risk of voluntarist subjectivism is apparently negligible, for Williams immediately elaborates its meaning in his account of the reasons for Lasswell's 'exclusion' of the question, 'with what purpose':

> the exclusion is not accidental. It is part of a general social model which abstracts social and cultural processes to such concepts as "socialization", "social function" or "interaction" ... [These] abstract notions ... have the effect of conferring normality on and in this sense legitimacy on any society in which a learning and relating process may occur. And when this is so, intention, in any full sense, cannot be recognised, let alone studied. To say that television is now a factor in socialisation, or that its controllers and communicators are exercising a particular social function, is to say very little until the forms of the society which determine any particular socialisation and which allocate the functions of control and communication have been precisely specified.
>
> *The central concepts of cultural science – understanding, value-judgement, the involvement of the investigator – have thus been excluded or circumvented.* (*TV1*, pp. 120–1; emphasis added)

In *The Sociology of Culture* Williams refers to an alternative tradition. This is largely composed of those authors discussed in Chapters 3 and 4, who have contributed to his social formalism. Moreover: '[t]he study of cultural forms and works continued, by an obvious affinity, to be practised by exponents of *verstehen*' (*SOC*, p. 16). Williams so effectively associates *verstehen* exclusively with the analysis of 'cultural forms and works'. One effect of this confinement is to sideline completely the main historical opponent of functionalism within US Sociology, the Chicago School. This is especially curious as that School produced a body of fieldwork-based sociology loyal to the principles of *verstehen* and of direct relevance to Williams's concerns.[7] Yet the discussion of functionalism in *Television* confirms that he was aware of at least the possibility of such hermeneutically informed empirical research.

Williams likewise recognizes the validity of reflective, theoretically informed quantitative empirical research. Crucially, he does not dismiss quantitative empirical research as necessarily tainted by an empiricist theory of knowledge, as has occurred within cultural studies and elsewhere.[8] His own early work on the media and intellectual formations had been dominated by the careful deployment of such techniques (often undertaken by Joy Williams). In *The Sociology of Culture* he explicitly cites such work and similarly endorses the emergent political economy of the media.[9]

In *Television* Williams provides an even more explicit critique of naïve methodological empiricism as part of his critique of the undeclared normative assumptions of functionalism:

> A particular version of empiricism – not the general reliance on experience and evidence, but a particular reliance on evidence within the terms of these assumed functions (socialisation, social function, mass communications) – has largely taken over the practice of social and cultural inquiry, and within the terms of its distortion of cultural science claims the abstract authority of "social science" and "scientific method" as against all other modes of experience and analysis. Against this confident and institutionalised practice it cannot be said too often that the work of social and cultural science is only secondarily a matter of methodological procedures; it is primarily the establishment of a consciousness of process, which will include consciousness of intentions as well as methods and working concepts. (*TV1*, p. 121)

'Intention', once again, is effectively equated with a self-reflective normative orientation with at least a hint of the future role of formations in Williams's practice. Yet undoubtedly the larger goal of the historical reconstruction of methodological debates in sociology in *The Sociology of Culture* is to draw from Williams's alternative quasi-hermeneutic tradition a linkage with formal analysis and so a 'new' sociology of culture. As can be seen in

Figure 5.1, the common ground of formal analysis also allows Williams to draw in the 'new convergence' (culture as a signifying system).

His assessment of the formalist methods that sustain this convergence is, as we saw in Chapter 4, very stringent. As we shall see in the next chapter, McLuhan's formalism was subjected to one of his sharpest polemics in *Television*.

Conspicuous by its absence from this initial mapping in *The Sociology of Culture*, however, is any reflection on the production paradigm.[10] Yet if one looks at the other categories of Williams's sociology of culture (at the bottom of Figure 5.1), that paradigm is pervasive. Moreover, as with his early work, Williams practises an undeclared method here. This time it is *typologization*. Williams's introduction and setting aside of Max Weber – and so the loss of a potential discussion of his 'ideal types' – is thus regrettable. For typologization is the prime mode of exposition Williams provides for the entire mature project. Categories informed by the production paradigm meet social formalist categories, which in turn provide accounts of the historically existent, currently existent, and even not yet existent but possible, forms of cultural practice. The demonstration of the existence of such variability is one of Williams's chief means of challenging the unilinearity of more reductivist modes of analysis. To use language closer to Williams's own, he insists on opening any analysis to historical variability. He thus seeks to avoid the methodological danger of inserting 'philosophical' categories which prevent the formation of appropriate sociological ones (*SOC*, p. 183). But there is a further danger for him that:

the very concepts which need to be constructed by historical and sociological analysis are assumed, often in received forms, either as the necessary grounds of theoretical proof or at best as the framework for any investigation which has intentions beyond the most scattered empiricism. The difficulty then is that all analytic construction has to begin from some...concepts, and yet they can so easily come to direct all stages of the inquiry, or, as has happened recently, in general cultural theory, to absorb research into their own forms. (*SOC*, p. 183)

Accordingly, the first step for Williams is usually the unlocking of any sedimented set of meanings of the 'historical or sociological fact' that is under analysis. Here the historical semantics of the *Keywords* approach plays its role in demonstrating the contingency of the particular 'definition' in question, either by revealing competing contemporary meanings or by recovering 'lost' ones.

What is so produced is a *range* of meanings. It is by this means that Williams 'equalizes' the otherwise discrete 'theoretical objects' of analysis posited by positivist and non-positivist methods. That is, he tends to develop a range of 'practices' that in turn *require* typologization as a precondition of any concrete analysis. These may be entirely derived by social-formal means, or conceptually or hermeneutically or, more rarely, by way of (theoretically informed) statistical calculation. In short, this is a further critically reflective 'control' Williams places on all his sociological research. But let us look more closely at this 'new convergence'.

5.2 'Culture': the final settlement?

Williams sees the new convergence of 'culture', outlined in Table 5.1, as one between a quasi-sociological 'whole way of life' sense, and another sense based in a semiotic-formalist expansion of signifying practice beyond 'the arts'. This is consistent with his hostility to the formal-textualist reduction of 'practices to forms'. Williams elaborates this position towards the end of *The Sociology of Culture* in this reworked conception of culture:

> Thus the distinction of culture, in the broadest or in the narrowest senses, as a realized signifying system, is meant not only to make room for study of manifestly signifying institutions, practices and works, but by this emphasis to activate study of the relations between these and other institutions, practices and work[s]. The key to these relations turns twice. It activates these relations by insisting that signifying practice is deeply present in all those other activities, while preserving the distinction that in those others quite different human needs and actions are substantially and irreducibly present: the necessary signification, as it were, more or less completely dissolved into other needs and actions. It then activates the relations in an opposite direction, by insisting that those other needs and actions are deeply present in all manifest signifying activities, while preserving the distinction that in these practices those other needs and actions are, in their turn, more or less completely dissolved. The metaphor of solution is crucial to this way of looking at culture, and the qualification "more or less" is not a casual phrase but a way of indicating a true range, in which relatively complete and relatively incomplete degrees of solution, either way, can be practically defined. (*SOC*, pp. 208–9)

This conception is explicitly offered by Williams as an alternative to 'whole way of life' as it facilitates more easily a linkage with 'significant relational terms beyond it'. 'Whole way of life', he believes, is constrained by its anthropological association with less complex societies in which a culture versus nature heuristic opposition is more plausible than it is in more complex societies, where 'there are so many levels of social and material transformation that the polarized "culture–nature" relation becomes insufficient' (*SOC*, p. 210). These levels of transformation include those covered by the 'relative degrees of solution' thesis in the above but also imply a role for the Marxian conception of production.

Accordingly, Williams provides examples of liminal cases – money, dwellings and modern communications – where either signifying or 'other' relations are dominant. Crucially, these examples are intended to refer respectively to other 'social systems': economic, kinship and political. Williams's elaboration of this position is open to a charge of ambiguity. In one of the few published commentaries on this thesis, Catherine Gallagher has argued that Williams is confused.[11] Her chief evidence for this accusation lies in the first example Williams provides of a modern 'complex transformation', money. Williams suggests that although coinage can be studied as a specific sign-system and even 'analyzed aesthetically', there is no doubt that 'the needs and actions of trade and payment are dominant' in its systemic role as currency. But he goes further and states, ambiguously, that 'the signifying factor, though intrinsic, is in this sense dissolved' (*SOC*, p. 210).[12] For Gallagher this amounts to an admission of ignorance that money's economic role is, precisely, to signify value. Rather, Williams explicitly notes this point. There is no doubt that Williams's opening choice is eccentric and questionably formulated, but it is not confused. His most likely intended meaning of 'in this sense dissolved' is that the economic 'system' is dominant over the 'aesthetically' signifying (numismatic) in all active currencies. But this is more appropriately conceptualized as a difference in available uses, not one of action and need versus 'the signifying factor'. Had Williams been able to tie this example more completely to the production paradigm rather than to his Mukařovskýan 'dominant', then his case could have been made more easily. That is, rather than proposing a division between signifying and 'other needs and actions', he could have employed a distinction like Márkus's between social conventions of 'proper' and 'other' uses'.[13]

Moreover, Gallagher misses completely Williams's emphasis on social 'systems' rather than 'objects'.[14] That is, he so attempts to distinguish 'manifestly signifying' and social 'systems' which may or may not be mutually embedded. Admittedly, these social 'systems' are very loosely formulated. They are lifted almost directly from the similar categories Williams proffered in *The Long Revolution* – that is, systems of decision, maintenance, learning and generation – and which he had conceded in *Politics and Letters* were in need of revision.[15] His failing in this section of *The Sociology of Culture* is his underdeveloped account of social theory, and not the ontological confusion Gallagher implies.

And yet, as we have seen, by 1974 Williams was quite capable of articulating a complex social theoretical argument in his well-informed critique of (Parsonian) functionalism in *Television*. Likewise, he was quite clear in *Politics and Letters* about the social theoretical gains he felt he had made already, within and since *The Long Revolution* formulations. The *NLR* interviewers had taken him to task for the way in which his historicist emphasis on the reconstruction of 'experience' tended to be used as a justification for avoiding questions of structural determination, most obviously of the 'classical Marxist' kind. Williams concedes the central criticism regarding the illegitimately epistemological role granted to the category of 'experience' in some formulations in *The Long Revolution*. He stresses that part of his rationale for *The Long Revolution*'s 'systems' was that he did not want to confine his analysis historically to the capitalist mode of production, nor to contemporary capitalist societies. However, his most pertinent response is the following:

> Paradoxically, I think that in those earlier books I myself tended to counterpose the notion of cultural process, which seemed to me to be so extraordinarily overlooked, to what I took to be a previously emphasized and adequately expounded economic or political process. The result was that I in turn abstracted my area of emphasis from the whole historical process. In the effort of establishing that cultural production was a primary activity, I think at times I gave the impression – especially given the ambiguity of my use of 'experience' – that I was denying determinations altogether, although the empirical studies scarcely suggest that. It took a long time to find the key move to the notion of cultural production as itself material, which was implicit in a lot of my empirical work but it would have been better understood if it had been made explicit. But because once cultural production is seen as itself social and material, then this indissolubility of the whole social process has a different theoretical ground. It is no longer based on experience, but on *the common character of the respective processes of production*. (*P&L*, p. 139; emphasis added)

As we have seen already in Section 4.3, however, this commonality is by no means uniform. For part of its development relies on the rejection of an objectivation model of culture for a processual one of practice. Williams's apparent ontological ambiguities here are in part a result of his insistence on his use of the notational model in his speech/writing distinction and in his conception of artistic practice. The 'degrees of solution' model is partly necessitated by a theoretical need for some means of *identifying* culture when most normative criteria for doing so have been marginalized.

Yet within its own terms, the degrees of solution model plainly 'works'. It is entirely consistent with Williams's method of typologization. The passage above rightly points towards the ways in which Williams would 'activate' it within his sociology of culture, by seeking the common character of the respective processes of production – *in combination with* the degree of signifying practice – within the range of categories presented in Figure 5.1.[16] These 'cultural production typologies' are elaborated in the next chapter.

In *Politics and Letters*, Williams makes another self-criticism in response to the same question concerning *The Long Revolution*:

> However, at the time my effort to reinstate what had been the radically neglected area of cultural practice was taken by others, both in support (which I did not want) and in opposition (which was very easy), as a

claim for its primacy over the other processes. Then, of course, the organization of [*The Long Revolution*] could be seen in that light, since it contained a prolonged history of various cultural institutions but no account
of the other kinds of practice which created very different institutions,
which were inseparable from them. In other words, my work was subject
to some of the same criticisms, that it was an approach from a sectoral
definition, that I had made of others. (*P&L*, p. 139)

This is clearly a continuation of Williams's response to Eagleton's and Hall's
critiques of *The Long Revolution* discussed in previous chapters, especially
Hall's charge of culturalism. It is also consistent with one of the aims of this
book: to tease out others of Williams's undeclared or insufficiently explicit
methodological assumptions. Yet this passage also suggests much about the
approach Williams may have taken in writing *The Sociology of Culture*. It too
is vulnerable to such a criticism of 'sectoralism'. It is as if this book and
Towards 2000 are 'torn halves' of an updating of *The Long Revolution*.
Towards 2000 is theoretically 'loose' as it is plainly aimed at a broad lay
audience as it ranges across the full diversity of Williams's political interests
and normative concerns. He resumes there some of the highly personalized
forms of presentation of his normative vision. In contrast, *The Sociology of
Culture* not only attempts an extremely tight theoretical closure within its
ostensible topic – in contrast with the arguably even more difficult *Marxism
and Literature* – *it also lacks normative declarations almost entirely*. The result is
an unintended 'instrumentalization' of Williams's sociology of culture, very
likely due to his concern to limit his former 'experiential' excesses. It is this
set of publication circumstances, I would suggest, that underpins his resort
to the 'degrees of solution of signifying practice' as a means of delimiting
his 'object' of analysis without any immediate normative reference.

Another of Williams's undeclared conceptual apparatuses is especially
worthy of note in this context, as it addresses both this 'normative deficit' –
and consequently the 'degrees of solution' thesis – and the problem Márkus
raised concerning the risk of appeals to 'fundamental' cultural forms.[17]

This under-elaborated concept is *disembedding*. It has already arisen in
a number of the exegeses in Chapter 4; for example I suggested its use in
Section 4.2 as a means of clarifying some underelaborated dimensions of
Williams's account of language. Williams uses it himself in introducing his
typology of cultural forms:

We have to recognize that there can be no absolute separation between
those social relationships which are evident or discoverable as the immediate conditions of a practice – the signalled places, occasions and terms
of specifically indicated types of cultural activity – and those which are
so embedded within the practice, as particular formal articulations, *that they
are at once social and formal*, and can in one kind of analysis be treated as
relatively autonomous. (*SOC*, p. 148; emphasis added)

We saw in Section 3.4 that Williams viewed the 'conditions of a practice' – a phrase first employed in the final section of 'Base and Superstructure' – as the most revealing indication of the social role of cultural forms and means of cultural production. A central task of his 'post-criticism' critique of literature became the elucidation of those embedded conditions which were, in that instance, unstated literary conventions. In *The Sociology of Culture* Williams develops this thesis into a component of a kind of philosophy of history of cultural forms. Significantly, this comment sets up the discussion of the emergence of acted dialogue in Greek tragedy, which in turn stimulates the comment – effectively his preliminary definition of 'mode' – upon which Márkus seized:

> This is an outstanding case of a highly conditioned specific form, of a deep kind, which became, as it were, a quite general cultural property, in the end belonging more to the sociology of our species, at a certain level of cultural development, than to the specific sociology of a given society at a certain place and time. (*SOC*, p. 150)

As noted in Section 2.5, Williams immediately qualifies this comment. Its relevance here is that it is the disembedding of the mode of acted dialogue from Greek tragedy that permits the 'species' speculation. The more substantial theoretical point is that it is the *deritualization of the embedded form that permits the emergence of the cultural mode as a cultural productive force*.[18]

Indeed, drama demonstrated for Williams not only a clear case of 'transformation' within modernity, but one which legitimates the prominence he attaches to signifying practices. His inaugural professorial lecture, 'Drama in a Dramatized Society', includes this stark statement concerning the fate of fragments of myth within modernity:

> Drama is a precise separation of certain common modes for new and specific ends. It is neither ritual which discloses the God, nor myth which requires and sustains repetition. It is specific, active, interactive composition: an action not an act; an open practice that has been deliberately abstracted from temporary practical or magical ends: a complex opening of ritual to public and variable action; a moving beyond myth to dramatic *versions* of myth and of history.... the basic social processes of presentation, representation, signification, have never been more important. Drama broke from the fixed signs, established its permanent distance from myth and ritual and from the hierarchical figures and processions of state; broke for precise historical and cultural reasons into a more complex, more active and more questioning world. (Williams, 1975, pp. 11–12)

Here Williams characterizes the freedom of the mode itself as it is enabled by its 'complete' disembedding from ritual and its development into a form of what the slightly later Williams would undoubtedly have called cultural production. But plainly Williams also sketches here the 'modern' importance of practices of signification that he emphasized in *The Sociology of Culture*. 'Embedded' also characterizes the 'anthropological' limits he placed on 'whole way of life' and the necessity of 'degrees of solution of signifying practice' in his modern 'transformations'. Indeed the degree of solution might be thought of as the degree of disembedding, or indeed of re-embedding.

But this linkage of demythologization and disembedding also returns us to the relevance of the comparison in Chapter 4 between Williams and Genette. Genette, as we saw, acknowledged the hermeneutic limit Ricoeur placed on the structuralist projection of totemic myth onto modern societies. Like Williams he found in genre analysis a more appropriate recognition of this 'anthropological' legacy. Both Williams and Genette recognize that modes are enduring 'fundamental genres'. Both are critical of an excessively synchronistic model of 'system'. Both also recognize that modes are dependent on available means of cultural production.[19] Williams even recognizes the 'cinematic' as a new mode.

Here is the key to Williams's view cited above that the 'indissolubility of the whole social process' lies in 'the common character of the respective processes of production' and here also lies the means of clarification of his ambiguous appeals to 'social systems'. As Williams elaborated this position in *The Sociology of Culture*, that common character also came to include *re*production, consistent with the redefinition of culture as a realized signifying system. A model of *multiple and potentially contradictory processes of reproduction* is Williams's sociological alternative to the excesses of formalism and synchronic structuralism and, in effect, the means of articulating his 'sectoralism' with existent social theory. As we have seen, he exposed the failings of what he called elsewhere the *projection* of formalist devices and systems as social processes, and likewise the comparable 'anti-sociological' *reduction* of practices to (formalist) forms and, especially, texts.

Indeed, it seems likely that such formulations were designed to offer a tactical 'correction' to the formalistic excesses within cultural studies while simultaneously challenging the limitations of the very term – 'whole way of life' – by which his own project had been misrepresented. If this version of 'the convergence' were accepted, it would be harder to ignore the social institutions Williams plainly believed had been too readily underplayed in the Birmingham research.

However, despite the inclusiveness of Williams's embrace of 'signifying practice', it is not entirely clear how Williams would analyse cultural phenomena that do not have any ready 'aesthetic' parallel. As we shall see in the next chapter, popular television programme conventions are relatively easily rendered compatible with Williams's typology of cultural forms. Yet Williams is silent on the issue of what alternative his sociology of culture might offer to the rejected, 'alienated' Birmingham 'unmasking' textualism of the code-based analysis of 'way of life' signifying practices of youth subcultures. The embedded/disembedded and practice/form distinctions

Table 5.2   Historical semantics of 'reproduction'

Sense of 'reproduction'	Elaboration
(a) (Technical) replication	Uniform 'mechanical' reproduction of precise copies
(b) Cultural replication	Formulaic product of the culture industries employing technical replication
(c) Formal production	Production of cultural objectivation made possible by the embedded conventions of a reproducible cultural form. Formal reproduction 'outweighs' specific content (*SOC*, p. 198)
(d) Formal 're-production'	Reverse of (c) in that innovations aid changes to the defining conventions of the form itself

would undoubtedly be an applicable starting point but Williams implies no more here.[20]

Williams generates his own multiple reproductive model via his historical semantics (Table 5.2). I have grouped elements of it within Table 5.3 alongside examples of the kinds of projection he rejected by way of contrast. I would contend that his contrast demonstrates Williams's more careful attention to social-theoretical protocols and thus avoids an immanent application of the charge of 'projection' against his alternative. Williams's key concern is to separate mechanico-technical 'replication' from his social-formal sense of reproduction that accommodates contradiction and innovation.

While Table 5.2 is largely self-explanatory, it begs the question of the role of means of communication and technical reproduction in Williams's sociology of culture. These are dealt with at length in the next chapter along with the relation between these 'sectoral' senses of reproduction and the conception of 'social reproduction' sketched in Table 5.3.

It is worth noting as a final point that Williams's better known 'social shaping' alternative to technological determinism can thus be seen to move in tandem with the social formalism of 'the new convergence'. That is, there is a strong resemblance between the failings of 'cultural' formalism – especially its fetishism of 'devices' – and technological determinism.[21] Williams closed his 1976 'Developments in the Sociology of Culture' by chiding sociology for not developing a 'sociology of systems of signs' and so providing 'the reason for the success of cultural structuralism'. He then painted this image of his sociology of culture, the first sentence of which prefigures his social formalist conception of 'mode':

A genuine sociology of systems of signs would be necessarily concerned, in historical and materialist ways, with the specific technologies which are now their dominant forms, but with these technologies as *systems of signs* and not at an abstracted technical level. Moreover, since at this level the technologies are necessarily seen as new and advanced forms of social organization, there is a basis for reworking not only the analysis of

Table 5.3 Transpositions and projections from 'the language paradigm' compared with Williams's schemas[a]

(Structural-) linguistic unit of analysis forming 'template' for transposition	Structuralist/formalist transposition	Social theoretical 'projection' from transposition
Sentence	Structuralist analysis of narrative (e.g. Propp)	(Poststructuralist) 'narrativization of history'
Phoneme (as unit of differentiation) (Jakobson)	Binary oppositions of 'mythemes' (as basis of analysis of totemic myths) (Lévi-Strauss)	Rendering of all 'discourse' as *bricolage* (Derrida)[b]
{Dominant 'medium' {(McLuhan)	Sense-ratio (hot/cool) (McLuhan)	Tribal/retribalized society} (McLuhan) (Table 6.7)}[c]
Williams's social formalism:		*Williams's sociology of culture*:
Embedded practical consciousness; Vološinovian signal	Disembedded and embedded cultural forms: mode/genre/type/form (Table 4.1)	Contradictory reproductive dynamics of:
		(i) Culture as realized signifying system(s) (including cultural forms)
		(ii) Technically replicative systems (general and cultural forces of production) and
		(iii) Reproduction of social order (hegemony)

[a] I have borrowed 'transposition' from Ricoeur (1974, p. 34).
[b] Derrida (1978, p. 285).
[c] The case of Mcluhan is presented in the next chapter, and in more detail in Jones (1998).

content (which is always a content of relationships) but also the analysis of institutions and formations (which are never independent of, though they are equally not controlled by, the technologies around which they now characteristically form.) It has taken a long time, and in adequate demonstration will still take a long time, to get through to this position, from which, developing several kinds of existing work but in a new theoretical perspective, a sociology of culture which will be a sociology of culture of advanced industrial societies can be foreseen and proposed. (1976b, pp. 505–6)

The typologies presented and discussed in Chapter 6 remain loyal to this vision.

6
Cultural Production and Means of Communication

This chapter contains more overtly exegetical material than the others. The first sections present the typologies based in Williams's production paradigm, employing *The Sociology of Culture* as the major point of reference. With the exception of the special place granted to means of communication, these follow fairly directly from the characterization of the paradigm and the mediating role of 'formations' developed in Chapters 2 and 3.

As we saw at the end of Chapter 5, Williams attempts to articulate his cultural production typologies with 'general' social relations by means of the category of reproduction (Table 5.2) and a related conception of contradictory asymmetry. Also it is by this means that Williams's approach to 'the culture industry' can be distinguished from that of Adorno. It is important to point out here too that Williams's typology of cultural institutions below is designed to include 'the culture industries'. Likewise, buried in this section of *The Sociology of Culture* is the very substantial claim that the relevant typologies, and especially those of cultural forms (Table 4.1) and means of cultural production, provide *'effective distinctions which should always be included at a very early stage in any analysis'* (*SOC*, p. 193; emphasis added).

The case of means of communication – most notably television – also enables consideration of the implications of 'new media' for Williams's social formalist typology of cultural forms. As was argued in the previous chapter, the 'sectoralism' of *The Sociology of Culture* tends to displace Williams's democratic norms. The related but separate late writings on means of communication 'restore' this normative dimension and thus facilitate the fuller discussion of Williams's normative project in the final chapter.

Finally, the reader should be reminded of what Robbins calls the 'sublimely unhelpful' classifications Williams employs as subheadings in *The Sociology of Culture* (Robbins, 1995, p. xi).[1] Much of the previous four chapters have been framed in order to demystify most of these categories but the remarkably ambitious scope of Williams's endeavours here means that some tabularized elements of this exegesis will be left to speak for themselves (including by means of their listed examples).

6.1 The cultural production typologies

As with the general argument of *The Sociology of Culture*, the cultural production thesis is considerably expanded in its potential historical reach over means of cultural production, as Table 6.1 demonstrates. The historical turning point, according to Williams's account, is the development of an objectivated *system* of signification in writing, and the simultaneous creation of a social division in cultural production by the creation of literacy as a skill threshold (e).[2] This and the categories in (f) are discussed later in this chapter. As we saw in Section 4.2, Williams exploits the distinction between bodily inherent and separable/objectivated means of cultural production in his social formalist conception of language.

The category of 'cultural producer' is pivotal and its typologization is latently informed by one of Williams's central norms, social access to the means of 'direct autonomous composition'. Accordingly *The Sociology of Culture* pays detailed attention to the available types of institutional relationships involving 'cultural producers', including their 'formations' of self-organization. These are Williams's key categories for the examination of 'relations of cultural production'.

It is worth noting first, however, that this was hardly a new set of concerns for Williams. From as early as *Culture and Society* he had begun to develop a sociology of writers. Significantly, it was in his chapter on 'The Romantic Artist' where he first articulated his analysis of the limitations of Romanticism. The principal purpose of that chapter was to locate the determinants of the contradictory character of the social criticism of the (English) Romantics prior to its later 'oversimplification' as the mass civilization/minority culture dichotomy.

Table 6.1 'Human and non-human' means of cultural production

Human resource/Means of production	Example
(a) Inherent (bodily) resources	Use of body in dance, song, speech
(b) Combination of inherent and related separated objects	Masks, body paint and so on.
(c) Instruments of performance	Musical instruments
(d) Separable objects which carry cultural significance	Use of clay, metal, stone and pigment in sculpture and painting
(e) Separable material systems of signification	Writing
(f) Complex amplificatory, extending and reproductive technical systems[a]	Subjection of any of above to amplification, extension or reproduction by 'means of communication'

[a] This typology slightly differs from that Williams used in his related writings on means of communication (cf. Table 6.11).

These determinants, he found, include:

(a) the change in relationship between writers and their reading publics due to the decline of patronage and the rise of a middle class reading public and a 'literary market';
(b) the increasing commodification of artworks which aided the rise of the novel but had disastrous consequences for poetry;
(c) the consequent alienation by 'habitual attitude' of the Romantic artist from the public (this was to be reformulated as the view of the audience as mass);
(d) the related retreat of the Romantic artists into an idealized (dematerialized) conception of both their artworks and themselves as 'imaginative' writers.

Williams does not see (c) and (d) as merely functions of (a) and (b). He argues that while these do articulate at times a professionalist pique, they are equally part of a genuine social criticism of industrial capitalism. This restoration of the contradictory character of an ideology is, as we saw in Chapter 1, typical of the strategy of that book.

While a tension is established between a stratum of writers and a reading public in the *Culture and Society* analysis, Williams does not raise the issue of the Romantics' social class position or origin as a 'negative' determinant. However, this issue is addressed in *The Long Revolution* where he sketches a preliminary analysis of 'The Social History of English Writers'. The method employed there is made deliberately straightforward as an explicit invitation to further research by others. It is based on a comparison of entries in the *Oxford Introduction to English Literature* and the *Dictionary of Biography*. Of more significance, of course, are the categories Williams uses to formulate relevant data from these sources. They are: social origin, education and 'method of living'. In the course of the analysis he expands these to include gender and (Anglo-Saxon versus Celtic) ethnicity.

As an *historical* analysis, the assembled data is also periodized into then commonly used literary 'ages' of fifty-year spans. More significantly, the positioning of writers within these 'ages' is achieved with the sociological criterion of educable age (ten) rather than any proposed literary correlate. This method is familiar from *Culture and Society*'s table designating the year in which each of the authors discussed in the book reached the age of twenty five.[3]

Accordingly, the results of the preliminary study in *The Long Revolution* indicate a shift in the social composition of the writers deemed selectable by the *Oxford Introduction*. The distinct pattern in the social origin of writers is one of change and expansion from a narrow 'gentry culture' (1480–1530) to a remarkable diversity during the Romantic period (including the entry of women writers), and then a relatively rapid contraction to 'merchant and professional families' in the period 1870–1950.

The interpretation of this shift is cautious but its implications are hard to miss. In discussing the Romantics in this context Williams notes that those from 'the families of tradesmen, craftsmen, poor farmers and labourers' constitute a group that made an 'especially distinguished' contribution to 'new ways of thinking' (*LR*, p. 260). In contrast the subsequent contraction in social origin is used to assess the 'relatively uncreative' fate of 'the majority pattern, the normal English mode':

> it seems to me there is some evidence of a social and imaginative narrowing which can be related to the emergence of a more standard social history of the principal contributors. The emergence of certain new elements in mood and content in more recent years might then be factually related to the limited variations which seem to have occurred in this standard pattern. (*LR*, p. 265)

Innovation had instead come from what Eagleton later called the 'exiles and émigrés', writers who had emerged from 'outside' the majority pattern of English bourgeois origin, grammar school and Oxbridge (Eagleton, 1970). The dominance of Oxbridge as the key institutional presence in the lives of English writers is the one empirico-historical constant in *The Long Revolution* analysis. The contemporary dilemma was thus one where no institution existed to facilitate the rising group of writers from working-class backgrounds.

So we are returned to the norm that emerges more explicitly in the later writings: social access to the means of autonomous composition (and distribution). It is useful to present here, as Table 6.2, Williams's remarkable attempt in *The Sociology of Culture* to typologize even social relations of innovation.

These categories speak 'forward' to those about to be detailed, but they also speak to the contradictory dimensions of the multiple reproduction processes presented in Table 5.2.

We saw in Section 1.6 that, by 1974, Williams had linked his 'internationalized' redefinitions of high and popular culture more systematically to 'the professional structures of high culture'. Accordingly, the production paradigm is applied to artists and intellectuals in *The Sociology of Culture* in conjunction with a typologization of cultural institutions (Table 6.3).

It is important that this table's numerical sequence not be misunderstood as a linear-historical one. For example, in *Towards 2000* Williams makes it plain that patronal relations based in corporate sponsorship within a 'para-national' capitalism are massively outweighing the 'post-market' patronal forms of the British nation-state.[4] During the course of the presentation of this typology, Williams also provides a brief assessment of some contemporary arts (Table 6.4) that further exemplifies the use of the categories in Table 6.3.

Table 6.2 Social relations of innovation[a]

Situational type of social relation of innovation	Example	Incorporated (into dominant) or emergent?
(a) *Rise* of new social classes, or fractions of classes, which brings new kinds of producer and interest, and/or support new work	Rise of English bourgeois drama	Emergent-incorporated
(b) *Redefinition*, by an existing social class or fraction, of its conditions and relations, or of the general order within which these exist and are changing, so that new kinds of work are necessary	Bloomsbury's oppositional but prefigurative role	Emergent-incorporated
(c) *Changes* in the means of cultural production, which provide new formal possibilities; these may or may not be initially linked with (a) or (b)	Development of the 'cinematic' *mode*, interacting with older and enabling new cultural forms	Open
(d) *Recognition*, by specific cultural movements, of the situations in (a) and (b), at a level preceding or not directly joined to their articulate social organization	Differences between Shakespearean and 'Jacobean' tragedy Failures of contemporary theoretical avant-gardism	'Very difficult to demonstrate any manifest relations between such work and otherwise registered social developments since the effective working is more wholly absorbed into the form' (*SOC*, p. 203)

[a] *SOC*, p. 202.

6.2 Formations, avant-gardes, intellectuals, autonomy

Yet Williams recognizes that for 'more precise analysis' he must also typologize the *self*-organization of cultural producers as *formations*. We have met this category earlier on several occasions, but *The Sociology of Culture* provides the only attempt at systematic typologization. This, as we see in Table 6.5, proves more difficult.

The initial typologization of formations follows that of cultural institutions almost point by point. During his discussion of cultural institutions of the present, Williams goes so far as to assert that 'it could be said (but with

Table 6.3   Forms of relationship between cultural producers and socio-cultural institutions

Societal-institutional form	(Sub-) type of relationship	Chief characteristics
1. Instituted artists (socially embedded)	Nil	A *social stratum* that is part of central social organization rather than differentiated as 'artist' (e.g. Celtic bards)
2. Patronage	(i) Institution to patronage	Transitional role between institutionalized order and dependency on patronage
	(ii) Retainer and commission	Individual artists retained or commissioned by aristocratic households or the Church
	(iii) Protection and support	'Milder' form of social support not necessarily involving economic exchange relations (e.g. theatrical companies of Elizabethan England)
	(iv) Sponsorship/ commercial sponsorship	First form of patronage that takes market for artworks as given, so patronage primarily monetary where formerly more commonly hospitality or social introduction and so on; commercial sponsorship is survival of this form of patronage into present era of full market dominance, but some corporate sponsorship is of sub-type (ii) and others a more overt form of self-promotion
	(v) The public as 'patron'	Replacement of patron with taxation-sourced revenue; potential contradiction in that power relation in earlier forms of patronage difficult to reconcile with public accountability; considerable confusion about which historical form of patronage is being emulated.
3. Market	(i) Artisanal	Producer wholly dependent on immediate market but retains ownership of work until sale
	(ii) Post-artisanal	'Next phase' of commodity production with two stages: (a) distributive: work sold by artist to distributive intermediary who then usually becomes effective employer of artist
		(b) productive: intermediary productive and invests in work for purposes of profit[a] and here 'typically capitalist social relations begin to be instituted' (*SOC*, p. 45). For examples, see Table 6.4

Table 6.3   (Continued)

Societal-institutional form	(Sub-) type of relationship	Chief characteristics
	(iii) Market professional	Further development of productive post-artisanal relations, pioneered by publishing because means of replication develop there first. Copyright struggles ensure general ownership of artwork remains with authors. Hence rise of negotiated contract and royalty as 'newly typical relationship'. However, this draws authors more fully into the 'organized professional market'
	(iv) Corporate professional	Productive post-artisanal organization now a modern corporation with strong tendency to reduce the role of artist to salaried professional but still compatible with market professional relationship (as in book publishing). Increases tendency to produce for market. 'New' (post-book) media most strongly corporate and so have become dominant and typical in late twentieth century. In this context, advertising has arisen as a new form of cultural production
4. Post-market	(i) Modern patronal and intermediate	Modern patronal are non-governmental institutions of public patronage (e.g. foundations) of arts that cannot self-sustain within market relations (cf. Section 2.5). Intermediate institutions (like BBC) depend on public revenue but 'direct their own production'. Employment modes range from patronal to corporate
	(ii) Governmental	The cultural institution as 'department of state' in some capitalist societies and 'most post-capitalist societies'

[a] By 'productive' Williams here appears to mean the 'further intermediate labour' involving 'mass' reproduction of original artwork – see also 'market professional' phase.

the qualitative difference of an epochal change) that cultural institutions are now integral parts of the general social organization' (*SOC*, p. 54). By 'integral' Williams means the form of highly regulated embeddedness characteristic of the earliest forms of cultural institution and self-organization. While the 'new media' and their salaried professionals best exemplify this reintegration for Williams, he chooses not to move down this path in his

Table 6.4   Institutional relations of exemplary contemporary (1981) artforms

Artform	Institutional relations
Painting	Patronal relations still strong (e.g. commissioned portraiture) but post-artisanal distributive relations common in gallery system
(Fine) music	Patronal relations in commissioned works; distributive post-artisanal in orchestral works and traditional sheet music
Popular music	Productive post-artisanal phase long established plus major moves to later phases (market professional and corporate) of market relations
Literature	Still some artisanal and distributive post-artisanal but long dominance of distributive post-artisanal and signs of later phases of market relations

Table 6.5   Modes of organization of formations (abandoned version)

Type	Sub-type	Characteristics	Example (where provided)
Early forms of 'integrated' internal organization	Bardic rules	Integrated singular order; strict internal self-regulation of rules of poetic composition	Welsh court poets (Gogynfeirdd)
	Craft guilds	Organization and training of artisans of specific craft; master–apprentice system developed into class system	
	Academies	Differentiation of arts from crafts; academies adopted model from liberal arts but applied especially to former crafts of painting and sculpture	Academia del Disegno of Vasari (est. 1563)
	Professional societies	Mode of self-organization of market professional hence primarily a business organization	

account of forms of self-organization of cultural producers, that is, towards an account of trade unions within the culture industries.

Here the analysis of formations radically shifts from the 'productionist' modes of self-organization to that of 'movements'. However his first attempt – based in the categories of existing scholarship (e.g. 'schools') – breaks down as Williams points to the failure of that scholarship to employ

Table 6.6   Types of modern formation

Forms of internal organization	Example	Forms of external relations with other groups and society	Example
(i) Formal membership	Emulation of guilds in German Brotherhood of St Luke	(a) Specializing in promotion of particular medium or style	Royal Society of Painters and Etchers
(ii) No formal membership but collective public manifestation – such as manifesto – instead	English Pre-Raphaelite Brotherhood; Futurists; Surrealists (cf. next columns)	(b) Alternative provision to that of dominant cultural institutions	Societé des Artistes Indépendants (1884)
(iii) Neither (i) nor (ii) but instead conscious association or group identification	French Nabis; Bloomsbury	(c) Oppositional relationship with established institutions and more general social conditions	Futurists; Dadaists; Surrealists

consistent criteria.[5] So he restarts from scratch with the categorizations in Table 6.6.

The distinction between alternative and oppositional formations is consistent with the brief appearance the category of formation makes in Williams's elaboration of his conception of hegemony in *Marxism and Literature*.[6] Equally consistently, Williams goes on in *The Sociology of Culture* to analyze such formations in conjunction with the concept of *class fraction*. Here he draws on his most detailed case study, 'The Bloomsbury Fraction'. As mentioned in Chapters 2 and 3, this analysis constitutes both an echo of Marx's *Eighteenth Brumaire* and an attempt to improve on Goldmann's genetic structuralism. Each of Williams's examples – with Bloomsbury again as the key case – is located within a class fractional origin.

In his initial analysis of the case of Bloomsbury, Williams traced the social determinants of the group's 'autonomy' from their largely shared class-fractional origin in the 'professional administrative sectors'. This sector is seen as part of a larger *ruling* 'dominant social class' based in industrial and agrarian capital. A major determinant of the group's dissident identity was the exclusion of women from full participation in that sector. The central representative feature ('limit' in *The Brumaire* sense) is the civilized individual as a generalizable ideal. Bloomsbury's critical ethos is thus positioned as the group's internal self-recognition as a dissidence *of conscience* uniting its members' diverse intellectual specializations, but in a displaced homologous structural relation with their class fraction of origin (cf. Table 3.2).[7]

When asked in 1978 by Krishan Kumar whether the Bloomsbury mode of 'internal' fractional dissidence (within a ruling social class) had evident successors, Williams admitted 'no, I don't have any idea' as his 'short answer' (Williams *et al.*, 1978, p. 87). Yet he immediately sketched a model that pointed towards an increasing role by '*oppositional* cultural groups' that develop within a far more complex set of class relations. *The Sociology of Culture* introduces a series of hypotheses concerning the role of avant-gardes that appears to build on this sketch:[8]

(a) that these formations are best understood within a 'para-national', that is, imperial metropolitan, context rather than a national or class-fractional one;

(b) that autonomy is provided by the imperial metropole, to which members of the avant-gardes were often immigrants;

(c) (yet) this autonomy risks becoming an alienating 'distance' – like that Williams identified in his 1977 formational study of the CCCS – grounded in the lack of any common language 'but that of the metropolis and whose other (including visual) received sign-systems have become distanced or irrelevant' (*SOC*, p. 84).

In particular:

> that such avant-garde formations, developing specific and distanced styles within the metropolis, at once reflect and compose kinds of consciousness and practice which become increasingly relevant to a social order itself developing in the directions of metropolitan and international significance beyond the nation-state and its provinces, and of a correspondingly high cultural mobility. (*SOC*, p. 84)

In effect the 'prefigurative' thesis concerning the class-fractional role of formations in the earlier analyses is extended to a global 'paranational' capitalism focussed on the metropoles. Each of these hypotheses was subsequently developed in a series of lectures and book chapters later collected posthumously in *The Politics of Modernism: against the new conformists.*[9] Indeed, the movement of this type of formation from an oppositional to dominant role appears to have provided that book's subtitle.[10] However, a Bloomsbury-style 'immanent dissidence' is not found to be a feature in these case studies. That dissidence is summarized in *The Sociology of Culture* as 'expressing at once the highest values of the bourgeois tradition and the necessary next phase of a bourgeois social and cultural order' (*SOC*, p. 81). Given the common avant-garde hostility to tradition and a remarkably expansive notion of 'bourgeois' norms in their 'anti-bourgeois revolt', such immanent criticism could hardly be expected. Rather, the liberation of the 'sovereign individual' includes that *from* 'the bourgeois family' which so 'translates desire as perpetually mobile'. In this sense Williams can recompose his 'prefigurative' formational thesis: 'a main element of modernism was that it was an authentic avant-garde, in personal desires and relationships, of the successful and evolving bourgeoisie itself' (1988a, pp. 8–9; *POM*, p. 56). Williams is thus able to sketch a formational complement to his brief critique of nihilism in *Modern Tragedy*.[11]

Williams returns to his cultural production and formational typologies later in *The Sociology of Culture* in his chapter on 'reproduction', in order to make a general claim about the *autonomy* of cultural producers. His conclusion concerning autonomy is fairly self-evident, given the above typologies: that (cultural) autonomy is tied to the variable distance of practices from each other, and that cultural reproduction might be distinguished from general social reproduction by the 'distance' of its practices from 'otherwise organized social relations'.[12] By 'otherwise organized' Williams means social relations not constituted in relation to the variable autonomy that some specific social relations of cultural production (e.g. the artisanal) make possible. The most obvious of these is the 'deep form' of conventional wage-labour. Such 'distances' are forms of '(a)symmetry' which will be addressed in the next section.

The separate discussion of 'the sociology of intellectuals' in *The Sociology of Culture* is extremely cautious. Williams initially appears to reject outright any notion of 'intellectuals', as 'a misleading specialization from a more general body of cultural producers', and 'a misleading extension from one type of cultural formation to a general social category' (*SOC*, p. 214). It soon emerges that this 'misleading extension' is the (Alfred) Weber/Mannheim conception of 'a relatively uncommitted intelligentsia' (*SOC*, p. 221).

Williams thus closely follows Gramsci's rejection of an 'intrinsic' definition for one that locates intellectuals 'within the ensemble of the system of relations' of 'intellectual' activities 'within the general complex of social relations' (Gramsci, 1971, p. 8). Plainly, Williams's conceptions of social and cultural reproduction – and, of course, hegemony – fulfil Gramsci's requirement of a 'general context' (though not Gramsci's own). Williams thus adopts Gramsci's famous argument that, as all human activities have an intellectual component, '[a]ll men are intellectuals...but not all men have in society the function of intellectuals' (Gramsci, 1971, p. 8).[13]

Williams also adopts the lesser known Gramscian 'disembedding' thesis that 'organic' intellectuals develop the 'embedded' social assumptions of the classes to which they are attached, as did, initially, the 'traditional' intellectuals of a previous order.[14] However, Williams makes it clear that he finds Gramsci's traditional/organic intellectual distinction inadequate. Apparently aware that Gramsci's 'solution' relied heavily on a conception of the (communist) party as itself an organic intellectual force, Williams confines the use of 'organic intellectual' to the forms of relations between 'intellectuals' and 'parties' at moments of radical social change.[15]

Williams makes much here of his own integration of the 'degrees of solution of signifying practice' and 'relative distance' theses.[16] The 'degrees of solution' thesis, however, chiefly concerns the cultural recognition of intellectuals 'as such', and hence almost corresponds with the modal sense of signal. So Gramsci's organic/traditional distinction is effectively replaced by Williams's own typology of modes of cultural producer–institution relations (Table 6.3). Williams then employs that typology to locate the 'uncommitted intelligentsia' thesis as a response to the increasing pressure of market-based relations upon, especially, universities. Accordingly, the autonomy of 'intellectual' cultural producers is sketched as generally dependent on:

(a) 'market asymmetry';
(b) the uneven practices of internal institutional reproduction of 'privileged institutions';[17] and
(c) alternative institutions.

It is tempting to reach for an easy 'biographical' explanation of this curious development in Williams's sociology of culture – that perhaps, as both successful novelist and cultural analyst, he saw little need for the artist/intellectual distinction. However, his goal here seems rather to be the placement within a sociological framework of the 'uncommitted intelligentsia' thesis (which, as we saw in Section 1.2, he had challenged in a different form in *Culture and Society*). Moreover, it seems highly likely that this strand of Williams's work was strongly influenced by formalist/structuralist cultural theories based in the 'projection' of avant-gardist aesthetic practices. Williams's usage of the concept of (quasi-avant-gardist) formation in contemporary debates, as in his critique of the CCCS, facilitated his critiques of this intellectual orientation and was a major component of his response to the contemporary influence of 'the language paradigm' in 'The Uses of Cultural Theory'. Finally, his formational analyses also tended to find or establish groupings that include both 'intellectuals' and 'artists': most notably J.M. Keynes's presence within Bloomsbury but Williams also casually pairs Nietzsche and Strindberg in his discussion of the politics of the avant-garde.[18] In short, Williams developed his own limited sociology of knowledge.[19]

6.3 Symmetries and asymmetries in cultural production and social reproduction

We saw in Section 3.4 that, in the course of an exchange with his interviewers in *Politics and Letters*, Williams highlights the contradictory development of the 'bourgeois press': that, while initially 'progressive', it became a negative force once it sought to suppress the radical presses during the nineteenth

century. We also saw in Section 5.2 that Williams's model of cultural reproduction develops from his social formalism.[20] (A)symmetricality is Williams's
term in *The Sociology of Culture* for the potentially contradictory relations
between such multiple systems of reproduction and social reproduction;
that is, the reproduction of a contingent social order (including modern
forms of hegemony).

Williams initially distinguishes between symmetrical and asymmetrical
relations but quickly focusses upon the latter. Symmetry equates with a
'homologous displaced connection' mode of correspondence (Table 3.2),
and asymmetry with 'contradiction'. Williams's central assertion is that 'the
crucial factor of asymmetry . . . became more and more evident in the fuller
development of the market' (*SOC*, p. 101). Early asymmetrical struggles
included the struggles against state censorship by newspapers including, of
course, the bourgeois press.

Williams's initial asymmetry is thus between 'the market and the official
reproductive institutions'; that is, how 'the older established institutions of
cultural and social reproduction (Church and State)' have been challenged
by 'the new institutions and forces both of the market and of professional
and cultural independence' (*SOC*, p. 101). This emphasis is significant because
it displaces the emphasis on the arrival of printing as the chief agent of
change within technologically determinist accounts.

Once the market became a more universalized form of organization
of cultural institutions, for example in cinema and broadcasting, a new
asymmetricality emerged over issues of morality and violence. For Williams
the 'basic complexity' now of asymmetricality is a 'deepseated contradiction
between the reproduction of market relations (both directly, within the
market, and indirectly, within the state and educational functions) and the
consequences of such reproduction in certain sensitive and perhaps crucial
areas of public morality, respect for authority and actual crime' (*SOC*,
pp. 102–3). Williams's chief example here is the previous twenty years of
struggle between market attempts at incorporation of youth cultures and
morally conservative responses to them. This is an interesting revision of
his hegemonic incorporation thesis. While the market was not actively
excluded as a means of incorporation in the 'Base and Superstructure' essay
and *Marxism and Literature*, the discussion tended to focus on the construction
of selective traditions within education and scholarship. It is possible to see
the influence here of the Birmingham research on youth subcultures –
which explicitly developed a market incorporation thesis – and related work
on moral panics.[21]

Williams certainly makes it explicit that one of his theoretical targets is
Althusser's Ideological State Apparatuses thesis – for its failure to distinguish
between 'the bourgeois state and the bourgeois market' (*SOC*, p. 102).[22]
However, he also gives an indication later in the book that he is re-posing
Gramsci's classical formulation of the problem of hegemony in which the

model agent of pre-modern hegemony was the Church. That is, the question of 'symmetry' refers implicitly to a lack of institutional preconditions for counter-hegemonic initiatives, while asymmetry offers correspondingly greater potential. Likewise, the struggle between the older and newer institutions can be seen as a further elaboration of the difference between the 'residual' and 'emergent' in Williams's previous revisions of Gramsci's key concept. However, here there is not even a gestural invocation of the significance of working-class democratic institutions as a counter-hegemonic force.

Yet Williams is not here attempting a contingent analysis of the present but, rather, a far more broadly historicized typologization. The categories of 'market' and 'professional independence' are re-employed in this discussion as defined in Table 6.3; that is, they are in turn vulnerable to the 'later phases' of corporate professional and 'post-market'. Accordingly, Williams also stresses the loss of professional independence (autonomy) that is possible in these later stages; that is, a restored 'symmetry'. High levels of capitalization require cost-minimization by improving technical means of production and alteration of 'the nature of the work'. In the case of the latter, 'manifest commercial modes of control and selection become, in effect, cultural *modes*', as a marketing function necessitates a level of pre-planning that acts as a form of selection of which cultural products will – and will not – be developed. (*SOC*, p. 104; emphasis added).

The above certainly seems consistent with Adorno's general arguments concerning the standardizing consequences of commodification within cultural production in Hollywood cinema and popular music. Williams nominates cinema and 'the popular newspaper' as 'the most extreme contemporary examples'. Likewise, he notes that the tendency towards marketizing in the corporate production of cultural commodities risks being 'internalized' and mistaken by 'primary producers' for their own artistic innovation. For this reason, in a further example of his distance from a celebration of an essentialized 'authenticity', he stresses that within the culture industries 'the contrast between market-originated and producer-originated work cannot be made absolute, once market conditions have been generalized' (*SOC*, p. 105).

However, the considerable nuances of Williams's production typologies reveal a capacity for attention to 'the less extreme' cases of cultural commodification and forms of 'asymmetrical' contradiction that tended to elude Adorno in his culture industry thesis.[23] Williams recognizes, for example, that 'new social classes, new age-groups and new minorities' complicate – but do not risk overriding – the market process in corporate cultural production (*SOC*, p. 106). Yet clearly those complications may result in significant restorations of 'the more normal process of cultural and artistic innovation', by which Williams presumably means, in part, artisanal and post-artisanal relations of cultural production. Subsequent research would appear to confirm many of Williams's observations about this corporate form.[24]

So Williams does not embrace total commodification in his rejection of an essentialized authenticity. Likewise, in *Towards 2000* he acknowledges – apparently for the first time – 'a very resilient area of a very different popular culture, much of it now marketed but much of it, also, not originated by the market' (*T 2000*, p. 145) which can also play an 'asymmetrical' role from outside the complete control of the culture industries. This provides the only occasion on which he speaks directly of 'the intense vitality of some kinds of popular music, always reached for by the market and often grasped and tamed, but repeatedly renewing its impulses in new and vigorous forms' (*T 2000*, p. 146). It will be remembered that Williams's critique of Hoggart rejected the equation of popular culture and working-class culture, but in doing so, it created a bifurcation between a 'self-made' institutional working-class culture and a necessarily marketized popular culture. Williams's lack of interest in developing the concept of 'popular culture' became a kind of blindspot for him.[25]

When Williams directly addresses 'reproduced and popular culture' in *The Sociology of Culture*, he largely recapitulates a set of arguments he had developed more extensively in his explicit writings on 'media'.[26] Indeed, while broadcasting and 'new media' are mentioned in *The Sociology of Culture*, they tend to be underplayed in comparison with Williams's 'extreme' cases of the corporate form. Ironically, his more detailed work on the asymmetries of modern popular culture is thus displaced from this central text to *Towards 2000*, so contributing further to the impression of an Adorno-like culture industry thesis.[27] One possible reason for this displacement is the complication of Williams's persistent *bête noire* in this field, Marshall McLuhan.

6.4   Overcoming conflations and 'projections' in McLuhan's 'media'

In *Marxism and Literature* Williams identifies his *Television: technology and cultural form* as the previous work to which the reader should turn for 'what I "really practically" mean' by 'material cultural production'. He states that 'I would now write some of these examples differently, from a more developed theoretical position and with the advantage of a more extended and a more consistent vocabulary (the latter itself exemplified in *Keywords*)' (*M&L*, p. 6). The reconstruction undertaken in the remainder of this chapter is strongly informed by *Television* in this manner, and employs not only the historical semantics, but also the conceptual framework of Williams's later discrete writings on means of communication, as well as the typologies above.[28]

As was argued in Section 5.1, historical semantic contestation of 'received terms' is a key step in all Williams's sociological work. His best known challenge in the case of communications was 'mass'. In 1962 he published

Communications with a fore-title that echoed *The Long Revolution*'s concluding prospective analysis, 'Britain in the sixties'. This echo made it evident that Williams did indeed regard 'communications' as a central element of the 'expanding culture' of his desired educated and participating democracy. Indeed the revolutionization of 'communications' was a central component of the third of Williams's 'long revolutions', a cultural revolution. Crucially, the location of these within that radical-democratic perspective moved hand in glove with the critique of Leavis's mass civilization/minority culture formulation and all similar uses of 'mass'.[29] For example, he immediately linked his famous comment in *Culture and Society* – 'There are in fact no masses; there are only ways of seeing people as masses' – to notions of 'mass communication', and even to a proffered neutral alternative to that term, 'multiple transmission' (*C&S*, pp. 300–5). This in turn led to his comparable hostility to the institutionalization of the category of 'mass communications' within functionalist sociology.

In hindsight it seems remarkable that Williams could compose *Communications* without any systematic reference to the category of 'media'. That is of course indicative of that category's contemporary semantic hegemony. Instead, the later Williams consistently employed 'means of communication' or 'means of modern communication'. These means are increasingly recognized as a cultural productive force. Yet the coinage of 'means *of communication*' also appears to have been a deliberate attempt to contest all forms of instrumentalized nomenclature. Williams's problems with the category of 'media' were addressed primarily in his critiques of Marshall McLuhan and some related texts.[30]

McLuhan's early career had more than passing parallels with Williams's. Even more than Williams, he had been drawn towards, without fully embracing, the marginal radicalism of the Leavises's *Scrutiny* circle. McLuhan's earliest popular cultural analyses, such as those in his first book, *The Mechanical Bride* (1951), bear considerable resemblance to Leavis's 'moral critique' of 'technologico-Benthamite civilization', Leavis's characterization of capitalist modernity.[31] These analyses, McLuhan later stated, were partly inspired by Leavis's and Thompson's 1933 *Culture and Environment*.[32] However, a precondition of *The Mechanical Bride* appears to have been the abandonment of Leavis's overt hostility to such popular cultural forms and, instead, their recognition as, in the words of its subtitle, 'the folklore of industrial man'.

Williams first showed interest in McLuhan in a review of *The Gutenberg Galaxy* in 1964.[33] In what was to become a familiar refrain, he welcomed McLuhan's attention to the specificity of communications but was wary of the causality he attributed to printing. He nonetheless expressed optimism about the arrival of McLuhan's *Understanding Media*.

Williams was to be disappointed. In a 1968 account, McLuhan expressed the belief that the moral critique of *The Mechanical Bride* was 'completely negated by TV' and that television had created in America an 'organic culture' (Stearn and McLuhan, 1968, pp. 302–3). Nothing could be more at odds with Williams's views than such an affirmative reinvention of the key Leavisite critical category he had so strongly criticized in *Culture and Society*. It was as if McLuhan had directly transferred Leavis's idealized function of the bearer of lost organic values from the literary canon to television.

Even so, the shift in Williams's view of McLuhan from the cautious 1964 review to the polemic in *Television* ten years later is dramatic. That uncompromising attack is fairly well-known but tends to be linked solely to Williams's charge of 'technological determinism'. The fact that the book opens with a famous critique of technological determinism, and the advancement of a 'social shaping' alternative, obviously lends support to this emphasis.

But Williams's chief charge against McLuhan in *Television* is *formalism*:

> The work of McLuhan was a particular culmination of an aesthetic theory which became, negatively, a social theory: a development and elaboration of a formalism which can be seen in many fields, from literary criticism and linguistics to psychology and anthropology, but which acquired its most significant popular influence in an isolating theory of "the media". (*TV2*, pp. 126–7)

The negative social theoretical role assumed by McLuhan's work is due, on Williams's account, to an absence created by the positivist sociological tradition that studied the media in terms of its 'effects' – especially in studies of violence – and the related functionalist conception of socialization. As we saw in Section 5.1, this tradition forms an important example for Williams in *The Sociology of Culture*, against which he contrasts the legacy of the alternative hermeneutic tradition. Crucially, Williams recast his hostility to 'mass communication' from the earlier 'only ways of seeing people as masses' to a critique of functionalist sociology's fetishism of description: 'What is really involved in that descriptive word "mass" is the whole contentious problem of the real social relations within which modern communications systems operate' (*TV2*, p. 121).

McLuhan's work appeared to provide an antidote to such empiricist descriptivism, precisely because of its apparent capacity to address the specificity of 'the medium' – print, radio, television – rather than the ideological construct of 'mass communications'. However, here we need to examine the conflations in McLuhan's 'medium' in order to understand why Williams rejected him so vehemently.

The historical semantic typologization of 'media' in the first edition of *Keywords* in 1976 was significantly revised the following year in *Marxism and Literature* but, strangely, these changes were not included in *Keywords*'s second edition. In *Keywords* Williams distinguishes three converging twentieth-century meanings for 'medium': an older sense (i) dating from the early seventeenth century from which two modern senses, (ii) and (iii), developed in the eighteenth and nineteenth centuries (Williams dates the pluralized form from the mid-twentieth century):

(i) 'intervening or immediate agency or substance' especially language
(ii) a modern conscious technical sense that distinguishes print from sound and vision
(iii) the 'specialized capitalist sense' in which a newspaper, broadcasting and so on are seen as a medium for something else. (That 'something else' is always, for Williams, advertising.)[34]

Williams contends in *Keywords* that the basis for (i) – where a physic-ally intermediate substance is considered essential to the expression of a thought – has declined 'in most modern science and philosophy'. This appears to be at odds with the rise of formalist and structuralist conceptions of language. This enigmatic position is revised in the discussion of 'medium' in *Marxism and Literature* where, crucially, a new sense or, rather a further variant of (i) not previously mentioned, is introduced:

> the notion of an intermediate substance was also extensively and simul-taneously developed, especially in the visual arts: "the medium of oils" or "the medium of water-colour"; in fact as a development from a relatively neutral scientific sense of the carrier of some active substance. The "medium" in painting had been any liquid with which pigments could be mixed; it was then extended to the active mixture and so to the specific practice...then... "[m]edium" became the specific material with which a particular kind of artist worked...Thus far there was not, and is not, any real difficulty. But a familiar process of reification occurred, reinforced by the influence of formalism. The properties of "the medium" were abstracted as if they defined the practice, rather than being its means. This interpretation then suppressed the full sense of practice...defined as work on a material for a specific purpose within certain necessary social conditions. Yet this real practice is easily displaced...to an activity defined, not by the material, which would be altogether too crude, but by that particular projection and reification of work on the material which is called "the medium". (*M&L*, pp. 159–60)

The reference to modern science is clarified as the supersession of former speculative beliefs in intermediate substances such as 'phlogiston' during research on oxygen. The *rise* of formalist conceptions of language is presented this time as a contrast to those natural scientific developments. Clearly, Williams's work on theories of language for *Marxism and Literature* played a role here.

Likewise, the account of sense (iii) above is revised so that another eighteenth-century sense – set aside in *Keywords*'s account of a twentieth-century convergence – is (properly) rendered as still active. This 'neutral' sense is 'a social organ or institution of general communication'. Sense (iii) above is thus revised as 'a secondary or derived use (as in advertising) of an organ or institution with another apparently primary purpose' (*M&L*, pp. 158–9). What remains debatable is why this conception should have been characterized as 'neutral'.

Nonetheless, this account is remarkably consistent with the conflations embedded within McLuhan's own practice. In McLuhan, however, this aesthetic sense of 'medium' is further conflated with 'communications technology'; in Williams's parlance, McLuhan conflates means of cultural production with cultural forms. In a single page of *Understanding Media*, for example, McLuhan treats 'a photograph', 'the movie', 'speech', 'the telephone', 'TV', 'a cartoon', 'typography' and 'the alphabet', all under the category of 'medium'.[35] The only distinction McLuhan wishes to make between these, famously, is whether they are 'hot' or 'cool'. Not insignificantly, this distinction relies on a highly formalist conception of reception whereby the audience 'completes' the meaning of certain media, so rendering 'cool' media high in 'participation' and 'hot' media low.[36]

Of course there is a sense in which it is legitimate to speak of all McLuhan's 'media' as possibly sharing some quasi-aesthetic formal properties or, at times, their being overtly turned to such uses. Williams tends to use the formulation, 'means of communicative production', to refer to such deployments. But McLuhan fails to delimit this characterization, thus over-generalizing his most famous slogan, 'the medium is the message'. Moreover, it is that very aesthetic inspiration that combines his formalism with his conceptions of 'sense ratios' and a Romantic remythologization, as in this extract from *The Gutenberg Galaxy* where he paraphrases a passage from the mythological discourse of William Blake's *Jerusalem* (while also arguing that this mythological vision 'remains quite opaque'):

Imagination is that ratio among the perceptions and faculties which exists when they are not embedded or outered in material technologies. When so outered, each sense and faculty becomes a closed system. Prior to such outering there is entire interplay among experiences. This interplay or synesthesia is a kind of tactility such as Blake sought in the bounding line of sculptural form and in engraving.

When the perverse ingenuity of man has outered some part of his being in material technology, his entire sense ratio is altered. He is then compelled to behold this fragment of himself "clothing itself as in steel". In beholding this new thing, man is compelled to become it. Such was the origin of lineal, fragmented analysis with its remorseless power of homogenization. (McLuhan, 1967a, pp. 265–6)

As Fekete has argued, this 'sensorium' and the related 'extension thesis' (developed from Harold Innis) is best characterized as an affirmative theory of alienation.[37] The norm against which this alienation thesis is measured is not, as in most Marxian versions, the conscious design of that which is objectified (or 'extended'), but instead a dream-like 'unconscious' tribal-organic state which the emerging 'electric age' will restore.

We can find the roots of Williams's charge of formalism in Table 6.7 and in the citation above from *The Gutenberg Galaxy*. McLuhan's 'method' – variously characterized by him as the use of 'probes', a 'field approach' or 'mozaicism' – is exemplified by his drawing from Blake not merely a mythologized source for his sensorium but a *'diagnosis* of the problem of his age' (1967a, p. 266; emphasis added). McLuhan makes very explicit his adoption of such 'insights' *from the aesthetic experimentation* of a series of artists and critics from Blake to McLuhan's chief source of inspiration, the French Symbolists. At one point he advocates this 'mythic' lineage as a rival to Williams's 'culture and society' tradition (1967a, p. 269). In later works, McLuhan usually does not reflect on such aesthetic insights but *practises* them in lieu of a discrete analytic discourse. By *The Medium is the Massage*, McLuhan was barely writing within such an analytic discourse at all but instead, in the main, *practising* photo-montage.[38]

A similar process of transformation of aesthetic practices into quasi-concepts was identified ten years later by Andreas Huyssen as a characteristic feature of 1970s and 1980s postmodernism and poststructuralism, more specifically, the recomposition of the modernist 'technical' initiatives within their aesthetic 'media' *as* poststructuralist theoretical ones and even as a form of contemporary intellectual avant-gardism.[39] This is also compatible with later theses concerning the anticipatory character of McLuhan's work.[40]

An intimation of some such linkages certainly underpins Williams's hostility to McLuhan. As we saw in the previous chapter, by 1976 Williams located him within the dominant formalist theoretical movement he wished to challenge. The case of McLuhan appears to have initiated Williams's

Table 6.7 McLuhan's historical typology of 'the media'

Dominant 'medium'	Resulting society	'Sensory balance' (sense-ratio)	'Hot/ cool'
Speech	Tribal	'Audile' (stable)	Cool
Writing based in phonetic alphabet	'Scribal'	Visual (unstable)	Hot
Mechanical printing	'Typographic man' linear, visual, rationality	Visual (unstable)	Hotter
'Electric' technology	'Re-tribalization'	Audile-tactile (envisioned new stabilization)	Coolest

suspicion of the potentially deleteriously affirmative consequences of quasi-theoretical avant-gardism.

Williams so sees the 'overextension' of McLuhan's visualist avant-gardism as intellectually illegitimate. For indeed McLuhan does not delimit his role to that of avant-gardist celebrant of the creative potentials of 'new media' – his 'probes' clearly have sociological, and of course socio-historical, pretensions (cf. Table 6.7):

> It is an apparently sophisticated technological determinism which has the significant effect of indicating a social and cultural determinism: a determinism, that is to say, which ratifies the society and culture we now have, and especially its most powerful internal directions. For if the medium – whether print or television – is the cause, all other causes, all that men [*sic*] ordinarily see as history, are at once reduced to effects. Similarly, what are elsewhere seen as effects, and as such subject to social, cultural, psychological and moral questioning, are excluded as irrelevant by comparison with the direct physiological and therefore "psychic" effects of the media as such. The initial formulation – "the medium is the message" – was a simple formalism. The subsequent formulation – "the medium is the massage" – is a direct and functioning ideology. (*TV2*, p. 127)

The 'direct and functioning ideology' Williams sees in this further projection is the legitimation of an existing social order by its affirmative characterization as a kind of technological utopia – the global village. This relies on a view of television, aided by satellite retransmission, as a restorer of 'organic culture' by means of a new sense-ratio. And so Williams moves on to characterize the McLuhanist 'projection':[41]

> If specific media are essentially psychic adjustments, coming not from relations between ourselves but between a generalised human organism and its general physical environment, then of course intention, in any general or particular case, is irrelevant, and with intention goes content, whether apparent or real. All media operations are in effect desocialised; they are simply physical events in an abstracted sensorium, and are distinguishable only by their variable sense-ratios. But it is then interesting that from this wholly unhistorical and asocial base McLuhan projects certain images of society: "retribalization" by the "electronic age"; the "global village". (*TV2*, pp. 127–8)

These citations confirm that for Williams the charge of technological determinism is subordinate to that of formalism. It seems very likely that the subtitle of *Television: technology and cultural form* was explicitly designed to reverse McLuhan's conflation of two distinct meanings of his 'medium'.

Of course this does not diminish the importance of Williams's critique of technological determinism (which will be presented next). But, as we shall see, it is an insufficient guide by itself to Williams's 'post-McLuhanist' conception of means of communication.

6.5   Overcoming technological determinism: the social shaping of means of communication

The first chapter of *Television*, 'The Technology and the Society', is justly famous. Accordingly, it has often been reproduced within teaching compilations as a textbook critique of technological determinism.[42] It contains a nine-stage breakdown of 'versions of cause and effect in technology and society'. Both this and Williams's redefinition of 'determination' were welcomed by the 'social shaping' school within the sociology of 'industrial' technology.[43]

Let us take first, then, Williams's primary definition of technological determinism that he somewhat inductively distils from the breakdown of his nine versions of cause and effect:

It is an immensely powerful and now largely orthodox view of the nature of social change. New technologies are discovered, by an essentially internal process of research and development, which then sets the conditions for social change and progress. Progress, in particular, is the history of these inventions, which "created the modern world". The effects of the technologies, whether direct or indirect, foreseen or unforeseen, are as it were the rest of history. The steam engine, the automobile, television, the atomic bomb, have *made* modern man [*sic*] and the modern condition. (*TV2*, p. 13)

Accordingly, he proposes an alternative for the case of television which is broadly consistent with the 'social shaping' approach:

it may be possible to outline a different kind of interpretation, which would allow us to see not only its history but also its uses in a more radical way. Such an interpretation would differ from technological determinism in that it would restore *intention* to the process of research and development. The technology would be seen, that is to say, as being looked for and developed with certain purposes and practices already in mind. At the same time the interpretation would differ from symptomatic technology in that these purposes would be seen as *direct*: as known social needs, purposes and practices to which the technology is not marginal but central. (*TV2*, p. 14)

We saw in Chapter 2 that Williams culturally duplicated elements of the Marxian 'base' to produce the category of means of cultural production

(Table 2.1). Determination here is still understood as the exertion of pressures and limits to be discovered by homological analysis, but now between distinct sets of productive forces and relations. It is this reworking that he applies more generally in the case of means of communication. As he argues in the pivotal essay, 'Means of Communication as Means of Production':

> first, ... the means of communication have a specific productive history, which is always more or less directly related to the general productive historical phases of productive and technical activity. ... second, ... the historically changing means of communication have variable relations to the general complex of productive forces and to the general social relationships which are produced by them and which the general productive forces both produce and reproduce. These historical variations include both relative homologies between the means of communication and more general social productive forces and relationships, and, most marked in certain periods, contradictions both of general and particular kinds. (*PMC*, p. 50)

More precisely in the case of communications technology, the reconceptualization finds determinacy operative in the historically variable *forms of relation between* the two sets of productive forces, means of communication and 'general', and their attendant social relations. Nor is there a naïve confidence in the necessarily 'progressive' character of the contradiction between communicative means of production and existent social relations.[44] Rather, as the passage above indicates, Williams considers there to be a range of historical variations in the mode of determination which is not arbitrary, and so is reproducible as a typology as displayed in Table 6.8.

'Relative homology' never appears again in Williams's work. It seems to be based on Goldmann's 'relative totality' (later referred to by Goldmann as 'homology') and is consistent with Williams's (later) conception of market symmetry discussed earlier in this chapter. The case study of the social development of broadcast television in Chapter 1 of *Television* locates causality within 'known social needs' arising within broader social relations

Table 6.8 Variants of determinacy involving means of communication as means of ('general') production

Relative homology (symmetry)	Contradiction (asymmetry)
Between means of communication as 'general' productive forces and social relations	(a) Between means of communication and social relations of cultural production
	(b) Between 'general' productive forces and social relations

of production, social institutions and the reproduction of a specific social order.[45] In terms of the categories in Table 6.8, the historical movement is from 'contradictory pressures' to a (re)stabilized symmetry between the two sets of productive forces and relations within the maintenance of a hegemonic order. In short, Williams proposes that the *institution of broadcasting* resolved 'at a certain level' the contradictory pressure which he conceptualizes in his famous concept, *mobile privatization*. The latter is a product of 'two apparently paradoxical yet deeply connected tendencies of modern urban industrial living: on the one hand mobility, on the other hand the more apparently self-sufficient family home' (*TV2*, p. 26).

The expanded, historically detailed, version of this argument, the only available in this context in Williams's work, is rarely discussed and is worthy of extended citation:

The new and larger settlements and industrial organisations required major internal mobility, at a primary level, and this was joined by secondary consequences in the dispersal of extended families and in the needs of new kinds of social organisation. Social processes long implicit in the revolution of industrial capitalism were greatly intensified: especially an increasing distance between immediate living and the directed places of work and government. No effective kinds of social control over these transformed industrial and political processes had come anywhere near being achieved or even foreseen. Most people were living in the fall-out area of processes determined beyond them. What had been gained, nevertheless, in intense social struggle, had been the improvement of immediate conditions, within the limits and pressures of these decisive large-scale processes. There was some relative improvement in wages and working conditions, and there was a qualitative change in the distribution of the day, the week and the year between work and off-work periods. These two effects combined in a major emphasis on improvement of the small family home. Yet this privatisation, which was at once an effective achievement and a defensive response, carried, as a consequence, an imperative need for new kinds of contact. The new home might appear new and "self-sufficient" but could be maintained only by regular funding and supply from external sources, and these, over a range from employment and prices to depressions and wars, had a decisive and often a disrupting influence on what was nevertheless seen as a separable "family" project. This relationship created both the need and the form of a new kind of "communication": news from "outside", from otherwise inaccessible sources.... The new "consumer" technology which reached its first decisive stage in the 1920s served this complex of needs within just these limits and pressures. There were immediate improvements of the condition and efficiency of the privatised home; there were new facilities, in private transport, for expeditions from the home; and then, in radio, there was a facility for a new kind of social input – news and entertainment brought into the home. Some people spoke of the new machines as gadgets, but they were always much more than this. They were the applied technology of a set of emphases and responses within the determining limits and pressures of industrial capitalist society. (*TV2*, pp. 26–7)

Here, the productive force of a means of communication achieves a specific correspondent social form in symmetry with the 'general' productive forces in a set of social relations more recently characterized as 'Fordist'.[46] This is a clear case of correspondence between displaced homologous structures (cf. Table 3.2). In this way Williams satisfies his own criterion of restoring to the historical account his understanding of 'intention' already cited: 'The technology would be seen, that is to say, as being looked for and developed with certain purposes and practices already in mind' (*TV2*, p. 14).

It is at this point of the development of Williams's position in 'Means of Communication as Means of Production' that McLuhan's work faces him as an 'ideological block' (*PMC*, p. 50). What McLuhan's project 'blocks' is precisely Williams's need to conceptualize broadcasting as a *social institution* consistent with the analysis above.

Three years later, Williams introduced a further set of considerations in a book he edited, *Contact: human communication and its history*.[47] There he draws a distinction between technique and technology:

A technique is a particular skill or application of a skill. A technical invention is then a development of such a skill or the development or invention of one of its devices. A technology by contrast is, first, the body of knowledge appropriate to the development of such skills and applications and, second, a body of knowledge and conditions for the practical use and application of a range of devices. (Williams, 1981c, pp. 226–7)

Once again, the clarification of a conceptual distinction leads to a reassertion of Williams's own model of determination that we have already met in *Television*'s account of what can now be called the *technology* of broadcast television.

What matters, in each stage, is that a technology is always, in a full sense, social. It is necessarily in complex and variable connection with other social relations and institutions, although a particular and isolated technical invention can be seen, and temporarily interpreted, as if it were autonomous. As we move into any general social inquiry, we then find that we have always to relate technical inventions to their technologies, in the full sense, and, further, that we are starting from one kind of social state or institution – a *technology* – and relating it to other kinds of social state and institution rather than to a generalized "society" so pre-defined as to separate or exclude it. (1981c, p. 227)

Consistent with this account, Table 6.9 lays out the main points of Williams's argument from the first chapter of *Television*.

The 'general' social institutions specific to nation-states within which the socially shaped technology of broadcasting is 'related' could easily be broadened. This could also be done by discussion of the forms of socio-cultural institution (Table 6.3) within which broadcasting is administered, as Williams had done for the British case in *Communications*. Similar 'institutions of the technology' are typologized in the second chapter of *Television*. These are certainly discussed within the above analysis, but it is the contradictory (asymmetrical) social needs of mobile privatization and 'the self sufficient family home' that receive the most prominence.

Conceptually, the recasting of the definition of technology to a socially shaped one allows Williams to employ 'technology' as what Adorno might consider the *mediation* of technical inventions and general social institutions and 'social states'. Yet the introduction of a distinction between technique/technical invention and technology was not new. It is the norm in French and German usage, and Williams's distinction is not the first such in English, the most notable precursor being Lewis Mumford.[48]

Indeed, as we saw in Section 3.3, the Adorno–Benjamin dispute over 'mechanical reproduction' turned heavily on the appropriate (German)

Table 6.9 The social shaping of broadcasting

Technical invention(s)	Social institution of technology	'Other' (general) social state or institution
Multiple inventions of devices which enable development of radio transmitter/receiver	Broadcast radio (single transmitter/multiple receivers)	Development of broadcast *technology* consolidates because it successfully responds to a 'new social need'; that is, the need for a means of reconciliation of contradiction between increased personal mobility (mobile privatization) and 'apparently self-sufficient family home' of the emergent consumer culture
Development of technical inventions required for television proceeds towards known 'intention' of broadcast technology	Broadcast television	As above

usage of 'technique' and 'technology' in assessing 'new media'. Moreover, the key issue at odds between them – whether such 'new media' could be optimistically celebrated as new means of cultural production within 'revolutionary' avant-garde art – is remarkably similar to that which set Williams against McLuhan. While Williams does not reconnect his technique/technology clarification with his discussions of 'medium' or those of Adorno and Benjamin, it is certainly used to inform his reintroduction of his critique of McLuhanism in *Towards 2000*.[49]

For Williams, this mediational moment opened up the prospect of policy intervention in the design of such technologies, at the point where techniques and technical inventions were developed into socially institutionalized technologies, and where socio-cultural institutions were developed to administer them. Williams does seem to have been the first to attempt self-consciously to extend such a 'social shaping' project to means of communication and, certainly, to the further issues of (hegemonic) social and cultural reproduction.

6.6   Means of communication and 'mediated' cultural forms

It is by means of medium as 'cultural form', however, that Williams establishes his most basic subtitular distinction in *Television* between television as technology and television as cultural form. In terms of the earlier discussion of 'medium', Williams regards 'the forms of television' as an 'intermediate communicative substance' but in a social formalist rather than 'McLuhanist formalist' sense. Indeed in shifting to his discussion of the cultural forms of television, Williams states: 'to regain the substance of the medium, we need to look more closely at television as a cultural form' (*TV2*, p. 43).[50] We can thus re-present the television component of Table 6.9 as Table 6.10.

The third column in Table 6.10 merely lists the elements of the typology of programme forms Williams undertakes in *Television*'s third chapter. The primary division is between 'received' forms (A) and 'the innovative forms of television itself' (B). However, unusually for Williams, there is no historical semantic 'contestation' of the received terminology. The forms identified are almost entirely consistent with contemporary television programme guides and 'industry' parlance. It is thus easy to mistake this typologization for a merely descriptive listing, especially as each form is dealt with succinctly. But that does not mean their treatment is superficial. 'Variety', for example, includes a remarkable history of the music hall and its place in the 'high/low' culture distinction, foreshadowing Williams's more detailed discussions of the underrated significance of melodrama several years later.[51] Such work considerably informed the vast literature on television soap opera in the 1980s.[52] The prioritization of news amongst this genre listing is also no coincidence and links directly with Williams's normative commitment to informed citizenship.

Table 6.10   Television: technology and cultural form(s)

Technical inventions/ techniques	Technology	Cultural forms	Simultaneously technology and cultural form

Technical inventions required for television *with broadcasting as goal*	'Free to air' broadcast television employing 'planned flow' programming	(A) *Combination and development of earlier forms*
		News
		  Sequences
		  Priorities
		  Presentation
		  Visualization
		Argument and discussion
		Education
		Drama
		Films
		Variety
		Sport
		Advertising
		Pastimes
		
		(B) *Mixed and new forms*
		Drama-documentary
		Education by seeing
		Features
		Discussion
		Sequences
		Television
			Planned flow – loss of specificity of 'programming' by progressive elimination of modal *signals* of distinction between forms of 'content'. Content tends towards extended sequence

But the genre typologization of *Television* has tended to be overlooked in favour of the much discussed conception of 'flow' – the non-discrete sequencing of televisual 'content' in programme 'distribution' – in the following chapter.[53] As Corner concludes in his recent thorough examination of the concept and its legacy, it was seized upon by the emergent 'television studies' and undoubtedly 'inflated' beyond reasonable expectations.[54] It could be added that 'flow' was taken up in the 1970s and 1980s with the same inappropriately selective overenthusiasm – and formational inclination towards formalism – as McLuhan's work was in the 1960s.

As Stuart Laing has emphasized, however, it is important to stress that Williams builds a case not just for 'flow' but for *planned flow* as a consequence of the different forms of social institutionalization of broadcasting, especially its more commercialized types.[55] Indeed, it cannot be stressed too strongly that flow operates in distinct contrast with the discreteness of the generic cultural forms of television Williams isolates in the previous chapter. Planned flow is instead 'simultaneously . . . a technology and a cultural form'

(*TV2*, p. 86). With the (hindsight) advantage of the typology displayed in Table 6.2, it becomes plain that Williams uses the term '*planned* flow' deliberately to indicate the pre-planning of 'programme' production characteristic of the corporate professional phase of producer–institutional relations.[56]

It is now also obvious that Williams was seeking to demonstrate a further symmetry between what he deliberately designates 'the mobile concept of flow' and the mobile privatization addressed by the institutional design of broadcasting technology (*TV2*, p. 72). Here Williams certainly acknowledges a specifically phenomenological 'experience' of viewing television confirmed, for him, by correspondence with readers of his television criticism.[57] Flow, Williams makes it plain, is also the product of the practices of 'selection and association' – analogous to, but far more dominant than, older cultural forms of miscellany – *from the available cultural forms of television* made within the socio-cultural institutions of television.[58]

But, most significantly, flow is primarily defined by what the later Williams would identify as *signals*. One of its chief characteristics is the increasing tendency towards destruction of the 'interval signals' previously employed to separate programming elements into discrete units, the last vestige of which in BBC television is the 'turning globe'.[59] This tendency towards programmed flow thus alters the *modal* cultural form of television. Worse, these changes are concealed under the ideological 'mask' of 'ordinary' programming schedules.

Table 4.1 showed that Williams regards 'the cinematic' as a new cultural *mode*. In *Television*, cinema is a key point of comparative reference in establishing the modal effects of televisual flow. Fundamentally, the autonomy of the generic cultural forms of television is seen to be so put at risk.

Understandably, this apparent pessimism has been challenged.[60] However, it needs to be re-stressed that this is less a judgement of television *per se* than tendencies within an institutionalized *mode* that Williams had discerned. As is relatively well known, Williams tirelessly participated in media policy debates that might change such modal configurations and was a strong advocate of particular televisual generic innovations.[61]

Spigel has pointed out that, while Williams was one of the first to propose that television should be regarded as 'part of our serious culture' (RWOT, p. 170), there is an assumed 'serious' recipient of television programming in these discussions, 'a viewer who is watching in a chair all night' (Spigel, 1992, p. xxvi). Likewise, Corner notes the clear linkage between Williams's development of 'flow' and his television reviewing.[62] In these Williams characteristically reviewed an evening's viewing in a single article.[63]

Despite these highly personalized conditions of composition, the case of television also provides perhaps the most significant demonstration of the potential for others to employ Williams's sociology of culture's conceptual repertoire. For example, a significant literature developed in the mid-1980s arguing for the recent emergence of 'quality television' in the United States.

Such research is compatible with Williams's late project in that it meets his criteria for artisanal and post-artisanal (autonomous) relations of cultural production in television, yet it would not necessarily meet his modal criteria, nor match the complexity of his social formal analysis of television's other cultural forms.[64]

However, there is another dimension to Williams's writing on means of communication that could be taken as evidence of an even more pessimistic view of reception possibilities.

6.7   Means of communication as means of socialization?

Williams clearly remained intrigued by the 'non-linear' consequences of McLuhan's extension thesis. McLuhan's is not a merely progressivist technological determinism that simply declares that the latest is the best. Williams thus attempts in 'Means of Communication as Means of Production' an alternative typologization of means of communication as represented in Table 6.11.

Table 6.11   Williams's typology of means of communication

Mode of communication	Type of 'communicative resource'	Means of communication	Required level of skill for effective social access to means of composition	Technical division of labour necessary?
Direct spoken language	Human-physical	Voice	'Primary' social communication	No
Direct non-verbal communication	Human-physical	Body/bodily gesture	As above	No
'Direct' mediated	Non-human material transformed by human labour but 'modally correspondent with' human-physical	(i) Amplificatory (ii) Durative	As above	No
'Indirect' mediated	Non-human material transformed by human labour but not 'modally correspondent with' human-physical	(i) Amplificatory (ii) Durative (iii) Instrumentally alternative (to human physical) material signifying systems	Requirement of further intermediate labour, for example writing, a/v editing	Yes

This understanding of means of communication is clearly informed by McLuhan's extension thesis for its basic 'technical' criterion, *the degree of independence from the human body*. Thus 'the type of communicative resource' exists in four modes: human-physical, amplificatory, durative and alternative. The second and, to a lesser extent, the third categories in this list are 'extensions'. The third is also the site of cultural replication (Table 5.2). The last is designed for fully objectivated signifying systems such as writing.[65] These are initially classified as 'instrumently alternative' (to bodily resources).

A further distinction is drawn within this 'instrumently alternative' group, between those which are *modally correspondent* with the primary bodily communicative means, and those which are not. By this conceptualization, another homologous relation, Williams absorbs but critically reconstructs the gains of McLuhan's extension thesis. The modal correspondence is seen to take place between existent bodily resourced *modes of communication*, rather than body parts (as in Innis) or sense-ratios (as in McLuhan).

There appears to be a conceptual correspondence – if not identity – between 'mode of communication' and the social formalist conception of mode developed within the typology of cultural forms (Table 4.1). As we have already seen, the case of television 'flow' points in this direction. Certainly the features Williams isolates in 'mode of communication' would appear to include the modal signals that form the 'formal infrastructure' of other cultural forms. This, I would suggest, is what Williams meant when he raised the prospect of a sociological recognition of technologies as sign systems in 1976.[66]

Thus amplificatory and durative means of communication are certainly seen to exist in resembling correspondences with bodily resourced communicative modes. For example, the usage of a simple megaphone resembles the amplification of the pitched projected voice; painting and sculpture render durable some means of non-verbal communication in painted or sculpted gesture, and so on. Williams classifies these forms of correspondence as 'direct' in the sense of socially transparent (and/or 'unmediated' – see below). The human labour of their composition, at least when contained within artisanal or post-artisanal relations of cultural production, is readily discernible. Williams also tends to categorize human-physical communicative means as direct as well.

Amplificatory and durative means of communication – such as broadcasting and cinema – make possible 'much closer' modal correspondence with bodily resourced modes such as speaking, listening, gesturing and even 'observing' (*PMC*, p. 57). These modal correspondences appear socially transparent in the very directness of the audio-visual reproduction they facilitate. But they are also, of course, the product of 'further intermediate labour' such as audio-visual editing.

However, Williams's priority is not only to make evident in this typologization the role of such 'obscured' human labour at all stages of cultural production. It is, more significantly, to investigate potential obstacles posed to greater social access by a 'technical division of labour'. He thus concludes that all such modes are actually indirect.

It is here that the case of writing becomes crucial. Williams activates the distinction between 'separable systems' and other 'objects' employed as means of communication. As in Table 6.1, writing is his prime example of a 'separable material system of signification' (*SOC*, p. 90). Unlike mere objects of communication and 'direct' communicative modes, it necessitates a considerable apprenticeship in order to acquire effective participation. Of course, this applies to both writing and reading.[67] There is, in short, no modal correspondence between literacy and bodily resourced modes which provides a point of ready social access.

Thus the social significance of the 'technology' of writing is that it is the first communicative mode in which a technical division of labour can be *fully* utilized as the basis of a social division of (intellectual) labour.[68] That is, the necessity of education enables control of the access to literacy.

We are thus returned to the initial differences between Williams's and McLuhan's 'post-Leavisite' approaches to popular culture and 'the media'. Williams manages in his later work to reintroduce the criterion of literacy as, once again, a precondition of both effective modern cultural composition and reception and, by implication, a minimal requirement for citizenship in a participatory democracy.

Such a perspective certainly ratifies Williams's longstanding advocacy of the teaching of skills of critical analysis and its extension to compositional practice:

> Of critical importance, in this respect, and as the necessary ground for any effective transition, is sustained discussion and demonstration of the inherent transforming processes involved in, for example, television and film. The modes of 'naturalization' of these means of communicative production need to be repeatedly analyzed and emphasized, for they are indeed so powerful, and new generations are becoming so habituated to them, that here as strongly as anywhere, in the modern socio-economic process, the real activities and relations of men [*sic*] are hidden behind a reified form, a reified mode, a 'modern medium'.

> The critical demystification has indeed to continue, but always in association with practice: regular practice, as part of a normal education, in this transforming labour process itself; practice in the alternative production of "images" of the "same event"; practice in processes of basic editing and the making of sequences; practice, following this, in direct autonomous composition. (*PMC*, pp. 61–2)[69]

This carefully delimited construction of a case for the preconditions of 'direct autonomous composition' is characteristic of the normative statements that the engagement with McLuhan continued to stimulate in Williams. With this norm in place, he goes further and so provides one of the most forthright restatements of his normative commitments within his later work:

> But socialism is not only about the theoretical and practical "recovery" of those means of production, including the means of communicative production, which have been expropriated by capitalism. In the case of communications, especially, it is not only, though it may certainly include, the recovery of a "primitive" directness and community. Even in the direct modes, it should be institution much more than recovery, for it will have to include the transforming elements of access and extension over an unprecedentedly wide social and inter-cultural range.

> In this, but even more in the advanced indirect communicative modes, socialism is then not only the general "recovery" of specifically alienated human capacities but is also, and much more decisively, the necessary institution of new and very complex communicative capacities and relationships. In this it is above all a production of new means (new forces and new relations) of production, in a central part of the social material process; and through these new means of production a more advanced and more complex realization of the decisive productive relationships between communications and community. (*PMC*, pp. 62–3)

Thus Williams employs the case of literacy paradigmatically to develop a position which articulates the need for appropriately planned social institutions which do not merely reproduce the 'hidden' history of broadcasting he has uncovered. Beyond this, in his rearticulation of the norm of 'community' he provides perhaps the most precise reply to those who would continue to conflate his position as one coterminous with Leavis's and/or Hoggart's nostalgia for lost 'ways of life'.

This is easily the most overlooked dimension of Williams's mature writing on 'the media'. Cinema, radio and television are indeed seen as 'powerful' because, as McLuhan argues, they break the dominance of print-based literacy. For Williams, however, the significance of this break is not the transcendence of the linear thinking of 'typographic man', or a reversion into pre-modern 'tribalism', but rather the *risk of reversal* of the democratic-educational gains towards a participatory democracy achieved by the expansion of literacy.

Of course the educational project implicit here for Williams is not the paternalist one of Leavis or others, but the empowering radical-democratic one he advocated from his earliest days in adult education.[70] For Williams never shifted from his earliest contention that a popular culture worthy of the name required democratic organization of the cultural means and skills of cultural composition so that all societal members might be 'direct autonomous composers'. His early policy formulations such as the following from *Communications* indicate this clearly:

> Where the means of communication can be personally owned, it is the duty of society to guarantee this ownership and to ensure the distribution facilities are adequate, on terms compatible with the original freedom. Where the means of communication cannot be personally owned, because of their expense and size, it is the duty of society to hold these means in trust for the actual contributors, who for all practical purposes will control their use. (*COM1*, p. 122)

Without such provisions, however, the very features of modern broadcasting he delineated in his post-McLuhanist typology provide a critical account of an alternative 'training':

> Even with the eventual coming of general literacy, there was a continuing direct relation between a specific training and the uses of print. What then happened, or can appear to have happened, was a radical shift of the relation between systems of social training and access to the products of the new technologies. The most basic social skills, of a kind acquired in quite primary development and relationship, gave access to the motion picture, the radio broadcast, the television programme, at the level of reception, while very easily learned skills gave more general access, including some production, to the photograph and telephone.

> Thus the new technologies were inherently more general, and less apparently subject to systems of training.... It was not only that the institutions of the new technologies, in the very course of their development, and especially of autonomous production, became, in themselves, training systems. In immediate ways, types of speech, points of view, catch phrases, jingles, rhythms were in effect taught.... What had been true of all communications systems was now more generalized by the very fact that the new systems meshed so readily with *unspecialized receptive skills*. (1981c, pp. 236–7; emphasis added)

It should be stressed, however, that this comment still leaves open the possibility that even 'unspecialized receptive skills' might not 'mesh so readily' with some of the offerings of the 'new systems'. Another asymmetricality remains possible. Williams immediately argues nonetheless that the social configuration of the institutions of these means of communication is such that this symmetrical 'meshing' is more likely.

This perspective also reconnects interestingly with a more orthodox socio-logical conception of socialization (but not the narrowly functionalist one Williams criticized). Williams effectively locates these post-literate media in a dialectical relationship with 'primary groups', especially those based in kinship. It is precisely because such groups provide oral access to language that cinema and broadcasting could intersect with them so effectively. These modally correspondent means of communication thus could embed themselves far more effectively in the 'way of life' of primary groups than other social institutions such as, most obviously, formal education (the chief source of the skills of literacy). This was also related to Williams's concern about the modal changes to television threatened by planned flow since 'our most general modes of comprehension and judgement' were tied to the exercise of discrete periods of attention (*TV2*, p. 87).

Williams's assessment of 'modern' means of communication as means of cultural production and means of communicative production thus rests on the cusp of very sanguine judgement and recognition of outright utopian prospects. This, as I argue in the final chapter, is the characteristic normative 'mode' for Williams.

6.8 Excursus: the infrastructure of modernity?

Like Section 1.6, this section very briefly compares the reconstruction just undertaken with some 'fellow travellers'. Unlike that other excursus, however, the focus here is on 'common ground' rather than theoretical differences. As an excursus, it can be read as an 'addendum' or as a further linkage between this chapter and the next.

Williams's 'post-McLuhanist' typologization of means of communication anticipated recent attempts by John Thompson and Craig Calhoun to develop similar typologies based in the direct/indirect distinction between what they respectively term 'mediated interaction' and 'indirect social relations'.[71] Both Thompson's and Calhoun's understandings of 'indirectness' are based in a Weberian conception of action rather than Williams's Marxian social division of labour of cultural production. Thompson also works with a post-McLuhanist distinction between 'technical medium' and 'symbolic forms' where the former is 'the material substratum' of the latter (Thompson, 1995, p. 18).

Nonetheless, each of these three conceptual constructs provides a means of sociologically countering the excesses of technological determinism that tend to flourish in periods of technical innovation in means of communication. The recent case of the advent of 'the internet' is an obvious example. Much initial discussion of this 'new medium' failed to discriminate between what Williams would have distinguished as technical inventions (digitalization of data and its means of global transmission), the socially instituted technology ('the internet') and its attendant cultural forms (in a preliminary typo-logization: e-mail, websites, reactive and interactional interactivity, online newspapers etc). The relevance of the direct/indirect distinction to these developments is even more obvious.[72]

Calhoun categorizes 'information technology' (broadly, all durative and amplificatory means of communication) – together with markets and administered organizations – as 'the infrastructure of modernity'. By this term he means those practices which facilitated the rise of indirect social relations as the dominant form of social integration, so displacing the pre-modern dominance of face-to-face direct social relations, especially those based in kinship systems.[73] As we saw, Williams's recognition of the complex relation between institutional forms and indirect communication as opposed to 'primitive' directness draws much the same conclusion.

Graham Murdock's and Thompson's similar discussions of the role of 'communications' and 'the media' in modernity – both influenced by Anthony Giddens – stress a broader process of detraditionalization. Giddens, like Williams, works with a conception of 'mediated' disembedding but he has a particular emphasis on 'space–time distanciation'; that is, the 'experiential' – even ontological – consequences of the loss of specificity of temporal and spatial locales.[74]

What confronts contemporary social theorization of these issues is, as Thompson openly admits, a remarkably undertheorized conception of 'tradition' that speaks chiefly to a contrast between 'modern' and 'traditional' societies rather than the survival of aesthetic (and other) traditions into modernity. Yet even Thompson has little to say about the sociological relevance of aesthetic traditions.[75] As we saw in Section 5.1, Williams identified this sociological lacuna in 1981. His complex typology of cultural forms and social reproduction – especially its emphasis on 'trans-epochal' cultural forms – thus also speaks directly to this need.

The break from pre-modern myth and ritual into modernity assumed by Williams is, in contrast, consistent with an 'orthodox' Weberian conception of disenchantment or deritualization.[76] Yet it does not endorse the pessimism of Weber's ongoing processes of rationalization towards an 'iron cage' that in turn informs Adorno's culture industry thesis. Nor, however, does it endorse Benjamin's naïve surrealist confidence that a technically induced 'deritualization' of the aura he attaches to aesthetic objects necessarily leads to a revolutionary politics.[77]

Williams's critique of McLuhan's own aesthetic modernist naïvete so resembles, as we have seen, Adorno's critique of Benjamin. Williams was as wary as Adorno of the failure to distinguish between avant-gardist deployment of new technics as 'modern(ist)' aesthetic 'media' – means of communicative production – and their very different incorporation into the factory-like 'technology' of the production of cultural commodities.

In his *Late Marxism: Adorno, or, the persistence of the dialectic* Fredric Jameson employs Williams's 'theory of culture' as a counterpoint. For Jameson, Williams provides the missing element of Adorno's culture industry thesis: a theory of culture.[78] Jameson's purpose in this provocative assertion is to argue that Adorno provided an account of an industry that exploited what had been autonomous 'culture', rather than a social theory of contemporary culture *per se*. In this sense, the hostility that has been exhibited towards the alleged élitism of the famous culture industry chapter of *The Dialectic of Enlightenment* has been misplaced: the references to the 'manipulation' of media audiences are the product of a similar undertheorization rather than a serious thesis.[79] This is a reasonable defence of Adorno, versions of which first became prominent outside critical theory (in English at least) within the sociology of popular music and even within the Birmingham cultural studies project.[80]

Jameson's more surprising move is to suggest that Williams's account of hegemony redresses the inadequacies in Adorno's emphases on manipulation.[81] Jameson's underdeveloped suggestions are quite compatible with not only Williams's version of hegemony but also with his version of emancipatory ideology critique introduced at the end of Chapter 3.[82] Moreover, Jameson's further insight that what Williams's view of hegemony offers is a means of locating 'the culture industry' within a conception of 'stable' social reproduction is compatible with the discussion in Section 6.3.[83]

For it is precisely at this point that Williams's conception of the potentially asymmetrical relationship between hegemony, means of communication and cultural forms comes into effect. Williams's establishment of a 'displaced' correspondence between broadcasting and the emergent consumerist order strongly resembles what Andrew Feenberg has more recently called the hermeneutic role of the 'cultural horizon of technology' in social hegemony.[84] Feenberg's thesis moves from the same premisses as Williams's social shaping approach to technology. Like Williams he provides a critique of technological determinism which leaves open the determinate possibility of social intervention 'between' what Williams distinguishes as a technical invention and socially instituted technology. In direct opposition to Weberian pessimism, Feenberg calls this possibility 'subversive rationalization'.[85]

This dimension of Williams's conception of hegemony so situates technology as an additional 'unstable equilibrium'. Williams's confidence in technical and cultural innovation was not blunted by the failures of avant-gardism. This was certainly the case with the prospects for 'new media'. Having noted in 'Communications Technologies and Social Institutions' that the advent of the video camera and recorder mark a phase in which 'the means of production are themselves being distributed', he concludes with this similar speculation:

> The epochal change, if it could indeed be achieved, would be a movement beyond the two previous major stages of communications technologies and institutions. The stage of minority instrumental systems (writing and printing) has already been joined and in some sectors succeeded by majority systems (print in generally literate societies, cinema, radio,

television) in which the typical relation is one of a few producers to many consumers: a repetition, in new technical forms, of a major division of labour...In this second stage, the limited distribution of specialized products has been overtaken by the wide distribution of generalized products. What now may be possible is a qualitative change to the wide distribution of *processes*: the provision of equitable access to the means and resources of directly-determined communication, serving immediate personal and social needs. (1981c, p. 238)

It is not difficult to see this as a revision of the policy commitment cited in the previous section of this chapter from *Communications*. The indirectness of institutional provision would be replaced with the more utopian vision of appropriate technologies enabling the directness of 'direct autonomous composition' and 'qualitatively different social life'. However, it must be remembered that this is Williams at his most self-consciously speculative and still more sanguinely specific than Benjamin in the 'Work of Art' essay.

Williams's last major writing on this topic published two years later in 1983, the 'Culture and Technology' chapter of *Towards 2000*, posits a more modest but still radical-democratic version of this possibility. As noted in Section 6.3, the limited innovations within commodified popular culture are acknowledged but only those independent of market standardization and/or produced by those who 'look to live beyond the routines which attempt to control and reduce them' (*T2000*, p. 146) are valorized. It is these sectors that Williams wishes to see privileged in the institutionalization of 'post-broadcasting' communications technologies. Further, if 'interactivity' were understood as 'interaction' rather than 'reaction' to pre-programmed marketized 'choices', then the envisioned 'necessary institution of new and very complex communicative capacities and relationships' might take shape thus:

Again, one of the major benefits of the new technologies could be a significant improvement in the practicability of every kind of voluntary association: *the fibres of civil society* as distinct from both the market and the state.... This could be, in practice, the achievement of full social and cultural powers by civil society, as opposed to their appropriation or marginalisation by the corporations or by the state. (*T2000*, p. 150; emphasis added)

These comments speak directly to the recent discussions around the relationship between the internet and the democratic norm of a public sphere.[86] Williams's typology of means of communication so points to a distinct normative goal: the design of communications systems in which post-literate media too might reach the stage of 'majority instrumental systems'.

Williams's consideration of the role of means of communication in modernity thus consistently draws him towards overt articulation of his radical democratic norms. Yet once again we see him hovering between sanguinity and utopianism. The final chapter highlights this apparently contradictory pattern of articulation of Williams's emancipatory goals and, also, its relation to conceptions of modernity, public sphere and modernism in his sociology of culture.

7
The Long Revolution(s) of Modernity

> A very large part of our intellectual life, to say nothing of our social practice, is, however, devoted to criticizing the long revolution, in this or that aspect, by many powerful selective techniques. But as the revolution itself extends, until nobody can escape it, this whole drift seems increasingly irrelevant. In naming the great process of change the long revolution, I am trying to learn assent to it, an adequate assent of mind and spirit. I find increasingly that the values and meanings I need are all in this process of change. If it is pointed out, in traditional terms, that democracy, industry and extended communication are all means rather than ends, I reply that this, precisely, is their revolutionary character. (*LR*, p. 13)

Williams's embrace of his 'long revolution' undercuts any easy prospect of 'narrative closure' in any study of his work. His remarkable act of completely republishing and reassessing *The Long Revolution*'s final chapter in *Towards 2000*, five years before his death, also problematizes any easy periodization of his work into early and 'mature' writings. Yet, of course there were shifts and changes in his emancipatory goals as elsewhere in his work.

Most notably, his rapprochement with the Marxian tradition – which made possible the entire 'cultural production' paradigm and the grounding of his social formalism – was matched by a resumption of his reflections on the prospects for the forms of social change in which he had expressed such confidence in the above passage in 1961. The consolidated capitalism that had defeated his early 'first and second New Left' hopes was later acknowledged, as we saw, in *The May Day Manifesto*. Nonetheless, he always saw some form of non-prescriptive socialism as a necessary component of the completed long revolution.

Williams's death in 1988 came just prior to the 'changes in system' from 'actually existing socialism' in Europe that are now commonsensically benchmarked by the watershed of '1989'. Undoubtedly, he would have welcomed those initial changes, as he had the previous uprisings, as evidence of hope against what he saw as Orwell's pessimism.[1] Today, Williams's 'assent' to the long revolution's widening embrace in the passage above might superficially connote an all too familiar kind of intellectual conformism to the uncritical embrace of all or most aspects of global capitalism. That comment did come at a high point in Williams's public wariness about Marxism, but its critical edge remains plain. Undoubtedly, had he lived, he would have addressed as another form of 'conformism' the modish variant of 'post-Marxism' that swept the western academies during the 1990s. Yet it is likely he would also have sought dialogue with the 'post-Marxist' intellectual avant-gardes, and perhaps even further elucidated the critical sociological project that this book has attempted to reconstruct.

This brief final chapter does not speculate about that possible elucidation but, rather, aims to articulate Williams's emancipatory goals more deliberately with the sociology of culture presented in the previous chapters.

7.1   Modernity, modernism and public sphere

The year 1989 also marked the arrival of the first English translation of Habermas's 1962 work, *The Structural Transformation of the Public Sphere*.[2] A considerable literature has built up seeking to link Williams's project with this aspect of Habermas's work, some even arguing that Habermas was influenced by Williams.[3] A common characteristic of this literature is its focus on the early Williams, most obviously *The Long Revolution* and *Communications*.[4] This is an entirely understandable emphasis but it fails to take into account Williams's later sociology of culture. What I wish to briefly assess here is the extent to which this dimension of Habermas's work might provide a useful means of drawing out Williams's normative project within his later work, not only as it is rearticulated in *Towards 2000* and in his related reflections in his last planned work, *The Politics of Modernism*, but also some of its latent components within the sociology of culture.

It is not difficult to see the appeal of the comparison with Habermas. Despite its grounding in characteristically philosophical Frankfurt concerns, Habermas's book tries to locate the ideal of a public sphere within an historical contextualization of its emergence, with Britain as the paradigmatic case study. At the very least Williams's radical-democratic vision undoubtedly shared Habermas's emphasis on the virtues of informed citizenship and deliberative decision-making.

A brief account of Habermas's public sphere thesis is necessary here. The advocacy of peaceful reconciliation of diverse *informed* opinions is argued by Habermas to be the central politico-cultural achievement of liberalism which cannot be brushed aside as 'mere ideology' disguising a class interest or other ulterior purpose. Rational-critical debate initially emerges, in Habermas's 1962 account, from the 'audience-oriented privateness' of letter writing within the bourgeois family through to the literary critical discussion in the eighteenth-century London coffee houses. It then grows from a literary public sphere into a public sphere which exists 'between state and society', so making possible the emergence of the modern 'public use of reason'. This mediating sphere was able, via 'the vehicle of public opinion' to 'put the state in touch with the needs of society' where the latter is unmistakeably the civil society of the rising bourgeoisie (Habermas, 1991, p. 31). The transition to democratic parliaments can thus be seen as the development of a 'political public sphere' inside the state itself. Habermas distinguishes the political public sphere from the literary public sphere, defining the former in terms of 'public discussion deal[ing] with objects connected to activities of the state' (Habermas, 1974, p. 49).

In the wake of the belated influence of the English translation, Habermas stressed that his initial articulation of his public sphere thesis 'moved totally within the circle of a classical Marxian *critique* of ideology' (Habermas *et al.*, 1993, p. 463). This approach is identical to that introduced in Section 3.1 as emancipatory ideology critique. Habermas wishes to acknowledge the utopian prospect of the public sphere, while remaining fully aware of both its dramatic failure as an empirical account of 'realpolitik', and its possible success as a means of legitimation of ongoing domination. But he also wishes to acknowledge that such an unfulfilled promise retains a normative potential as a court of appeal.

There is thus considerable resemblance between Habermas's emancipatory ideology critique of the ideal of a rational-critical public opinion and Williams's immanent critique of 'culture'. It is perhaps not surprising then, that Habermas briefly cites Williams in *The Structural Transformation*. This is more likely due to Williams's and the Frankfurt School's overlapping methodological interests in an historical semantics than any greater interest by Habermas in Williams. Habermas's chief acknowledged interest in *Culture and Society* is in Williams's historical semantic analyses of 'art' and 'culture'.[5]

However, Habermas's historical account of the relationship between literary and political public spheres not only overlaps with Williams's early sociohistorical interests, but strongly resembles the later Williams's emphasis on the 'emergent' capacities of cultural forms and formations. Habermas has recently revived the model of the literary public sphere as a means of recognizing more fully the role of emergent social movements.[6]

Williams similarly endorsed the role of 'new social movements' (especially feminism and environmentalism) in *Towards 2000*. However, this was not his first such recognition. His long critique of Daniel Bell's *The Cultural Contradictions of Capitalism* in 1976 mounted a strong defence of new social movements against Bell's neo-conservative rejection of them as evidence of the 'hedonistic' success of modernist avant-gardism over the everyday routinization of the Protestant ethic.[7] Habermas mounted a very similar critique of Bell in his influential 1980 speech on the unfinished 'Enlightenment' project of modernity.[8] As we saw in Section 1.6, Williams recognized this Enlightenment project initially in *The Long Revolution* and more fully in his later writings on culture. Habermas, like Williams, argued that Bell had recognized but misconstrued a significant tension between what Habermas distinguished as societal modernization and cultural modernity.

The confusions between the Enlightenment sense of 'modernity' and the aesthetic senses of 'modern' – and indeed also a reduced technicist notion of 'modernization' – are well documented but are also, of course, indicative of a crucial terrain of semantic contestation.[9] Part of Habermas's 1980 strategy was plainly to 'outflank' some notions of the postmodern by shifting the core conception of 'modern' from its aesthetic to its Enlightenment meaning. Neo-conservatives like Bell – Habermas's chief 'target' – are so revealed to be blaming cultural modernity (especially aesthetic modernism and the avant-gardes) for social phenomena more reasonably attributable to (mainly capitalist) societal modernization. Despite their opposing assessments of avant-gardism, Bell's conflation thus strongly resembles McLuhan's 'projection'.

In a 1987 lecture Williams contests the usual periodization of aesthetic modernism. He advocates a strategy familiar from *Culture and Society*: the creation of an alternative 'tradition' – this time of the modern – that is different from the selective tradition from which 'postmodernism' has been derived. His alternative tradition would broaden the 'usual' periodization of aesthetic modernism (1890–1940) to include at least the Romantics in order to reopen 'a modern *future*' (*POM*, p. 35).[10] This strategy is put into practice in one of the late essays on avant-gardism, 'The Metropolis and the Emergence of Modernism', where Wordsworth and Dickens are given pride of place.[11]

Such a reconfiguration explains why the discussion of avant-gardist formations in *The Sociology of Culture* so strongly resembles that of the Romantic artist in *Culture and Society*. In effect, the latter's formational chapter on the Romantics could be seen as a fundamental component of Williams's move towards emancipatory ideology critique in that it sketched the preconditions of the Romantics' establishment of culture as that 'court of appeal' where emancipatory critique could lodge its normative claims to a possible future.

In one of his few references to 'modernity' in its quasi-Habermasian sense, Williams repositions T.S. Eliot formationally as part of 'a literally reactionary tendency', 'an *arrière* garde', that is 'a modernism, as so often, against modernity' (1985, p. 43; *POM*, p. 76).[12] As we saw in Chapter 1, by recovering culture's 'post-Romantic' role as a 'court of appeal', Williams began the restoration of its Enlightenment dynamic that Eliot, more than anyone else except perhaps Arnold, had sought to reverse in the English tradition. The key 'modern' issue that so set Williams against Eliot was equitable access to education, a central component of Williams's 'expanding culture'.

In the 'Culture and Technology' chapter of *Towards 2000* – apparently planned to be republished in *The Politics of Modernism*[13] – Williams reintroduces Leavis's mass/minority formulation within the terms of his semantically expanded 'modernism'. The figure of the metropolis is employed to mediate the 'displaced' ways in which the 'two faces of this "modernism" could literally not recognize each other': the 'energetic minority art of a time of reduction and dislocation' and 'the routines of a technologized "mass" culture' (*T2000*, pp. 142–3). If taken as a general account of aesthetic modernism, this is plainly inadequate; it would indeed be 'infelicitously using a synchronic term to cover a diachronic process' (Pinkney, 1989b, p. 23). However, Williams is here instead attempting to rescue his *potential allies* against a common foe from an analytical failing; that is, from a perspective formed from an 'unholy combination' of technological determinism and cultural pessimism that Williams wishes to 'disentangle and explain' (*T2000*, p. 129). Those who held to this view regarded, for example, the approaching satellite broadcasting as both inevitable in its institutional forms *and* contaminated by 'mass culture'. Critics of capitalist societal modernization thus increasingly resembled cultural neo-conservatives.

If so, then who or what is that foe? The broadly correct – but too easy – answer is the 'paranational capitalism' – today usually located within the category of globalization – that increasingly figures in Williams's last writings. But that hardly answers the question of why the whole project of *The Politics of Modernism* appears to have been positioned 'against the new conformists'. Yet Williams is reasonably explicit in 'Culture and Technology':

> a new class of intellectuals are [*sic*] already occupying and directing the sites of the new cultural and information technologies. They are talking confidently of their "product" and its planned marketing, and are closely engaged with the major supplying corporations and the myriad of new specialist agencies in their interstices. They are oriented, within exposed and declining primary economies, to a new phase of expanded "post-industrial" consumerism ... (*T2000*, pp. 128–9)

Williams's 'new conformists', I would suggest, are those who would 'conform' with *this future projection*. Undoubtedly, the exemplary case here is McLuhanism. The 'two faces of modernism' discussion is prefaced by a reprise of *Television*'s critique of 'the fantastic projection' of the 'global village'. The 'real' two faces of modernism are accordingly revealed as the 'monopolizing corporations' that made the global village projection plausible, and the latter's affirmative theorization by (presumably conformist) metropolitan intellectuals.[14] In his essays on avant-gardism, Williams added to the latter the incorporation of many avant-gardist practices.

The republication of 'Culture and Technology' in *The Politics of Modernism* divorced it from the explicit critique of the post-industrial society thesis that opened *Towards 2000*'s reconsideration of *The Long Revolution*'s 'Britain in the sixties' analysis. In what is tantamount to an auto-critique, Williams makes it plain that any attempt to understand his former invocation of 'industrial revolution' as a component of his 'long revolution' must be subject to his later critique of technological determinism. Most significantly, he states in explicitly Marxian terms that the technologically determinist focus on (new) forces of production divorced from relations of production in the post-industrial society thesis must be rejected.[15] Although Daniel Bell is not mentioned, Williams's criticism is consistent with other critiques of Bell's *The Coming of Post-Industrial Society*.[16] Indeed, the separation of forces from relations of production is a position Bell recently reasserted.[17]

So the rejection of intellectual conformism with neo-conservative – in Habermas's sense above – 'post-industrial consumerist' projections could be understood as a chief target of both *Towards 2000* and *The Politics of Modernism*. Williams's more immediate concern is the susceptibility of 'nonconformists' to technological determinism and cultural pessimism.

Where might all this leave Williams's own 'long revolutionary' emancipatory goals? Could all the values Williams needed still be found 'in the process of change' as he states in the opening citation above?

His rejection of any naïve confidence in the revolutionary character of the technical forces of production is obviously a considerable qualification of any optimism about 'industry' and, indeed, such means rather than ends. As we saw in the previous chapter, Williams's later position would regard technical innovation as a site of considerable contestation where the norms in play were more likely to be externally democratic rather than internal to industrial change.

Deepening democratization, of course, endures as a continuing norm throughout Williams's work, albeit apparently shorn of its early guarantor, working-class democratic institutions, by incorporation. An educated and participatory democracy – and its extension into other forms of social life such as workplace self-management – never seems to have wavered as part of his vision. In the more specific case of means of 'extended communications', Williams plainly remained more open to his earlier optimism that each new revolutionization opened up the immanent but determinate possibility of radical social reinstitutionalization tied to deepening democratization.

The critique of technological determinism is thus a useful critical reference point in signalling Williams's revisions of his long revolution. All the more reason, then, for his contesting technological determinism's presence amongst his fellow travellers.

What then of that other contemporary failing amongst the fellow travellers, cultural pessimism? The immediate example Williams provides suggests merely a continuation of a fear of mass culture. But the frequent references to the future in Williams's last works suggest something far deeper. He rejects being 'stuck in the post' in contemporary discussions of modernism precisely because of their implicit denial of the prospects for significant social change in the future (*POM*, p. 35). Cultural pessimism is, in short, conformism with the *arrière garde*'s rejection of modernity's 'incomplete project' – in Habermas's sense of the fulfillment of the Enlightenment's promises – in favour of Eliot-like reaction *or* neo-conservative accommodation with 'post-industrial consumerism' as a kind of legitimatively utopian 'end of history'. Here especially Williams would posit a resembling correspondence with that strain of avant-gardism that focussed on personal liberation at all costs.[18]

We are so returned, in effect, to Williams's interest in the alternative as opposed to the incorporated or residual, the innovative rather than the merely replicative. As we have seen, *The Sociology of Culture* also acknow-ledged this distinction but characterized the tension in terms of contradictory relations between social and cultural reproduction (in its multiple senses) that took conjunctural forms of asymmetry and symmetry. At its strongest this thesis asserts that without innovation the bourgeois epoch is 'at total risk' (*SOC*, p. 201). So innovation too becomes a site of hegemonic contest-ation. Formational analyses (as summarized in Table 6.2) were required to assess the plausibility of the modes of correspondence implied in Williams's suggested correspondence between intellectual conformism and hegemonic future projections.

In the previous chapter we saw that Williams's own specific assessments of the future on issues close to these concerns – democratization of the means of communication – hovered on the cusp of a remarkably sanguine revelation of risks and dangers of reversals of his long revolution's achieve-ments and the envisioning of openly utopian prospects for its completion. This 'tragic utopianism' can also be contextualized within a larger body of his work.

7.2   Tragic utopianism

Habermas's public sphere thesis is, in brief, an emancipatory ideology critique of the Enlightenment and liberal promise of deliberative 'rational-critical' democracy. As I noted in Section 3.1, emancipatory ideology critique can be loosely characterized as the pursuit of the 'utopian promise' of an emancipatory ideology. As Habermas pursues the promise of the public sphere, the early Williams pursues that of culture.

Moreover, as Williams does not merely seek to revive a lost organic com-munity of cultural unity, so Habermas does not seek to revive the agora of Athenian democracy. *The Structural Transformation* is, as its subtitle plainly states: 'an inquiry into a category of *bourgeois* society'.[19] It is for this reason that Habermas places so much emphasis on the audience-oriented privateness of letter-writing and indeed, the pre-political literary public sphere as a precursor to the *bourgeois* public sphere. The emergent bourgeois subjectivity within an intimate sphere entailed an immanent intersubjectivity that Habermas would later 'ontologize' in his theory of communicative action.[20]

Another motive for this shift was Habermas's initial assessment of the histor-ical decline into a 'power infiltrated public sphere' and 'culture-consuming public' that owes much to Adorno's conception of the 'naked' power relations that prevail in the *absence* of an (emancipatory) ideology worthy of immanent critique.[21]

Similarly, Williams's late hostility to the legitimative utopia of 'post-industrial consumerism' renews a long-standing theme in his work that first emerges in 'Culture is Ordinary''s vitriolic attack on both the 'old cheapjacks' and the 'dangerous new class' of advertisers and publicists (*ROH*, pp. 6–7), continues in the 'missing chapter' on advertising planned for *The Long Revolution*[22] and remains near the surface of his subsequent writings on means of communication.

There is then a striking similarity between Habermas's and Williams's estimates of the threats to their ideals of a deliberative public sphere and an edu-cated and participatory democracy. However, while for the Habermas of *The Structural Transformation* the 'manufactured public sphere' appeared to have arrived, Williams's 'British Chemicals [sponsored] general election' was only a dystopian prospect (*T2000*, p. 138). Likewise, while Williams too had an abiding interest in the forms of intersubjectivity that facilitated the formation of bourgeois ideals – and especially, the obstacles to their enactment – he saw no need to theoretically ground these, as Habermas had done, 'at a deeper level' (Habermas, 1993, p. 442).

Williams's conception of this intersubjectivity arises in the discussion of 'liberal tragedy' in *Modern Tragedy* examined in Chapter 1. He had there linked that strain of tragedy to what he called in *The Long Revolution* 'the deadlocks of modern society'. By 'deadlock' Williams means, in part, the incomplete bourgeois revolutions (*MT2*, p. 68). But liberal tragedy refers to more than the masking and emancipatory senses of liberalism as an ideology. As we saw in Section 3.2, Williams's thesis here resembles Goldmann's 'innerworldly refusal' in *The Hidden God*. A key component of 'liberal tragedy' is a 'liberal self' and 'liberal consciousness' that is 'trapped'. Part of this entrapment is a recognition of the falsity of all or some liberal values within 'the existing compromise order' (*MT2*, p. 96). Ibsen's plays are seen as the first full articulation of this recognition. As we saw in Section 4.4, it is in Ibsen that Williams first identifies a fully self-conscious *recognition* of the contradictions of the private/public divide. The tragic hero is no longer ennobled by suffering, nor dies struggling against this falsity, but, crucially for Williams, internalizes the deadlock in the form of an unfulfillable aspiration:

> And this is the heart of liberal tragedy, for we have moved from the heroic position of the individual liberator, the aspiring self against society, to a tragic position, of the self against the self. Guilt, that is to say, has become internal and personal, just as aspiration was internal and personal. The internal and personal fact is the only general fact, in the end. Liberalism, in its heroic phase, begins to pass into its twentieth century breakdown: the self-enclosed, guilty and isolated world; the time of man [*sic*] his own victim.

> We are still in this world, and it is doubtful if we can clearly name all its pressures. A characteristic ideology has presented it as truth and even as science, until argument against it has come to seem hopeless. A structure of feeling as deep as this enacts a world, as well as interpreting it, so that we learn it from experience as well as from ideology. (*MT2*, p. 100)

This tragic figure is a familiar one within Williams's later work. The retreat into such a pessimistic assessment of future prospects, underwritten by an equally pessimistic conception of 'modern' subjectivity, is a major motif Williams discerns in modern cultural formations. It is the key thematic link between his critique of formalist linguistic and cultural theories (and, indeed, technological determinism) and his formational studies. It is perhaps the ultimate 'limit' Williams finds in a dissident bourgeois consciousness whether it manifests in dystopias or 'bourgeois cultural theory'.[23]

Yet what equally seems to have attracted Williams to Bloomsbury's bourgeois dissidence was that its ethic successfully combined its attention to personal liberation – most notably of women – with an alternative to the tragic liberal self: a *conscience* that facilitated public engagement, so redeeming part of the liberal promise.

But what does Williams mean in the above citation by enacting a world as well as interpreting it? Is this a genre confusion or perhaps even an ontological confusion of 'art' and 'reality'? Not so. Williams is here practising the reconstruction of a 'structure of feeling' examined in Section 1.4 and the critique of active conventions examined in Section 3.4. As we saw, the critically reflective capacities of autonomous cultural practice reveal the structure of feeling as *unrealized possibilities* while conventions may indeed 'produce an action'. In *The Sociology of Culture* these two perspectives are briefly conjoined, in another discussion of tragedy. There Williams argues that new formal conventions may objectivate 'sooner' – rather than merely 'anticipate' – emergent forms of social recognition that later might become fully articulated ideologies.[24] As in *The Long Revolution* analysis, it is the common social preconditions to which both modes (here drama and philosophy) speak – as in a 'resembling correspondence' (Table 3.2). However, the modal capacity of drama to enact a completed action allows a different form of social recognition. Moreover, in the particular instance above, Williams is also stressing the containment of possible forms of social action that follows from the lack of such social recognition. Liberal tragedy is Williams's characterization of this entrapment within a form of public *inaction* that indeed 'enacts a world'. Its pervasiveness so operates hegemonically and its socio-cultural reproduction requires formations that practise such withdrawal from, at least, Bloomsbury-like conscience.

Whether these are more accurately classified as modes or genres, Williams is here not confusing aesthetico-cultural forms with, for example, political ideologies. Rather, he is suggesting that the utopian and tragic may be determinate 'modal' components of aesthetic cultural forms, ideologies, practices of interpretation and cultural theories. In a related but distinct example, we met in Section 4.3 Williams's hostility to the dystopian modal choices of Orwell's fiction and Stuart Hall's politico-cultural theory. Similarly, Williams's approving citation from John Fekete in 'The Uses of Cultural Theory' states this position (here addressed to individuated theorists) plainly: "the intention of emancipatory praxis is prior to interpretive practice" (1986, p. 29; *POM*, p. 174).[25]

Plainly, the tragic liberal self that shrinks from such commitment is also a very different bourgeois 'self' from that which Habermas initially celebrated. Habermas too recognizes something like this development in his character-ization of an increasingly privatized intimate sphere that no longer looked outwards. What Habermas saw evidenced in changing domestic architecture and urban design Williams would later recognize in its socially extended form as mobile privatization.[26]

A tragic 'broken liberalism' would not be an ideology easily susceptible to emancipatory critique. Liberal inaction might even be thought as a form of 'tragic conformism'. Of course, it is also this tragic subjectivity that successive social movements – most obviously variants of feminism but also civil rights movements – have sought to change, often 'from within' in something like the Bloomsbury mode. While both Williams and Habermas were slow to recognize the role of such 'counter publics' – except of course in the case of class for Williams – each subsequently acknowledged these failings. Habermas had certainly recognized the patriarchal character of the bourgeois family from which the intersubjectivity of bourgeois letter-writing emerged in his initial account. Williams appears not to have reached a similar recognition concerning his conception of bourgeois intersubjectivity, his closest being an account of the contradictory forms of domination within the bourgeois family in 'The Politics of the Avant-garde'.[27]

Williams even subheads part of this discussion in *Modern Tragedy* – written in 1962 – 'the end of liberalism' (*MT2*, p. 73). The crucial linkage with the political project we met in Chapter 1 is Williams's appeal to a non-violent revolution 'by a process of argument and consensus', if only for 'some Western societies' (*MT2*, p. 78). However, the likely (British) institutional bearers of this demo-cratic project were hegemonically incorporated by 1966 and were recognized as failed in comparison with the new social movements in *Towards 2000*.[28]

As Eagleton has recently pointed out, Williams weighs up with equal seri-ousness in *Modern Tragedy* the potentially tragic necessity of violent revolution, so setting aside 'what is properly called utopianism, or revolutioniary romantic-ism' as 'the suppression or dilution of this quite inevitable fact' (*MT2*, p. 77).[29] Yet it is this position that Williams appears to have most significantly revised in subsequent years. In the 1979 Afterword to *Modern Tragedy* he identified an 'overwhelming' contemporary tragic form: 'a widespread loss of the future' (*MT2*, p. 208), so providing a clear linkage between the tragic liberal self and his later rejection of contemporary intellectual conformisms discussed above.[30] Acccordingly, he reassessed the utopian mode:

> It has been argued that it is time now to move from a tragic to a utopian mode, and there is some strength in this; it is also a classical form of invigoration and hopeful protest; it is also, at any time, a necessary mode of one area of social thought. But it is not, when we look into it, a question of this or that prescription. The fact is that neither the frankly utopian form, nor even the more qualified outlines of practicable futures, which are now so urgently needed, can begin to flow until we have faced, at the necessary depth, the divisions and contradictions which now inhibit them. (*MT2*, p. 218)

It is this 'tragic utopianism', I would suggest, that strongly informs Williams's last works and accounts for the tension between normative and 'sanguine' modes of writing we have met in his sociology of culture.[31]

Williams's implication later on in *Modern Tragedy*'s (1962) analysis of liberal tragedy – that only a socialist principle of cooperation offers an alternative to this crisis of subjectivity – is consistent with, if a somewhat glib summary of, his early normative vision and so implies his larger project of democratization. Of more enduring significance is the foundation he lays for a critique of what he explicitly articulates in his last writings as a retreat into 'negations' with no reconstructive referent – especially by the avant-gardes. He thus alludes to the classic liberal distinction – between negative freedoms (from constraint and obligation) and positive freedoms (enabling fuller social participation). Another 'way out' of liberal tragedy, then, might be the pursuit of the positive freedoms of an educated and participatory democracy that Williams celebrated – in the same year as the *Modern Tragedy* analysis – in *Communications* and renewed in *Towards 2000*.[32] Habermas's work has moved in this direction in recent years as well, so effectively renewing his practice of immanent ideology critique.[33]

The late renewal of the utopian mode in Williams informs *Towards 2000*'s opening reconsideration of 'Britain in the sixties'. Entirely focussed on discussions of the future, he activates his 1978 analysis of utopian forms of writing in 'Utopia and Science Fiction'.[34] In so doing he also provides an effective challenge to Daniel Bell's project of redefining the utopian mode in *The End of Ideology* as an instrumentally 'empirical one' (Bell, 1962, p. 405).[35]

Williams distinguishes between systematic and heuristic utopias. The distinction is best exemplified for him by that famous clash of late nineteenth-century socialist classics, Edward Bellamy's *Looking Backwards* and William Morris's reply, *News From Nowhere*. While Bellamy's systematic work achieves an account of a projected 'social machinery', it lacks the heuristic dimension of *News From Nowhere*, which Williams characterizes, following E.P. Thompson following Abensour, as 'the education of desire' (*PMC*, p. 202).

Williams thus regards 'Britain in the sixties' and *Towards 2000* as 'prospective analyses' which attempt to combine both modes of utopian writing. These analyses hold to the key systematic projection of a plausible alternative social order, while maintaining the heuristic mode's aim to establish what Williams calls, in a now famous phrase, 'resources of hope'. Such 'resources' necessarily include social agents such as those within new social movements. Moreover, the heuristic mode's 'utopian impulse' might also challenge not only 'a more generalized despair, but also . . . the incorporated and marketed version of a libertarian capitalist cornucopia' (*T2000*, p. 14) which, as we have seen, he also calls 'post-industrial consumerism'. For this reason Williams is drawn towards fictional utopias like Ursula Le Guinn's *The Dispossessed* and prospective analyses like *The Limits to Growth* whose 'content' offers a prospect that implies a preferable future outside the over-resourced parameters of the managed affluence of late capitalism.[36] Le Guinn demonstrates for Williams 'not the education but the learning of desire' for a new mode of social change that plainly speaks to Williams's postulated 'tragic self' (1978g, p. 213; *PMC*, p. 211).

It is by such means that Williams 'reinvented' the normative dimension of his critical sociology in times that bear more than a passing resemblance to the present. This position still shares much with emancipatory ideology critique but also attends to the dimensions that have tended to limit its effectiveness. In its 'Frankfurt' form at least it implied a formalism of its own – that the act of critique was sufficient in itself to unleash the utopian energies of the emancipatory ideology. Williams's heuristic utopianism – and its attempt to overcome the imaginative deadlock of the tragic liberal self – restores a dimension well known to Marx, that social agents were required who might act on this potentiality. In one of his very last writings, for example, Williams recognized and supported a reactivation of the Romantic critique of capitalism by ecological social movements that might recognize the Romantics as 'voices of fellow strugglers rather than of historically outdated or periodised thinkers' (*C&S*, p. viii).[37]

But Williams's reconstruction goes further. By placing the practice of prospective critical analysis on the cusp of two modal forms – tragedy and utopia – he provides a more satisfactory means of linking emancipatory critique and empirical research. Prospective analysis informed by the typologies and methods of his sociology of culture becomes a practicable intellectual option.

The tragic liberal self certainly was not the self Raymond Williams inhabited.[38] Yet he was aware that whatever the prospects for those formed as 'organic' intellectuals like himself to escape the tragic liberal self, he would always need to address formations of bourgeois fractional composition. His account of the expansion of education in *The Long Revolution*, for example, had provided a very precise class-fractional analysis of the alliance of social forces that had brought about this component of his 'expanding culture'.

Likewise, the addressees of the first edition of *Communications* were plainly Leavisite school teachers.

Each time he faced subsequent setbacks he carefully assessed the contradictory components of the existent balance of forces.[39] These sites included those he had first identified in *The Long Revolution*, and then reconceptualized in his later work as sites of contradiction in social and cultural reproduction. They rested on the inability of any social system to control completely the cultural productive forces and social relations necessary for innovation. They thus provided a schematic checklist for his counter-hegemonic 'resources of hope' within his 'cultural revolution' of expanding democratization.

Still, is all this sufficient to persuade the tragically guilty modern self to look outwards towards positive freedoms and perhaps embrace more? The continuing appeals to Williams's exemplary life are perhaps the most obvious suggestive evidence of his success here. Yet we have few records of Williams's own 'experience' in dealing face-to-face with this tragically withdrawn 'self'. One such is his account of his final major cultural policy involvement: as a 'mole' on the British Arts Council during the term of the Callaghan Labour government. His 'brief', negotiated with the Minister, was the development of strategies for the Council's democratic reform based on lessons learnt during his membership. Despite his brief he still found it necessary to offer his resignation twice. His retrospective assessment of the Council's limitations harks back to the micropolitical reforms to the 'managerialist' committee procedure he proposed in *The Long Revolution*, to his critique of the ideology of service in *Culture and Society*, and to his long-standing proposals for democratic intermediary bodies in the reform of cultural institutions.

His own most Adorno-like formulations are developed in this policy critique. He characterizes the typical form of control of the Council and its panels – being told 'you have arrived when you sit at this table' and so on – as 'administered consensus by co-option'. Likewise, the typical pseudo-consensual decision-making which results from the lack of formal voting is 'a bewildered consensus'.

Yet, unsurprisingly, he does see such an administered culture as nonetheless open to reform towards his goal of fully democratic intermediacy and even the more radical demand for 'the concession of the practice of democracy':

> "Isn't that syndicalism?", asked the present Chairman, a former Labour minister, when I outlined these ideas. In fact it is not, and could not be. The proposals are conceived as applicable within the existing social order, without necessary changes in the ownership of means of production, and may indeed, if only for that reason, be impracticable: making a reality of democratic management is very difficult in this kind of centralized and minority-controlled society, and its proposals are, understandably, very fiercely resisted. Not syndicalism, then, but a degree of self-management,

of diversity and openness of representation, and of vigorous public argument. If we have to go further, we shall go further. (*ROH*, p. 55)

This Williams speaks to our present. Whether and how 'to go further' depends on continuing prospective analysis of the balance of forces between the project of deepening democratization and/or its challenge by such forces as contemporary '*arrière* gardes'. The resources Williams provided for this task within his sociology of culture remain some of his most enduring legacies.

Notes

Preface: looking both ways

1. Jones (1994).
2. Murdock (1997, p. 87). Cf. Garnham's complaint that the key citation from Williams in one of Garnham's defining essays 'is hidden, gnomically, in a book of literary theory' (Garnham, 1986, p. 9). Garnham was one of the few to actively promote Williams's mature cultural materialism within this field during Williams's lifetime (Garnham, 1983). I say 'often called political economists of the media' because it seems to me that many such authors now write within wider fields, notably social theory (e.g. Garnham, 2000).
3. Robbins (1995, p. xvi).
4. This – and the related status of the redeemability of the category of 'culturalism' – is probably my major interpretative difference with the work of Andrew Milner with whom I otherwise largely agree.
5. Lash (1993, pp. 193–4).
6. Kellner (1997a). Cf. Kellner's parallel argument for an end to the polarized debate between 'political economy' and cultural studies (1997b).
7. Here my position closely resembles that advocated by Goodwin and Wolff (1997) on the relation between a post-functionalist critical sociology and a 'conserved' cultural studies, and shares much with Rojek's and Turner's recent critique of the cultural turn (2000).
8. I should note too here the increasing commonality between the later work of Williams's most stringent critic, Terry Eagleton, and the early work of Williams. Two of his most recent books (Eagleton, 2000, 2003) suggest a quite methodical revisitation of the key elements of the early Williams.
9. Table 5.3 might also be considered such an excursus.

1 Settling accounts with 'culture'

1. Williams (1958); citations shall be from the more accessible *ROH* republication. This section has benefited from my exchange with John Corner: Corner (1994); Jones (1995).
2. Williams (1968a); citations from *ROH*.
3. *Conviction*, the 1958 collection that included 'Culture is Ordinary' and an essay by Hoggart, was designed as a successor to the most famous collection of writings by 'the angry young men', *Declaration*. Accordingly its flap jacket opens with: 'More Angry Young Men? No ... emphatically not. The contributors to this book might well be called the Thoughtful Young Men.' Cf. Ritchie (1988).
4. Knights (1978).
5. See the further discussion of Arnold in Section 1.5.

6. Baldick (1983, pp. 186–93).
7. Leavis (1966).
8. *R&C*; Hoggart (1963).
9. Passeron (1972); Jones (1982, pp. 92–6).
10. Williams (1957a, b); *C&S*, pp. 319–28. This method is discussed in the next section.
11. *COM1*, p. 75; *C&C*, p. xx; *T2000*, pp. 145–6; cf. Section 6.3.
12. Indeed, there is an uncannily similar phrase in Leavis's 'Literature and Society' (1966, p. 192).
13. Boyes (1993, pp. 125–35). I am indebted to Boyes's discussion of Williams for clarifying the role of Sharp and for pointing me to the next two citations from Williams. It is significant that Hoggart's defence of sentimental commercial popular songs in *The Uses of Literacy* also positions itself – more gently – against Sharp (Hoggart, 1976, p. 163). Laing (1994) has also traced this linkage from similar sources through to the CCCS's subcultural research. See Section 1.4 for greater detail on Romantic folkloricism.
14. Sharp (1966).
15. Boyes is surely correct in arguing that Williams chose to confine the recording of this 'experience' to his novels.
16. Cf. Section 3.2.
17. Even the later reference in *The Long Revolution* to *Culture and Society*'s 'redefinition' passage cited above assiduously avoids its use (*LR*, p. 328).
18. See Jones (1994).
19. Williams (1953, p. 239).
20. Accordingly, unless otherwise stated, my references to an 'anthropological' sense of 'culture' are to the legacy of this sense initiated by Eliot rather than to any anthropological literatures *per se*.
21. Emphasis in original.
22. Eliot (1948, pp. 41–2).
23. This description is changed in *Culture and Society* to 'a difficult work to assess' (*C&S*, p. 231).
24. Eliot (1948, p. 37); Mannheim (1960, p. 81).
25. *C&S*, p. 241.
26. Even this heuristic role, as we shall see in Section 5.2, is eventually questioned in *The Sociology of Culture*.
27. Hall (1980a).
28. Turner (1996). But cf. Andrew Milner's commentary which suggests Hall's own position can be read as much less sympathetic to culturalism than Turner's (Milner, 1993, p. 80).
29. Hall (1997, p. 25).
30. Althusserian structuralist Marxism has considerably diminished as an influence on contemporary sociological discussion (e.g. Benton, 1984) but is still routinely cited within literary studies (e.g. Kavanagh, 1995). Each of the critiques of Williams discussed below adopted some version of Althusser's structuralist reinterpretation of Marx's conception of ideology as its most fundamental starting point.
31. *P&L*, p. 133.
32. See Chapter 3 for further discussion of Anderson's thesis.
33. Althusser (1977a, pp. 169ff).
34. *P&L*, pp. 97–8.
35. *LR*, pp. 56–9.

36. Eldridge and Eldridge also tabularize this discussion but limit their presentation to the first two columns. Their discussion thus does not move to the same conclusion as mine and places, for example, a greater emphasis on the influence of Ruth Benedict (Eldridge and Eldridge, 1994, pp. 78ff).

37. Hall (1980a, p. 64); Johnson (1979a, b); Barnett (1976). Eagleton's critique is dealt with in more detail in Chapter 2.

38. Johnson footnotes at this point a passage from *Marxism and Literature* where Williams approvingly contrasts the emphasis on class domination within Gramsci's hegemony with any conception of culture as 'cooperative shaping' (*M&L*, p. 112). I would not read this as an admission of any former neglect of politics but rather a reassessment of his former political strategy – see Section 1.6.

39. See especially Williams (1976c).

40. *LR*, p. 62. The phrase recurs as 'the problem is always one of method' in the 1971 lecture, 'Literature and Sociology: in memory of Lucien Goldmann' (1971, p. 15). Its implications are discussed in detail in Chapter 3.

41. Eliot (1948, p. 25). Williams draws here on his earlier analysis of this play in his *Drama in Performance*.

42. This was not Williams's first use of the concept, cf. Williams and Orrom (1954) . See, for example, Higgins's reconstruction of its earlier uses (1999, pp. 39–42) which contests Williams's own reconstruction in *Politics and Letters* (*P&L*, pp. 158ff).

43. *LR*, p. 64.

44. *C&S*, p. xiii; *KW1*, p. 9.

45. Williams nonetheless did employ – normatively but circumspectly – the concept of the knowable community within his own work on the nineteenth-century novel. See his summary of this position in his comparison of Hardy and Lawrence in *The English Novel: from Dickens to Lawrence* in *Politics and Letters* (*P&L*, p. 247).

46. *LR*, pp. 70–88.

47. The debates around the Poor Laws are one of Williams's major points of reference here.

48. *C&S*, pp. 330–2.

49. *Britain in the Sixties: communications* was also the full title of the first edition of *Communications*.

50. See Chapter 7.

51. *LR*, p. 14.

52. *C&S*, pp. 87–109.

53. O'Neill (2000). This shift was not a linear one, but it is interesting to contrast the 1950 *Reading and Criticism* (*R&C*), with the 1953 essay, 'The Idea of Culture' (Williams, 1953), which rehearsed several of the arguments of *Culture and Society*.

54. Italicization added by Williams.

55. Anderson (1964, p. 27).

56. Cf. Chapter 3 for Williams and hegemony. Williams also responded to Anderson's account of the role of 'moral critique' and 'utilitarianism' in the British Left the following year (Williams, 1965). In Chapter 3, I argue that Anderson also influenced Williams's discussion of Goldmann and the sociology of literature. All this well preceded Eagleton's better known critique (Eagleton, 1976a) which largely recapitulated or exaggerated these issues without recognizing the technique of immanent critique. Eagleton so misrecognized Williams's immanent critiques as decontextualization and 'manipulation' by 'selective quotation and sentimental

misconception' (1976b, p. 25). More recently – in what is possibly another implicit auto-critique – Eagleton has acknowledged the practice of immanent critique within a more complex rendering of the 'English "Culture and Society" lineage' (2000, p. 8, cf. 22).

57. *P&L*, pp. 372–3.
58. I have examined the last of these in detail in Jones (1994).
59. Williams (1968c).
60. *M&L*, pp. 11–20; Williams (1974a). Williams's 'final' redefinition of culture – as a 'realized signifying system' – is discussed in Section 5.2.
61. Herder (undated, pp. 225–31); cf. also Darcy (1987). On Herder and folklore, see Cocchiara (1981, pp. 168–84); Clark (1955, pp. 251–81).
62. Burke (1978). 'Discovery of the people' is Burke's phrase.
63. Schick (1971).
64. Cocchiara (1981, pp. 201–19).
65. For example, Therborn (1976, pp. 179–86). Commentators such as Eagleton have recently pointed to this Romantic anticipation of similar themes within postmodernism (Eagleton, 2000, pp. 13–14). In *Modern Tragedy* Williams addresses the 'anti-Enlightenment' dimension of Romanticism explictly, arguing that, rather than being anti-reason, the (English) Romantics were anti-utilitarian, and so operated within a 'curious dialectic' that eventually allowed the positing of the 'self-making' individual against alienation to collapse into a mere (eventually irrationalist) subjectivism (*MT1*, pp. 71–3).
66. Young (1995, pp. 40–1).
67. Tony Bennett's recent attempt to establish an homology between Tylor's *Primitive Culture* and Williams's mature position thus seems particularly misplaced, especially when compared with Young's exhaustive assessment (Bennett, 1998, pp. 92–101).
68. This certainly arrives in *The Sociology of Culture* – cf. Chapter 6.
69. *MT1*, pp. 74–84; *M&L*, p. 18; *WICTS*, pp. 200–1.

2　Cultural materialism versus 'received Marxist theory'

1. This sentence was added to the 1980 version in *PMC*. The original version states: 'it is spelled out in a forthcoming book, *Marxism and Literature*' (1976c, p. 89).
2. Cf. Section 1.3. In subsequent writings Eagleton has significantly revised this assessment of Williams, and even in part recanted it (e.g. 1981, p. 97), but it has been republished many times without emendation, as recently as 1998.
3. The major critiques are: Eagleton (1976a) (cf. also the version in Eagleton, 1976b); Eagleton (1989); Hall (1980a, b, c); cf. also Neale (1984).
4. I thus set aside here those commentaries which tend to move from the former assumption for example, Stevenson (1995, p. 48) and Eagleton (1989, pp. 168–9). Stevenson attributes a strong influence to Williams's reading of Timpanaro, especially his *On Materialism* (1975). Williams was undoubtedly impressed by Timpanaro but there is no evidence that he revised the emphasis in his 1976 'manifesto'. His 1978 essay on Timpanaro critically emphasizes the polemical character of Timpanaro's project and appears to endorse only Timpanaro's polemic against 'objective idealism' in structural linguistics and structuralism (and even then the former more than the latter) (Williams, 1978f, pp. 5, 15; *PMC*, pp. 106, 119; cf. *P&L*, p. 167). Within his social formalist work, however, Williams does not employ Timpanaro, apparently having gained more from other critiques of 'objective idealism' that provided viable alternatives such as those by Goldmann and Vološinov (cf. Chapters 3 and 4).

5. Eagleton too briefly advocates a kind of production paradigm in the chapter following his critique of Williams in *Criticism and Ideology*, 'Categories for a Materialist Criticism'. These categories include a 'literary mode of production' developed analogically from a 'general mode of production'. Eagleton ostensibly develops this from Williams's conception of 'material practice' (elaborated below) which he correctly recognizes as a rejection of 'that pervasive form of critical idealism which would repress the whole material infrastructure of artistic production' even though, in his view, it 'retains strong residual elements of humanism' (Eagleton, 1976b, p. 44). However, Eagleton's emphasis is on *mode* of production and its 'precise articulations' and his greater debt is to Althusser's structuralist conception of mode of production and Althusser's advocacy of such analogies therefrom (e.g. Althusser and Balibar, 1977, p. 317). Williams, as argued below, was extremely wary of the reductivist potential of any undifferentiated conception of mode of production. Eagleton does, however, recognize the need for specification of further analogical subcategories such as 'artisanal literary production'. Althusser aside, perhaps the crucial difference between the two at this point was that Williams was already thinking outside the practice of literary criticism and so applied his production paradigm to 'culture' rather than 'literature'.
6. *PL*, pp. 50–2.
7. *P&L*, p. 144; Caudwell (1947, pp. 55ff). John Higgins highlights Williams's shifting evaluations of Caudwell (a fact Williams conceded in *P&L*, p. 144) because they 'perfectly mirrored his complex relations to Marxist cultural theory as a whole' (Higgins, 1999, p. 102). This comment marks my chief difference with Higgins's account – an overestimation of the significance of the (nonetheless evident) elements of continuity between the early work and the mature project.
8. As my practice in these instances will be to reproduce Williams's commentaries immediately after citations from Marx, I have where possible employed the same translations of Marx's work as those used by Williams (if not always the same editions).
9. *P&L*, p. 138; Hall (1980b, p. 101); cf. Eagleton (1988, p. 8).
10. Cf. Section 1.3.
11. Williams (1973a, 1983a). The latter essay was originally called 'Culture' as it appeared in a 1983 collection on the work of Marx. Citations of it from *WICTS*.
12. Hall conducted an almost simultaneous survey of key texts of Marx in Hall (1974, 1977a, b, c, 1983a).
13. For example, Cohen (1978).
14. Feher (1984).
15. This passage is pitted against the one in 'The 1859 Preface' in both *Culture and Society* (*C&S*, pp. 266–7) and *Marxism and Literature* (*M&L*, p. 76). I use here the translation cited by Williams in *Culture and Society*. He sources the citation in *Marxism and Literature* to the *Selected Writings* (cf. Marx, 1958b) but it is actually identical to this version.
16. For exegetical purposes I refer to the usage in *The Brumaire* as more developed than 'The 1859 Preface', although it was actually written seven years before.
17. This is the 'literal' interpretation of 'determination' to which Williams's gives strongest endorsement. Cf. *M&L*, pp. 84–7.
18. In this citation Williams has included the previous sentence from the text as the 'extra' citation in brackets.
19. This is most likely because of his reflections on the work of the Western Marxists discussed in the next chapter.

20. This is especially ironic given the dependence placed on *The Brumaire* in their own work by both Hall and Eagleton, largely following Poulantzas. See Section 4.3 for Hall's usage. Higgins's (over)emphasis on continuity in Williams's work also questions this orthodoxy but in the end appears to agree with the substance of Hall's critique (1999, p. 123).

21. Especially Williams (1978a). I will use the revised title, 'The Bloomsbury Fraction' in future references.

22. Cf. the recent criticism along these lines by Joseph (2002, p. 72).

23. Williams also problematizes the concept of mediation by using the 'positive/ negative' distinction (*M&L*, pp. 95–100). This discussion is closely related to his assessment of the Frankfurt School, so I deal with it in the next chapter.

24. This conceptualization also addresses Márkus's accurate critique of the vagueness of the role of the category of 'intention' in the earlier version of this argument in the 1973 article, 'Base and Superstructure in Marxist Theory'. Intention is introduced in that article in order to problematize the relation between 'determination' and 'totality' (Márkus, 1994a, pp. 434–6).

25. 'Marx on Culture' was unavailable at the time of Eagleton's and Hall's major critiques. But it is most curious that Eagleton neglected it in his 'Base and Superstructure in Raymond Williams' (Eagleton, 1989a).

26. Even though Williams employs an English translation of *The German Ideology* for other passages in this article, he here cites the German text, *Historisch-kritische Gesamtausgabe* [*MEGA*] (Moscow, 1927–35) vol. 1, part 5, 15–17. Cf. Marx and Engels (1976, p. 36).

27. Lest the reader conclude from this that Marx here reintroduces a material/immaterial bifurcation, this alternative translation of the same clause should be considered: 'the architect builds the cell in his mind before he constructs it in wax' (Marx, 1976, p. 284). There is a related continuing problem with the translation of the German 'geistig' which may be rendered in English as 'intellectual' or 'ideal'.

28. The citation is from *The Poverty of Philosophy* which was written shortly after *The German Ideology* in 1846–7; cf. Marx (1973a, p. 116). Williams sources this translation (presumably his own) to '*MEGA* vol. 1, part 6, 197' (*WICTS*, p. 211).

29. The chapter on 'productive forces' in *Marxism and Literature* is particularly frustrating in this regard in that it makes the case for this concept without actually employing the formulation (*M&L*, pp. 90–4).

30. For a typical mobilization of this charge of essentialism in favour of an Althusserian structuralism, see Bennett (1981). Márkus notes explicitly that Marx's 'thesis about the "primacy" of social existence understood as the material production and material intercourse of men (*sic*) has nothing to do with the traditional metaphysics problem of the relation of mind to body, or matter in general' (1986, p. 43).

31. The principal precursors are Adorno and Benjamin. See the discussions in Chapters 3 and 6.

32. See Table 3.2 and Section 6.3.

33. For example, Gramsci (1971, pp. 210–23).

34. Márkus (1990).

35. Márkus (1986, p. 43).

36. Márkus (1986, pp. 51ff). Márkus provides the example of a wine glass which may be 'properly' used to drink from, but which may also be used as a paperweight, and so on.

37. Márkus (1986, p. 54). Márkus thus rejects those interpretations which would reduce the Marxian production paradigm to 'an instrumentalistic understanding of all

human activities, with their reduction to labour as goal-rational activity'. Rather, he insists on the three dimensions just recounted: objectivation, the material content/social form distinction and, thirdly, the comprehension of any act of production as a moment within a broader process of reproduction (Márkus, 1990, p. 98).

38. Márkus (1990, pp. 99–101).

39. Williams does not cite the passage in square brackets. He works here from the version of *The German Ideology* edited by McLellan, so he may have not seen an earlier sentence in the prior paragraph which was not included by McLellan, and which immediately follows Marx's citation of Stirner's comment: '[He] surely must have known, however, that it was not Mozart himself, but someone else who composed the greater part of Mozart's *Requiem* and finished it, and that Raphael himself "completed" only an insignificant part of his own frescoes' (Marx and Engels, 1976, p. 393).

40. *WICTS*, p. 217.

41. Márkus (1995, pp. 76–9).

42. For Williams's distinction between these categories see Table 4.1.

43. *SOC*, pp. 187–8.

44. *M&L*, pp. 115–27. Cf. Table 3.1.

45. *PMC*, pp. 47–9.

46. Williams's motives for this formulation probably came from a very different concern. He sources 'notation' to his *Drama in Performance* (*M&L*, p. 6) which is strongly focussed on the disjunction between a 'literary work' and its performance. Williams conceded in *Politics and Letters* that that book was written in part to extend practical criticism to drama but that unlike the practical critical emphasis on reading, his interest was in the process of composition. It seems reasonable to speculate that by emphasizing the difference between a literary 'work' and a dramatic notation with this later formulation, Williams was also seeking to challenge the 'ideological capture' of the work as *text* that he regards as persisting from practical criticism to New Criticism to Literary Structuralism (*P&L*, p. 231).

47. See Chapter 4.

48. See Section 4.1.

49. See Section 5.2.

50. See especially the work of its chief advocate, Richard Peterson (Peterson, 1976, 1994).

51. See, respectively, Tuchman (1983) and Wolff (1999, pp. 502–3).

52. Williams was clearly impressed by Bourdieu's and Passeron's *Reproduction* (1977), as indicated both by a contemporary review and by his use of it in *The Sociology of Culture*. Williams states in that review that, when he collaborated with Bourdieu in a seminar, he found both 'deep differences' and an 'extraordinary convergence of themes and interests' (1977g, p. 240). Bourdieu subsequently emphasized only the former. In recent years he twice referred disparagingly to Williams's work on the Romantic artist (without citation, but the chapter on the Romantic artist in *Culture and Society* is the only likely text) (Bourdieu, 1993, p. 195, 1996, p. 55). Bourdieu's criticism – that Williams reduces the contradictory position of the Romantic artists to 'its alienating effects' – suggests at the very least a complete misunderstanding of the relation between that chapter and the book as a whole. Williams also co-authored an exegesis of Bourdieu with Nicholas Garnham (Garnham and Williams, 1980), although it was Garnham who wrote the draft to which Williams assented (personal conversation with Nicholas Garnham, April, 1995).

53. Bourdieu (1977). See Section 4.3 for elaboration of Vološinov.
54. This is despite its titular use in at least one collection of English translations (Bourdieu, 1993). Significantly, this text has no French antecedent in book form.
55. For example, Calhoun (1993, p. 69).
56. So Bourdieu's position here has more in common with Veblen than Marx.
57. See Chapter 7.
58. For an early backgrounding of Habermas's theory of communicative interaction, see Held (1980, pp. 256–9). For Habermas's explicit rejection of the production paradigm, see Habermas (1995). This is a reply to the critique in the first chapter of Márkus (1986). For an assessment of this debate, see Grumley (1991).

3   From criticism to critique

1. The category of 'Western Marxist' is usually sourced to Anderson (1976).
2. Williams (1976c). This is the source of the cultural materialist 'manifesto' that heads Chapter 2.
3. Williams (1971, 1973a). Cf. O'Connor (1989, p. 106); Higgins (1999, p. 112).
4. Williams appears to repudiate part of this position in a 1977 interview. However, the discussion moves from the interviewer's false assumption that Anderson's comments celebrated the role of *Culture and Society*, rather than that of *The Long Revolution*. Crucially, while Williams reconfigures the role of Leavis in Anderson's thesis (and takes personal responsibility for Anderson's misconceptions), he endorses the absent centre thesis itself (Williams, 1977a, pp. 13–14).
5. The interviewing team was Anderson, Anthony Barnett and Francis Mulhern.
6. Williams (1969a, 1973b, 1974b).
7. For an elaboration of Williams's position on 'mass', see Section 6.4.
8. Frankfurt Institute for Social Research (1973).
9. Marcuse (1965).
10. Marcuse (1972, p. 120).
11. Three recent reviews of the concept of ideology in English all fail to include discussion of this 'emancipatory' conception of ideology or the related conception of immanent (emancipatory) critique: Thompson (1990); Eagleton (1991) and Hawkes (1996). In contrast, see Davis and Schleifer (1991) (especially Chapter 1), and Young (1996). Russell Jacoby's *The End of Utopia* eloquently traces the absence of immanent ideology critique within much 'post-universalist' cultural criticism (Jacoby, 1999, pp. 125–54). On the establishment of a basis for this conception of ideology critique within Marx's own practice, see Márkus (1995) and Márkus's debate with Jorge Larrain (Márkus, 1983, 1987; Larrain, 1984). On the emergence of the conception of critique as such, see Benhabib (1986). For advocacy of immanent critique within sociology, see Antonio (1981). Cf. also Ricoeur's related use of (emancipatory) 'imagination' as the mediating link between his reconceptulization of the concepts of ideology and utopia (1986, pp. 265–6).
12. Márkus (1995, pp. 66–99).
13. Márkus (1995, p. 66).
14. Jay holds that the reproduction in Adorno's collected works of the chapter on 'Ideology' (in which this passage occurs) from this collectively authored book proves his authorship (Jay, 1984b, p. 180).
15. This immanent conception of 'truth' does not rely on a binary opposition between ideology and an externally guaranteed conception of 'science'.

16. Márkus (1995, pp. 69–70). It is this 'unmasking' sense that is the more common understanding of ideology critique today. Adorno's and Márkus's criterion of the necessary coherence of ideologies susceptible to emancipatory critique thus differs from the otherwise similar reconstruction in Fredric Jameson's *The Political Unconscious* of a Marxian 'positive hermeneutic' which recovers a utopian dimension in *all* ideologies and related forms of dominative cultural production (Jameson, 1981, pp. 281ff). Jameson also works with a contrast between this positive hermeneutic and a negative conception of ideology as 'structural limitation' similar to Márkus's 'unmasking' (Jameson, 1981, pp. 52–3).

17. See especially Adorno (1991a). Cf. Paddison (1996). Paddison's exegesis includes a third, philosophico-historical stage to Adorno's mode of ideology critique. I do not mean to suggest that all of Adorno's critical writings employ this method.

18. Goldmann and Adorno (1976).

19. But cf. his discussion of 'mediation' addressed in Section 3.3.

20. Mulhern (2002) in reply to Collini (2001), a review essay on Mulhern (2000).

21. Adorno's concessions here are minimal compared with Williams's. The key text is usually thought to be 'Transparencies on Film' (Adorno, 1991c). Cf., for example, Jay's assessment that there 'Adorno for the first time acknowledged a critical potential within the mainstream of the culture industry' (Jay, 1984b, p. 127) and Hansen's that 'undertones of élitism are refreshingly absent' (Hansen, 1981–82, p. 190).

22. Cf. Piaget (1970). I have borrowed some exegetical phrases in this paragraph from Jay's discussion of Goldmann (Jay, 1984a, pp. 319–20). A more detailed discussion of structuralism occurs in Chapter 4.

23. More accurately, Lévi-Strauss regards this formal correspondence as one of analogy. I use it because it is Stuart Hall's chosen example from Lévi-Strauss (Hall, 1978a, p. 25). This facilitates discussion of Hall's usage in Section 5.3.

24. For example, Derrida's highly influential critique of Lévi-Strauss in his 'Structure, Sign and Play in the Discourse of the Human Sciences' (Derrida, 1978); cf. Norris (1987, p. 242).

25. During an assessment of Williams's Goldmann essay, Edward Said asserts that: 'Homology is, after all, merely a refined version of the old Second International base-and-superstructure model' (Said, 1991, p. 239). This unsubstantiated claim completely misunderstands Williams's assessment of Goldmann. Bourdieu makes similar assertions about Goldmann's 'reflectionism' in his *The Rules of Art* (1996, pp. 202, 383[n. 24]).

26. This exegetical paragraph is indebted to Zima's account.

27. Eagleton (1976c, p. 34); Evans (1981, p. 55). Cf. Wolff (1993, p. 57); Milner (1996, p. 37). On this point, Márkus (1981) is a more stringent critic of Goldmann. For a spirited defence of Goldmann, see Boelhower (1980). For a recent critique of Goldmann by one of his former students, see Zima (1999).

28. See Goldmann and Adorno (1976).

29. I return to this theme in the final chapter.

30. For a detailed account of these conceptual transformations, see Márkus (1981). See also Goldmann (1967) for one of his clearest accounts.

31. Citations from the Goldmann and 'Base and Superstructure' essays will be double-sourced. However, the precise text has been taken from the original *NLR* versions rather than the revised ones in *PMC*. Significant textual changes are endnoted.

32. Changed to 'some of the greatest literature' in *PMC*.

33. 'Very seriously' changed to 'seriously' in *PMC*.

34. Zima (1999, pp. 92–3).
35. Cf. Section 4.4.
36. On this issue, see also Sections 2.5 and 4.4.
37. *M&L*, p. 108. Cf. Gramsci (1971, p. 80n). For an elaboration of this distinction in Gramsci, see Buci-Glucksmann (1982).
38. *M&L*, p. 113.
39. In the 1975 essay, 'You're a Marxist Aren't You', Williams renders his more overtly political position in similar terms, pointing specifically to the failures of the British Labour Party (*ROH*, pp. 65–76).
40. This passage is radically expanded and revised in *PMC*. For discussion of this, see Section 4.2.
41. See, for example, Hall *et al.* (1978b, pp. 56–65).
42. Gramsci (1971, pp. 6ff, 80ff). For Williams's view of the organic/traditional intellectual distinction, see Section 6.2.
43. Gramsci (1971, pp. 5–23).
44. Buci-Glucksmann (1980, pp. 276–82).
45. For more detail on the case of Bloomsbury, see Section 6.2. On Williams and 'ideology', see next section.
46. This version of mediation appears to be identical to that identified by Márkus as the 'unmasking' version of ideology critique (Márkus, 1995, pp. 69–70).
47. Williams's often eccentric citation process in these chapters of *Marxism and Literature* (II, 4 and 5) is particularly elusive, as he appears to slide from a Harvard to a traditional citation system, and on occasion overlooks citation of his sources altogether. The bibliography lists only Adorno's *Prisms* and *Negative Dialectics*, but in the discussion of mediation there is a footnoted reference to the original German version of 'Theses on the Sociology of Art' (Adorno, 1972; cf. *M&L*, p. 98). Later, a completely unsourced citation is made from Adorno's letter to Benjamin of 2 August 1935 (*M&L*, p. 103). This citation corresponds perfectly with the translation provided by Martin Jay in his *The Dialectical Imagination* (Jay, 1996, p. 207), and Williams's introduction of it does resemble Jay's. (Williams had reviewed Jay's book within his second 'Frankfurt School' review [Williams, 1974b].) The following chapter's discussion also alludes (without citation) to a thesis by Adorno, most likely from his *The Philosophy of Modern Music* (1973b). Williams lists a German edition of this text in his bibliography in *The Sociology of Culture*. One possible secondary source here is Jameson's citation of *The Philosophy of Modern Music* in his *Marxism and Form* (Jameson, 1974a, p. 7).
48. Adorno (1972, p. 128). (Williams's citation is sourced directly to the German original.)
49. Adorno (1989).
50. For example, Hohendahl (1995, p. 161).
51. Zuidervaart (1991, p. 104).
52. Adorno (1978) and (1997) respectively.
53. Cf. Adorno's discussion of the fate of the music score in 'Music and Technique' (Adorno, 1977).
54. Benjamin (1982). For Adorno's critique in the correspondence, see New Left Books (ed.) (1977), pp. 120–6, and the discussions below and in Section 6.3.
55. Cf. Hansen (1981–82, pp. 187–8); Livingstone *et al.* (1977, pp. 107–8). Williams made a similar analysis of film in 1983 (Williams, 1983b).
56. Cf. Table 2.1 and Chapter 6.
57. This is especially odd as Benjamin is singled out from the rest of the Frankfurt School as a special case of interest in the introduction to *Marxism and Literature*

(*M&L*, p. 4). Williams does allude to this essay in a brief reference to aesthetic 'aura' (*M&L*, p. 103).

58. See, for example, the discussions in Livingstone *et al.* (1977) and Sprinker (1999).
59. Benjamin (1973); Williams (1973b).
60. *TEN*, pp. 25–49; *C&C*, pp. 189–201. My argument here moves in close parallel with that of Pinkney (1989a). He suggests, correctly in my view, that the rejected 'idealism' Williams identifies in Benjamin's third analytic stage can be described as a cultural analysis that risks 'the danger of being absorbed precisely by that which it claims to be analysing' (Pinkney, 1989a, p. 12). Further, Pinkney validly argues that *The Country and the City* is vulnerable to an immanent application of this criticism, that is that while the treatment of Dickens resembles Benjamin's first two stages, that of Virginia Woolf and other modernist writers does not. For Pinkney, the required 'formational' analysis of modernism does not arrive until the relevant essays included in *The Politics of Modernism* (Pinkney, 1989a, pp. 12–14). However, as we have seen, 'The Bloomsbury Fraction' provided such an analysis of Woolf's 'formation', if not of modernism *per se*, in 1978. The significance of this oversight by Pinkney is considerable. It suggests that the formational analysis was not a late response to debates around (post)modernism, but a direct product of Williams's reflections on Goldmann, Gramsci and the Frankfurt School in the 1970s. As we shall see in Chapter 6, the criticism of Benjamin's 'idealism' *and* modernist avant-gardism was paralleled in Williams's 1974 critique of McLuhan.
61. Benjamin (1973, p. 50).
62. Livingstone *et al.* speculate that these elements did not survive to the published version due to the Institute's tendency in this period in the United States to euphemize any overtly political statements (Livingstone *et al.*, 1977, pp. 105–6).
63. Benjamin (1973, pp. 58–9).
64. See Wolin (1994, pp. 173–5) for Adorno's and Benjamin's earlier understanding of the Arcades project.
65. More than this, Adorno is also practising an autocritique of 'the sociology of the interior' section of his early study of Kierkegaard where he made much of Kierkegaard's 'promenades in his own parlour' (Adorno, 1994, pp. 41ff).
66. Although such a juxtaposition was arguably always a feature of Williams's analytic approach, it becomes particularly prominent in the period after *Marxism and Literature*. One of the most methodologically explicit is a late essay on the history of cinema which 'lays beside each other' four such processes (Williams, 1983b).
67. See Section 6.5.
68. *M&L*, p. 65.
69. See, as an example of such a rejection, Barrett (1991).
70. I allude here to the discussion in Section 1.5.
71. Indeed, in the foreword to the first edition, Williams explicitly links this section with *Culture and Society* and *The Long Revolution* (*MT1*, p. 9).
72. *MT1*, p. 48. What follows is a summary account prone to oversimplification. The substance of this critique is discussed further in Chapter 7.
73. On the distinction between practical critical and (social) formalist approaches see Williams (1977d).
74. See Chapter 4 for further discussion of this distinction.
75. *C&C*, pp. 42–3.
76. For example, Williams (1970b).

77. Williams (1978b, c).
78. These are briefly discussed in Chapter 7.
79. Cf. Section 3.2.
80. Lest this still seem somewhat reductive, it is important to add that Williams was a tireless participant in the minutiae of advocating democratizing reforms in press policy and broadcasting in particular. See Jones (1994) and Chapter 6.

4 Social formalism

1. For example, Glucksmann, A. (1972); Glucksmann, M. (1974).
2. Cf. also the discussion at the end of Section 5.2 and in Chapter 2, fn. 4.
3. See the citation that heads Section 4.3.
4. *RWOT*, p. 11; cf. Preface.
5. Williams (1976b) and (1986) respectively.
6. In this instance at least he is almost certainly drawing on Fekete (1984), from which he quotes later in the article. Cf. Chapter 7.
7. The phrase is Ricoeur's (1974, p. 31); cf. Glucksmann (1974, p. 62); Sturrock (1986, pp. 26–31).
8. Cf. Leach (1974, pp. 27ff).
9. Barthes (1967, 1972).
10. For standard exegeses, see Culler (1975) and Hawkes (1977) but cf. Doložel's (1994) criticism of these discussed below.
11. Bakhtin and Medvedev (1985, pp. 54ff) cf. *POM*, p. 167.
12. See Section 4.3 for a fuller version of and the source of, this citation and Section 6.4 for McLuhan.
13. *KW2*, p. 139.
14. Doložel (1994, p. 503). On Goldmann's minimal Parisian influence, see Jay (1984a, pp. 328–9) and the revealing discussion at the end of Goldmann's contribution to the influential 1966 Johns Hopkins symposium on structuralism (Goldmann, 1972).
15. Doložel cites especially Culler (1975) and Hawkes (1977). As Doložel notes, one reason for this emphasis is the presence of Jakobson within both the Russian and the Prague formations. Jakobson's work in Prague, even where acknowledged as such, could thus be treated under 'Russian formalism' (e.g. Bennett, 1979, p. 45). Another factor is the focus on literature in all these texts.
16. The first subsequent English language texts that positioned Mukařovský, for example, in a similar way to Williams's 1977 discussions would appear to be Frow (1986) (who is far more critical of Mukařovský) and Swingewood (1987).
17. Vološinov (1973).
18. Saussure (1966, pp. 65–70).
19. Saussure (1966, p. 74).
20. *M&L*, pp. 27–8; Vološinov (1973, p. 61).
21. *M&L*, p. 24; cf. Section 1.6.
22. *M&L*, pp. 24–5, 32.
23. Matejka (1973, p. 168); Vološinov (1973, pp. 48–9, 98).
24. Vološinov (1973, p. 57).
25. In his important (and unique) review of Williams's writings in this area, Michael Moriarty makes the valid point that this is hardly an original criticism of Saussure as it was anticipated by non-Marxists like Jakobson and Benveniste. However, Moriarty tends to assume that the only alternative view is that developed by

Benveniste and eventually adopted by Lacan; that is, that 'individual identity is intersubjectively created through language' (Moriarty, 1995, p. 95). A similar position was taken in a brief discussion in Barrett *et al.* (1979, p. 13).

26. Vološinov (1973, p. 10). (Williams does not provide citation sources.)
27. Vološinov (1973, p. 11).
28. Vološinov (1976).
29. Cf. for example, Norris (1982, p. 32).
30. Norris's comments are based on a discussion of *Keywords* which was an improvised talk.
31. *M&L*, p. 170.
32. Although it does seem likely that Williams relied entirely on Vološinov's account of Humboldt's linguistics.
33. *M&L*, p. 43. This expectation was soon confirmed by Williams's inclusion of an essay by Rossi-Landi on language as the opening chapter of the collection he edited, *Contact: human communication and its history* (Rossi-Landi and Pesaresi, 1981). Williams also expressed his approval of Rossi-Landi's work on ideologies of linguistic relativity (Rossi-Landi, 1973; *P&L*, p. 182).
34. Rossi-Landi (1977, pp. 72–8). Rossi-Landi also employs a distinction between bodily and 'externally' resourced means of communication similar to Williams's.
35. Márkus (1986, p. 36).
36. Márkus (1986, p. 38).
37. This goes some way towards clarifying the confusing ambiguity noted by Wolff (1993a, pp. 63–4) in Williams's invocations of 'material' when designating both aesthetic objectivations and the 'materiality' of language. Contrary to Wolff's reading, Williams really does wish to insist on the equal 'materiality' of *written* linguistic notations and fully material aesthetic objectivations. Speech acts, in contrast, are an 'activity' which, while not durably objectivated (unless by 'oral tradition'), nonetheless rely on the 'material' 'bodily inherent resource' of the voice box. However, as noted in Section 2.1, Williams's insistence on 'materiality' is usually tied to an elaboration of his conception of cultural production rather than a mere ontological assertion.
38. See Section 4.4.
39. Anthony Giddens's account of his structuration theory in *The Constitution of Society* also took this term as 'a leading theme'. Giddens's opening definition states that it 'consists of all the things which actors know tacitly about how to "go on" in social life without being able to give them direct discursive expression' (Giddens, 1984, p. xxiii). While not coterminous with Williams's understanding, it is broadly compatible. Giddens does not source the term to Marx or Williams, but rather presents it as a neologism. He was certainly familiar with Williams's work, having reviewed both *Politics and Letters* (Giddens, 1979) and *The Sociology of Culture* (Giddens, 1981). In the earlier review he recognizes *Marxism and Literature* as Williams's crucial turning point, and regards its position on language and signification as 'essentially correct' (Giddens, 1979, p. 12). At the very least this suggests there is a body of contemporary social theory with which Williams's sociology of culture could be fruitfully linked.
40. Italicization of 'is' not present in the version cited by Williams.
41. For ease of exposition I shall refer to Marx, rather than Marx and Engels.
42. Although he does acknowledge that such a risk exists.
43. Marx makes a marginal note referring to priests as 'the first form of ideologists' at this point (Marx and Engels, 1976, p. 45). Cf. the argument on this point in

Neale (1984, pp. 204–6). Neale's perceptive and relatively early critique is flawed by a curious insistence that Williams did not show sufficient attention to class analysis.

44. In his most elaborate analyses, Goldmann defended his notion of the 'collective subject' with examples consistent with this description. Indeed, Williams's adoption of 'practical consciousness' can plausibly be seen as an attempt to find a substitute for the limitations of this concept.

45. Eagleton (1976b, pp. 22–3).

46. Dates have been changed for these texts to be consistent with those in Bibliography.

47. Williams (1977b); CCCS (1978).

48. The passage just cited is perhaps where Timpanaro's influence is at its strongest. Cf. *P&L*, p. 167 and footnote 4 of Chapter 2.

49. See Clarke *et al.* (1977, p. 66).

50. On the 'first' new left, see Hall (1989) and Kenny (1995).

51. Barthes (1972, pp. 109–58).

52. On the development of the conception of 'code' in early French structuralism, see Descombes (1986, pp. 92ff).

53. On the distinction between emancipatory and unmasking ideology critique, see Section 3.1. For problems with Hall's conception of ideology, see Section 3.4.

54. Hall (1972). Cf. Barthes (1977a). Barthes had already addressed the news-photo in 1961 (Barthes, 1977b), but this essay was then unavailable in translation. The CCCS had published a translation of 'Rhetoric of the Image' in the first issue of its *Working Papers* in 1971.

55. Hall (1972, pp. 66–7).

56. Hall (1973) and Hall *et al.* (1976). For ease of exposition I refer to Hall as the author of both individually and collaboratively published works. Hall relied in part on the developing empirical work of David Morley, which pursued the decoding typology in empirical research on televison audiences and had an enormous influence on the growing field of 'media studies'. See Morley (1975) & Morley (1980). On the reception of this work in cultural studies, see Storey (1996), and in media studies, see Nightingale (1996).

57. Hall (1973, p. 16).

58. Hall *et al.* (1976, pp. 67–8).

59. Williams (1976a, p. 36).

60. Hall later played on this ambiguity of the term – the linguistic sense and the other sense as in an 'articulated lorry' – in a much-cited interview (1986). But outside the discussion of Bourdieu, its initial sourcing in the late 1970s was to his own reading of Marx's '1857 Introduction' (1977a, p. 48; 1977b, p. 327); cf. Hall (1974), which in turn was influenced by Althusser's reading.

61. Bourdieu's apparent hostility to Marxian approaches is consistent with the incompatibility of his and Williams's conceptions of cultural production (discussed in Section 2.6), and with his antipathy towards Goldmann's homological analysis (see footnoted reference in Section 3.2).

62. It should be stressed that the analysis in the following citation makes no reference to Bourdieu. The precise source of 'homology' is not sourced but is compatible with Hall's reflections in Hall (1978a). Nor does he source his reference to Poulantzas below. Such imprecision is a common problem in what were openly acknowledged, of course, to be working papers.

63. Poulantzas's work had a considerable influence on Hall. But Poulantzas (at the time of *Political Power and Social Classes*) rejected any equation of the structuralist

conception of homology with his and Althusser's use of 'correspondence' (Poulantzas, 1976, pp. 27–8). Hall appears to equate these on at least one occasion (Hall, 1977a).

64. Hall formulated this proposition even more strongly the following year (1978b).
65. Hall (1977b, p. 320).
66. Hall and Jefferson (1977). Andrew Milner's witty suggestion that Hall's related 'two paradigms' discussion (Section 1.3) almost constructed a 'myth of Claude Althusser' as the opponent of 'Raymond Hoggart' is relevant here (Milner, 2002, p. 2). For Hall's recognition of the distinction between the two, see Hall (1978a, pp. 26–7). *Resistance Through Rituals* also acknowledged a conception of homology between the 'infrastructrue' of the group and its style, derived from the work of Paul Willis. Willis's recent account of his recollections of the CCCS's usage of the term 'homology' (2000, pp. 127–30) is relevant here. Willis validly complains that discussion in the subcultural literature has tended to source 'homology' directly to Lévi-Strauss without acknowledgement of his own usage of it in his early field-work based publications such as *Profane Culture* (Willis, 1978). He has no recollection of sourcing it from Lévi-Strauss but, rather, believes it arose in collective discussions of *Goldmann's* work at Birmingham. However, a related tendency within such accounts is more consistent with one strain of Willis's own practice (Willis, 1990). That is, a conception of subcultural *bricoleurs* that emphasizes a 'resistant reception' dimension that effectively re-establishes a kind of authorship, albeit tied to a denial of pristine authenticity (e.g. Barker, 2002, p. 70).
67. Some subcultural researchers would validly argue that there were indeed spectacular youth subcultures in Britain in the 1950s, most notably the Teds.
68. I have traced the sociological contexts of this research programme as it developed via Stan Cohen's conception of 'moral panic' in Jones (1997).
69. Cf. Section 3.1.
70. *M&L*, p. 169.
71. Frow (1995, p. 11). Frow's comment arises in a sympathetic discussion of Ian Hunter's Foucaultian critiques of Williams (e.g. Hunter, 1988, pp. 85ff). For my critique of Hunter's view, see Jones (1994).
72. Moriarty's suggestion of a possible parallel between Barthes and Williams is especially relevant here (Moriarty, 1995, pp. 106–13).
73. Most of these are collected in Hall (1988).
74. Hall *et al.* (1978a, pp. viii–ix).
75. Cf. discussion of Williams and 'empiricism' in Section 5.1.
76. However he fails to paginate his sourcing of Poulantzas. It would seem Hall refers here to Poulantzas's characterization of the 'juridico-political superstructure' (Poulantzas, 1976, pp. 133–4).
77. Williams had sketched an alternative conception of 'constitutional authoritarianism' in the 1979 afterword to *Modern Tragedy* (*MT2*, pp. 207–19).
78. Cf. Milner (1993, p. 88). There appears to be an ironic 'injoke' in this title – in much the same pitch as the critique of the CCCS's *On Ideology* – that I have not seen 'unpacked' anywhere. I take the title to be an allusion to Hoggart's *The Uses of Literacy*. Williams is thus ironically echoing Hoggart's Leavisian doubts about the corrupting consequences of literacy in so titling his own doubts about the consequences of contemporary cultural theory.
79. Jessop *et al.* (1984); Hall (1985).
80. Norris has argued that Williams's critique of Orwell is based in an empiricist conception of truth (Norris, 1984). This underestimates Williams's mode of argument

(unlike Norris's later essay on *KeyWords*). Williams's criterion is characteristically immanent. He believes Orwell's 'projections' of fictional characters should have been imbued with the courage Orwell the observer witnessed in Catalonia and elsewhere, rather than merely presenting the passivity of his own cultural formation.

81. Williams established a parallel between the dystopian mode and 'bourgeois cultural theory' in his 'Utopia and Science Fiction' (1978g, p. 211; *PMC*, p. 207).

82. Hall (1997, pp. 30–1). This is made in response to the interviewers' allusion to Jorge Larrain's critique of Hall's 'neutral' conception (Larrain, 1991). Larrain, however, has vigorously resisted the very notion of any emancipatory conception of ideology (cf. Section 3.1). For a critique of the anti-democratic consequences of such strategic pragmatism in Gramsci, see Cohen and Arato (1992, pp. 142–59).

83. The effects of this displacement are far more serious in Hall's linkage of his (mis)understanding of Williams's conception of culture with Paul Gilroy's gross misreading of Williams's discussion of racism in *Towards 2000* (Hall, 1993, p. 360; Gilroy, 1987). Space does not permit adequate reconstruction of the evidence that would demonstrate the scale of Gilroy's and Hall's misrepresentation of Williams. However, Andrew Milner has generously conveyed my core argument from a paper by me within his own recent treatment of this matter (Milner, 2002, pp. 118–22).

84. As we saw in Section 3.4 Hall still recently accepted 'the Althusserian argument about the impossibility of getting outside of ideology' (Hall, 1997, p. 30). Yet even Althusser did not 'rank real art among the ideologies' (Althusser, 1977c, p. 203).

85. See Chapter 6 and Brunsdon (1990).

86. The recent Open University teaching series edited by Stuart Hall, *Culture Media and Identities*, provides some good examples of the continuity of this legacy, for example Du Gay *et al.* (1997) and Du Gay (1997). The chief qualification, however, lies in the emphasis on 'creative autonomy' of those researching popular music (e.g. the work of Keith Negus in Du Gay [ed.], 1997) which tempers the reductivism of Hall's initial formulation of the role of cultural producers. More broadly, there is a huge literature that debates the populist dimensions of the 'resistant reception' model as it was selectively developed outside Hall's 'hegemonic' framework. Cf. McGuigan's (1992) account of this transition as, in Curran's phrase, a 'new revisionism' (cf. Curran, 1990). See also Section 6.6.

87. *M&L*, pp. 140–1.

88. *P&L*, pp. 325, 335.

89. Although this is not meant to eliminate the normative judgement Williams endorses in its stead.

90. *P&L*, p. 340.

91. Williams presumably has Shklovsky (e.g. 1965) and Eichenbaum in mind but does not name them here, as he does in 'The Uses of Cultural Theory'.

92. See Section 6.4.

93. Indeed, Jakobson had developed his model as a critique of the limitations of 'devices'. Cf. Swingewood (1987, p. 17).

94. Suino (1979, pp. 97–8).

95. Mukařovský (1979).

96. Mukařovský (1979, pp. 88–9; 1986, p. 6).

97. Swingewood (1987, pp. 71–2).

98. I have cited the entire paragraph from which Williams directly cites only the last nineteen words.

99. Cf. Propp (1968).
100. Ricoeur (1974, pp. 33–4) and Lévi-Strauss (1970). Ricoeur was one of several interviewers in the latter. Both pieces were published together in *Esprit* in 1963.
101. Genette (1982a, pp. 13–15).
102. Pettit (1975, p. 43); Barthes (1977c).
103. Compare, for instance, his assessment of the early work of Barthes (Genette, 1982b).
104. It should be stressed, however, that neither appears to have read the other, and Williams would have been dissatisfied with Genette's continuing adherence to the linguistic paradigm as in, for example, his linguistic understanding of mode discussed below.
105. But Genette also discusses many twentieth-century examples of this misattribution, including Bakhtin's (Genette, 1992).
106. Cf. Section 2.5.
107. Genette (1992, p. 12).
108. Cf. the discussion of Adorno's conception of cultural productive force in Section 3.3.
109. *PMC*, p. 48. Cf. Section 2.5.
110. *M&L*, pp. 180–91.
111. Milner (2002, p. 100) reads Williams's typology as consisting of three, not four, categories. I did too until quite recently (cf. Jones, 2002). It is fair to attribute this interpretative difficulty to the notorious problems of Williams's style in *The Sociology of Culture*. Cf. (*SOC*, p. 196) for the key passage.
112. Goldmann (1977, pp. 371ff); cf. Genette (1992, p. 17).
113. Cf. Table 6.1.
114. For example, for the discussion that follows, 'Realism, Naturalism and their Alternatives' (1977c).
115. Cf. Table 3.2.
116. Williams provides a remarkable expansion of this case in material drawn from some of his last Cambridge lectures and published as 'On Dramatic Dialogue and Monologue' (*WIS*, pp. 31–64). While the analysis tends to remain within the formal 'column', it provides an extraordinary synthesis of historical semantics, formal typologization and statistical empirical analysis. Moreover, while Williams provides a critique of the orthodox definition of soliloquy as 'speaking aloud to oneself', he chooses to render this as 'inner speech', clearly alluding to Vološinov (*WIS*, p. 43; cf. Section 4.2).
117. *SOC*, pp. 169–71. For Williams's use of 'fraction' in his analysis of cultural formations, see Sections 3.2 and 6.2.
118. Milner (2002, p. 101).
119. Derrida (1980). Significantly, Derrida's critique (or deconstruction) of Genette (based on an earlier publication of Genette's argument) relies heavily on the (re)assertion of the primacy of the concept of *text*.

5   Towards a sociology of culture

1. O'Connor lists only one review in his usually reliable bibliography, that by Anthony Giddens (O'Connor, 1989, p. 170; Giddens, 1981).
2. A major influence on the conception of sociology amongst Hall and others in Birmingham cultural studies was Bramson's *The Political Context of Sociology*

(Bramson, 1967) which, significantly, focusses on sociology's complicity in the development of the mass society/mass culture theses.

3. By 1990, Hall could reflect: 'When I was offered a chair in sociology, I said, "Now that sociology does not exist as a discipline, I am prepared to profess it"' (Hall, 1990, p. 11).

4. Respectively: *TV*, pp. 119–26; 1976a, b; *M&L*, pp. 136–41; *SOC*, pp. 9–32.

5. Lasswell (1948). Williams was apparently citing the question from memory as he does not provide a source and abbreviates to 'how' Lasswell's third dimension, 'in what channel'.

6. See Section 2.3.

7. For such an assessment of the Chicago School, see Bleicher (1982, pp. 105ff).

8. This is significant because of the implicit charges of empiricism made, for different (Althusserian) reasons, by Hall and Eagleton against Williams's (over) use of the category of 'experience'. Williams's historical semantic analyses of 'empirical' and 'positivist' in *Keywords* make it plain that he understood the difference between an empiricist theory of knowledge that privileges sense-data over all else, and the use of empirical methods within a non-empiricist critical-theoretically informed frame. Indeed, he is also obviously aware of the positivist extension of the empiricist case to an advocacy of observational and experimental methods as the only valid scientific procedure (*KW2*, p. 116 cf. 239). This is the probable source of Williams's use of the category of 'observational sociology' rather than 'positivist sociology'. The most glaring conflation by a cultural studies practitioner of an empiricist theory of knowledge with all empirical methods (as part of a defence of the superiority of semiotics) comes in Fiske's *Introduction to Communication Studies* (1991, p. 135). Cf. also the discussion of this issue in the next section.

9. Williams's chief references here are Murdock and Golding (1974) and Garnham (1977).

10. However, Williams's most developed discussion of the production paradigm, 'Marx on Culture' (discussed in Chapter 2), was published two years after *The Sociology of Culture* in 1983.

11. Gallagher (1995, pp. 312–15).

12. See Section 2.2's explanation of Williams's usage of 'indissolubility'.

13. Cf. Section 2.5.

14. Gallagher's critique rests on a contrast (that she attributes to Williams) with the case of food which I cannot find in any edition of *The Sociology of Culture*.

15. *LR*, p. 136; *P&L*, pp. 136ff.

16. For interestingly convergent more recent accounts which rely on a typology very similar to Williams's own late one for meanings of 'culture' (including those presented in Chapter 1), see Bocock (1992, pp. 230–4)) and the related discussion in Lury (1992, p. 369). See also the remarkably anticipatory 'degrees of solution' model in Mulhern (1980).

17. Cf. Section 2.5.

18. Williams notes, for example, the shift in choral singing from embedded component of religious occasion to competitive performance (*SOC*, p. 151).

19. See Genette's speculations at the end of Genette (1982a).

20. Cf. Corrigan's and Willis's suggestive contemporary discussion (1980) that moves partially in parallel with Williams's here; see also Section 6.3.

21. For detailed discussion of this issue, see Section 6.5.

6 Cultural production and means of communication

1. I argued similarly at the time of the book's publication (Jones, 1981).
2. For a sympathetic elaboration of this position, see Lury (1992).
3. *C&S*, p. xi.
4. *T2000*, pp. 138–43.
5. However, this 'existing scholarship' remains unnamed.
6. *M&L*, pp. 119–20; cf. Table 3.1.
7. This account draws on both 'The Bloomsbury Fraction' and *The Sociology of Culture*. It should be noted that Williams uses 'fraction' to refer to both fraction of class origin and also to the formation itself as a means of stressing its break from the ideological and political orthodoxy of that origin.
8. Williams asserts that 'no full social analysis of avant-gardes has yet, to my knowledge, been undertaken' (*SOC*, p. 83). He was writing before the translation of the influential work of Bürger (1984), but it is odd that he did not employ Poggioli's *The Theory of the Avant-Garde* (1968) which certainly anticipates some of his arguments.
9. These are: Williams (1985, 1987, 1988a, b) and the 1987 lecture, 'When Was Modernism?' (*POM*, pp. 31–5). Cf. Chapter 7.
10. Although it is worth noting that Adorno's *Philosophy of Modern Music* uses exactly the same term ('new conformism') to exactly the same purpose (Adorno, 1973b, pp. 5–7). This text is cited in *The Sociology of Culture* as an exercise in comparative social formal analysis that Williams sees as comparable with his own (*SOC*, p. 179).
11. See Section 3.4.
12. This conception of distance emerged first in the critique of the Birmingham CCCS.
13. *SOC*, pp. 216–17.
14. Gramsci (1971, pp. 5–6).
15. *SOC*, p. 226.
16. See Section 5.2 for the former.
17. Prophetically, Williams notes how vulnerable 'critical sociology' is to the internal reproductive priorities of these institutions.
18. (1988a, p. 9); *POM*, p. 56.
19. See the productive use made of Williams's analysis in Longhurst (1989). Steve Fuller's social epistemology would also appear to cry out for the mediating role of 'formations' – cf. his own recent use of the category of 'fantasist vanguardism' (Fuller, 2002).
20. *SOC*, pp. 98ff. Undoubtedly, Althusser's 'ISA essay' was an influence here in posing the 'reproduction' problematic (1977b), but Williams was equally – and far more sympathetically – attentive to Bourdieu's and Passeron's *Reproduction* (1977); cf. Williams (1977g). He had also published a long critique of Daniel Bell's *The Cultural Contradictions of Capitalism* (1996) (see Chapter 7). However, I would argue that the most significant impetus was the dynamic of Williams's own research on the cultural reproduction of aesthetic genres and the technically replicative capacities of communications technologies.
21. The key moment appears to be in John Clarke's work on subcultural 'diffusion and defusion' (Clarke, 1977, pp. 188–90), and its reworking by Hebdige (1979, pp. 92–9). Clarke *et al.* (1977, pp. 72–4) interpreted the contradictory 'dominant' responses to groups like the Mods – commodification and moral panic – as part of the contradictory dynamic of the unstable equilibria of hegemony.

22. Cf. Althusser (1977b).
23. Cf. Sections 3.1 and 3.3.
24. See especially Ryan (1991), one of the few efforts to build directly, in part, from *The Sociology of Culture*. Cf. also the related footnoted 1990 reassessments of *Television*'s similar predictions and arguments by Ederyn Williams throughout *TV2*.
25. Cf. Section 1.2.
26. *SOC*, pp. 108–12.
27. In a 1983 essay (Williams, 1983b) and a 1985 lecture, 'Cinema and Socialism' (*POM*, pp. 107–18), Williams applied his work on market asymmetry, melodrama and popular culture to the case of cinema, so correcting its negative exemplary role in *The Sociology of Culture*: 'there is no technological determinism running from "film" to "Hollywood"' (1983b, p. 22).
28. Those other discrete writings (not including those on mediated cultural forms) are: 1978c, 1981b, c.
29. I can thus only broadly endorse the existing analyses of Williams's media writings that emphasize this informing dimension: for example, Sparks (1993). Eldridge and Eldridge (1994, pp. 98–110) also quite validly use the 1961 public lecture, 'Communications and Community', as a linking text to make a similar case (*ROH*, pp. 19–31). Williams used the same title for a subsection of the conclusion of *Culture and Society*. However, I would also stress the tendency within these estimations to focus on the early Williams rather than the mature sociology of culture. See also Williams (1962, 1969b, 1970b, 1977f, 1978a). I have discussed such literature at length in Jones (1994). See also McGuigan (1997).
30. McLuhan may not have coined the term 'media', as Tom Wolfe has claimed (Wolfe, 1984), but he certainly did more than any other intellectual to legitimate it.
31. Mulhern (1979).
32. Leavis and Thompson (1937); cf. Stearn and McLuhan (1968, p. 303).
33. Williams (1968b); McLuhan (1967a).
34. *KW1*, p. 169; *KW2*, p. 203.
35. McLuhan (1967b, p. 31).
36. Fekete has plausibly traced this view to McLuhan's drawing a thesis of 'creative passivity' from Keats's conception of 'negative capability' and T.S. Eliot's 'catalyst' conception of creativity (1977, p. 159).
37. Fekete (1977, pp. 136–7). It is a commonplace observation that McLuhan's theses concerning the relation between 'media' and spatio-temporal orders were at the very least heavily indebted to Innis (cf. Carey, 1969; Thompson, 1995, p. 7). Likewise he readily adopted Innis's extension thesis concerning the relation between communications media and human 'senses', thus rendering printing, for example, a 'visual technology'. McLuhan admits as much in his introduction to Innis's *The Bias of Communication* where he locates his own *The Gutenberg Galaxy* as 'a footnote to the observations of Innis on the subject of the psychic and social consequences, first of writing, then of printing' (McLuhan, 1964, p. ix). See also Jones (2000a).
38. McLuhan and Fiore (1967). Cf. Fekete's description of this text as a 'pedagogic art' derived from Rimbaud's painted slides (1982, pp. 60–1).
39. Huyssen (1986, pp. 178–221). More specifically, McLuhan and Susan Sontag (who wrote a remarkably sympathetic avant-gardist celebration of McLuhan [Sontag, 1968]) are regarded by Huyssen as members of the 'American avant-garde' who revive 1920s avant-gardism, so making 'theoretical' initiatives such as McLuhan's more likely.

40. For example, Ferguson (1991). For an account of McLuhan that moves affirmatively from similar premises to Williams's critique (which is briefly acknowledged), see Willmott (1996).
41. It seems likely that this conception of avant-gardist 'projection' was influenced by the work of Williams's then doctoral student, John Fekete (later published as Fekete [1977]). Fekete receives recognition in the acknowledgements of both *Television* and *Marxism and Literature* and is cited approvingly in 'The Uses of Cultural Theory'. Another relevant parallel here is Jameson's use of 'projection' in the organization of his *The Prison House of Language* (1974b).
42. For example, Corner and Hawthorne (1980); Mackay and O'Sullivan (1999).
43. McKenzie (1996). See also the welcome fuller recognition of William's place in these arguments in Preston's recent critique of the role of technological determinism within the information society thesis and related literatures (Preston, 2001).
44. This codicil broadly distinguishes Williams's position from that advocated by Enzensberger in his famous critique of McLuhan and 'left archaism'. Enzensberger may have been an influence, however, on Williams's critique of what Enzensberger calls McLuhan's 'apolitical avant-gardism' (Enzensberger, 1970).
45. *TV2*, pp. 14–31.
46. See, for example, Harvey's account (1991, pp. 125–97).
47. Williams (1981a).
48. MacKenzie and Wajcman (1985, pp. 24–5n).
49. *T2000*, pp. 129–30. See also the discussion in Chapter 7.
50. Cf. Laing (1991, p. 163). Williams also notes in the introduction to *Television* that Joy Williams's work on Chapters 3, 4 and 6 was 'at once primary and indispensable' (*TV1*, p. 8).
51. Williams (1977d, 1983b).
52. The literature here is indeed vast. Illustrative examples are Longhurst (1987) and Gledhill (1987).
53. For example, Fiske (1987, pp. 99–100).
54. Corner (1999, pp. 60–9); Stuart Laing reached the same conclusion in an earlier assessment (1991, p. 167).
55. Laing (1991, p. 167). This is very clear from its earlier use in one of Williams's television criticisms as 'general flow', ('Programmes and Sequences', 11 March 1971) although here the institutional target is the BBC (*RWOT*, pp. 133–6).
56. *TV2*, pp. 86–7.
57. *TV2*, pp. 89–90.
58. *TV2*, p. 72. In principle at least, Williams so anticipates work on televisual genre hybridity such as that of Todd Gitlin (Gitlin, 1985).
59. *TV2*, pp. 83–4.
60. Corner is again the best guide here. He complains that Williams does not develop the implications for 'the new structuring of cultural perception' of this thesis (1999, p. 64). This is true of *Television* but see the next section for Williams's later fulfilment of Corner's requirement.
61. See the citations regarding Williams's policy work in fn. 29 above and, on his specific advocacy of, most famously realism, see Williams (1977c, e).
62. Corner (1999, pp. 61–3); cf. *TV2*, p. 95.
63. *RWOT*, passim.
64. Feuer, J. *et al.* (1984) and the related discussion in Brunsdon (1990). But note the relative simplicity of Feuer's nonetheless useful account of genre analysis (1992)

compared to Williams's. One recent primer on such genre analysis is indicative of the continuing dominance of the formalism Williams challenged (Lacey, 2000).

65. The durative and amplificatory dimensions thus also capture the issue of 'space–time distanciation' that figures prominently in what is now called 'medium theory' within contemporary communication theory; cf. Meyrowitz (1985, 1996, 1999); for a more critical view, see Ferguson (1990). See also next section.

66. (1976b, p. 505).

67. *WIS*, p. 3.

68. Williams deals with the obvious objections to this claim by a reliance on the completeness of the break between writing and bodily resourced modes. Thus dance, for example, no matter how immanently sophisticated or culturally unfamiliar, still provides a dimension of accessibility impossible in the case of literacy (*SOC*, p. 92).

69. In the elided section Williams emphasizes the inadequacy of formalist semiotics to such an educative project.

70. See the materials collected in McIlroy and Westwood (1993).

71. Thompson (1995); Calhoun (1992).

72. For further discussion of this point, see Jones (2000a).

73. Calhoun (1992, pp. 210–13).

74. Murdock (1993); Giddens (1990). Of these commentators, only Murdock acknowledges the relevance of Williams's work. Giddens surprisingly does not acknowledge the similar arguments of Meyrowitz, who, as noted earlier, relies on McLuhan and Innis for his 'medium theory'. Thompson and Calhoun do acknowledge Meyrowitz.

75. Thompson (1995, p. 181). Murdock is again the exception here. Cf. also the more recent work of Garnham (2000).

76. Cf. the citation from 'Drama in a Dramatized Society' in Section 5.2.

77. Cf. Lunn (1985, p. 152).

78. Jameson (1990, pp. 107, 230).

79. Adorno and Horkheimer (1986, pp. 120–67).

80. Bradley (1979). For more recent receptions of Adorno within the sociology of popular music, see Goodwin (1992) and Paddison (1996).

81. Jameson (1990, p. 143)

82. Jameson's own view, that classical ideology critique needs to be modified to suit the needs of a 'postmodern social order' (Jameson, 1990, p. 144) would appear to be vulnerable to critiques like Keane's of Habermas (cf. Jones, 2000b).

83. Jameson (1990, p. 143).

84. Feenberg (1992, 1999, pp. 86–7).

85. It is here that Feenberg sees a possible role for organized social movements, providing examples in the user/consumer 'redefinition' of the 'technical code' of the Minitel computer network in France and the challenge to the technical code of technocratic medicine posed by organized AIDS patients (Feenberg, 1992, p. 319; cf. Feenberg, 1995).

86. For example, Buchstein (1997).

7   The Long Revolution(s) of modernity

1. *O*, p. 78.
2. Habermas (1991).

3. Eley (1993, pp. 294–5). The first such detailed comparison – that effectively predates the translation of *The Structural Transformation* – is Brantlinger (1990, pp. 195–8). But cf. Eagleton's juxtapositions of Williams and Habermas in his *The Function of Criticism* (Eagleton, 1984).

4. See especially Nieminen (1997).

5. Habermas (1991, p. 37).

6. Habermas (1996b, pp. 365–70).

7. Williams (1976d); Bell (1996).

8. Habermas (1996a, pp. 42–4).

9. See, for example, Calinescu (1995, pp. 41–94), Kumar (1995, pp. 66–100), Giles (1993) and Jameson (2002).

10. I cite directly here from the published version of 'When Was Modernism?' but this text is a reconstruction undertaken by Fred Inglis from his own notes and those from which Williams lectured.

11. Williams (1985).

12. Similar references to Eliot occur in the 'Metropolitan Perceptions' essay (*POM*, p. 43) and 'Theatre as a Political Forum' (*POM*, p. 94).

13. *POM*, frontispiece.

14. *T2000*, p. 143.

15. *T2000*, pp. 83–5.

16. For example, Kumar (1981, pp. 199ff); Bell (1999a).

17. Bell (1999b).

18. Cf. Section 6.2.

19. Emphasis added.

20. Cf. Keane (1988, p. 219).

21. Habermas's subsequent self-critical characterization of this part of *The Structural Transformation* bears an uncanny resemblance to the passage from *Aspects of Sociology* by Adorno on ideology cited in Section 3.1 (Habermas, 1993, p. 442).

22. Williams (1960).

23. 1978g (211); *PMC*, p. 207.

24. *SOC*, p. 158.

25. Cf. Fekete (1984, p. 244).

26. Habermas (1991, p. 158).

27. Habermas (1991, pp. 43–51) cf. Habermas (1993, pp. 427–9). The comparable recognition of patriarchy in Williams might have been expected to have come from what he called his 'long involvement' with Ibsen which started with his Tripos thesis at Cambridge later published in *Drama from Ibsen to Eliot* (*P&L*, p. 62). Ibsen's tragic heroes are often women. However, Williams plainly saw his 1952 task of 'revaluation' of Ibsen as beginning by setting aside existing critical reception (especially Shaw's) that focussed on Ibsen's attention to social issues of the day and thus on 'elements of Ibsen that were in fact incidental'. The first of these Williams lists is 'the Emancipation of Women' (*DFIE*, pp. 41–2). Williams revised his view of Ibsen with his conception of liberal tragedy in *Modern Tragedy* but did not overtly reverse there his 'setting aside' of the role of patriarchy. When a similar contradiction in his assessment of Ibsen's *A Doll's House* was pointed out to him in *Politics and Letters* he offered an arguably 'token' corrective and reasserted his key thesis concerning Ibsen's role in liberal tragedy; that is, that he was 'the drama-tist of blockages of liberation' (*P&L*, p. 199). The key conceptual difference between Habermas (in 1989) and Williams (in 1985) here is that while Habermas accepts that the historical exclusion of women from the public sphere had 'structuring

significance' in that it also structured the public sphere's relation to the (patriarchal) private sphere – so 'modernizing patriarchy' (*pace* Carol Pateman) – Williams regards the bourgeois family as a 'hybrid fusion' of residual feudal-patriarchal and emergent-hegemonic bourgeois propertied modes of dominance (Habermas, 1993, p. 428; cf. Williams, 1988a, p. 8).

28. *T2000*, pp. 172–24.
29. Eagleton (2003, p. 59).
30. This would appear to be the basis of Williams's plan to republish this afterword in *The Politics of Modernism* (*POM*, frontispiece).
31. In so doing Williams 'reinvented' one of the classic motifs in the formation of German sociology (Liebersohn, 1988).
32. *COM1*, pp. 92–6; *T2000*, p. 120.
33. Habermas (1996b). See Jones (2000b) for further elaboration of this point.
34. Williams (1978g); *PMC*, 196–212. The significance of 'utopianism' to any reassessment of Williams was first raised by Francis Mulhern in his still highly relevant review of *Towards 2000* (Mulhern, 1998). Patrick Brantlinger's comparison of Williams and Habermas implies a similar position (1990, pp. 182–98). Eldridge and Eldridge briefly discuss a 'wary utopianism' (1994, pp. 215–26). See also the discussion by Levitas (1990, pp. 114–30).
35. On the enduring 'dystopian' legacy of Bell's formulations, see Jacoby (1999).
36. In an interesting anticipation of the contradictory dilemmas faced within 'post-89' Eastern Europe, Williams acknowledges that while such a utopia might be the only one that might appeal to those 'who have known affluence and with it social injustice and moral corruption' it would not be so for 'those still subject to extreme exploitation' (1978g, p. 214; *PMC*, p. 212).
37. 'Foreword to 1987 Edition' of *Culture and Society*.
38. Although a more fully biographical study might speculate about a linkage with Williams's period of withdrawal while writing *Culture and Society*. Higgins (1999), for example, draws something like this from Williams's comments about that period in *Politics and Letters* during his opening biographical chapter. Perhaps this sentence would then refer to 'the mature Williams'.
39. For example, the afterword to the third edition of *Communications* (*COM3*, pp. 180–9) and of course the extended discussions in *Politics and Letters*.

Bibliography

Adorno, T. (1972) 'Theses on the Sociology of Art'. *Working Papers in Cultural Studies* 3: 120–8. First published 1967.

Adorno, T. (1973a) 'Correspondence with Benjamin'. *New Left Review* 81: 55–80.

Adorno, T. (1973b) *Philosophy of Modern Music*. NY: Seabury Press. First published 1948.

Adorno, T. (1977) 'Music and Technique'. *Telos* 32 (Summer): 73–95.

Adorno, T. (1978) 'On the Social Situation of Music'. *Telos* 35 (Spring): 128–64. First published 1932.

Adorno, T. (1984a) 'Cultural Criticism and Society'. In his *Prisms*. Cambridge, Mass.: MIT Press. First published 1955. English translation 1967.

Adorno, T. (1984b) *Aesthetic Theory*. Trans. C. Lenhardt. London: RKP. First published 1970.

Adorno, T. (1989) *Introduction to the Sociology of Music*. NY: Continuum. First English translation published 1976 from revised 1968 German edition.

Adorno, T. (1991a) 'On Lyric Poetry and Society'. In his *Notes to Literature vol 1*. NY: Columbia University Press. First published 1957.

Adorno, T. (1991b) 'Culture and Administration'. In his *The Culture Industry: Selected Essays on Mass Culture*. London: Routledge. First published 1960.

Adorno, T. (1991c) 'Transparencies on Film'. In his *The Culture Industry: Selected Essays on Mass Culture*. London: Routledge. First published 1966.

Adorno, T. (1992) 'Commitment'. In his *Notes to Literature vol 2*. NY: Columbia University Press. First published 1974.

Adorno, T. (1994) *Kierkegaard: Construction of the Aesthetic*. Minneapolis: University of Minnesota Press. First published 1933.

Adorno, T. (1997) *Aesthetic Theory*. Minneapolis: University of Minnesota Press. R. Hullot-Kentor (trans.).

Adorno, T. and Horkheimer, M. (1986) *The Dialectic of Enlightenment*. London: Verso. First published 1944.

Althusser, L. (1976) *Essays in Self-Criticism*. London: NLB.

Althusser, L. (1977a) 'On the Materialist Dialectic'. In his *For Marx*. London: New Left Books. First published 1963.

Althusser, L. (1977b) 'Ideology and the Ideological State Apparatuses'. In his *Lenin and Philosophy*. London: NLB. First published 1969.

Althusser, L. (1977c) 'A Letter on Art'. In his *Lenin and Philosophy*. London: NLB. First published 1966.

Althusser, L. and Balibar, E. (1977) *Reading Capital*. London: NLB. First published 1968.

Anderson, P. (1964) 'Origins of the Present Crisis'. *New Left Review* 23: 26–53. Revised and republished in his (1992) *English Questions*. London: Verso.

Anderson, P. (1968) 'Components of the National Culture'. *New Left Review* 50: 3–57. Revised and republished in his (1992) *English Questions*. London: Verso.

Anderson, P. (1976) *Considerations on Western Marxism*. London: NLB.

Antonio, R. (1981) 'Immanent Critique as the Core of Critical Theory: Its Origins and Developments in Hegel, Marx and Contemporary Thought'. *British Journal of Sociology* 32(3): 330–45.

Arnold, M. (1971) *Culture and Anarchy*. Cambridge: Cambridge UP. First published 1869.

Bakhtin, M. and Medvedev, P. (1985) *The Formal Method in Literary Scholarship: A Critical Introduction to Sociological Poetics*. A. Wehrle (trans.) Cambridge, Mass.: Harvard UP. First published 1928.

Baldick, C. (1983) *The Social Mission of English Criticism 1848–1932*. Oxford: Clarendon.

Barker, C. (2002) *Making Sense of Cultural Studies*. London: Sage.

Barnett, A. (1976) 'Raymond Williams and Marxism: A Rejoinder to Terry Eagleton'. *New Left Review* 99: 47–64.

Barrett, M. (1991) *The Politics of Truth: From Marx to Foucault*. Cambridge: Polity.

Barrett, M., Corrigan, P., Kuhn, A. and Wolff, J. (1979) 'Representation and Cultural Production'. In M. Barrett *et al*. (eds) *Ideology and Cultural Production*. London: Croom Helm.

Barthes, R. (1967) *Elements of Semiology*. NY: Hill and Wang. First published 1964.

Barthes, R. (1972) *Mythologies*. St Albans: Paladin. First published 1957.

Barthes, R. (1977a) 'Rhetoric of the Image'. In S. Heath (ed./trans.) *Image, Music Text*. London: Fontana. First published 1964.

Barthes, R. (1977b) 'The Photographic Message'. In S. Heath (ed./trans.) *Image, Music Text*. London: Fontana. First published 1961.

Barthes, R. (1977c) 'Introduction to the Structural Analysis of Narratives'. In S. Heath (ed./trans.) *Image, Music Text*. London: Fontana. First published 1966.

Bell, D. (1962) *The End of Ideology: On the Exhaustion of Political Ideas in the Fifties*. NY: Free Press.

Bell, D. (1996) *The Cultural Contradictions of Capitalism*. NY: Basic Books. First published 1976.

Bell, D. (1999a) *The Coming of Post-Industrial Society*. NY: Basic Books. First published 1973.

Bell, D. (1999b) 'The Axial Age of Technology; Foreword: 1999'. In D. Bell, *The Coming of Post-Industrial Society*. NY: Basic Books.

Benhabib, S. (1986) *Critique, Norm and Utopia: A Study of the Foundations of Critical Theory*. NY: Columbia UP.

Benjamin, W. (1973) *Charles Baudelaire: A Lyric Poet in the Era of High Capitalism*. London: NLB.

Benjamin, W. (1982) 'The Work of Art in the Age of Mechanical Reproduction'. In H. Arendt (ed.) *Illuminations*. London: Fontana. First published 1936.

Bennett, T. (1979) *Formalism and Marxism*. London: Methuen.

Bennett, T. (1981) 'Producing Art' (review essay on Wolff, 1981). *Screen Education* 39: 86–93.

Bennett, T. (1998) *Culture: A Reformer's Science*. Sydney: Allen & Unwin.

Benton, T. (1984) *The Rise and Fall of Structural Marxism: Althusser and his Influence*. London: Macmillan.

Bleicher, J. (1982) *The Hermeneutic Imagination: Outline of a Positive Critique of Scientism and Sociology*. London: RKP.

Bloch, E., Lukács, G., Brecht, B., Benjamin, W. and Adorno, T. (1977) *Aesthetics and Politics*. R. Taylor (ed./trans.). London: NLB.

Bocock, R. (1992) 'The Cultural Formations of Modern Society'. In S. Hall and B. Gieben (eds) *Formations of Modernity*. Cambridge: Polity/Open University Press.

Boelhower, W. (1980) 'Introduction' to L. Goldmann *Essays on Method in the Sociology of Literature*. St Louis, Mo.: Telos Press.

Bourdieu, P. (1977) *Outline of a Theory of Practice*. Cambridge: Cambridge UP.

Bourdieu, P. (1984) *Distinction*. London: RKP. First published 1979.

Bourdieu, P. (1991a) 'Symbolic Power'. In J. Thompson (ed.) P. Bourdieu, *Language and Symbolic Power*. Cambridge, Mass.: Harvard UP. Previously published translation in R. Nice (trans.) (1977) 'Two Bourdieu Texts'. *CCCS Stencilled Occasional Paper* No. 46.

Bourdieu, P. (1991b) 'Delegation and Political Fetishism'. In J. Thompson (ed.) P. Bourdieu, *Language and Symbolic Power*. Cambridge, Mass.: Harvard UP.

Bourdieu, P. (1993) *The Field of Cultural Production*. NY: Columbia UP.

Bourdieu, P. (1996) *The Rules of Art*. Stanford: Stanford UP. First published 1992.

Bourdieu, P. and Passeron, J.-P. (1977) *Reproduction in Education, Society and Culture*. London: Sage.

Boyes, G. (1993) *The Imagined Village: Culture, Ideology and the English Folk Revival*. Manchester: Manchester UP.

Bradley, D. (1979) 'The Cultural Study of Music'. *CCCS Stencilled Occasional Paper* No. 61.

Bramson, L. (1967) *The Political Context of Sociology*. Princeton: Princeton UP.

Brantlinger, P. (1990) *Crusoe's Footprints: Cultural Studies in Britain and America*. NY: Routledge.

Brunsdon, C. (1990) 'Quality in Television'. *Screen* **31**(1): 67–90.

Buchstein, H. (1997) 'Bytes that Bite: The Internet and Deliberative Democracy' *Constellations* **4**(2): 248–63.

Buci-Glucksmann, C. (1980) *Gramsci and the State*. London: Lawrence and Wishart.

Buci-Glucksmann, C. (1982) 'Hegemony and Consent: A Political Strategy'. In A. Showstack Sassoon (ed.) *Approaches to Gramsci*. London: Writers and Readers.

Bürger, P. (1984) *Theory of the Avant-Garde*. Minneapolis: University of Minnesota.

Burke, P. (1978) *Popular Culture in Early Modern Europe*. London: T. Smith.

Calhoun, C. (1992) 'The Infrastructure of Modernity: Indirect Social Relationships, Information Technology, and Social Integration'. In H. Haferkampf and N. Smelser (eds) *Social Change and Modernity*. Berkeley: UCLA Press.

Calhoun, C. (1993) 'Habitus, Field and Capital: The Question of Historical Specificity'. In C. Calhoun *et al.* (eds) *Bourdieu: Critical Perspectives*. Cambridge: Polity.

Calinescu, M. (1995) *Five Faces of Modernity: Modernism, Avant-Garde, Decadence, Kitsch, Postmodernism*. Durham: Duke University Press. First edition 1977. Second edition 1987.

Carey, J. (1969) 'Harold Innis and Marshall McLuhan'. In R. Rosenthal (ed.) *McLuhan: Pro & Con*. London: Pelican.

Caudwell, C. (1947) *Illusion and Reality: A Study of the Sources of Poetry*. NY: International Publishers.

CCCS (Centre for Contemporary Cultural Studies) (1978) *On Ideology*. London: Hutchinson. First published in 1977 as *WPCS 10*.

Clark, R. (1955) *Herder*. Berkeley: UCLA Press.

Clarke, J. (1977) 'Style'. In S. Hall and T. Jefferson (eds) *Resistance through Rituals: Youth Subcultures in Post-war Britain*. London: Hutchinson. First published 1974 as *WPCS 7/8*.

Clarke, J., Hall, S., Jefferson, T. and Roberts, B. (1977) 'Subcultures, Cultures and Class'. In S. Hall and T. Jefferson (eds) *Resistance through Rituals: Youth Subcultures in Post-war Britain*. London: Hutchinson.

Cocchiara, G. (1981) *The History of Folklore in Europe*. Philadelphia: Institute for the Study of Human Issues. First published 1952.

Cohen, G. (1978) *Karl Marx's Theory of History: A Defence*. NJ: Princeton UP.

Cohen, J. and Arato, A. (1992) *Civil Society and Political Theory*. Cambridge, Mass.: MIT Press.

Coleridge, S. (1852) *On The Constitution of Church and State*. London: Edward Moxon. First published 1830.

Collini, S. (2001) 'Culture Talk'. *New Left Review: Second Series* 7: 43–54.

Corner, J. (1994) 'Debating Culture: Quality and Inequality'. *Media, Culture and Society* **16**(1): 141–8.

Corner, J. (1999) *Critical Ideas in Television Studies*. Oxford: OUP.

Corner, J. and Hawthorne, J. (1980) *Communications Studies: An Introductory Reader*. London: Edward Arnold.

Corrigan, P. and Willis, P. (1980) 'Cultural Forms and Class Mediations'. *Media, Culture and Society* **2**: 297–312.

Culler, J. (1975) *Structuralist Poetics: Structuralism, Linguistics and the Study of Literature*. London: RKP.

Curran, J. (1990) 'The New Revisionism in Mass Communication Research: A Reappraisal'. *European Journal of Communication* **5**: 135–64.

Darcy, A. (1987) 'Franz Boas and the Concept of Culture: A Genealogy'. In D. Austin-Broos (ed.) *Creating Culture*. Sydney: Allen and Unwin.

Davis, R. and Schleifer, R. (1991) *Criticism and Culture: The Role of Critique in Modern Literary Theory*. Harlow, Essex: Longman.

Derrida, J. (1978) 'Structure, Sign and Play in the Discourse of the Human Sciences'. In his *Writing and Difference*. Chicago: University of Chicago Press. Lecture delivered in 1966.

Derrida, J. (1980) 'The Law of Genre'. In S. Weber (ed.) *Glyph 7: The Strasburg Colloquium: genre*. Baltimore: Johns Hopkins U.P.

Descombes, V. (1986) *Modern French Philosophy*. Cambridge: Cambridge UP.

Doložel, L. (1994) 'Prague School Structuralism'. In M. Groden and M. Kreisworth (eds) *The Johns Hopkins Guide to Literary Theory and Criticism*. Baltimore: Johns Hopkins UP.

Du Gay, P. (ed.) (1997) *Production of Culture/Cultures of Production*. London: Sage.

Du Gay, P., Hall, S., James, L., Mackay, H. and Negus, K. (1997) *Doing Cultural Studies: The Story of the Sony Walkman*. London: Sage.

Eagleton, T. (1970) *Exiles and Emigres*. London: Chatto & Windus.

Eagleton, T. (1976a) 'Criticism and Politics: The Work of Raymond Williams'. *New Left Review* **95**: 3–23. Republished in his 1976b.

Eagleton, T. (1976b) *Criticism and Ideology*. London: NLB.

Eagleton, T. (1976c) *Marxism and Literary Criticism*. London: Methuen.

Eagleton, T. (1981) *Walter Benjamin or, Towards a Revolutionary Criticism*. London: Verso.

Eagleton, T. (1984) *The Function of Criticism*. London: Verso.

Eagleton, T. (1988) 'Resources for a Journey of Hope: The Significance of Raymond Williams'. *New Left Review* **168**: 3–11.

Eagleton, T. (1989a) 'Base and Superstructure in Raymond Williams'. In Eagleton (ed.) (1989b).

Eagleton, T. (ed.) (1989b) *Raymond Williams: Critical Perspectives*. Cambridge: Polity.

Eagleton, T. (1991) *Ideology: An Introduction*. London: Verso.

Eagleton, T. (2000) *The Idea of Culture*. London: Blackwell.

Eagleton, T. (2003) *Sweet Violence: The Idea of the Tragic*. London: Blackwell.

Eagleton, T. and Wicker, B. (eds) (1968) *From Culture to Revolution*. London: Sheed & Ward.

Eldridge, J. and Eldridge, L. (1994) *Raymond Williams: Making Connections*. London: Routledge.

Eley, G. (1993) 'Nations, Publics, and Political Cultures: placing Habermas in the Nineteenth Century'. In C. Calhoun (ed.) *Habermas and the Public Sphere*. Cambridge, Massachusetts: MIT Press. Paper given in 1989.

Eliot, T.S. (1948) *Notes Towards the Definition of Culture*. London: Faber.

Enzensberger, H. (1970) 'Constituents of a Theory of the Media'. *New Left Review* **64** (November/December): 12–36.

Evans, M. (1981) *Lucien Goldmann*. Brighton: Harvester.

Feenberg, A. (1992) 'Subversive Rationalisation: Technology, Power and Democracy'. *Inquiry* **35**(3/4): 301–22.

Feenberg, A. (1995) *Alternative Modernity: The Technical Turn in Philosophy and Social Theory*. Berkeley: University of California Press.

Feenberg, A. (1999) *Questioning Technology*. London: Routledge.

Feher, F. (1984) 'The French Revolutions as Models for Marx's Conception of Politics'. *Thesis Eleven* **8**: 59–76.

Fekete, J. (1977) *The Critical Twilight: Explorations in the Ideology of Anglo-American Literary Theory from Eliot to McLuhan*. London: RKP.

Fekete, J. (1982) 'Massage in the Mass Age: Remembering the McLuhan Matrix'. *Canadian Journal of Political and Social Theory* **6**(3): 50–67.

Fekete, J. (1984) 'Modernity and the Literary Institution: Strategic Anti-foundational Moves'. In J. Fekete (ed.) *The Structural Allegory: Reconstructive Encounters with the New French Thought*. Manchester: Manchester University Press.

Ferguson, M. (1990) 'Electronic Media and the Redefining of Time and Space'. In M. Ferguson (ed.) *Public Communication: The New Imperatives*. London: Sage.

Ferguson, M. (1991) 'Marshall McLuhan Revisited: 1960s Zeitgeist Victim or Pioneer Postmodernist?'. *Media, Culture and Society* **13**: 71–90.

Feuer, J. (1992) 'Genre Study and Television'. In R. Allen (ed.) *Channels of Discourse, Reassembled: Television and Contemporary Criticism*. 2nd Edn. London: Routledge.

Feuer, J., Kerr, P. and Vahimagi, T. (eds) (1984) *MTM: 'Quality Television'*. London: BFI.

Fiske, J. (1987) *Television Culture*. London: Routledge.

Fiske, J. (1991) *Introduction to Communication Studies*. 2nd Edn. London: Routledge.

Frankfurt Institute for Social Research (1973) *Aspects of Sociology*. London: Heinemann. First published 1956.

Frow, J. (1986) *Marxism and Literary History*. London: Blackwell.

Frow, J. (1995) *Cultural Studies and Cultural Value*. Oxford: Clarendon Press.

Frye, N. (1973) *Anatomy of Criticism*. Princeton, NJ: Princeton UP.

Fuller, S. (2002) Plenary Address. International Sociological Association Congress, Brisbane, July.

Gallagher, C. (1995) 'Raymond Williams and Cultural Studies'. In Prendergast (1995).

Garnham, N. (1977) 'Towards a Political Economy of Culture'. *New Universities Quarterly* (Summer): 341–57.

Garnham, N. (1983) 'Toward a Theory of Cultural Materialism'. *Journal of Communication*. Summer: 314–29.

Garnham, N. (1986) 'Contribution to a Political Economy of Mass Communication'. In R. Collins *et al.* (eds) *Media Culture and Society: A Critical Reader*. London: Sage.

Garnham, N. (2000) *Emancipation, the Media and Modernity: Arguments about the Media and Social Theory*. Oxford: OUP.

Garnham, N. and Williams, R. (1980) 'Pierre Bourdieu and the Sociology of Culture: an introduction'. *Media, Culture and Society* **2**(3): 209–23.

Genette, G. (1982a) 'Structuralism and Literary Criticism'. In his *Figures of Literary Discourse*. NY: Columbia UP. First published 1964.

Genette, G. (1982b) 'The Obverse of Signs'. In his *Figures of Literary Discourse*. NY: Columbia UP. First published 1964.

Genette, G. (1992) *The Architext: An Introduction*. Berkeley: University of California Press. First published 1979.

Giddens, A. (1979) 'Raymond Williams's Long Revolution' (review of *Politics and Letters*). *Times Higher Education Supplement*, December 14: 11–12. Revised and republished in his *Profiles and Critiques in Social Theory* and also in his *In Defence of Sociology*.

Giddens, A. (1981) 'The State of Sociology' (review of Fontana's 'New Sociology' series including Williams's *The Sociology of Culture*). *Times Literary Supplement*. February 27: 215.

Giddens, A. (1984) *The Constitution of Society*. Berkeley: University of California Press.

Giddens, A. (1990) *The Consequences of Modernity*. Stanford: Stanford UP.

Giles, S. (1993) 'Afterword: Avant-Garde, Modernism, Modernity: A Theoretical Overview'. In S. Giles (ed.) *Theorizing Modernism: Essays in Critical Theory*. London: Routledge.

Gilroy, P. (1987) *There Ain't No Black in the Union Jack*. London: Hutchinson.

Gitlin, T. (1985) *Inside Prime Time*. NY: Pantheon.

Gledhill, C. (1987) 'The Melodramatic Field: An Investigation'. In C. Gledhill (ed.) *Home is Where the Heart is: Studies in Melodrama and the Woman's Film*. London: BFI.

Glucksmann, A. (1972) 'A Ventriliquist Structuralism'. *New Left Review* 72: 68–92. First published 1967.

Glucksmann, M. (1974) *Structuralist Analysis in Contemporary Social Thought*. London: RKP.

Goldmann, L. (1967) 'Ideology and Writing'. *Times Literary Supplement*. September 28: 903–5.

Goldmann, L. (1972) 'Structure: Human Reality and Methodological Concept'. In R. Macksey and E. Donato (eds) *The Structuralist Controversy*. Baltimore: Johns Hopkins UP. Paper delivered in 1966.

Goldmann, L. (1973) *The Human Sciences and Philosophy*. London: Cape. First published 1966.

Goldmann, L. (1977) *The Hidden God: A Study of the Tragic Vision in the Pensées of Pascal and the Tragedies of Racine*. London: RKP. First published 1956. First English translation 1964.

Goldmann, L. (1986) *Towards a Sociology of the Novel*. London: Tavistock. First published 1964. First English translation 1975.

Goldmann, L. and Adorno,T. (1976) 'Goldmann and Adorno: To Describe, Understand and Explain'. In L. Goldmann, *Cultural Creation in Modern Society*. St Louis: Telos Press. First published 1971.

Goodwin, A. (1992) *Dancing in the Distraction Factory*. Minneapolis: University of Minnesota Press.

Goodwin, A. and Wolff, J. (1997) 'Conserving Cultural Studies'. In E. Long (ed.) *From Sociology to Cultural Studies*. London: Blackwell.

Gramsci, A. (1971) *Selections From the Prison Notebooks* (ed.) Q. Hoare and G. Smith. London: Lawrence and Wishart. First English translation of these selections.

Grumley, J. (1991) 'Marx and the Philosophy of the Subject: Márkus contra Habermas'. *Thesis Eleven* 28: 53–69.

Habermas, J. (1974) 'The Public Sphere: An Encyclopedia Article'. *New German Critique* 1(3): 49–55. First published 1964.

Habermas, J. (1991) *The Structural Transformation of the Public Sphere*. Cambridge, Massachusetts: MIT Press. First published 1962. First English translation 1989.

Habermas, J. (1993) 'Further Reflections on the Public Sphere'. In C. Calhoun (ed.) *Habermas and the Public Sphere*. Cambridge, Massachusetts: MIT Press. Paper given in 1989.

Habermas, J. (1995) 'Excursus on the Obsolescence of the Production Paradigm'. In his *The Philosophical Discourse of Modernity*. Cambridge, Massachusetts: MIT Press. First published 1985. First English translation 1987.

Habermas, J. (1996a) 'Modernity: An Unfinished Project'. In M. D'Entreves and S. Benhabib (eds) *Habermas and the Unfinished Project of Modernity*. Cambridge: Polity. First published 1981.

Habermas, J. (1996b) *Between Facts and Norms: Contributions to a Discourse Theory of Law and Democracy*. Cambridge: Polity. First published 1992. First English translation 1996.

Habermas, J. *et al.* (1993) 'Concluding Remarks'. In C. Calhoun (ed.) *Habermas and the Public Sphere*. Cambridge, Massachusetts: MIT Press.

Hall, S. (1971) 'Deviancy, Politics and the Media'. *CCCS Stencilled Occasional Paper* No. 11.

Hall, S. (1972) 'The Determinations of News Photographs'. *Working Papers in Cultural Studies* 3: 53–87.

Hall, S. (1973) 'Encoding and Decoding in the Television Discourse'. *CCCS Stencilled Occasional Paper* No. 7.

Hall, S. (1974) 'Marx's Notes on Method: A "Reading" of the "1857 Introduction"'. *Working Papers in Cultural Studies* 6: 132–71.

Hall, S. (1977a) 'The "Political" and "Economic" in Marx's Theory of Classes'. In A. Hunt (ed.) *Class and Class Structure*. London: Lawrence and Wishart.

Hall, S. (1977b) 'Culture, the Media and the "Ideological Effect"'. In J. Curran *et al.* (eds) *Mass Communication and Society*. London: Edward Arnold/Open University Press.

Hall, S. (1977c) 'Rethinking the "Base-and-Superstructure" Metaphor'. In J. Bloomfield (ed.) *Class, Hegemony and Party*. London: Lawrence and Wishart.

Hall, S. (1978a) 'The Hinterland of Science: Ideology and the "Sociology of Knowledge"'. In CCCS (1978).

Hall, S. (1978b) 'Newspapers, Parties and Classes'. In J. Curran (ed.) *The British Press: a manifesto*. London: Macmillan.

Hall, S. (1980a) 'Cultural Studies: Two Paradigms'. *Media, Culture and Society* 2(2): 57–72.

Hall, S. (1980b) 'The Williams Interviews' (review of Williams's *Politics and Letters*). *Screen Education* 34: 94–104. Republished in Eagleton (ed.) (1989b).

Hall, S. (1980c), 'Cultural Studies and the Centre: Some Problematics and Problems'. In S.Hall *et al.*s (eds) *Culture, Media, Language*. London: Hutchinson.

Hall, S. (1983a) 'The Problem of Ideology: Marxism without Guarantees'. In B. Matthews (ed.) *Marx 100 Years On*. London: Lawrence and Wishart.

Hall, S. (1983b) 'Unpacking Orwell: The Shape of States to Come?'. In S. Hall (ed.) *The State and Society: Block 1*. Milton Keynes: Open University Press.

Hall, S. (1985) 'Authoritarian Populism: A Reply'. *New Left Review* 151: 115–24.

Hall, S. (1986) 'On Postmodernism and Articulation: An Interview with Stuart Hall' (interviewer: Lawrence Grossberg). *Journal of Communication Inquiry* 10(2): 45–60.

Hall, S. (1988) *The Hard Road to Renewal: Thatcherism and the Crisis of the Left*. London: Verso.

Hall, S. (1989) 'The "First" New Left: Life and Times'. In R. Archer *et al.* (eds) *Out of Apathy*. London: Verso.

Hall, S. (1990) 'The Emergence of Cultural Studies and the Crisis of the Humanities'. *October* 53: 11–23.

Hall, S. (1993) 'Culture, Community, Nation'. *Cultural Studies* 7(3): 349–63.

Hall, S. (1997) 'Interview: Culture and Power' (interviewers: Peter Osborne and Lynn Segal). *Radical Philosophy* 86 (November/December): 24–41.

Hall, S. and Jefferson, T. (eds) (1977) *Resistance through Rituals: Youth Subcultures in Post-war Britain*. London: Hutchinson. First published 1974 as *WPCS 7/8*.

Hall, S., Connell, I. and Curti, L. (1976) 'The "Unity" of Current Affairs Television'. *Working Papers in Cultural Studies* 9: 51–92.

Hall, S., Critcher, C., Jefferson, T., Clarke, J. and Roberts, B. (1978a) *Policing the Crisis: Mugging, the State and Law 'n' Order*. Houndmills: Macmillan.

Hall, S., Lumley, B. and McLennan, G. (1978b) 'Politics and Ideology: Gramsci'. In *CCCS* (1978).

Hansen, M. (1981–82) 'Introduction to Adorno, "Transparencies on Film"'. *New German Critique* 24(25): 186–98.

Harvey, D. (1991) *The Condition of Postmodernity*. Oxford: Blackwell.

Hawkes, D. (1996) *Ideology*. London: Routledge.

Hawkes, J. (1977) *Structuralism and Semiotics*. London: Methuen.

Hebdige, D. (1979) *Subculture: the Meaning of Style*. London: Methuen.

Held, D. (1980) *Introduction to Critical Theory*. Oxford: Polity.

Herder, J. (n.d.) *Outlines of a Philosophy of the History of Man*. NY: Bergman (facsimilie reproduction of 1800 English translation by T. Churchill).

Higgins, J. (1999) *Raymond Williams: Literature, Marxism and Cultural Materialism*. London: Routledge.

Hoggart, R. (1963) *Teaching Literature*. London: National Institute of Adult Education.

Hoggart, R. (1976) *The Uses of Literacy: Aspects of Working-class Life with Special Reference to Publications and Entertainments*. Harmondsworth, UK: Penguin. First published 1957.

Hohendahl, P. (1995) *Prismatic Thought: Theodor W. Adorno*. Lincoln: University of Nebraska Press.

Hunter, I. (1988) *Culture and Government*. London: Macmillan.

Huyssen, A. (1986) *After the Great Divide: Modernism, Mass Culture, Postmodernism*. Bloomington: Indiana University Press.

Jacoby, R. (1999) *The End of Utopia*. NY: Basic Books.

Jakobson, R. and Tynjanov, J. (1971) 'Problems in the Study of Literature and Language'. In L. Matejka and K. Pomorska (eds) *Readings in Russian Poetics*. Cambridge, Mass.: MIT Press. First published 1928.

Jameson, F. (1974a) *Marxism and Form*. Princeton: Princeton UP. First published 1971.

Jameson, F. (1974b) *The Prison-House of Language*. Princeton: Princeton UP. First published 1972.

Jameson, F. (1981) *The Political Unconscious*. Cornell: Cornell UP.

Jameson, F. (1990) *Late Marxism: Adorno, or, the Persistence of the Dialectic*. London: Routledge.

Jameson, F. (2002) *A Singular Modernity*. London: Verso.

Jay, M. (1984a) *Marxism and Totality: The Adventures of a Concept from Lukács to Habermas*. Berkeley: University of California Press.

Jay, M. (1984b) *Adorno*. London: Fontana.

Jay, M. (1996) *The Dialectical Imagination*. Berkeley: University of California Press. First published 1973.

Jessop, B., Bonnett, K., Bromley, S. and Ling, T. (1984) 'Authoritarian populism, two nations and Thatcherism'. *New Left Review* 147: 32–60.

Johnson, R. (1979a) 'Three Problematics: Elements of a Theory of Working Class Culture'. In J. Clarke *et al.* (eds) *Working Class Culture: Studies in History and Theory*. London: Hutchinson/CCCS.

Johnson, R. (1979b) 'Histories of Culture/Theories of Ideology: Notes on an Impasse'. In M. Barrett *et al.* (eds) *Ideology and Cultural Production*. London: Croom Helm.

Jones, P. (1981) 'Three Books by Raymond Williams'. *Thesis Eleven* **3**: 187–93.

Jones, P. (1982) '"Organic" Intellectuals and the Generation of English Cultural Studies'. *Thesis Eleven* **5**(6): 85–124.

Jones, P. (1994) 'The Myth of "Raymond Hoggart": on "Founding Fathers" and Cultural Policy'. *Cultural Studies* **8**(3): 394–416.

Jones, P. (1995) 'Williams and "Quality": A Response to John Corner'. *Media, Culture and Society* **17**(2): 317–22 (reply to Corner [1994]).

Jones, P. (1997) 'Moral Panic: The Legacy of Stan Cohen and Stuart Hall'. *Media International Australia* **85**: 6–16.

Jones, P. (1998) 'The Technology is Not the Cultural Form? Raymond Williams's Sociological Critique of Marshall McLuhan'. *Canadian Journal of Communication* **23**(4): 423–454.

Jones, P. (1999) '"The Problem is Always One of Method . . .": Cultural Materialism, Political Economy and Cultural Studies'. *Key Words* **2**: 28–46.

Jones, P. (2000a) '"McLuhanist" Projections and Social Theory: Some Reflections'. *Media International Australia* **94** February: 39–55.

Jones, P. (2000b) 'Democratic Norms and Means of Communication: Public Sphere, Fourth Estate, Freedom of Communication'. *Critical Horizons* **1**(2) August: 307–39.

Jones, P. (2002) 'Williams and Márkus on Production'. In J. Grumley, P. Crittenden and P. Johnson (eds) *Culture and Enlightenment: Essays for George Márkus*. Aldershot: Ashgate.

Joseph, J. (2002) *Hegemony: A Realist Analysis*. London: Routledge.

Kavanagh, J. (1995) 'Ideology'. In F. Lentricchia and T. McLaughlin (eds) (1995) *Critical Terms for Literary Study*. 2nd Edn. Chicago: University of Chicago Press.

Keane, J. (1988) *Democracy and Civil Society*. London: Verso.

Kellner, D. (1997a) 'Critical Theory and Cultural Studies: The Missed Articulation'. In J. McGuigan (ed.) *Cultural Methodologies*. London: Sage.

Kellner, D. (1997b) 'Overcoming the Divide: Cultural Studies and Political Economy'. In M. Ferguson and P. Golding (eds) *Cultural Studies in Question*. London: Sage.

Kenny, M. (1995) *The First New Left*. London: Lawrence and Wishart.

Knights, B. (1978) *The Idea of the Clerisy in the Nineteenth Century*. Cambridge: Cambridge UP.

Kumar, K. (1981) *Prophecy and Progress: The Sociology of Industrial and Post-industrial Society*. Harmondsworth: Penguin.

Kumar, K. (1995) *From Post-industrial to Post-modern Society*. Oxford: Blackwell.

Lacey, N. (2000) *Narrative and Genre: Key Concepts in Media Studies*. Houndmills: Palgrave.

Laing, D. (1994) '*Scrutiny* to Subcultures: Notes on Literary Criticism and Popular Music'. *Popular Music* **13**(2): 179–90.

Laing, S. (1991) 'Raymond Williams and the Cultural Analysis of Television'. *Media, Culture and Society* **13**: 153–69.

Larrain, J. (1984) 'Three Different Concepts of Ideology in Marx? A Rejoinder to Márkus'. *Canadian Journal of Political and Social Theory* **8**(3): 151–61.

Larrain, J. (1991) 'Stuart Hall and the Marxist Concept of Ideology'. *Theory, Culture and Society* **8**: 1–28.

Lash, S. (1993) 'Pierre Bourdieu: Cultural Economy and Social Change'. In C. Calhoun *et al.* (eds) *Bourdieu: Critical Perspectives*. Cambridge: Polity.

Lasswell, H. (1948) 'The Structure and Function of Communication in Society'. In L. Bryson (ed.). *The Communication of Ideas*. NY: Harper.

Leach, E. (1974) *Lévi-Strauss*. London: Fontana.

Leavis, F. (ed.) (1966) 'Literature and Society'. In *The Common Pursuit*. Harmondsworth: Penguin.

Leavis, F. and Thompson, D. (1937) *Culture and Environment*. London: Chatto and Windus. First published 1933.

Lévi-Strauss, C. (1963) 'Structural Analysis in Linguistics and Anthropology'. In his *Structural Anthropology*. NY: Basic. First published 1945.

Lévi-Strauss, C. (1970) 'A Confrontation'. *New Left Review* **62**: 57–74. First published 1963.

Lévi-Strauss, C. (1973) *Totemism*. Harmondsworth: Penguin. First published 1962.

Lévi-Strauss, C. (1976) 'Structure and Form: Reflections on a Work by Vladimir Propp'. In his *Structural Anthropology vol 2*. NY: Basic Books. First published 1960.

Levitas, R. (1990) *The Concept of Utopia*. NY: Syracuse UP.

Liebersohn, H. (1988) *Fate and Utopia in German Sociology, 1870–1923*. Cambridge, Massachusetts: MIT Press.

Livingstone, R., Anderson, P. and Mulhern, F. (1977) 'Presentation III'. In Bloch, E., Lukács, G., Brecht, B., Benjamin, W. and Adorno, T. (1977) *Aesthetics and Politics*. R. Taylor (ed./trans.). London: NLB.

Longhurst, B. (1987) 'Realism, Naturalism and Television Soap Opera'. *Theory, Culture and Society* **4**: 633–49.

Longhurst, B. (1989) *Karl Mannheim and the Contemporary Sociology of Knowledge*. Houndmills: Macmillan.

Lunn, E. (1985) *Marxism and Modernism: An Historical Study of Lukács, Brecht, Benjamin and Adorno*. London: Verso.

Lury, C. (1992) 'Popular Culture and the Mass Media'. In R. Bocock and K. Thompson (eds) *Social and Cultural Forms of Modernity*. Cambridge: Polity/Open University Press.

McGuigan, J. (1992) *Cultural Populism*. London: Routledge.

McGuigan, J. (1997) 'A Slow Reach Again for Control: Raymond Williams and the Vicissitudes of Cultural Policy'. In J. Wallace *et al.* (eds) *Raymond Williams Now: Knowledge, Limits and the Future*. NY: St Martin's Press.

McIlroy, J. and Westwood, S. (eds) (1993) *Border Country: Raymond Williams in Adult Education*. Leicester: National Institute of Adult Continuing Education.

MacKay, H. and O'Sullivan, T. (eds) (1999) *The Media Reader: Continuity and Transformation*. London: Sage/Open UP.

MacKenzie, D. (1996) 'Marx and the Machine'. In his *Knowing Machines: Essays on Technical Change*. Cambridge, Mass.: MIT Press.

MacKenzie, D. and Wajcman, J. (1985) 'Introductory Essay'. In D. MacKenzie and J. Wajcman (eds) *The Social Shaping of Technology*. Milton Keynes: Open UP.

McLuhan, M. (1951) *The Mechanical Bride*. Boston: Beacon Press.

McLuhan, M. (1964) 'Introduction' to H. Innis, *The Bias of Communication*. Toronto: University of Toronto Press.

McLuhan, M. (1967a) *The Gutenberg Galaxy: The Making of Typographic Man*. London: RKP. First published 1962.

McLuhan, M. (1967b) *Understanding Media: The Extensions of Man*. London: Sphere. First published 1964.

McLuhan, M. and Fiore, Q. (1967) *The Medium is the Massage: An Inventory of Effects*. London: Penguin.

Mannheim, K. (1960) *Man and Society in an Age of Reconstruction: Studies in Modern Social Structure*. First published 1940. London: RKP.

Marcuse, H. (1965) 'Remarks on a Redefinition of Culture'. *Daedalus* **94**(1): 190–207.

Marcuse, H. (1972) *Negations: Essays in Critical Theory*. Harmondsworth: Penguin. First published in English in 1968.

Márkus, G. (1981) '"Ideology" and its Ideologies: Lukács and Goldmann on Kant'. *Philosophy and Social Criticism* **2**(8): 125–47.

Márkus, G. (1983) 'Concepts of Ideology in Marx'. *Canadian Journal of Political and Social Theory* **7**(1–2): 84–103.

Márkus, G. (1986) *Language and Production: A Critique of the Paradigms*. Dordrecht, Holland: D. Reidel.

Márkus, G. (1987) 'Ideology, Critique and Contradiction in Marx: An Answer to J. Larrain'. *Canadian Journal of Political and Social Theory* **11**(3): 74–88.

Márkus, G. (1990) 'Marxism and Theories of Culture'. *Thesis Eleven* **25**: 91–106.

Márkus, G. (1994a) 'The End of a Metaphor: The Base and the Superstructure'. In C. Gould and R. Cohen (eds) *Artifacts, Representations and Social Practice: Essays for Marx Wartofsky*. Dordrecht, Holland: Kluher.

Márkus, G. (1994b) 'A Society of Culture: The Constitution of Modernity'. In G. Robinson and J. Rundell (eds) *Rethinking Imagination: Culture and Creativity*. London: Routledge.

Márkus, G. (1995) 'On Ideology-Critique – Critically'. *Thesis Eleven* **43**: 66–99.

Marx, K. (1951) *The Eighteenth Brumaire of Louis Bonaparte*. D. de Leon (trans.). New York Labor News Co.

Marx, K. (1958a) 'Preface to a Contribution to the Critique of Political Economy (1859 Preface)'. In K. Marx and F. Engels, *Selected Works Volume 1* Moscow: Foreign Languages Publishing House (overprinted: London: Lawrence and Wishart).

Marx, K. (1958b) *The Eighteenth Brumaire of Louis Bonaparte*. In K. Marx and F. Engels, *Selected Works Volume 1*. Moscow: Foreign Languages Publishing House (overprinted: London: Lawrence and Wishart).

Marx, K. (1973a) *The Poverty of Philosophy*. Moscow: Progress Publishers.

Marx, K. (1973b) *Grundrisse: Foundations of the Critique of Political Economy (rough draft)*. London: Pelican (Allen Lane)/ NLB.

Marx, K. (1974) *Capital Volume One*. London: Lawrence and Wishart.

Marx, K. (1976) *Capital Volume One*. Harmondsworth: Penguin.

Marx, K. and Engels, F. (1976) The German Ideology. In K. Marx and F. Engels, *Collected Works Volume 5: 1845–1847*. London: Lawrence and Wishart.

Marx, K. and Engels, F. (1977) The German Ideology (extracts). In K. Marx, *Selected Writings*, D. McLellan (ed.) Oxford: OUP.

Matejka, L. (1973) 'On the First Russian Prolegomena to Semiotics'. In Vološinov (1973).

Meyrowitz, J. (1985) *No Sense of Place: The Impact of Electronic Media on Social Behaviour*. NY: OUP.

Meyrowitz, J. (1996) 'Taking McLuhan and "Medium Theory" Seriously: Technological Change and the Evolution of Education'. In S. Kerr (ed.) *Technology and the Future of Schooling*. Chicago: University of Chicago Press.

Meyrowitz, J. (1999) 'Understandings of Media (three images of media)'. *ETC: A Review of General Semantics* **56**(1): 1–4.

Milner, A. (1993) *Cultural Materialism*. Melbourne: Melbourne UP.

Milner, A. (1996) *Literature, Culture and Society*. London: UCL Press.

Milner, A. (2002) *Re-Imagining Cultural Studies: The Promise of Cultual Materialism*. London: Sage.

Moriarty, M. (1995) '"The Longest Cultural Journey": Raymond Williams and French Theory'. In Prendergast (1995).

Morley, D. (1975) 'Reconceptualising the Media Audience: Towards an Ethnography of Audiences'. *CCCS Stencilled Occasional Paper* No. 9.

Morley, D. (1980) *The Nationwide Audience: Structure and Decoding*. London: BFI.

Mukařovský, J. (1979) *Aesthetic Function, Norm and Value as Social Facts*. Ann Arbor: University of Michigan. First published 1936.

Mukařovský, J. (1986) 'Art as Semiotic Fact'. In L. Matejka and I. Tutinik (eds) *Semiotics of Art: Prague School Contributions*. Cambridge, Mass.: MIT Press. First published 1934.

Mulhern, F. (1979) *The Moment of 'Scrutiny'*. London: NLB.

Mulhern, F. (1980) 'On Culture and Cultural Struggle'. *Screen Education* **34**: 31–5.

Mulhern, F. (1998) 'Towards 2000, or News from You-Know-where'. In his *The Present Lasts a Long Time: Essays in Cultural Politics*. Cork University Press/Field Day.

Mulhern, F. (2000) *Culture/Metaculture*. London: Routledge.

Mulhern, F. (2002) 'Beyond Metaculture'. *New Left Review: Second Series* **16**: 86–104.

Murdock, G. (1993) 'Communications and the Constitution of Modernity'. *Media, Culture and Society* **15**(4): 521–39.

Murdock, G. (1997) 'Base Notes: The Conditions of Cultural Practice'. In M. Ferguson and P. Golding (eds) *Cultural Studies in Question*. London: Sage.

Murdock, G. and Golding, P. (1974) 'For a Political Economy of Communication'. In R. Miliband and J. Saville (eds) *The Socialist Register 1973*. London: Merlin.

Neale, R. (1984) 'Cultural Materialism: A Critique'. *Social History* **9**(2): 199–215.

Nieminen, H. (1997) *Communication and Democracy: Habermas, Williams and the British Case*. Finnish Academy of Science and Letters.

Nightingale, V. (1996) *Studying Audiences: The Shock of the Real*. London: Routledge.

Norris, C. (1982) *Deconstruction: Theory and Practice*. London: Methuen.

Norris, C. (1984) 'Language, Ideology and Truth: Orwell and the Post-war Left'. In C. Norris (ed.) *Inside the Myth. Orwell: Views from the Left*. London: Lawrence and Wishart.

Norris, C. (1987) *Derrida*. Cambridge, Mass.: Harvard UP.

Norris, C. (1997) 'Keywords, Ideology and Critical Theory'. In J. Wallace *et al.* (eds) *Raymond Williams Now: Knowledge, Limits and the Future*. NY: St Martin's Press.

O'Connor, A. (1989) *Raymond Williams: Writing, Culture, Politics*. London: Blackwell.

O'Neill, D. (2000) 'The Importance of the Concept of Attachment in Raymond Williams's *Culture and Society*'. Paper presented to 'Raymond Williams: After 2000' Conference, Melbourne, 10–11 June.

Paddison, M. (1996) *Adorno, Modernism and Mass Culture*. London: Kahn and Averill.

Passeron, J.-C. (1972) 'Introduction to the French Edition of *The Uses of Literacy*'. *Working Papers in Cultural Studies* **1**: 120–31.

Peterson, R. (1976) 'The Production of Culture: A Prolegomenon'. In R. Peterson (ed.) *The Production of Culture*. Beverly Hills, Cal.: Sage.

Peterson, R. (1994) 'Culture Studies Through the Production Perspective: Progress and Prospects'. In D. Crane (ed.) *The Sociology of Culture: Emerging Theoretical Perspectives*. London: Blackwell.

Pettit, P. (1975) *The Concept of Structuralism: A Critical Appraisal*. Dublin: Gill and Macmillan.

Piaget, J. (1970) *Structuralism*. NY: Harper Colophon. First published 1968.

Pinkney, T. (1989a) 'Editor's Introduction: Modernism and Cultural Theory'. In *POM*.

Pinkney, T. (1989b) 'Raymond Williams and the "Two Faces of Modernism"'. In T. Eagleton (ed.) (1989b).

Poggioli, R. (1968) *The Theory of the Avant-Garde*. Cambridge, Mass.: Belknap. First published 1962.

Poulantzas, N. (1976) *Political Power and Social Classes*. London: NLB.

Prendergast, C. (ed.) (1995) *Cultural Materialism: on Raymond Williams*. Minneapolis: University of Minnesota Press.

Preston, P. (2001) *Reshaping Communications: Technology, Information and Social Change.* London: Sage.

Propp, V. (1968) *Morphology of the Russian Folktale.* Austin: University of Texas Press. First published 1928.

Ricoeur, P. (1974) 'Structure and Hermeneutics'. In his *The Conflict of Interpretations.* Evanston: Northwestern UP. First published in 1963.

Ricoeur, P. (1986) *Lectures on Ideology and Utopia.* NY: Columbia UP. Delivered in 1975.

Ritchie, H. (1988) *Success Stories: Literature and the Media in England, 1950–1959.* London: Faber.

Robbins, B. (1995) 'Foreword'. In *SOC.*

Rojek, C. and Turner, B. (2000) 'Decorative Sociology: Towards a Critique of the Cultural Turn'. *The Sociological Review* **48**(4): 629–48.

Rossi-Landi, F. (1973) *Ideologies of Linguistic Relativity.* The Hague: Mouton.

Rossi-Landi, F. (1977) *Linguistics and Economics.* The Hague: Mouton.

Rossi-Landi, F. and Pesaresi, M. (1981) 'Language'. In R. Williams (ed.) *Contact: Human Communication and its History.* London: Thames and Hudson.

Rundell, J. (1987) *Origins of Modernity: The Origins of Modern Social Theory from Kant to Hegel to Marx.* Cambridge: Polity.

Ryan, B. (1991) *Making Capital from Culture: The Corporate Form of Capitalist Cultural Production.* Berlin: Walter de Gruyter.

Said, E. (1991) *The World, the Text and the Critic.* London: Vintage. First published 1983.

Saussure, F. de (1966) *Course in General Linguistics.* NY: McGraw Hill. First published 1915.

Schick, E. (1971) *Metaphorical Organicism in Herder's Early Works.* The Hague: Mouton.

Sharp, C. (1966) 'Introduction to the First Edition, 1917'. In his *English Folk Songs from the Appalachian Mountains.* London: OUP.

Shklovsky, V. (1965) 'Art As Technique'. In L. Lemon and M. Reis (eds) *Russian Formalist Criticism: Four Essays.* Essay first published in 1917.

Sontag, S. (1968) 'One Culture and the New Sensibility'. In G. Stearn (ed.) *McLuhan: Hot and Cool.* Harmondsworth: Penguin. First published 1965.

Sparks, C. (1993) 'Raymond Williams and the Theory of Democratic Communication'. In S. Splichal and J. Wasko (eds) *Communication and Democracy.* Norwood, NJ: Ablex.

Spigel, L. (1992) 'Introduction' to R. Williams, *TV: Technology and Cultural Form.* Hanover, NH: Wesleyan University Press.

Sprinker, M. (1999) 'The Grand Hotel Abyss'. *New Left Review* **237**: 115–36.

Stearn, G. and McLuhan, M. (1968) 'A Dialogue'. In G. Stearn (ed.) *McLuhan: Hot and Cool.* Harmondsworth: Penguin.

Stevenson, N. (1995) *Culture, Ideology and Socialism: Raymond Williams and E.P. Thompson.* Aldershot, UK: Avebury.

Storey, J. (1996) *Cultural Studies and the Study of Popular Culture.* Edinburgh: Edinburgh UP.

Sturrock, J. (1986) *Structuralism.* London: Paladin.

Suino, M. (1979) 'Afterword'. In Mukařovský (1979).

Swingewood, A. (1987) *Sociological Poetics and Aesthetic Theory.* NY: St Martin's Press.

Swingewood, A. (1998) *Cultural Theory and the Problem of Modernity.* NY: St Martin's Press.

Therborn, G. (1976) *Science, Class and Society.* London: NLB.

Thompson, E.P. (1961) 'The Long Revolution' (review of Williams's *The Long Revolution*). *New Left Review* 9 & **10**: 24–33(pt 1) & 34–9(pt 2).

Thompson, J. (1990) *Ideology and Modern Culture.* Cambridge: Polity.

Thompson, J. (1995) *The Media and Modernity: A Social Theory of the Media*. Stanford: Stanford University Press/Polity.

Timpanaro, S. (1975) *On Materialism*. London: NLB.

Tuchman, G. (1983) 'Consciousness Industries and the Production of Culture'. *Journal of Communication* (Summer): 330–41.

Turner, G. (1996) *British Cultural Studies: An Introduction* (2nd Edn) Unwin Hyman, London.

Vološinov, V. (1973) *Marxism and the Philosophy of Language*. NY: Seminar Press. First published 1930.

Vološinov, V. (1976) *Freudianism: A Marxist Critique*. NY: Seminar Press. First published 1927.

Williams, R. (1953) 'The Idea of Culture'. *Essays in Criticism* 3: 239–66.

Williams, R. (1956) 'T.S. Eliot on Culture'. *Essays in Criticism* 6: 302–18.

Williams, R. (1957a) 'Fiction and the Writing Public'. *Essays in Criticism* 7: 422–8. Republished in *WICTS*.

Williams, R. (1957b) '*The Uses of Literacy*: Working Class Culture'. *Universities and Left Review* 1(2): 29–32.

Williams, R. (1958) 'Culture is Ordinary'. In N. McKenzie (ed.) *Conviction*. London: MacGibbon & Kee. Republished in *ROH*.

Williams, R. (1960) 'Advertising; The Magic System'. *New Left Review* 4(July/August): 27–32. Revised and republished in *PMC*.

Williams, R. (1962) 'The Existing Alternatives in Communications'. *Fabian Tract* 337 (June). London: The Fabian Society.

Williams, R. (1965) 'The British Left'. *New Left Review* 30: 18–26. Republished in *ROH*.

Williams, R. (1968a) 'Culture and Revolution: a Comment'. In T. Eagleton and B. Wicken (eds) (1968). Republished in *ROH* as 'The Idea of a Common Culture'.

Williams, R. (1968b) 'A Structure of Insights' (review of McLuhan's *Gutenberg Galaxy*). In G. Stearn (ed.) *McLuhan: Hot and Cool*. Harmondsworth: Penguin. First published 1964.

Williams, R. (1968c) (ed.) *The May Day Manifesto*. Harmondsworth: Penguin.

Williams, R. (1969a) 'On Reading Marcuse' (review of Marcuse's *Negations*). *Cambridge Review* (May 30): 366–8.

Williams, R. (1969b) 'Crisis in Communications'. *The Listener* 82 (July 31): 138, 140.

Williams, R. (1970a) 'A Hundred Years of Culture and Anarchy'. *The Spokesman* (December): 8. Based on a 1969 lecture. Revised and republished in *PMC*.

Williams, R. (1970b) 'Radical and/or Respectable'. In R. Boston (ed.) *The Press We Deserve*. London: RKP.

Williams, R. (1971) 'Literature and Sociology: In Memory of Lucien Goldmann'. *New Left Review* 67: 3–18. Revised and republished in *PMC*.

Williams, R. (1972) 'Lucien Goldmann and Marxism's Alternative Tradition'. *The Listener* 87 (23 March): 375–6.

Williams, R. (1973a) 'Base and Superstructure in Marxist Cultural Theory'. *New Left Review* 82: 5–16. Revised and republished in *PMC*.

Williams, R. (1973b) 'Baudelaire's Paris' (review of Benjamin, 1973). *The Guardian Weekly*. September 8: 22.

Williams, R. (1974a) 'On High and Popular Culture'. *New Republic*. (November) 171 (23): 13–16.

Williams, R. (1974b) 'The Frankfurt School'. *The Guardian*. February 14: 14.

Williams, R. (1975) 'Drama in a Dramatised Society: An Inaugural Lecture'. (Delivered 29 October, 1974) Cambridge: Cambridge University Press. Republished in *RWOT*.

Williams, R. (1976a) 'Communications as Cultural Science'. In C. Bigsby (ed.) *Approaches to Popular Culture*. London: Arnold. First published 1974.

Williams, R. (1976b) 'Developments in the Sociology of Culture'. *Sociology* **10**: 497–506.

Williams, R. (1976c) 'Notes on Marxism in Britain Since 1945'. *New Left Review* **100**: 81–94. Revised and republished in *PMC*.

Williams, R. (1976d) 'How Can We Sell the Protestant Ethic at a Psychedelic Bazaar? (review of D. Bell, *The Cultural Contradictions of Capitalism*). *The New York Times Book Review* February 1: 3.

Williams, R. (1977a) 'Interview with Raymond Williams (Part One)'. *Red Shift* **2**: 12–17.

Williams, R. (1977b) 'The Paths and Pitfalls of Ideology as an Ideology'. (review of CCCS, 1978). *Times Higher Education Supplement* June 10: 13.

Williams, R. (1977c) 'Realism, Naturalism and their Alternatives'. *Cine-tracts* **1**(3): 1–6.

Williams, R. (1977d) 'Social Environment and Theatrical Environment: The Case of English Naturalism'. In M. Axton and R. Williams (eds) *English Drama: Forms and Development*. Cambridge: CUP. Revised and republished in *PMC*.

Williams, R. (1977e) 'A Lecture on Realism'. *Screen* **18**(1): 61–74.

Williams, R. (1977f) 'Television and the Mandarins' (critique of the Annan Report on the Future of Broadcasting). *New Society* March 31: 651–2.

Williams, R. (1977g) 'French Connection' (review of, in part, Bourdieu and Passeron, 1977). *New Society* May 5: 239–40.

Williams, R. (1978a) 'The Significance of "Bloomsbury" as a Social and Cultural Group'. In D. Crabtree and A. Thirlwall (eds) *Keynes and The Bloomsbury Group*. London: Macmillan. Revised and republished as 'The Bloomsbury Fraction' in *PMC*.

Williams, R. (1978b) 'The Press We Don't Deserve'. In J. Curran (ed.) *The British Press: A Manifesto*. London: Macmillan.

Williams, R. (1978c) 'The Press and Popular Culture: An Historical Perspective'. In G. Boyce *et al.* (eds) *Newspaper History: From the Seventeenth Century to the Present*. London: Constable. Republished in *WICTS*.

Williams, R. (1978d) 'Class of the Conscious'. *New Society* January 5: 26–7.

Williams, R. (1978e) 'Explaining the Word' (review of Bloch *et al.* [1977]). *The Guardian* March 23: 11.

Williams, R. (1978f) 'Problems of Materialism'. *New Left Review* **109**: 3–17. Revised and republished in *PMC*.

Williams, R. (1978g) 'Utopia and Science Fiction'. *Science Fiction Studies* **5**(3): 203–14. Revised and republished in *PMC*.

Williams, R. (1980) 'Means of Communication as Means of Production'. In *PMC*. First published 1978.

Williams, R. (1981a) (ed.) *Contact: Human Communication and its History*. London: Thames and Hudson.

Williams, R. (1981b) 'Introduction' to R. Williams (ed.) (1981a).

Williams, R. (1981c) 'Communications Technologies and Social Institutions'. In R. Williams (ed.) (1981a). Republished in *WICTS*.

Williams, R. (1983a) 'Culture'. In D. McLellan (ed.) *Marx: The First Hundred Years*. London: Fontana. Republished as 'Marx on Culture' in *WICTS*.

Williams, R. (1983b) 'British Film History: New Perspectives'. In J. Curran and V. Porter (eds) *British Cinema History*. NJ: Barnes & Noble.

Williams, R. (1984) *Raymond Williams with Michael Ignatieff* (video recording of interview). London: ICA.

Williams, R. (1985) 'The Metropolis and the Emergence of Modernism'. In E. Timms and D. Kelley (eds) *Unreal City*. Manchester: Manchester UP. Republished as 'Metropolitan Perceptions and the Emergence of Modernism' in *POM*.

Williams, R. (1986) 'The Uses of Cultural Theory'. *New Left Review* **158**: 19–31 Republished in *POM*.

Williams, R. (1987) 'Language and the Avant-Garde'. In N. Fabb *et al.* (eds) *The Linguistics of Writing*. Manchester: Manchester UP. Republished in *POM*.

Williams, R. (1988a) 'The Politics of the Avant-Garde'. In E. Timms and P. Collier (eds) *Visions and Blueprints: Avant-Garde Culture and Radical Politics in Early Twentieth Century Europe*. Manchester: Manchester UP. Republished in *POM*.

Williams, R. (1988b) 'Theatre as Political Forum'. In E. Timms and P. Collier (eds) *Visions and Blueprints: Avant-Garde Culture and Radical Politics in Early Twentieth Century Europe*. Manchester: Manchester UP. Republished in *POM*.

Williams, R. and Orrom, M. (1954) *Preface to Film*. London: Film Drama Ltd.

Williams, R. *et al.* (1978) 'Discussion: Session 2'. In D. Crabtree and A. Thirlwall (eds) *Keynes and The Bloomsbury Group*. London: Macmillan.

Willis, P. (1978) *Profane Culture*. London: Routledge.

Willis, P. (1990) *Common Culture*. Milton Keynes: Open University Press.

Willis, P. (2000) *The Ethnographic Imagination*. Oxford: Polity.

Willmott, G. (1996) *McLuhan, or Modernism in Reverse*. Toronto: University of Toronto Press.

Wolfe, T. (1984) *Marshall McLuhan: The Man and his Message* (video). McLuhan Productions/Canadian Broadcasting Corp.

Wolff, J. (1981) *The Social Production of Art*. London: Macmillan.

Wolff, J. (1993a) *The Social Production of Art* (2nd Edn). London: Macmillan.

Wolff, J. (1993b) *Aesthetics and the Sociology of Art* (2nd Edn). London: Macmillan.

Wolff, J. (1999) 'Cultural Studies and the Sociology of Culture'. *Contemporary Sociology* **28**(5): 499–507.

Wolin, R. (1994) *Walter Benjamin: An Aesthetic of Redemption*. Berkeley: UCLA Press.

Young, R. (1995) *Colonial Desire: Hybridity in Theory, Culture and Race*. London: Routledge.

Young, R. (1996) *Torn Halves: Political Conflict in Literary and Cultural Theory*. Manchester: Manchester UP.

Zima, P. (1999) *The Philosophy of Modern Literary Theory*. London: Athlone Press.

Zuidervaart, L. (1991) *Adorno's Aesthetic Theory: The Redemption of Illusion*. Cambridge, Mass.: MIT Press.

Index

Note: Page numbers in **bold** refer to Tables and Figures.

Sub-categories under Williams's name have been confined to titles of his books and select articles. His own concepts (e.g. 'notation') and issues addressed by him (e.g. 'base and superstructure metaphor') have been categorized under their own alphabetical entries.